The Monotheisation of Pontic-Caspian Eurasia

Edinburgh Byzantine Studies
Innovative approaches to the medieval Eastern Roman empire and its neighbours
Edinburgh Byzantine Studies promotes new, theory-driven approaches to the empire commonly called Byzantium. The series looks at the literary, historical, material and visual remains of this long-living political order and its neighbours, often from a multi-disciplinary and/or cross-cultural vantage point. Its innovative readings highlight the connectivity of Byzantine culture as well as of Byzantine Studies.

Series Editors
Louise Blanke, The University of Edinburgh
Ivan Drpić, University of Pennsylvania
Niels Gaul, The University of Edinburgh
Alexander Riehle, Harvard University
Yannis Stouraitis, The University of Edinburgh
Alicia Walker, Bryn Mawr College

Books available in the series
Identities and Ideologies in the Medieval East Roman World
Yannis Stouraitis

The Monotheisation of Pontic-Caspian Eurasia: From the Eighth to the Thirteenth Century
Alex M. Feldman

Imperial Visions of Late Byzantium: Manuel II Palaiologos and Rhetoric in Purple
Florin Leonte

Books forthcoming
Saints, Relics and Identity in Medieval and Modern Caucasia: The Cult of Saints and the Body Politic
Nikoloz Aleksidze

Social Stratification in Late Byzantium
Christos Malatras

Visit the Edinburgh Byzantine Studies website at
edinburghuniversitypress.com/series-edinburgh-byzantine-studies.html

The Monotheisation of Pontic-Caspian Eurasia

From the Eighth to the Thirteenth Century

Alex M. Feldman

EDINBURGH
University Press

Edinburgh University Press is one of the leading university presses in the UK. We publish academic books and journals in our selected subject areas across the humanities and social sciences, combining cutting-edge scholarship with high editorial and production values to produce academic works of lasting importance. For more information visit our website: edinburghuniversitypress.com

© Alex M. Feldman, 2022, 2024

Edinburgh University Press Ltd
The Tun – Holyrood Road
12(2f) Jackson's Entry
Edinburgh EH8 8PJ

First published in hardback by Edinburgh University Press 2022

Typeset in 10.5/13 Warnock Pro by

IDSUK (DataConnection) Ltd

A CIP record for this book is available from the British Library

ISBN 978 1 4744 7810 6 (hardback)
ISBN 978 1 4744 7811 3 (paperback)
ISBN 978 1 4744 7812 0 (webready PDF)
ISBN 978 1 4744 7813 7 (epub)

The right of Alex M. Feldman to be identified as the author of this work has been asserted in accordance with the Copyright, Designs and Patents Act 1988, and the Copyright and Related Rights Regulations 2003 (SI No. 2498).

Contents

List of Figures	vii
Acknowledgements	viii
Abbreviations	xiii
Note on Transcription and Transliteration	xv
A Proposition	1
1 The Monotheisation of Khazaria	18
The Earliest Textual Sources on Khazaria	19
The Advent of Khazarian Judaism	31
Monotheisation and Sedentarisation in Khazaria	59
Approximate Conclusions	78
2 A Commonwealth Inchoate: Byzantium and Pontic-Caspian Eurasia in the Tenth Century	83
Khazaria's Decline and Disappearance	84
Reinterpreting Northern Peoples in the *DAI*	90
3 Case Studies of Monotheisation in Eighth- to-Thirteenth-Century Pontic-Caspian Eurasia	97
Volga Bulgaria	98
Magyars, Pečenegs and Cumans	107
Rus': Byzantine Christianisation	135
4 Monotheisation in Metal	151
Empires of Faith and their Finances	151
Coinage and 'Commonwealth' (Eighth to Thirteenth Century): the *Ummah* and the *Oikoumene*	157

A Reassessment of Civilisation in Pontic-Caspian Eurasia 167
    Monotheisation Revisited 168
    Periodisation and Civilisation 176

Appendices 185
    Appendix 1 Gog and Magog's Association with Khazaria 187
    Appendix 2 Steppe Nomadism and Gumilëv's Eurasian Ideology 190
    Appendix 3 The Khazar-Ashkenazi Descent Theory 193

Bibliography 206
    Primary Sources 206
    Secondary and Archaeological Literature 213

Index 276

Figures

I.1 A map of Eurasia with outlines of Pontic-Caspian Eurasia.   4

3.1 An image of the Khazar tamga, potentially one of the symbols of the Āšĭnà dynasty, which appears on certain Khazar dirhams.   142

Acknowledgements

'Ad fontes!' The battlecry of the historian.[1]

For many years, I read the acknowledgements sections of history books as a sort of mild listing of various persons involved with the author who deserved thanks and praise: little more than a list of shout-outs. Yet acknowledgements are much more than about gratitude and commendation; they are about the very intricate process by which a book – history itself – is produced. In fact, the process of producing history depends on the contingent forces of bottom-up markets, top-down regulation, office politics and the puzzling cycles of history itself, and the product itself is sometimes capable of altering the very history it seeks to retell. It's easy to say that 'history is written by the winners' – this cliché reveals little more than window dressing for a process of individual and collective memory which are as intertwined in the present as they are in the past. I suppose the production of history is as much about the personal stories of the men and women who produce it as it is about the stories they narrate. Hence, the *true* weight of acknowledgements.

You may not choose your family, but you can choose whether or not to internalise (or recognise) your family ethos within yourself – after all, you are as much a product as you are a producer. My grandparents (Annette and Abraham Feldman; Eudice and Hugh Mesibov) were staunch members of the Greatest and the Silent Generations – they came of age amidst the decadence of the 1920s (a decade which began with a worldwide pandemic and ended in an economic crash – the reverse of the 2010s), the misery of the 1930s and the crucible of the 1940s. They inherited a world of chaos;

---

[1] Feldbrugge, *History of Russian Law*, 49.

they left it superior, if imperfect. After painting in the WPA, building ships, bridges and global governing structures, they became fashion designers, pharmacists, opera singers and art and art history professors – the Western middle classes. Their modernist sensibilities left them comfortable with the prosaic mid-century Western dogmas (it all began with Greece and Rome, then the Middle Ages, the Renaissance, Columbus, Washington, etc.). Yet this all began to change as my parents' generation (Baby Boomers) came of age, as challenging the modernist archetypes (hence, postmodernism) became fashionable and some questioned whether Western civilisation itself even exists (it does). My grandmother Eudice Mesibov even left her career singing Bizet's *Carmen* in Marshall-planned post-war European opera halls to write a doctorate arguing that the second commandment was not always taken seriously. It was a great work of art history – and it also revealed something else. By the time I noticed it, the last bastions of traditional Western civilisational dogma, a tiny, self-reproducing caste, preserved the product at all costs.

The story of this story (the meta-story?) commenced in the autumn of 2010, when I began my first Greek class at Roger Williams University of Rhode Island. Like many post-industrialised Western universities (specifically the liberal arts kind) in the 2010s, History, Classics, Philosophy and all the social sciences (or humanities) were haemorrhaging students, and therefore funding, since few parents allowed for such extravagance after 2008's Big Short. Production and consumption had become the domain of economists, not historians. I was fortunate to have parents who approved such pedagogical indulgence, but everywhere were the signs of unavoidable unravelling: economics, finance, law and business departments were ballooning with money and students were taking out exorbitant loans for vocational degrees in the faint hope that they might come in handy. Still, our consistently 15-minutes-late-for-every-class professor of Greek discouraged us from pursuing Classics as a career – there wasn't enough room left in the bastion and most of us would need to scrape and scrounge producing or selling something else in the corporate world as the waters rose. Returning to him after living in Athens and witnessing the turmoil caused by uncontrolled financial markets, I was told that nothing written in Greek after the era of St Augustine of Hippo and St John Chrysostom was worth reading – the Classical canon ended in the fifth century. It was *his* bastion and *he* was the department head, so that was that. I suppose his words were one of the earliest reasons for the book you're holding.

If the villain plays a major role, luck is indispensable. This project was conceived in the final stages of my MRes at the University of Birmingham

(UoB) in 2013, where I had been writing a tedious argument against the conventional story of Vladimir's baptism in 987–9 in the Crimean city of Cherson. At the time, I was reading Paul Stephenson's *Byzantium's Balkan Frontier* and wondering whether the processes and forces which define Western civilisation (Christianisation and ethnogenesis) which he was discussing in the ninth- to thirteenth-century Balkans were applicable further east into Eurasia. What would that mean for Western Civilisation? The result was a topic that got me back into UoB in 2014 to continue working with my long-time supervisor, mentor and dear friend, Archie Dunn. I thank Archie for his constant support, everlasting patience, rivers of reference letters and limitless editing ever since our first emails in 2012. I also thank my advisor, guide and the social glue who held the entire department together (the Centre for Byzantine, Ottoman and Modern Greek Studies – CBOMGS – at UoB), Ruth Macrides, who steadfastly prodded me towards better expression in English and better reading in Greek, and who was continually patient through countless drafts of many articles with 'Teutonic' footnotes. Ruth could also grease the gears of historical production – she made 'diasporic' connections that allowed for publications and even my link to Edinburgh University Press (EUP). Ευχαριστώ πολύ για όλα. When she sadly passed away in 2019, CBOMGS was devastated – we (and myself personally) will always feel her loss. Archie and Ruth have been almost like family to me. And they both intimately know/knew the delicate process by which history is produced.

Yet it takes more than Greek to scale a cliff. Russian did not come naturally – my ancestors had renounced the language almost as soon as they left Odessa, Riga and Antwerp for new lives in New York. Mike Berry, of Birmingham's Centre for Russian, European and Eurasian Studies, serendipitously appeared one day as I was struggling with Russian. Over several years, he guided me through seas of Russian translations with persistence and serenity. Гора благодарности.

Yet the story of the production of history is still more elaborate. Along the way, many others offered professional advice and correspondence. I thank Peter Rogers, Jonathan Shepard, Marek Jankowiak, Maria Vrij, Günter Prinzing and Dionysios Stathakopoulos for their input. Peter has been a steadfast friend and guide – as much for 'real life' as in Byzantium; I appreciate so much all our conversations and correspondence. Jonathan has made many recommendations, written several letters and answered many of my questions throughout this process. Marek's input has been vital regarding comparative coinage and the movement of precious metals through ninth- to thirteenth-century Pontic-Caspian Eurasia. Maria, aside from facilitating many long hours in the UoB Barber coin study room, has generously provided much needed guidance on sixth- to eighth-century Byzantine coinage. Ever since we met in Belgrade in August 2016, Günter has offered his reference and crucial ideas. Finally, Dionysios has been a staunch advocate with a strong sense of justice throughout the odyssey of producing history.

Friends and colleagues from everywhere, many of them long-time experts in the process of producing history – from the US, Ukraine, the Russian Federation, and everywhere in between at CBOMGS (friends who have been there through thick and thin, such as Francisco López-Santos Kornberger) – must be thanked, including Florin Curta, Anthony Kaldellis, Nikita Khrapunov, Peter Golden and Ian Wood for personal communications and suggestions (and for *Byzantine and Rus' Seals*, Nikita).

Special thanks go to John Haldon and Paul Stephenson, seasoned veterans of the process of producing history, who read through an original PhD thesis which went to over 600 pages, not to mention writing many reference letters. I understand that it was exhausting to read, but I didn't want to take any chances at the viva in 2018. Without John's and Paul's suggestions and advocacy, this book would not be in your hands.

The homestretch began when EUP agreed to take on a relatively unknown young historian with no prior books nor fellowships. Being an impure Classicist, then a Byzantinist, dabbling in Central European, East European, Russian and Eurasian history and archaeology is not the most palatable background in a world where funding is jealously guarded and flags are firmly planted in thoroughly demarcated disciplines with self-reproducing, torch-passing fiefdoms. Yet I must earnestly thank Carol MacDonald at EUP for taking the chance and Niels Gaul, Yannis Stouraitis, Rachel Bridgewater, Louise Hutton, Fiona Conn, Fiona Sewell, Jane Burkowski and the whole EUP review committee for their help and suggestions to improve this book. Luck reappeared early in 2020 right before the COVID-19 outbreak when I found out from Sarah Wells at the Warburg Institute at the University of London that my project had been chosen for a Yates fellowship, without which this product would have been long bogged down in the machinery of historical production. So many thanks go to Bill Sherman, Michelle O'Malley and everyone else at the Warburg. Feeling like an exile lost in a sea of ill-advised trajectories in the social sciences, I have been delighted to find refuge at the Warburg.

Finally, none of this would have been possible without the eternal support, inspiration and encouragement (even from afar) of my parents, Deborah Mesibov and Richard Feldman, my grandparents, and the rest of the Mesibov and Feldman clans – my whole family. I must also recognise my lifelong friends who rarely laughed at my career choice: Thomas, Warren, Corey, Michael, Jarred, Jonathan, Maria and Jill. And for all her patience, strength, support and faith, I thank my partner and companion, Pilar Hernández Mateos – *y toda la familia de Hernández y Mateos, saludos grandes de la página.*

History is a laborious product – to consume and to produce. It requires long-term, structural evaluation; its investment in the past is tantamount to its investment in the future. Yet I am certain the era is approaching when the discipline of history, and of the social sciences generally, returns to its rightful place,[2] not among the last bastions of a decayed structure, awash in a sea of economic hazard, but as the lights of learning astride civilisations they've always been, where humans can once again take refuge trying to make sense of it all.

Alex Mesibov Feldman

---

[2] Guldi and Armitrage, *History Manifesto*.

Abbreviations

The following lists are abbreviations used in the bibliography. Sources such as the Russian Primary Chronicle, or the *Povest' Vremennÿkh Let* (*PVL*) and the *De Administrando Imperio* (*DAI*) are abbreviated as such in the main text.

Latin-Alphabet Abbreviations

AAoE	*Anthropology & Archeology of Eurasia*
ActaAntHung	*Acta Orientalia Academiae Scientiarum Hungaricae*
AEMA	*Archivum Eurasiae Medii Aevi*
BMGS	*Byzantine and Modern Greek Studies*
BSO[A]S	*Bulletin of the School of Oriental [and African] Studies*
BZ	*Byzantinische Zeitschrift*
CFHB	*Corpus Fontium Historiae Byzantinae*
CSHB	*Corpus Scriptorum Historiae Byzantinae*
CSSH	*Comparative Studies in Society and History*
DOP	*Dumbarton Oaks Papers*
EHR	*English Historical Review*
EJA	*European Journal of Archaeology*
EtBalk	*Études Balkaniques*
EtByz	*Études Byzantines et Post-Byzantines*
GOTR	*Greek Orthodox Theological Review*
HA	*Hungarian Archaeology*
HUkSt	*Harvard Ukrainian Studies*
JbGOst	*Jahrbücher für Geschichte Osteuropas*
JESHO	*Journal of the Economic and Social History of the Orient*
JMedHist	*Journal of Medieval History*
JSS	*Journal of Semitic Studies*

MGH	*Monumenta Germaniae Historica*
MQ	*Mankind Quarterly*
NC	*Numismatic Chronicle*
RH	*Russian History*
SBS	*Studies in Byzantine Sigillography*
SEER	*Slavonic and East European Review*
VizVrem	*Византийский Временник*
VoprIst	*Вопросы Истории*

Cyrillic-Alphabet Abbreviations

ВК	*Восточная коллекция*
ЗРВИ	*Зборник радова Византолошког института*
НиЭ	*Нумизматика и Эпиграфика*
РА	*Российская Археология*
СА	*Советская Археология*
СЩ	*Сфрагістичний Щорічник*
ХΘИиП	*ΧΕΡΣΩΝΟΣ ΘΕΜΑΤΑ: Империя и Полис. Сборник научных трудов*

Note on Transcription and Transliteration

When transcribing Greek names, I have tried to render them through strict transliteration (e.g., Konstantinos VII Porphyrogennetos; Theodoros Laskaris; Ioannes Tzetzes). As for transliterating Russian names, ethnonyms, posts and titles into English, I have opted to adhere to what are, in my opinion, the most accurate representational characters available in the Latin alphabet. Therefore, I have listed below the most common letters in the Cyrillic alphabet whose transcriptions are not directly self-evident and the equivalent transcriptions of which I use frequently in this inquiry.

Cyrillic letters (on the left) with the corresponding Latin characters (on the right):

ц	c
ш	š
щ	šč
х	kh
ы	ÿ
й	j
и	i
ж	ž
я	ja
ч	č
ь	ʼ
ю	ju
ё	ë
ъ	ă
i	y

Regarding the Cyrillic letters э and е, I have made no distinction between them and have largely transliterated them with the Latin letter *e*.

Byzantine, Khazar and Rus' titles and posts, such as *protevon, strategos, metropolites, el'teber, knjaz'* and *khağan*, I have rendered in italics to distinguish them as such to prevent them from being confused with both proper place names and personal names, which I have left in a normal font. The same goes for commonly used contemporaneous concepts such as the Byzantine *oikoumene* or the Islamic *ummah*.

Για τους γονείς και τους παππούδες μου,
Por todos nuestros antepasados,
За всіх мертвих. Пусть они останутся мертвыми.

וְאָנֹכִ֗י מַעֲשֵׂיהֶם֙ וּמַחְשְׁבֹ֣תֵיהֶ֔ם בָּאָ֕ה לְקַבֵּ֥ץ אֶת־כָּל־הַגּוֹיִ֖ם וְהַלְּשֹׁנ֑וֹת וּבָ֖אוּ וְרָא֥וּ אֶת־כְּבוֹדִֽי׃

וְשַׂמְתִּ֨י בָהֶ֜ם א֗וֹת וְשִׁלַּחְתִּ֣י מֵהֶ֣ם ׀ פְּלֵיטִ֡ים אֶֽל־הַגּוֹיִ֡ם תַּרְשִׁ֨ישׁ פּ֥וּל וְל֛וּד מֹ֥שְׁכֵי קֶ֖שֶׁת תֻּבַ֣ל וְיָוָ֑ן הָאִיִּ֣ים הָרְחֹקִ֗ים אֲשֶׁ֨ר לֹא־שָׁמְע֤וּ אֶת־שִׁמְעִי֙ וְלֹא־רָא֣וּ אֶת־כְּבוֹדִ֔י וְהִגִּ֥ידוּ אֶת־כְּבוֹדִ֖י בַּגּוֹיִֽם׃

> And I, because of what they have planned and done, am about to come and gather the people of all nations and languages, and they will come and see my glory.
>
> I will set a sign among them, and I will send some of those who survive to the nations – to Tarshish, to the Libyans and Lydians (famous as archers), to Tubal and Greece, and to the distant islands that have not heard of my fame or seen my glory. They will proclaim my glory among the nations.
>
> Isaiah 66:18–19 (*NIV*)

ἕκαστοι τὰ πάτρια, ὁποῖά ποτ' ἂν τύχῃ <καθεστηκότα>, περιέπουσι. Δοκεῖ δ' οὕτως καὶ συμφέρειν, οὐ μόνον καθότι ἐπὶ νοῦν ἦλθεν ἄλλοις ἄλλως νομίσαι καὶ δεῖ φυλάττειν τὰ ἐς κοινὸν κεκυρωμένα, ἀλλὰ καὶ ὅτι ὡς εἰκὸς τὰ μέρη τῆς γῆς ἐξ ἀρχῆς ἄλλα ἄλλοις ἐπόπταις νενεμημένα καὶ κατά τινας ἐπικρατείας διειλημμένα ταύτῃ καὶ διοικεῖται. Καὶ δὴ τὰ παρ' ἑκάστοις ὀρθῶς ἂν πράττοιτο ταύτῃ δρώμενα, ὅπῃ ἐκείνοις φίλον· παραλύειν δὲ οὐχ ὅσιον εἶναι τὰ ἐξ ἀρχῆς κατὰ τόπους νενομισμένα.

> Koetschau (ed.), *Origenes Gegen Celsus*, §V.XXV. This is translated by Chadwick, *Origen: Contra Celsum*, 283.

In the Western World the philosophy of history was founded in the Christian faith. In a grandiose sequence of works ranging from St Augustine to Hegel this faith visualised the movement of God through history. God's acts of revelation represent the decisive dividing lines. Thus Hegel could still say: All history goes toward and comes from Christ. The appearance of the Son of God is the axis of world history. Our chronology bears daily witness to this Christian structure of history. But the Christian faith is only one faith, not the faith of mankind. This view of universal history therefore suffers from the defect that it can only be valid for believing Christians.

> Jaspers, *The Origin and Goal of History*, 1.

מַה־שֶּׁהָיָה כְּבָר הוּא וַאֲשֶׁר לִהְיוֹת כְּבָר הָיָה וְהָאֱלֹהִים יְבַקֵּשׁ אֶת־נִרְדָּף

Whatever is has already been, and what will be has been before; and God will call the past to account.

Ecclesiastes 3:15 (*NIV*)

A Proposition

The tradition of all dead generations weighs like a nightmare on the brains of the living. And just as they seem to be occupied with revolutionizing themselves and things, creating something that did not exist before, precisely in such epochs of revolutionary crisis they anxiously conjure up the spirits of the past to their service, borrowing from them names, battle slogans, and costumes in order to present this new scene in world history in time-honored disguise and borrowed language.

Karl Marx, *18th Brumaire of Louis Napoleon*

За десять лет меняется всё, а за двести лет ничего не меняется.
In ten years, everything changes; in two hundred years, nothing changes.

Pjotr Stolypin

In the year 987, the Roman emperor Basileios II Porphyrogennetos was surrounded on all sides in his palace in Constantinople – New Rome (Nova Roma). His bookish progenitors had allowed caudillos and generalissimos (in Greek, κηδεμόνες) to rule in their stead for the past several generations, and his misguided attempt in 986 to prove his mettle against the Bulgars at the Battle of Trajan's Gate resulted in the disgruntlement of the military officers who had once fought for his predecessors' generalissimos. Now two of them (Bardas Skleros and Bardas Phokas) were steadily bearing down on Constantinople from the Anatolian heartland, bolstered by thousands of Armenian crack troops unhappy with imperial Chalcedonian Christianity. All of Anatolia seemed to have deserted Basileios, and with it, imperial provinces in Crimea most likely seeking greater autonomy. Court historians like Leon Diakonos looked back to the times of the generalissimos with nostalgia while poets like Ioannes Geometres lamented the sullying of imperial authority and berated the Romans as 'Thracians'. Cornered, Basileios sent a desperate delegation to some Viking named Vladimir faraway in Kiev asking for military support in exchange for the hand of his sister – the princess Anna Porphyrogennete – a prize so valuable that not even the western emperor, Otto III, was allowed her. The price? Accept Christianity immediately and conquer Cherson (Sevastopol') – most probably on Basileios' behalf.

No one knows exactly how many inhabitants of Kiev were baptised in the Dniepr that day; sources differ on the exact story. In the *Russian Primary Chronicle (Povest' Vremennÿkh Let* – hereafter, *PVL*), a source containing so much mythology about Christianisation that its historical reliability is subject to permanent concern, nearly all of Kiev's population accepted Christianity (although there were already many Christians among them). In far more reliable Byzantine sources, there is barely a peep. Yet one thing is certain: enough people have been Christianised since then that over a thousand years later, Orthodox onion domes still dot the landscape from Sevastopol' to Vladivostok.

The stories of medieval conversions have been told many times and frequently focus on the story of the individual ruler's conversion; the process is also usually set in Europe and couched in terms of Christianisation, to either Latin or Byzantine Christianity. Yet similar processes occurred further east as dynasties such as the Sāmānids or Almušids chose Islam in central Asia, resulting in what can be called Islamisation. Much less well known, but perhaps even more strikingly, Judaism has also been chosen – as when the Khazar rulers, presumably the Āšĭnà dynasty, selected Judaism from the three Abrahamic faiths. Each dynast had his reasons of political opportunism for making his choice, which was later mythologised. If Paris is worth a mass, then for Vladimir, Anna was worth a siege of Cherson. It was also a way for him to crush dissent and provide a safety valve for incoming Vikings seeking plunder further south. For Almuš in his capital of Bolgar on the middle Volga, Islam healed his family; it also provided security, better fortifications and enhanced commerce. For the Khazarian Āšĭnà dynasty in Itīl' in the Volga delta, Judaism was a third way between Islam and Christianity to avoid subservience to either. For all of these dynasties, however, the process of adopting one brand of monotheism or another was never as simple as an individual's baptism or *Shahada* (the Islamic creed) incantation for a king or prince. Joining one club or another brought an entire constitutional package, typically including urbanisation and sedentarisation, sacred liturgical scripts, textual and historical traditions and most importantly, *law* – which sealed the security, legitimacy and wealth of the ruling dynasty in perpetuity. The entire top-down package, I believe, can therefore be deemed *monotheisation*.

As it occurred in Europe, this process has been described as Christianisation; in the Middle East and North Africa, Islamisation. But these geographic regions, which are now commonly understood to describe these two faiths respectively, need not have turned out as indeed they have. For centuries, Islamisation was a process occurring in Europe just as Christianisation occurred in the Middle East and further in Asia. Judaisation, as in Khazaria, also occurred. And although many conversions from paganism to monotheism are often conceived as late antique or medieval phenomena, these processes were certainly not confined to commonly used periodisations like 'late antiquity' or the 'Middle Ages'. They range across many centuries – from Rome's Christianisation after Constantine to far-flung attempts at Islamisation after Mohammed, Christianisation in the Americas, and even into the eighteenth to twentieth centuries.

Therefore, geographical labels like 'Europe' and the 'Middle East', and periodisational labels like 'late antiquity' or 'Middle Ages', are arbitrary: they tend to obfuscate the substantial historical developments occurring in the process of monotheisation. This book is about both the short-term and long-term consequences of monotheism in Eurasia; it is about globalising these terms (or at least putting them into a broader context), which had previously only applied to Western Civilisation. Namely, this book is primarily concerned with the growth and development of monotheism in a place and time where Europe and Asia, and when late antiquity and the Middle Ages, cannot be truly distinguished. Hence the book specifically focuses on Pontic-Caspian Eurasia during the eighth to thirteenth centuries. But what is Pontic-Caspian Eurasia exactly?

Pontic-Caspian Eurasia encompasses the forests, forest-steppe and steppe regions of Eastern Europe, the northern Black Sea and Caspian littorals, from the Lower Danube to the Western Carpathians to the Baltic; from the Northern Caucasus to the Lower Volga (and points east along the Silk Roads) to the Urals to the White Sea. It is an admittedly ambiguous and vast realm. Yet its ambiguity and scale are precisely what make Pontic-Caspian Eurasia such a valuable object for consideration: the ambiguity and scale of these periods and regions make for exceptional overlapping 'Petri dishes' from which to understand the development of monotheism, without beginning from preconceived ideas about ethnicity or sovereignty (teleological history).

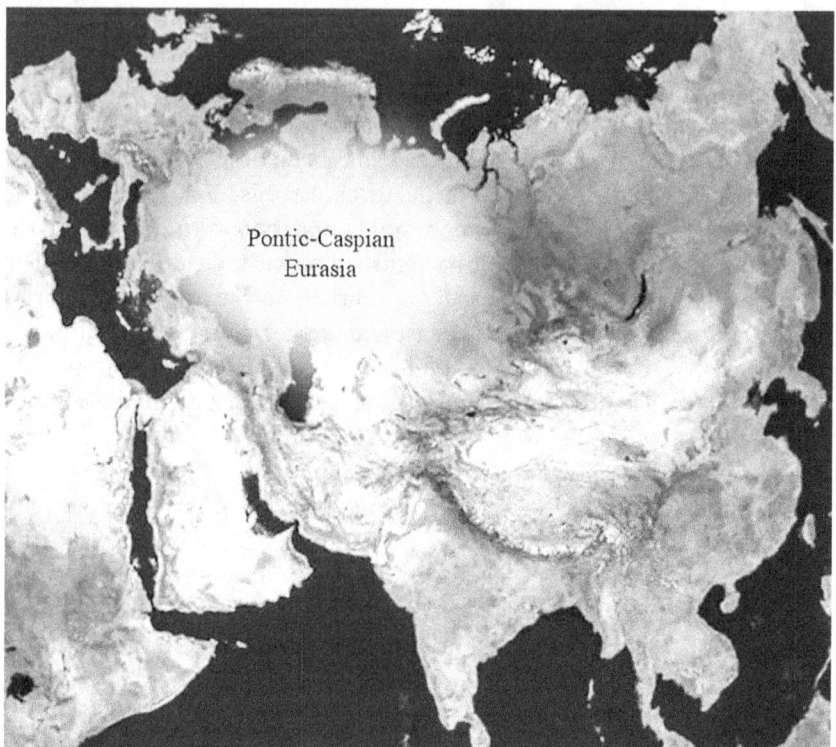

Figure I.1 A map of Eurasia with outlines of Pontic-Caspian Eurasia.

Pontic-Caspian Eurasia is also a useful region for inquiry because it avoids retelling the stories of various current nation-states like Ukraine, Hungary, Bulgaria, Kazakhstan or Russia – each of which has been abundantly conceived in some form or another corresponding to the ancient and medieval periodisational paradigms. Instead, this book views these stories backwards in time, involving the textual and archaeological data garnered from the geographical territories of these countries while simultaneously considering that the past can only ever be a province of the present, despite any attempt to perceive history regardless of present interpretation.

Since interpreting the past is a perpetual enterprise, many old interpretations linger on, having fermented into modern consensuses or conventions, which remain frequently unchallenged. Specifically, the story of how antiquity became late antiquity and then the Middle Ages (often taken for granted by the very historians whose task it is to deconstruct and defy such convention) endures either unchallenged or through incremental revisions. Such is the standard fare for history courses in Western high schools and universities: continuing to employ intellectually valuable concepts and scholarly shorthands, yet which either have taken on lives of their own, or have proven to be inapplicable beyond the self-described 'West'. For instance, one might ask: where is the geographical line beyond which the difference between late antiquity and the Middle Ages does not apply? The same may be said for concepts such as 'tribe', 'ethnicity' or 'nationality', which, albeit frequently confronted, linger on confusedly, and often supposed as either primordial or circumstantial in the imaginations of many. These are examples of modern conventions (sometimes even taken for granted in modern scholarship) which are yet to be fully stripped from the twenty-first-century consciousness, whose underpinnings still carry the vestiges of the awesome twentieth century. This is not to contend that structural concepts such as ethnicity and sovereignty in history have no value; they do. The problem is rather that such scholarly shorthand easily takes on a life of its own. Projecting today's notions onto the past is a practice we are undoubtedly familiar with, yet the question remains: what new consensuses can satisfactorily replace the old? Since conventions can hardly be altogether forfeited, but rather replaced, I propose to make a new contribution to the debates of periodisation, with particular regard to ethnicity and sovereignty in Pontic-Caspian Eurasia, in which neither the respective emergences of the above-mentioned countries, nor the differentiation of the late antique from the medieval, is taken for granted.

Because the various regions of Pontic-Caspian Eurasia, when considered in context with each other, may constitute Petri dishes for examining the processes of monotheisation, we can view monotheisation not simply as an individual enterprise of conversion, but as a societal endeavour of all the attendant processes accompanying conversion, in which the individual and the collective are bound by the same fate for the sake of replicating the divine will. While bottom-up conversion movements were important, the top-down adoptions of monotheism by various rulers, whether Christianity, Islam or Judaism, is the primary foundation for what we now consider ethnicity. This is not to say that ethnicity did not exist before monotheisation – it did. But it did not have monotheism as a binding agent (to use a chemical metaphor) and was therefore far more fluid, or what we may call circumstantial, based on the changing circumstances which formed individual and group identities. By contrast, after generations of monotheisation, which solidified monotheistic identities into a more viscous substance, ethnicity began to seem primordial – as if it were set in amber from the pre-monotheistic past, even if it was not. In other words, primary sources considered pagans as *ethne* until, after generations of top-down monotheisation, ethnicity seemed a primordial phenomenon, although it was not so originally.

Therefore, late antiquity, as a periodisational paradigm describing the gradual top-down adoption of monotheistic law by various rulers, extends much later into the eighth to thirteenth centuries as we move our geographical focus much further east, into Pontic-Caspian Eurasia. Given a more expansive view of the roots of civilisation, in resolutely monotheistic firmaments in a wider region including Europe, Asia and the Middle East, we are left with implications about the place of the West within a broader lineage of Abrahamic civilisation. Ultimately, by demystifying the transition from the ancient to the medieval world, I propose that the processes of monotheisation can be applicable beyond just the Western European late antiquity or Middle Ages. And we may even approach a more holistic definition of civilisation itself.

Pontic-Caspian Eurasia: Overlapping 'Petri Dishes'

This book will address these historiographical and periodisational challenges using the various case studies available in Pontic-Caspian Eurasia as overlapping 'Petri dishes' in which to identify, confront and reassess our understanding of the world of the eighth to thirteenth centuries.

While the admittedly ambiguous term 'Pontic-Caspian Eurasia' may necessarily be vast and perhaps slightly confusing, it is nevertheless useful as a geographical concept since it proves simultaneously immense and yet exclusive. For example, Pontic-Caspian Eurasia may include case studies and debates within the histories of Russia, Hungary, Khazaria, Tatarstan, Bulgaria, Kazakhstan and even the Caucasus. In terms of monotheistic adherence, because it incorporates communities and rulers practising paganism, Judaism, Christianity (Latin and Orthodox) and Islam, 'Pontic-Caspian Eurasia' is a viable term as a structurally confined geographic area during the eighth to thirteenth centuries. It is not a geographical term which exclusively evokes Latin or Orthodox Christianity, or Islam, like 'Europe' (Christianity) or 'the Middle East' (Islam). Pontic-Caspian Eurasia also includes the Pontic-Caspian steppe and its long-time nomadic inhabitants, which admittedly extends it to East Asia. The term's geography is useful, being necessarily large enough to transcend national, climatic and geographic boundaries, without being universal.

Pontic-Caspian Eurasia is also as useful chronologically as it is geographically. Periodisations like late antiquity and the Middle Ages *cannot* be satisfactorily applied in Pontic-Caspian Eurasia, as they typically carry the normative paradigms of 'Roman' and 'Post-Roman' Western European (Latin-Christian) history. Therefore, Pontic-Caspian Eurasia is particular enough to favourably lend itself to drawing specifically local conclusions, but simultaneously general enough to imply certain universally applicable conclusions about the process of monotheisation. Because Pontic-Caspian Eurasia challenges periodisational concepts like late antiquity and the Middle Ages, and even geographical concepts like Europe and Asia, it also has implications for divisions between academic disciplines.

Although I was trained as a Byzantinist, it hardly seems that such a rigid notion of discipline easily applies to the era and area. For example, Anthony Bryer, the eminent Birmingham historian of Byzantium, is said to have declared that a historian of Russia is equally a historian of Byzantium.[1] Simultaneously, while a Medievalist's field is different from that of a Byzantinist, the question arises: where is the line? What defines the disciplinary parameters of the Byzantinist versus the Medievalist? What about a Medievalist versus a Classicist? These distinctions did not structurally exist in the sources by which we define them; instead, they are much more recent creations, and particularly have been applied as a Western yardstick, while historians and archaeologists frequently disagree on how such Western terms can apply beyond European space. Ultimately, it is merely recent convention to view the works of Augustine of Hippo (fourth to fifth centuries) as the bookend to a classical canon which may otherwise extend to the works of Maximos of Arta (fifteenth to sixteenth centuries) or later still.

Meanwhile, although historians talk of multidisciplinarity, collaboration and contextualisation, all these disciplines often remain needlessly divided. It seems these disciplinary divisions require less distinction, not more, lest they verge on anachronism at best, or worse, obsolescence. Because of divisions between these fields, their methodologies differ while sources are approached with resulting inconsistencies (which is not necessarily problematic). This is not to say that conventionally separate methodologies, whether in Eastern Europe or in the West, whether within the purview of Classicists, Medievalists, Byzantinists or Russologists or another discipline, ought to be discarded. I am *not* advocating a 'good old common-sense' approach. But to avoid teleological interpretations of historical processes, I intend to transcend arbitrary chronological, geographical and methodological tendencies, and instead combine them.

[1] Paraphrased by Milner-Gulland, 'Ultimate Russia, Ultimate Byzantium'.

For example, I will challenge the overly schematic, dominant ideas about the formations of both ethnicity and chronology – is ethnicity either a primordial or a circumstantial phenomenon? Can the tripartite division of history (ancient–medieval–modern), particularly common in the West, be imposed on non-Western traditions? What even constitutes 'the West'? What does this imply about how we define civilisations? The reason for addressing ethnicity together with conventional periodisation is that jointly, I believe these concepts (beginning as scholarly shorthand) have taken on lives of their own, becoming excessively schematised, ultimately rendering history as an easily reproducible teleological package, ready to be deployed to substantiate recent political agendas.

As an example of the generic, combined usages of ethnicity and chronology in many historiographies, let us consider the case of the 'Ruritanian people' (to use the common placeholder ethnonym [after Ernest Gellner]). In this easily replicable package, the Ruritanians migrated, as an entire ethnicity, from their ancient homeland to their medieval homeland. There, they created a medieval state and converted to Christianity (or Islam in other cases) at some debatable, if stable date. Archaeological finds, with their specific ethnic markings, of certain types of ceramics, arrowheads, ritual symbols and swords, confirm their ethnic attachment to their homeland. Ruritanian runes, attested epigraphically on ancient gravestones, indicate the continuity of the Ruritanian language. Their first national dynasty, the Parstids, conquered the surrounding populations and expanded the borders of the medieval state. They commissioned medieval historical works to glorify the nation, minted coins and seals to exhibit their ethnic exclusivity and cohesion, and their ethnically homogeneous descendants happily reside in their modern state to this day.

Certainly this is an egregious oversimplification of the way history has been understood for generations both before and since World War II. And historians have been scrutinising and revising portions of it ever since, according to their respective specialisms and fields.[2] I propose to bind these erstwhile separate fields together by integrating various methods, techniques and sources, both textual and archaeological.

The Proposal

This book proposes to reconsider the historical narratives and counter-narratives of the establishment of monotheism (and by extension,

---

[2] According to Siapkas, 'Ancient Ethnicity and Modern Identity', 66: 'Every generation rewrites history ... Classical antiquity does not exist independently of us, but is constructed and maintained by our engagements with it in the present.'

ethnicity and sovereignty) during the eighth to thirteenth centuries in Pontic-Caspian Eurasia. Many of these narratives and counter-narratives remain conflicted due to the dismissal, unawareness or decontextualisation of the underlying forces and processes involved in monotheisation in both Western and Soviet/post-Soviet historiography. For example, some English-language histories, while often important, may be outdated, narrow in scope or, frequently, unfamiliar with recent archaeological discoveries, usually reported in Russian. Conversely, Russian-language literature sometimes bears other inclinations, such as towards Soviet-era Marxist historical analyses and, more recently, towards adapting the past to construct ethnocentric narratives (for example, conceptions of Ukrainian or Russian ancient and medieval histories). Although these foundations are indispensable, they also serve as a commencement point from typical twentieth-century historiography.

In exploring the monotheisation of Pontic-Caspian Eurasia, we cannot escape the imposing nature of Byzantine imperialism and sovereignty. After all, Byzantium was the Eastern Roman Empire – whose emperors were theoretically sovereign over all Christendom. Due to imperial restructuring into internal provinces termed *themata*, it has been supposed that Byzantium had become a kind of medieval nation-state during the eighth to thirteenth centuries.[3] To describe their polity, Byzantine sources use words like *politeia* – an ambiguous term which can be translated as polity, kingdom, empire, dominion and so on. Byzantine sources also frequently use the term *oikoumene* (the inhabited world) to describe their domain.[4] The two terms denoted slightly different meanings of state and sovereignty in the imperial imagination. For example, while *oikoumene* initially meant

---

[3] Kaldellis, *Romanland*.
[4] There are two overlapping definitions of the term *oikoumene*: the inhabited, or known, world, and the specifically Christian world, or Christendom, which was gradually repurposed by imperial sources to refer expressly to the world subject to imperial law – the Orthodox world. There is little reason to believe that the concept of the *oikoumene* is a current ideological construct foisted onto Byzantium. Quite simply, as Magoulias writes (*Byzantine Christianity*, 89): 'If the emperor was the monarch of the Byzantine oikoumene, meaning the inhabited Christian empire, then the patriarch of the empire's capital city was the "ecumenical" ecclesiastical leader of that empire.' This statement is not a recent ideological construct so much as recognising a Byzantine one. According to Kaldellis (*Hellenism in Byzantium*, 100), 'the methodology by which the "universalist" interpretation has been constructed is problematic. First, it rests on the fiction of the "multi-ethnic empire", which was partly devised to serve the needs of modern national identities competing against that of Byzantium itself.' I agree with him that the concept of the 'multi-ethnic empire' is hollow – but only up to a point (cf. Kaldellis, *Romanland*; Websdale, 'Remarks on *Romanland*', 319–34). Yet I do not believe that the term *oikoumene* is to blame.

the inhabited, or known, world, later, in the eleventh to fifteenth centuries, it came to express the Orthodox Christian world slightly more specifically (but not simply Byzantium as distinct from the rest of Orthodoxy) – much like the Islamic *ummah*. Conversely, the term *politeia* denotes more the imperial Orthodox sovereignty, but again, not simply Byzantium as distinct from the rest of Orthodoxy (else the more specific term *Rhomaion politeia* could be used). Ultimately, the discussion will take both concepts into account, but with the recognition that neither satisfactorily separates Byzantium from any other Orthodox 'state' (such as the Rus').

Two ways of interpreting Byzantium are therefore visible: the Byzantium of the *themata* (based on Kaldellis' idea of a medieval nation-state which incorporated various subgroups within, such as Armenians and Bulgars), and the Byzantium of the *oikoumene* (an entire Orthodox civilisation). Questions arise: was the *oikoumene* meant to describe the entire known world, or just the part legally or theoretically subject to the emperor?[5] Was imperial sovereignty as absolute outside Constantinople as Byzantine sources have indicated? Can we veritably apply recent distinctions between 'church' and 'state' (likewise, 'ecclesiastical' versus 'secular') to eighth- to thirteenth-century Pontic-Caspian Eurasia? As eleventh- to thirteenth-century Byzantine ecclesiastical structures spread throughout much (though not all) of Pontic-Caspian Eurasia, it is helpful to think of Byzantium not just as a nation-state, but also as a civilisation – the *oikoumene* – which offers far more in terms of understanding the past as it was conceived by contemporaries (especially in Byzantium's relationship with northern peoples) rather than recently imagined.[6]

Therefore, the concepts of sovereignty and ethnicity are primary concerns in eighth- to thirteenth-century Pontic-Caspian Eurasia. Some historians have projected Rus', Bulgarian or Khazarian sovereignty or ethnicity as early as possible, bordering on the anachronistic. Similarly, others imagine various ethnicities as early as possible, while the very concept of ethnicity itself is often conflated with pagan tribalism (termed primordial ethnicity).[7] Ethnolinguistic cohesion and continuity are often taken for granted,

---

[5] Koder, 'Die räumlichen Vorstellungen der Byzantiner von der Ökumene', 15–34.

[6] This is a point made by many historians, including: Zuckerman, 'Byzantium's Pontic Policy in *Notitiae Episcopatuum*', 201–30; Shepard, 'Khazars' Formal Adoption of Judaism', 9–34; Androshchuk, 'Byzantine Imperial Seals in Rus'', 43–54; Vachkova, 'Danube Bulgaria and Khazaria', 339–62; Wasserstein, 'Khazars and Islam', 373–86; Prinzing, 'Die autokephale Kirchenprovinz Bulgarien/Ohrid', 389–413.

[7] See for example the historiographical discussions of the Volga Bulgars, Magyars, Pečenegs, Cuman-Qıpčaqs and Rus' in Chapter 3.

especially when applied to archaeological discoveries, which have often been categorised by types – archaeological typologies – resulting in 'culture-history', like the pseudo-case of the Ruritanian people. Instead, I will propose alternatives to such arbitrary assumptions of pre-monotheistic ethnicity and sovereignty, which are better summarised as shifting allegiance networks, within which individual and communal agents operated regardless of recent periodisational conventions like the transition of a given sovereignty or ethnicity from late antiquity to the early Middle Ages.

It is helpful to begin with underpinning thematic dichotomies like nomadism and sedentarism, centrality and periphery, literacy and non-literacy, and paganism versus monotheism. Although these schematic binaries may admittedly be easily and frequently oversimplified, these themes are useful for making comparisons between processes occurring in different times and places. For example, due to the Christianisation and sedentarisation of previously pagan migrations during the *völkerwanderung* (the migration period), can we truly assume that this period ended at some stable, if debatable date in the seventh to eighth centuries, when we have myriad archaeological and textual data ascribing many more migrations in the Pontic-Caspian Eurasia continuing much later? Conversely, if late antiquity can be supposed to have ended and the Middle Ages begun when various dynasties adopted Christianity, Latin or Orthodox, where does that leave those who adopted Islam or Judaism? Alternatively, can we distil Russian or Hungarian identity down to ethnolinguistic exclusivity (of the Magyars, Slavs or Scandinavians) and contrive these respective labels as ethnically primordial and/or permanent as early as the eighth to ninth centuries? While many are preoccupied with defining the characteristics of one nation or another, or the changes within one predefined era or another (for example: late antique versus early medieval), the continuities between various peoples and periods are very often overlooked. In other words, attempts to establish the ethnicities and/or sovereignties (like ancient Ukrainians) and periodisations (for instance: ancient Bulgaria versus medieval Bulgaria), as static instead of as processual phenomena, while once popular, have grown increasingly limited in scope as some historians, working in the confines of various schools of thought, have sought to narrow their fields of study or to disengage from such contentious topics altogether.[8]

Building on Dimitri Obolensky's *Byzantine Commonwealth* (1971), I suggest that during the eighth to thirteenth centuries, several significant

---

[8] See for example the historiographical discussions in the concluding chapter, 'A Reassessment of Civilisation in Pontic-Caspian Eurasia'.

developments occurred (namely, monotheisation and its attendant processes), which I believe spelled the waning of a much longer late antique 'migration period' than has been previously defined. By employing this comparative framework with which to chart the successes and failures of various eighth- to thirteenth-century dynasties in Pontic-Caspian Eurasia, I hope to recontextualise understandings of the roots of today's civilisations and periodisations – not as grounded in the ancient world of Greece, Rome and Persia, but rather in the monotheistic world of Orthodox and Latin Christianity, Sunni and Shi'a Islam, and Judaism. In short, the goal of this book is to demonstrate that the phenomena of ethnicity and sovereignty, as currently defined, are layered, and the base layer is none other than monotheism itself.

Methods

In surveying the eighth- to thirteenth-century monotheisation of Pontic-Caspian Eurasia, the book's basic methodology is the comparative analysis of dynasties, groups and monotheisms – and by extension, sovereignties and ethnicities. Several major cases will be compared in chronological order: the Khazars, Volga Bulgars, Magyars, Pečenegs, Cuman-Qıpčaqs and Rus'. Comparative analysis as methodology is important due to scale, especially when employing both textual and archaeological evidence. It is meant to challenge broad notions like ethnicity and sovereignty, rather than to presuppose them in pursuit of more limited aims. That said, the devil is, as always, in the methodological, if proverbial, detail.

Textual methodologies

Texts like hagiographies, chronicles, legal codes, ecclesiastical records and personal missives can be read through several theoretical lenses permitting various inferences about the audiences and purposes of the authors. For example, early Rus' law codes have been read from Marxist angles; Anna Komnene's *Alexiad* can be viewed via feminist perspectives. Although these interpretations would not have been accessible to the original authors, such lenses have developed based on myriad examinations of texts; they are neither easily nor advisably dismissible. A minimalist approach to theory might sacrifice context on the altar of purity in textual interpretation. The question is not whether theoretical frameworks should be considered while examining sources, but how much theory? Not all sources are viewable the same way. Chronicles written by or for newly monotheistic dynasties ('barbarian histories') cannot be read the same way as imperial court histories. For example, the foundational literature in peripheral centres of the *oikoumene*, like Kiev, Gnezdun (Gniezno) or Esztergom, should be approached differently from the contemporary court histories in Rome or Constantinople. Such chronicles' authors had different goals in their narratives. By extension, our own historical interpretations would necessarily account for how these chronicles were conceived by contemporaries.

Walter Goffart pioneered this method, separating sixth- to eighth-century 'barbarian histories' like those written by Jordanes, Gregory of Tours, Paul the Deacon and so on from those written in the imperial court, since contemporaries bore similar conceptions when writing primarily about contemporary events.[9] However, his 'barbarian histories' range up to the early ninth century: 'the trough of the curve' between the fall of Rome and the rise of Christian Europe. On the contrary, the same source interpretations may be made even later. For example, the first sources written from the perspective of the Arian Goths (Jordanes' *Getica*), Latin Franks (Gregory of Tours' *Historia Francorum*) and so on are easily comparable to those of the Judaic Khazars (*Schechter Text*), Islamic Volga Bulgars (*Tārīkh-i-Bulghār*), Latin Magyars (*Gesta Hungarorum*) and Orthodox Rus' (*Povest' Vremennÿkh Let*). Due to similar rhetoric (praise of rulers credited with monotheisation, extravagant conversion stories, common usage of scriptural parallelisms and chiasmus,[10] etc.), these sources shared similar goals: instilling the new faith in the ruling elites and their subjects, which secured the legitimacy of the ruling dynasty.

Conversely, saintly hagiographies, histories, legal codes, clerical lists and epistles ought to be approached differently, due to their presence within far older literary traditions. For example, two texts pertaining to the attempted conversions of the Khazar and Volga Bulgar rulers clarify this point: the late ninth-century Slavonic *Vita Constantini* and the mid-tenth-century *diary (Risāla) of ibn Fadlān*. The Slavonic *Vita Constantini* tells the story of the missionary, Constantine-Cyril (Sts Kyrillos and Methodios, apostles to the Slavs), in his attempt to convert the Khazar *khağan* in a confessional court debate (c. 860–1). *Ibn Fadlān's diary*, by contrast, was written in the first person, telling the remarkably frank story of his meeting

---

[9] Goffart, *Narrators of Barbarian History*.
[10] Lund, 'Chiasmus in Old Testament', 104–26; Ostrowski, 'Volodimer's Conversion in "Povest' Vremennykh Let"', 567–80; Feldman, 'Autonomy and Rebellion in Cherson', 47–60.

the Volga Bulgar ruler, Almuš, who after considerable negotiations agreed to convert to Sunni Islam (c. 921–2). Compared to the *Tārīkh-i-Bulghār*, ibn Fadlān's narrative is characteristic of the more developed Arabic literary tradition of the Caliphate.

Finally, two Christian imperial documents, the mid-tenth-century *De Administrando Imperio* (hereafter *DAI*), compiled under the auspices of the emperor Konstantinos VII Porphyrogennetos, and several iterations of the *Notitiae Episcopatuum* (hereafter *NE*), are contentiously used as mines for information about eighth- to thirteenth-century ethnicities and sovereignties. For example, Konstantinos' ubiquitous usage of the term *ethnos* in the *DAI* has been accepted by generations of historians, keen to trace various ethnicities (Hungarian, Serbian, Ukrainian, etc.) as far into the past as possible. However, Konstantinos' own concept of ethnicity was hardly consistent not only in his *DAI*, but also in his other works, like his *De Thematibus*, *Vita Basilii* or *De Ceremoniis*. Elsewhere, although some historians characterise Kievan Rus' as a sort-of independently sovereign country since the tenth century, the eleventh- to twelfth-century versions of the *NE* record the Rus' metropolitanate as subject to imperial ecclesiastical administration. If Kievan Rus' was within the imperial *oikoumene*, alongside other metropolitanates and *themata* in Italy, Anatolia or the Balkans, then what does that imply about the sovereignty of Kievan Rus' and many other regions?

While answers to these questions will be attempted, in order to renegotiate the history of the time and place, sources cannot continue to be read in the light of recent ideological trends (national, intersectional, etc.); rather, they should be read in the light of their own contemporaneous world views. Ultimately, the comparative analysis of sources should cast doubt on conventional habits of taking simple models of ethnicity, sovereignty and periodisation for granted. This is equally true when examining archaeological evidence.

Archaeological methodologies

Like texts, archaeological material is equally susceptible to inadvisable exploitation. One of the most common forms of misusing archaeological evidence is through archaeological typologies, often found in burial assemblages and mounds (kurgans). For decades before and after World War II, it was common for archaeological discoveries to be typologised based on visible similarities: analogous-seeming glass beads, ceramic jars or even spearheads would commonly be assumed as materials used by ancient ethnicities, corresponding to recent nations. Thus, archaeologists could use material culture to reconstruct the prehistoric past for some presumed nation, a method known as 'culture-history'. It was also abused by nationalists to justify twentieth-century wars, for example, when objects with swastika markings were used to substantiate Nazi conquests.

Common everywhere, burial mounds can date from the eighteenth century CE back to the remotest antiquity. Archaeological typologies have also been used to speculate on the ethnicity of the deceased buried in kurgans, but this is frequently oversimplistic.[11] For example, the ethnicity of the deceased cannot necessarily be proven (like those of a Pečeneg, Magyar, Oğuz, etc.) based on typologies of material culture (namely, ceramics, weapons, jewellery, etc.) found in eighth- to thirteenth-century kurgans in Pontic-Caspian Eurasia. Ultimately, we cannot ask the deceased themselves if they identified as one ethnicity or another.

Interpreting archaeological finds of settlements and fortifications can be equally contentious: clusters of hill forts (*gorodišči*) on waterways throughout Pontic-Caspian Eurasia are sometimes assumed as borders between imagined ethnicities like Khazaria, Volga Bulgaria, or Rus'. Centuries-old borders are not always as explicit as archaeologists have imagined; rather, these settlements and fortifications may equally suggest gradual sedentarisation.[12]

Numismatics – the study of coins and money – is equally important since coins typically bear specific dates and mint marks. Two basic numismatic approaches are taken: the first being how changes on coins themselves demonstrate how various rulers and dynasties legitimised their reigns. For example, coins of tenth- to thirteenth-century Christian dynasties, conventionally deemed as the founding dynasties of Poland, Hungary and Russia (the Piasts, Árpáds and Rjurikids, respectively), are comparable to the coins of the contemporaneous Islamic dynasties

---

[11] Pálóczi Horváth, *Pechenegs, Cumans, Iasians*, 13; *Ḥudūd al-ʿĀlam*, tr. Minorsky, 160; Somogyi, 'Byzantine Coins in Avaria and Walachia', 111; Zhivkov, *Khazaria*, 113, 235; Matyushko, 'Nomads of Steppe', 155–67; Davis-Kimball, 'Excavations in Lower Don', 11–13; Curta, 'Burials in Prehistoric Mounds', 269–85; CSEN, '2001 Report'; CSEN, '2004 Report'.

[12] Petrukhin, 'Sacral Kingship and Judaism of Khazars', 292–5; Schorkowitz, 'Cultural Contact and Transfer', 85; Afanas'ev, 'Где археологические свидетельства хазарского государства', 43–55; Tortika, *Северо-западная хазария*, 90; Zhivkov, *Khazaria*, 201–33; Franklin and Shepard, *Emergence of Rus*, 81; Kovalev, 'Khazar Identity through Coins', 222; Romašov, 'Историческая география Хазарского каганата', 81–4; Stepanov, *Българите и степната империя*, 9–10.

like the Ṭāhirids, Ṣaffārids and Sāmānids, which have no corresponding current nation-states.

Second, coins are also useful for demonstrating monetary flows – from their place of minting to their place of discovery – in gold, silver or base-metal denominations found in hoards or solo. In this way, coin finds can suggest circulation models and can even, eventually, be used to reconstruct entire economies. This is especially helpful when exploring tribute and taxation in Pontic-Caspian Eurasia, as eighth- to eleventh-century Islamic and Christian silver coinage from several regions flowed consistently northward towards Scandinavia.[13] In this regard, Rus' coins, which have long been used to justify interpretations of Rus' sovereignty, can equally be used to challenge assumptions of Rus' sovereignty when juxtaposed, for example, with the twelfth- to fourteenth-century Rus' coinless period. In the same vein, tenth- to eleventh-century Byzantine and Islamic coin finds in nominally Rus' territory do not necessarily correspond to such assumptions of 'Rus' territoriality', meaning that often, notions of Rus' sovereignty territory can be anachronistic. Instead, coins help demonstrate Pontic-Caspian Eurasia as a broad area of competing allegiance networks, including both the Rus' and Khazar *khağans*, which is frequently more helpful than anachronistic assumptions of so-called sovereign territories.

Finally, sigillography, or the study of seals, is particularly pertinent to the development of monotheism in Pontic-Caspian Eurasia. The Byzantine propensity to authorise most official correspondence via small lead seals containing names, titles and patron saints produced a world of small artefacts ripe for exploration. When these are compiled, social networks can be partially reconstructed in this trans-Black Sea cultural context.[14] Frequently, seals' information about their owners and inferences about their addressees (based on find-sites), which express family names, titles, offices and appeals to various saints, are applicable not so much in terms of sovereignty or ethnicity as in terms of the ever-changing complexes of allegiance networks throughout the time and place.

---

[13] Haldon, *State and Tributary Mode of Production*; Stoljarik, *Monetary Circulation*; Franklin and Shepard, *Emergence of Rus*, 3–70; Pritsak, *Old Rus' Weights and Monetary Systems*; Zuckerman, 'Formation de l'ancien état russe', 95–120; Kovalev, 'Northern Silk Road', 55–105; Kovalev, 'Output of Sāmānid Samarqand', 197–216; Kovalev, '"Official" Volga Bulğār Coins', 193–207; Jankowiak, 'Two Systems of Trade', 137–48; and Thomas Noonan's works on historical economics, which are vital to many fields of this time and place.

[14] Brătianu, *Mer Noire*; King, *Black Sea*; Ascherson, *Black Sea*.

Format

The book begins with the eighth- to ninth-century adoption of Judaism by the Khazarian *khağans*, which is a suitable case study, since this process functions as a historical exception which proves the rule – that current ethnicity is largely the residue of top-down monotheistic internalisation, as demonstrated in later case studies (such as the Volga Bulgars, Magyars and Rus'). Unlike these other cases, Khazaria's attempted Judaisation did not result in a residual Khazarian-Jewish population. Khazarian Judaism also elicits much debate due to the so-called 'Khazar-Ashkenazi descent theory' (the idea that Ashkenazi Jews descend exclusively from Khazars – see Appendix 3). This has become a historiographical tug of war between those who believe, at one extreme, that today's Ashkenazi Jews are truly Khazars and not descendants of the post-Bar-Kokhba diaspora, and, at the other extreme, that the Khazarian *khağans* never embraced Judaism at all. The implications for Jews are obvious. Chapter 2 explores Khazaria's tenth- to eleventh-century disappearance in the context of Byzantine imperial policy. Chapter 3 assesses the textual and archaeological underpinnings of other case studies of monotheisation in tenth- to thirteenth-century Pontic-Caspian Eurasia (that is, by the rulers of the Volga Bulgars, Magyars and Rus'), along with other groups which remained largely pagan, like the Pečenegs and Cuman-Qıpčaqs. Chapter 4 contextualises Khazarian coinage alongside Byzantine and Islamic coinage of roughly similar periods, before delving deeper into Pontic-Caspian Eurasia to comparatively examine the coinages of other peripheral dynasties in both the Christian *oikoumene* and Islamic *ummah*. Finally, 'A Reassessment of Civilisation in Pontic-Caspian Eurasia' consolidates all the deductions regarding ethnicity, sovereignty and periodisation based on the various case studies of the monotheisation of Pontic-Caspian Eurasia during the eighth to thirteenth centuries.

1

The Monotheisation of Khazaria

לֹא הִגְלָה הַקָּדוֹשׁ בָּרוּךְ הוּא אֶת יִשְׂרָאֵלְלְבֵין הָאוּמוֹת אֶלָּא כְּדֵי שֶׁיִּתּוֹסְפוּ עֲלֵיהֶם גֵּרִים

The Holy One, Blessed be He, exiled Israel among the nations only so that converts would join them.

Talmud, Pesachim, 87b:14.

This chapter will explore the monotheisation of Khazaria, from the first seventh-century mentions of Khazaria in the textual sources, through the adoption of Judaism allegedly occurring in the eighth to ninth centuries, up to the tenth-century Khazarian texts. There are many disagreements within the field of Khazar studies: when, where, why and how did the *khağan* convert to Judaism - and did it even happen in the first place? Perhaps more controversially, is there incontrovertible evidence linking modern Ashkenazi Jews to ninth- to tenth-century Khazarian Jews? Furthermore, can the process of monotheisation be linked to the process of sedentarisation? And finally, can the process of Khazarian monotheisation shed light on other monotheisation processes in Pontic-Caspian Eurasia?

I use the term 'monotheisation' because the *khağans*' conversion to Judaism was neither inevitable, nor a consensus: rather, Islam or Christianity could have won out, and the map of the world could now look very different. In other words, had the *khağans* adopted Islam or Christianity, the term 'monotheisation' would still apply. I use the term 'sedentarisation' to refer to the adoption of a settled, agrarian and urbanised regime. These two processes may have at times been correlated, but were not necessarily mutually causal (*cum hoc ergo propter hoc*).

This study begins with Khazaria because although it disappeared politically, its lessons are essential to avoiding teleological interpretations of the subsequent history of Pontic-Caspian Eurasia.

Khazaria functions as an initial 'Petri dish' for examining the processes surrounding monotheisation in eighth- to thirteenth-century Pontic-Caspian Eurasia. Contextualised between the Islamic Caliphate and Christian Rome (Byzantium), this chapter will address the three most heated debates about Khazaria: (1) the dating of conversion, (2) the extent of conversion and (3) the location of Itīl, the 'Jewish' Khazar capital. As for the original reason for adopting Judaism, most historians agree that the reason was to avoid being politically subjugated to Islam or Christianity, and I see no reason to disagree.

The Earliest Textual Sources on Khazaria

A considerable number of textual sources refer to the Khazars and Khazaria. To clarify, the label 'Khazars' would most easily fit the political elite, that is, the collectors, rather than providers, of tribute. 'Khazaria' therefore implies the lands and peoples over which this elite held authority.

The earliest references to Khazars and Khazaria come primarily from Chinese, Greek, Arabic and Persian sources. They also appeared in Latin in the earliest Slavonic sources. There were three Khazar sources, written in Hebrew and self-referencing; however, their reliability or even authenticity is debated, and they occur only in the mid-tenth century, a time by which the Khazars are alleged to have converted to Judaism.

In the first great monograph on Khazar history, Dunlop claimed that the name 'Khazar' derived from Chinese references to Uiğur nomads, who were designated as 'Kosa' and arrived in the Pontic-Caspian steppe in the 650s.[1] Others posited a derivation from the Old Turkic root 'qaz-', meaning 'to wander',[2] which became the consensus until 1982. That year saw the publication of the Terkhin Inscription, a stele found in 1957 in northern Mongolia dating to the mid-eighth century under the Uiğur *khağanate*, on which the name *Qasar* appeared in Turkic runiform.[3] The new source provoked new theories, such as linking the name to the Old Turkic 'qas-', meaning 'to oppress, or subjugate'.[4] It was also linked to the title

---

[1] Dunlop, *History of Jewish Khazars*, 37–8.
[2] Gombocz, 'Bulgarisch-türkischen Lehnwörter', 199; Németh, *A honfoglaló magyarság kialakulása*, 94.
[3] Golden, 'Khazar Studies', 16 n37; Brook, *Jews of Khazaria*, 6; Zhivkov, *Khazaria*, 40–1; Klyashtorny, 'Terkhin Inscription', 335–66.
[4] Bazin, 'L'origine des Khazar', 51–71.

caesar in Middle Persian: '*kesar*', then garbled into '*qasar*'.⁵ This was then reconnected to Dunlop's original supposition.⁶

Regardless of the name's origins, most historians agree that the Khazar ruling Āšĭnà dynasty descended from the western half of the Gökturk *khağanate*, preserving the Khazars' legitimacy⁷ and the nomads' allegiances who paid them tribute. The first mentions of the Āšĭnà dynasty, preserved in sixth-century Chinese sources,⁸ describe Chinese interference in a Gökturk civil war between two clans called the Nušibi and Dulu upon the death of *khağan* Taspar in 581. Whether Khazaria emerged from these events has elicited plenty of debate.⁹

The first Greek mention of the name 'Khazar' in Theophanes Omologetes (the Confessor's) *Chronographia* refers to the Khazars as Turks (for example, Gökturks) a year before the 626 siege of Constantinople,¹⁰ which itself garnered considerable debate.¹¹ Theophanes mentions Khazaria in subsequent episodes such as the emperor Justinian II's adventure there in 704 and marriage to the *khağan*'s sister, and again in 732–3 with the marriage of emperor Konstantinos V to the Khazar princess Tzitzak (Čiček), baptised Eirene. These episodes are also covered by Nikephoros, writing in the 780s, who later became patriarch of Constantinople.¹² The Khazars, so named, are also mentioned by Theophilos of Edessa regarding their wars

---

⁵ Golden, *Introduction to Turkic Peoples*, 134; Róna-Tas, 'A kazár népnévről', 349–79; Kovalev, 'Khazar Identity through Coins', 243 n8.
⁶ Senga, 'Toquz Oghuz Problem and Origin of Khazars', 57.
⁷ Semënov, 'Образование хазарского каганата', 118–27; Zhivkov, *Khazaria*, 23.
⁸ Zongzheng, *History of Turks*, 39–85; Woods et al., 'Chinese Chroniclers of Khazars', 231–61.
⁹ Obolensky, *Byzantine Commonwealth*, 172; Magomedov, *Образование хазарского каганата*, 176–7; Artamonov, *История хазар*, 114–32; Dunlop, *History of Jewish Khazars*, 3–33; Semënov, 'Образование хазарского каганата', 118–27. Zuckerman, Zhivkov and Novosel'cev disagree: Novosel'cev, *Хазарское государство*, 83–91; Zhivkov, *Khazaria*, 51–3; Zuckerman, 'Khazars and Byzantium', 411–17. Novosel'cev argues that Khazaria derived from a melange of tribes, with the Sabirs ('proto-Hungarians') predominating. Zhivkov characterises the Nušibi–Dulu conflict as equating to the mid-sixth-century Khazar–Bulgar conflict and Old Great Bulgaria's disintegration.
¹⁰ Theophanes, *Chronographia*, ed. de Boor, 315: τὸ δὲ τρίτον μέρος αὐτὸς λαβὼω ἐπὶ Λαζικὴν ἐχώρει, καὶ ἐν ταύτῃ διατρίβων τοὺς Τούρκους ἐκ τῆς ἑῴας, οὓς Χάζαρεις ὀνομάζουσιν, εἰς συμμαχίαν προσεκαλέσατο, tr. Mango et al., *Chronicle of Theophanes*, 446–7: 'During [Erakleios'] stay [in Lazika] he invited the eastern Turks, who are called Chazars, to become his allies'.
¹¹ Howard-Johnston, 'Byzantine Sources for Khazar History', 167 n17; Zuckerman, 'Khazars and Byzantium', 411–17; Kwanten, *Imperial Nomads*, 39–40.
¹² Nikephoros, *Brevarium*, ed. and tr. Mango, *Short History*, §35.28, §42.8–75, §45.36–67, §63.2, §75.23; Afinogenov, 'History of Justinian and Leo', 181–200.

against the Caliphate.[13] They are discussed too in the Slavonic *Vita Constantini* (c. 870s–880s), which details Konstantinos-Kyrillos' mission to Khazaria and his fraught endeavour to convert the Khazars to Christianity in a Khazarian theological court debate.[14] Two epistles of the early-tenth-century Constantinopolitan patriarch Nicholas Mystikos also indicate the mission for alliance and conversion in Khazaria,[15] along with the third version of the (eighth-century) *Notitia Episcopatuum*.[16] By the tenth to eleventh centuries, the Khazars are discussed by Leon Diakonos and Ioannes Skylitzes, extensively in the works of emperor Konstantinos VII Porphyrogennetos and later by Georgios Akropolites.

A number of Persian and Arabic sources mention Turks and Khazars from the seventh century. The earliest, an anonymous pre-Islamic Sasanian Persian source, describes the 'land of the Turks', which the scholar Shapira characterises as present-day Tatarstan or Bašqortostan:

> Turkestān is a vast place and all of it is cold, it is forests, they have few fruit-trees and edible fruits and [other edible] things. There are some among them who worship the Moon and there are some who are sorcerers, and there are some who are of the Good Religion ... They till the land. When they die, they throw (their dead) in forests, and there are some who go to Paradise, and there are some who go to Hell and the Middle Abode (Purgatory).[17]

Shapira asserts that the 'Good Religion' here is Zoroastrianism, which the writer probably practised.

Shapira also presents a Zoroastrian apocalyptic work called the *Zand ī Wahman Yasn*, where the name 'Khazaria' appears in an anachronistic list of nations which, unsurprisingly, sought the destruction of Persia, although not in the year 624/625, but in 588/589 instead.[18]

Another anonymous Persian source mentions Khazaria specifically, and hints at Khazarian Judaism:

> just like the faith of Jesus from [Rome], and the faith of Moses from the Khazars, and the faith of Mani from the Uigurs took away the strength

---

[13] Theophilos of Edessa, *Chronicle*, tr. Hoyland, 228–9; 305–6.
[14] *Vita Constantini*, eds Grivec and Tomišić, *Constantinus et Methodius*, 109; tr. Kantor, *Slavonic Lives*, 25–33; 65–81.
[15] Nicholas Mystikos, *Epistles*, eds and tr. Jenkins and Westerink, *Letters*, 390–1.
[16] *Notitiae Episcopatuum Ecclesiae Constantinopolitanae*, ed. Darrouzès, 241–2.
[17] Shapira, 'Iranian Sources on Khazars', 293.
[18] Ibid., 296–7.

and vigor they had previously possessed, threw them into vileness and decadence amongst their rivals, and the faith of Mani even frustrated the [Roman] philosophy.[19]

Shapira asserts that this Zoroastrian testimony to Khazarian Judaism is channelled through a Muslim medium. Judging by the reference to Khazarian Judaism, this excerpt probably dates to the ninth century.

Several other Islamic Persian authors also mentioned the Khazars between the seventh and ninth centuries. One of the best-known is the ninth-century Persian geographer and bureaucrat ibn Khurradādhbih, whose grandfather converted to Islam and was posted to northwestern Persia, a crucial frontier from which to view Khazaria. His work, the *Book of Roads and Kingdoms*,[20] dating to the 870s, is referenced by later Islamic bookmen, although only a fragment of it survives.

In a passage detailing the story of an Islamic traveller named Sallām the Interpreter who journeyed on behalf of the caliph to report on the people of Gog and Magog in c. 844, Khurradādhbih mentions a Khazarian *tarkhān*.[21] According to Khurradādhbih, the Khazars are not equivalent to the people of Gog and Magog, since the Khazarian *tarkhān* gave Sallām's entourage five guides to continue his journey after their rendezvous with the governor of Armenia in Tiflis (T'blisi). Khurradādhbih again mentions Khazaria relating to the routes of the Rus' and the Radanite Jewish merchants. First he indicates the Rus' routes through Khazaria:

> [The Rus'] follow another route, descending the River Tanais (Don), the river of the Ṣaqāliba, and passing by Khamlīj, the capital of the Khazars, where the ruler of the country levies a ten per cent duty. There they embark on the Caspian Sea, heading for a point they know.[22]

Next, he indicates the Radanites' routes through Khazaria:

> Sometimes they take a route north of Rome, heading for Khamlīj via the lands of the Ṣaqāliba. Khamlīj is the Khazar capital.[23]

---

[19] Ibid., 294–5.
[20] Ibn Khurradādhbih, *Livre des routes et provinces*, ed. and tr. de Meynard; tr. Lunde and Stone, *Ibn Fadlān*, 99–104; 111–12.
[21] Ibn Khurradādhbih, *Sallām the Interpreter*, tr. Lunde and Stone, *Ibn Fadlān*, 99–104. This is presumably the king, or Khazarian *beg*.
[22] Ibid., 111–12; 233 n15. The translators date this text to c. 830.
[23] Ibid., 112.

Later, ibn al-Faqīh, in his *Kitāb al-Buldān* (Hamadan, 902–3[24]), and ibn Rusta, in his *Kitāb al-A'Lāk an-Nafāsa* (Isfahan, c. 903–13[25]), are the very first Muslim authors who explicitly mention an official form of Judaism within Khazaria. Al-Faqīh derived much of his information from ibn Khurradādhbih, whereas ibn Rusta relied on Khwārazmian sources.[26] According to ibn al-Faqīh, 'All of the Khazars are Jews. But they have been Judaized recently.'[27] Conversely, ibn Rusta reported, 'Their supreme chief professes the religion of the Jews and so do Isha and the leaders and great ones who side with him. And the rest of them profess a religion similar to the religion of the Turks.'[28]

In the mid-tenth century, the well-known Persian geographer al-Istakhrī compiled several earlier sources, describing Khazaria and its neighbours in his *Book of Roads and Kingdoms*. Al-Istakhrī was also personally familiar with the northern frontier of the Caliphate, travelling throughout Transoxiana and Khwārazmia, which enhances his work's reliability. I will briefly summarise his text in thirds, as it was apparently joined together from three previous sources. His three sections cover essentially the basic, domestic and foreign aspects of Khazaria in that order. His first section on the Khazars deals with the physical aspects of Khazaria: where it is, what rivers run through it, the physical and demographic size of the capital (Itīl'), construction materials, martial strength, the dispensation of their laws, the levying of tolls and duties on foreign merchants and the religion of the king, called their *bāk* (*beg*). His second passage depicts daily life in Khazaria, that is, the peoples incorporated within the *khağanate* and subjected to the *khağan*, these peoples' religious lives, economic considerations, the relationship between the *khağan* and *beg* and the customs of succession. His third segment discusses the relations between Khazaria and its neighbours such as the Burtās, Baškīrs, Volga Bulgars, Rus' and Pečenegs.[29]

The last Persian source is the anonymous geography the *Ḥudūd al-'Ālam*, or *The Regions of the World*, written in 982. In its discussions on the Khazars, the *Ḥudūd al-'Ālam* repeats much information from previous authors on Khazaria like ibn Khurradādhbih, ibn Rusta and al-Istakhrī.[30]

---

[24] Ibid., 113; Golden, 'Conversion of Khazars to Judaism', 142.
[25] Ibid., 116.
[26] Pritsak, 'Khazar Kingdom's Conversion to Judaism', 279.
[27] Ibn al-Faqīh, *Kitâb al-Buldân*, ed. de Goeje, 298.
[28] Ibn Rusta, *Kitāb al-A'lāk an-Nafīsa*, ed. de Goeje, *Bibliothecarum Geographicorum Arabicorum*, 139.
[29] Al-Istakhrī, *Book of Roads and Kingdoms*, tr. Lunde and Stone, *Ibn Fadlān*, 152–9.
[30] *Ḥudūd al-'Ālam*, tr. Minorsky, 40–4 (Barthold's preface).

This is the first source where the Caspian Sea is called the 'Khazar Sea',[31] setting a centuries-long trend.[32] It is also the only Islamic source mentioning the name of the dynasty, *Ansā*[33] (presumably a garbled version of Āšĭnà), and the 'Khazarian Pečenegs', as if they were a branch of the Pečenegs which paid tribute to the Khazars or as if the author thought the two groups indistinguishable.[34]

Most of our textual information on Khazaria comes from Arabic texts. The earliest Arabic mention of the Khazars belongs to the historian al-Mas'ūdī (mid-tenth century) in his *Murūj aḏ-Ḏahab wa-Maʿādin al-Jawhar* (*Meadows of Gold*). His discussion of Khazaria is extensive and regarded by some scholars as one of the most reliable sources.[35]

The next Arabic text, written by ibn Hauqal, a contemporary and personal acquaintance of al-Istakhrī, is entitled *Ṣūrat al-'Arḍ* (*The Face of the Earth*), which was composed between 967 and 988.[36] He builds on al-Istakhrī's work and describes the commercial affairs around the lands of the Ṣaqāliba, the Khwārazmians (south of the Aral Sea), and reports that by his time, Khazaria had disappeared and these lands were used as a source of slaves along with the Ṣaqāliba.[37]

The late-tenth-century work of al-Muqaddasī, entitled *Aḥsan al-Taqāsim fī Maʿrifat al-Aqālīm* (*The Best Divisions in the Knowledge of the Regions*), compiles the works of previously mentioned geographers such as Khurradādhbih, al-Istakhrī, and Hauqal. Al-Muqaddasī wrote: 'Beyond the Caspian Sea (lake) is a large region called Khazar, a grim, forbidding place, and full of herd animals, honey and Jews.'[38] Like ibn Hauqal, al-Muqaddasī claims that the Khazar king was once Jewish, but is so no longer.[39] While some of al-Muqaddasī's assertions are dubious – for example, that the shah of Khwārazmia invaded Khazaria and forced the king to accept Islam – he also indicates that Rus' later conquered Khazaria, which

---

[31] Ibid., 53.
[32] The early-twelfth-century Selčuq physician Marwazī also used the term 'Khazar Sea': *Sharaf al-Zamān Ṭāhir Marvazī*, tr. Minorsky, *On China, Turks and India*, 36.
[33] *Ḥudūd al-ʿĀlam*, tr. Minorsky, 162.
[34] Ibid., 160–1.
[35] Al-Mas'ūdī, *Meadows of Gold*, tr. Minorsky, *Sharvān and Darband*; tr. Lunde and Stone, *Ibn Fadlān*, 128–46; Wasserstein, 'Khazars and Islam', 377.
[36] Ibn Hauqal, *Ṣūrat al-'Arḍ*, tr. Lunde and Stone, *Ibn Fadlān*, 173.
[37] Ibid., 167.
[38] Al-Muqaddasī, *Aḥsan al-Taqāsim fī Maʿrifat al-Aqālīm*, tr. Collins, 289.
[39] Al-Muqaddasī, *Aḥsan al-Taqāsim fī Maʿrifat al-Aqālīm*, tr. Lunde and Stone, *Ibn Fadlān*, 171–2.

is supported independently, as in the well-known passage in the *PVL*, dating this event to 965.⁴⁰

The most important Islamic source for Khazaria dates to the early 920s, when the traveller ibn Fadlān returned from his famous journey on behalf of the 'Abbasid caliph al-Muqtadir to Volga Bulgaria (a people he calls Ṣaqāliba) on the middle Volga. Summoned to instruct them on proper Islamic worship, Fadlān began his journey to the middle Volga in 921 at the head of a formidable caravan laden with assets, guardsmen, interpreters and a personal letter from the caliph. Departing Baghdad, he bypassed Persia to travel to Bukhārā, then northward through Khwārazmia, moving southwest of the Aral Sea, where he encountered nomads, presumably Oğuz. Continuing northward, he encountered Baškīrs and Pečenegs until arriving at the Volga Bulgarian capital, Bolgar in what is now the Spasskij district, at the vast confluence of the Kama and Volga, in May 922. The king, named Almuš, entitled Yïltawār (*el'teber*⁴¹), wanted cash bullion from Fadlān so he could build a fortress to protect himself against the Khazars, who had by that time reduced him and his kingdom to tributary status. Fadlān recounts his conversation with Almuš:

> You all came together and my master [the caliph] paid all your expenses, and the only reason was so that you could bring me this money to have a fortress built to protect me from the Jews, who have tried to reduce me to slavery.⁴²

Later, Fadlān extrapolates on the arrangement between the Ṣaqāliba (Volga Bulgars) and the Khazars: although Almuš was powerful, he had to pay tribute to Khazaria and send his daughter to the Khazarian *khağan*, who, Fadlān explains, was Jewish while he and his daughters would be Muslim. Fadlān then goes on to detail Rus' funerary practices including a boat-burning burial, and presents a considerable portion on Khazaria.

Fadlān's journey account (*Risāla*) is invaluable, despite his not meeting the Khazarian *khağan* himself. Since Volga Bulgaria paid tribute to Khazaria, like other subordinates to the Khazar *khağan*, Fadlān can be considered as visiting Khazaria, albeit not visiting the capital of Itīl' specifically. Finally, Fadlān, like many other Islamic authors, gives his

---

⁴⁰ *Povest' Vremennÿkh Let*, tr. Cross and Sherbowitz-Wetzor, *Russian Primary Chronicle*, 84.
⁴¹ Semënov, 'Происхождение титула "хазар-эльтебер"', 160–3.
⁴² Ibn Fadlān, *Risāla*, tr. Lunde and Stone, *Ibn Fadlān*, 29.

own description of the lands of Gog and Magog, a monotheistic myth that persisted for centuries and spread throughout the lands of Islam and Christendom:

> The Khazars and their king are Jews. The Ṣaqālibah and those who live on the Khazar border are under his rule. He addresses them as slaves and they owe him their obedience. Some claim that the Khazars are the tribes of Gog and Magog.[43]

It was from here that Khazaria took on the quasi-legendary status of a Jewish kingdom – a legendary third force, an unbelievable occurrence, and therefore symbolised by Gog and Magog in the minds of others, Muslim, Christian or even Jewish in the case of mid-twelfth-century Sephardic author Yehuda HaLevi, when seeking to explain why and how a ruler could adopt, in his words, the 'despised' faith.[44]

The attribution of Gog and Magog to the Khazars appears in Christian sources as well. One of the most important sources for the Khazarian adoption of Judaism is a brief note by Christian of Stavelot (or Stablo, Druthmar of Aquitaine, or Christian Druthmar), a ninth-century monk famed for his grammatical skills living in the Stavelot monastery in Lorraine. He mentions Khazaria in his 'Expositio in Mattheaum Evangelistam':

> We are not aware of any nation under the sky that would not have Christians among them. For even in Gog and Magog, the Hunnic people who call themselves Gazari, those whom Alexander confined, there was a tribe more brave than the others. This tribe has already been circumcised, and they profess all dogmata of Judaism. However, the Bulgars, who are also from these seven tribes, are now becoming baptized.[45]

The attribution of Gog and Magog to the Khazars is understandable given Christian's cultural milieu and knowledge of Greek and possibly Hebrew. For him, Gog and Magog could denote a realm such as Khazaria at the peripheries of the known world. In this light, Gog and Magog would

---

[43] Ibn Fadlān, *Risāla*, tr. Montgomery, *Mission to Volga*, 53.
[44] Yehuda HaLevi, *Kuzari*, tr. Korobkin, 350–7.
[45] Christian of Stavelot, 'Expositio in Mattheaum Evangelistam', tr. Chekin, 'Judaism among Khazars', 17–18; ed. Migne, t.106, c.1456: 'Nescimus jam gentem sub cœlo in qua Christiani non habeantur. Nam et in Gog et in Magog, quæ sunt gentes Hunnorum, quæ ab eis Gazari vocantur, jam una gens quæ fortior erat ex his quas Alexander conduxerat, circumcisa est, et omnem Judaismum observat. Bulgarii quoque, qui et ipsi ex ipsis gentibus sunt, quotidie bapizantur.'

unavoidably make Khazaria an 'other', especially given the Khazars' recent nomadic paganism and adoption of Judaism in Christian's time.[46]

Nevertheless, the dating of the passage above is vital. As the translator, Chekin dates the passage to between 864 and 881, judging from the baptism of Bulgarian *khağan* Boris on the former date and the destruction of Christian's monastery on the latter date by Viking raiders.[47] Given Christian's personal contacts in the Byzantine world through the Italian town of Benevento, his is a reliable source.[48] As a ninth-century mention of Khazaria, including a reference to its Judaism, this source has considerable importance for Khazar studies, especially due to its independence from Islamic references to Judaism within Khazaria.

Finally, the earliest Rus' source, the *PVL*, written in Slavonic at the earliest in the early twelfth century, mentions Khazaria and its Jews, although the source in general is considered dubious by many historians. The *PVL*'s first mention of Khazars equates them to the generic term 'Scythians',[49] which is fairly normal for most Christian texts. The *PVL*'s first references to Khazaria, from even before the 'historical' timeline up to entries given by the 880s, express a broad, if relatively latent conflict between the southbound Rus' and the incumbent Khazar authority competing for tribute among the indigenous inhabitants of the middle Dniepr region.[50] However, the *PVL*'s most important mention of Khazars comes during the famous story about Vladimir's conversion,[51] beginning in 986 with the cavalcade of foreign missions seeking to convert him to one or another monotheism. The source relates the following conversation between Vladimir and the Khazarian Jews:

> The Prince then asked where their native land was, and they replied that it was in Jerusalem. When Vladimir inquired where that was, they

[46] For a broader discussion of Khazaria's mythical affiliation with Gog and Magog, see Appendix 1.
[47] Christian of Stavelot, 'Expositio in Mattheaum Evangelistam', tr. Chekin, 'Judaism among Khazars', 18–19; Shepard, 'Khazars' Formal Adoption of Judaism', 14; Golden, 'Khazar Studies', 17–18.
[48] Christian of Stavelot, 'Expositio in Mattheaum Evangelistam', tr. Chekin, 'Judaism among Khazars', 23.
[49] *Povest' Vremennÿkh Let*, tr. Cross and Sherbowitz-Wetzor, *Russian Primary Chronicle*, 55.
[50] Ibid., 58–61; Petrukhin, 'Normans and Khazars', 393–400; Kulik, 'Judeo-Greek Legacy', 51–64; Shepard, 'Viking Rus and Byzantium', 498; Franklin and Shepard, *Emergence of Rus*, 71–111.
[51] *Povest' Vremennÿkh Let*, tr. Cross and Sherbowitz-Wetzor, *Russian Primary Chronicle*, 96–119.

made answer, 'God was angry at our forefathers, and scattered us among the gentiles on account of our sins. Our land was then given to the Christians.' The Prince then demanded, 'How can you hope to teach others while you yourselves are cast out and scattered abroad by the hand of God? If God loved you and your faith, you would not be thus dispersed in foreign lands. Do you expect us to accept that fate also?'[52]

The significance of this passage is that the Khazars are presented as invariably Jewish, again by a source completely independent of others such as those mentioned above. Khazar sources themselves also explain the adoption of Judaism in Khazaria.

There are three principal Khazarian sources, all Hebrew and dated to the tenth century.[53] I will briefly discuss their contexts, details and proposed dates. The three sources are known as the *Kievan Letter*, the anonymous *Schechter Text* (or *Cambridge Document*), named after the scholar Solomon Schechter who found it in 1896 in the Cairo Geniza, and the Khazar king Joseph's mid-tenth-century letter to ar-Rahman III's (the Córdoban caliph's) Jewish advisor Hasdai ibn Šaprut (*King Joseph's Reply*). Šaprut had originally learned of Khazaria from what were presumably Radanite merchants travelling from Khwārazmia[54] and instructed his secretary, Menahem ibn Saruq (the author of the first Hebrew dictionary, the *Mahberet*), to draft the letter. Debate remains about whether

---

[52] Ibid., 97. In the Laurentian Redaction (eds Ostrowski and Birnbaum, *Повість временних літ*, 628–31):

'ѡн же реч̑ то гдѣ єсть землѧ ваша· ѡни же рѣша въ Єрс̑лмѣ· ѡнъ же реч̑ то тама ли єсть· ѡни же рѣша разъгнѣвасѧ Бъ҃ на ѡц҃и наши· и расточи ны по странамъ грѣхъ рад̑ нашихъ· и предана быс̑ землѧ наша хс̑еѧномъ· ѡн ж р̑е то како вы инѣх̑ оучители сами ѿвержени ѿ Ба҃ и расточени· аще бы Бъ҃ любилъ васъ и законъ вашь· то не бысте росточе[ни] по чюжимъ землѧмъ· еда намъ то же мыслите прињати::'

[53] The tenth-century Islamic author, ibn al-Nadim (*Fihrist of al-Nadim*, ed. and tr. Dodge, 36–7), independently verifies the Khazars' use of Hebrew script:

'The Turks, the Bulgar, Blaghā, the Burghaz, the Khazar, the Llān, and the types with small eyes and extreme blondness have no script, except that the Bulgarians and the Tibetans write with Chinese and Manichaean, whereas the Khazar write Hebrew.'

[54] Yehuda HaLevi, *Kuzari*, tr. Korobkin, 345.

king Joseph composed the original letter himself or it was possibly written on his behalf by another Khazar Jew.[55] The oldest extant manuscript containing the letter dates from the sixteenth century and is stored in Oxford.[56] Šaprut's letter and *King Joseph's Reply* are intimately connected to the *Schechter Text*. Together, these epistles are known as the *Khazar Correspondence*,[57] for which the Islamic world played a facilitative role.[58] However, distinctive Khazarian ties to Jewish communities in the Islamic world remain debated.[59]

The *Kievan Letter* and *Schechter Text* have been translated and contextualised by Golb and Pritsak,[60] who date them to about 930 and the mid-late-940s respectively.[61] While older scholarship ignored, downplayed or dismissed the *Kievan Letter*'s historicity or relevance, it is now validated as the principal affirmation of Judaism within Khazaria.[62] Briefly, this document is a letter sent by a community of Kievan Jews to other powerful Jews concerning personal misfortune and soliciting financial assistance,[63] probably from the Khazarian king, although its rediscovery in Cairo suggests that the Khazarian king could do little for the petitioner on whose behalf the letter was written. Most significantly, the text indicates that a number of people (in Kiev) adopted Judaism and Hebrew as their faith and script by the 930s. Also, several signatories' names on the document are originally Turkic and Turkic runes at the bottom relate: 'I have read (it).' The text also displays one of the earliest mentions of Kiev and thereby casts doubt on generations of scholarship deriving chronologies exclusively from the *PVL*.[64]

The *Schechter Text* is another anonymous composition which has survived albeit missing considerable portions, including the addresser

---

[55] Stampfer, 'Did Khazars Convert to Judaism?', 1–72. See Appendix 3 on the Khazar-Ashkenazi descent theory.
[56] *Schechter Text*, eds and tr. Golb and Pritsak, *Khazarian Hebrew Documents*, 76.
[57] Ibid., 94–5.
[58] Wasserstein, 'Khazars and Islam', 381.
[59] Ibid., 385; Stampfer, 'Did Khazars Convert to Judaism?', 27–8; Artamonov, *История хазар*, 265–6.
[60] *Kievan Letter*, eds and tr. Golb and Pritsak, *Khazarian Hebrew Documents*, 3–71.
[61] *Kievan Letter* and *Schechter Text*, eds and tr. Golb and Pritsak, *Khazarian Hebrew Documents*, 71, 94–5.
[62] Golden, 'Khazar Studies', 10–11; Wasserstein, 'Khazars and Islam', 381.
[63] Erdal ('Khazar Language', 95–7) suggests that the Kievan Jewish community was the *addressee*, not the *addresser*.
[64] *Kievan Letter*, eds and tr. Golb and Pritsak, *Khazarian Hebrew Documents*, 5–71; Zuckerman, 'Khazars' Conversion to Judaism', 237–70.

and addressee, so the source's agenda and intended audience remain unclear. Yet the text comprises the synopsis of a Khazarian 'peoplehood' story: the story of Khazarian Judaism in their own words. According to Golb and Pritsak, the letter was written in Constantinople by a 'Jewish subject of the Khazarian King Joseph'.[65] The text recounts a Jewish migration to what later became Khazaria and of subsequent intermarriages between Jews and Khazarian nomads whereby 'they became one people', routed their enemies and confounded the respective faiths of the Orthodox Christian Roman-Byzantines and the Muslim Saracens in a religious dispute. The narrative follows three Khazarian kings, Benjamin, Aaron and Joseph, whom Golb and Pritsak respectively date to c. 880–900, c. 900–20 and c. 920–60.[66] The text is the first Khazarian document mentioning a 'return' to Judaism (by a warrior-ruler named Sabriel) and the title *khağan*.[67] The letter also recounts hostilities with the Alanian king of the Caucasus, (mentioned too in the *DAI*[68]), so the text chronologically fits with other contemporaneous sources. As well, it offers context (and perhaps a follow-up letter) to the previously mentioned Khazarian king Joseph's epistle to Hasdai ibn Šaprut of Córdoba in the mid-940s.

King Joseph's Reply is a response to Šaprut's original epistle by the then-ruler of Khazaria, Joseph. It survives in two redactions: a long manuscript (thirteenth century), translated into Russian by Kokovcov[69] in 1932 and into English by Korobkin in 1998,[70] and a short manuscript (sixteenth-century) translated into English by Kobler[71] in 1953. It is typically dated as arriving in Córdoba c. 955. Like the *Schechter Text*, it is meant for diplomatic consumption, comprising a conversion story, blood lineage, top-down rule and ethnogenesis. *King Joseph's Reply* has withstood twentieth-century attempts to prove it a forgery.[72] Yet the source contains obvious exaggerations, such as Joseph's enumeration of subject peoples and tributaries, although the extent of the hyperbole remains debated.[73]

---

[65] *Schechter Text*, eds and tr. Golb and Pritsak, *Khazarian Hebrew Documents*, 130.
[66] Ibid., 107–37.
[67] Ibid., 113.
[68] Konstantinos VII Porphyrogennetos, *De Administrando Imperio*, ed. Moravcsik, tr. Jenkins, §10.
[69] *King Joseph's Reply*, ed. and tr. Kokovcov, Еврейско-хазарская переписка; eds and tr. Golb and Pritsak, *Khazarian Hebrew Documents*, 576.
[70] Yehuda HaLevi, *Kuzari*, tr. Korobkin, 350–7.
[71] *King Joseph's Reply*, tr. Kobler, *Letters of Jews*, 97–115.
[72] Komar, *Хазарское Время*, 183; Brutzkus, 'Khazar Origin of Kiev', 110–11.
[73] Galkina, 'Территория хазарского каганата', 141.

Also, the *Schechter Text* and *King Joseph's Reply* differ in three main ways. First, it is the Sabriel character of the *Schechter Text* who leads the 'return to Judaism', whereas he is called Bulan ('the wise') in *King Joseph's Reply*.[74] Bulan-Sabriel is an important figure in the Khazarian conversion process. Second, *King Joseph's Reply* reports the strengthening of Judaism by a king named Obadiah, whereas he does not appear in the *Schechter Text*. Third, biblical descent plays no role in the *Schechter Text*, whereas king Joseph claims descent from Cusar, son of Togarmah (brother of Ashkenaz), Noah's grandson.

Nearly two centuries later, the Sephardic rabbi Yehuda ben Barzillai (of Barcelona), who wrote the early-twelfth-century judicial exposition the *Sefer hā'Ittīm*, discussed the *Correspondence*, although he had access to the *Schechter Text* and *King Joseph's Reply* but not to Hasdai ibn Šaprut's original letter.[75] Then, in c. 1140, the famous rabbi Yehuda HaLevi completed his *Kuzari*,[76] which drew on the Khazars' historiosophical example as a defence of Judaism. The work is simultaneously a theological polemic, a spiritual autobiography and a series of Platonic dialogues, and therefore, unsurprisingly, theologians have debated it for centuries.[77] Regardless of later interpretations, it contains useful information about Khazaria.[78] Some of HaLevi's musings on Khazaria are undoubtedly his own fabrication,[79] and he dates the Khazarian adoption of Judaism to 400 years before his time, that is, about 740. This date has therefore become a traditional one for the Khazarian conversion to Judaism, although this dating has since fallen out of mainstream reference for good reason, which will be discussed below.

The Advent of Khazarian Judaism

This section discusses questions about where, when and how did Judaism first arrive in what later became Khazaria.

---

[74] *King Joseph's Reply*, tr. Kobler, *Letters of Jews*, 115 n29.
[75] *Schechter Text*, tr. Kokovcov, *Еврейско-хазарская переписка*, 127–8; eds and tr. Golb and Pritsak, *Khazarian Hebrew Documents*, 75, 127.
[76] Yehuda HaLevi, *Kuzari*, tr. Korobkin, xxiii.
[77] Alcalay, *Jews and Arabs*, 174; Silman, *Philosopher and Prophet*, 299–304.
[78] Contrary to Wasserstrom, 'Review: *Philosopher and Prophet*', 296, I would argue that as for any archaeological material, nothing exists without context, HaLevi's *Kuzari* included.
[79] Yehuda HaLevi, *Kuzari*, tr. Hirschfield, 35, 82; DeWeese, *Islamization*, 300–10.

Between Christianity and Islam

During the incessant warfare between the steppe-nomads and the Caliphate from the late seventh to ninth centuries, the Gökturk Āšĭnà dynasty consolidated power over a realm which later became known as Khazaria. It was to this realm, allegedly, that persecuted Jews fled from the lands of Christendom and Islam.

The *Schechter Text*, alone among Khazarian sources mentioning these phenomena, and without verifiable dates, refers to Jews emigrating to Khazaria presumably from Armenia.[80] While the Hebrew word ארמיניא (ARMYNYA – *fol.1r:1, 3*) could also be a metathetic for Byzantium, that is, Romanía,[81] I believe it is closer to the Arabic designation 'Arminiyya', which refers to the entire Caucasus region.[82] Although some have taken this passage literally,[83] the author acknowledges that wherever these newcomers emigrated from originally, they were Jews only by their observance of circumcision and the Sabbath. By intermarrying and allying with the indigenous inhabitants, they evidently 'became one people'.[84] Considerable time passed before a successful warrior (named Sabriel) 'returned' to Judaism at the behest of God, presaging only a nominal adoption of Judaism, the rhetoric of which meant to impose social cohesion.[85] The 'return' to Judaism was meant to pre-empt the respective politico-religious authority that Byzantium and the Caliphate sought to exercise within Khazaria among the *khağans*' subject populations, including many Christians and Muslims. It therefore served a dual purpose of imposing cohesion and precluding outside influences from exerting authority within the realm.

Yet Jewish migration to Khazaria was important only as far as later Jewish authors were concerned: because it represented Khazaria's placement on a Judaic historical timeline. In other words, by converting to Judaism, the *khağans* sought to place Khazarian history within the context of Jewish

---

[80] *Schechter Text*, eds and tr. Golb and Pritsak, *Khazarian Hebrew Documents*, 106–7.
[81] Ibid. This is because Byzantium is repeatedly mentioned later with the words: יון (YWN: Yunan/Ionia – *fol.1r:22, fol.2r:10, fol.1r:*), מקדון (MQDWN: Macedonia – *fol.1r:16, fol.2r:5, 6, fol.2v: 12*) and the Romans themselves as היוונים (HYWWNYM: Ha-Yunanim ['Ionians'] – *fol.1v:2, 5, 7*), which invites doubt that Romanía (Byzantium) would be the true meaning.
[82] Kulik, 'Judeo-Greek Legacy', 54.
[83] Schama, *Story of Jews*, 266; Zuckerman, 'Khazars' Conversion to Judaism', 241.
[84] Kulik, 'Judeo-Greek Legacy', 54; DeWeese, *Islamization*, 306–15; Schama, *Story of Jews*, 266.
[85] Zuckerman, 'Khazars' Conversion to Judaism', 242.

history.[86] This was a literary device for legitimising and nativising the new monotheism by presenting it as an older, locally established tradition.[87] While the historicity and legitimacy of the retrospective 'return' to Judaism in the *Schechter Text* are quite debatable,[88] we cannot entirely dismiss the migration of Jews into Khazaria. This migration may have been caused by various persecutions of Jews throughout the seventh to tenth centuries, mentioned in several Christian texts.

For example, as early as the seventh century, many forced baptisms and Jewish persecutions are attested, although Michael the Syrian's *Chronicle*[89] and the Syracusan bishop's *Vita* of *Zosimo*[90] directly indicate Jewish migrations beyond imperial jurisdiction. In the eighth century, Theophanes Omologetes (the Confessor's) *Chronographia* reports forced conversions under Leon III,[91] which were followed in the ninth century under Basileios I by persecutions recorded in the southern Italian *Chronicle of Ahima'az*[92]

---

[86] For example, references to rebuilding Jerusalem in the *Kievan Letter* (eds and tr. Golb and Pritsak, *Khazarian Hebrew Documents*, 14–15) clearly demonstrate the retrospective adoption of an undoubtedly Judaic historical timeline. The *Schechter Text* clearly refers to events in Genesis and Exodus (eds and tr. Golb and Pritsak, *Khazarian Hebrew Documents*, 110–11). *King Joseph's Reply* (tr. Kobler, *Letters of Jews*, 106–7; ed. and tr. Kokovcov, Еврейско-хазарская переписка, 92) clearly refers to the Genesis Table of Nations.

[87] DeWeese, *Islamization*, 307–8. Contrarily, Petrukhin, 'Sacral Kingship and Judaism of Khazars', 295, has argued that the *khağan*'s Turkicness was the vehicle of legitimacy, instead of his Jewishness. This is also supported by Komar, Хазарское время, 237; Zhivkov, *Khazaria*, 18.

[88] *Schechter Text*, eds and tr. Golb and Pritsak, *Khazarian Hebrew Documents*, 108–11. *King Joseph's Reply* portrays the figure of Bulan-Sabriel similarly to the Old Testament's description of Hezekiah and Josiah, linking Khazarian history to the Old Testament: 'He did what was right in the eyes of the LORD, just as his father David had done. He removed the high places, smashed the sacred stones and cut down the Asherah poles. [wooden female deity idol]' (Kings II, 18:3–4, *NIV*). According to *King Joseph's Reply* (tr. Kobler, *Letters of Jews*, 108), 'Another king rose up, named Bulan, who was a God-fearing man. He expelled wizards and idolaters from the land and trusted in God alone.' Petrukhin ('Sacral Kingship and Judaism of Khazars', 291) noticed that 'the Khazarian khagan is called "the judge" and can be associated with the Old Testament Israelite leaders of the period of Judges'.

[89] Michael the Syrian, *Chronicle*, ed. and tr. Chabot, *Chronique de Michel le Syrien*, II.413. Michael the Syrian was apparently a twelfth-century chronicler referencing a now-lost seventh-century Syrian chronicle (cited in MacMaster, 'Pogrom that Time Forgot', 223–8).

[90] Zosimus, *Vita*, eds Société des Bollandistes, *Vita S. Zosimo Episcopo Syracusano in Sicilia*, 19: 'Hebraei quidam advenae; peregrinis in ea civitate Hebraeis.'

[91] Theophanes, *Chronographia*, ed. de Boor, 401.

[92] Ahima'az, *Chronicle*, tr. Salzman, 70.

and the *Sefer Yuḥasin*.[93] While there are no Greek sources which indicate forcible baptisms and persecutions leading directly to migrations to Khazaria, they are accepted by a general consensus among historians.[94]

The next persecution of Jews, under Romanos Lakapenos in the 940s, is directly attested by both Christian[95] and Muslim sources, notably al-Mas'ūdī:

> The king of the Khazars had already become a Jew in the Caliphate of Hārūn al-Rashīd, and there joined him Jews from all the lands of Islam and from the country of the Greeks. Indeed the king of the Greeks at the present time, A.H. 332 [943–4], Armānūs [Romanus Lecapenus] had converted the Jews in his kingdom to Christianity and coerced them. [...] Many Jews took flight from the country of the Greeks to Khazaria, as we have described.[96]

The *Schechter Text* records the same event:

> Then returned Israel, with the people of Qazaria, (to Judaism) completely; the Jews began to come from Baghdad and from Khorasan, and from the land of Greece, and they strengthened the men of the land, so that (the latter) held fast to the covenant of the 'Father of a Multitude ...'

> ... In the days of Joseph the king, my master, [he sought] {Alan} help when the persecution befell during the days of Romanus the evil one. When the thing became [know]n to my master, he did away with many Christians. Moreover, Romanus [the evil o]ne sent great presents to HLGW {Oleg} king of RWSY' {Rus'} inciting him to (do) his evil.[97]

---

[93] *Sefer Yuḥasin*, ed. Niebuhr, 115–24.
[94] Holo, *Byzantine Jewry in Mediterranean Economy*, 43–4; Vasiliev, *Goths in Crimea*, 102; Starr, *Jews in Byzantine Empire*, 92–3; Sharf, *Byzantine Jewry*, 86–98.
[95] Peter, *Letters*, ed. Pertz, Peter, Doge of Venice, 'Epistola', 7.
[96] Cited in Dunlop, *History of Jewish Khazars*, 89; Zuckerman, 'Khazars' Conversion to Judaism', 246. Werbart ('Invisible Identities', 93) disagrees.
[97] *Schechter Text*, eds and tr. Golb and Pritsak, *Khazarian Hebrew Documents*, 110–11, 114–15.

(110, *fol.1v:12–15*)

וישובו / לבוא מן בגדד ומן כורסן ומארץ ינן והחזיקו [י]די אנשי / הארץ ויתחזקו בברית אב המון וישימו עליחם

(114, *fol.2r:15–19*)

בימי יוסף המלך / אדוני [דרש]ע בעזרת השמדה רומנוס הרשע / וכי [נוד]ע הדבר לאדוני סילה / רבים ערלים וגם רומנוס / [הרש]ע שלח מתנות גדולות להלגו מל[ך] רוסיא ויסיתו / לרעתו

These two documents clearly indicate tenth-century Byzantine persecutions of Jews and migrations of Jews to Khazaria from Byzantine and Islamic lands,[98] which were recounted in al-Dīmašqi's fourteenth-century chronicle.[99] Combining these independent accounts validates the *Schechter Text*'s historicity.[100] A generation later, following the reconquest of Crete in 961, another Geniza letter about a Byzantine Jew named Moshe Agura indicates another Jewish wave of emigration, and confirms substantial tenth-century Jewish persecutions in Byzantium.[101] Increasing populations of Jews (as well as Muslims and Christians) becoming subjects of the Khazarian *khağans* clearly implied increasing pressure to adopt one of these monotheisms.

Between the seventh and ninth centuries, the world was increasingly polarised between these two 'empires of faith'[102] (Christian Rome/Byzantium and the Islamic Caliphate) and their monotheistic affiliates, whose authorities derived from a single god and a duopoly on truth, law, legitimacy and literacy. It became apparent that sovereignty, power and authority were predicated on a given monotheism, dictated by a given perception of the divine, derived from a given interpretation of a divine scripture. Principally, only one form of monotheism could be correct and therefore only one ruler could wield ecumenical authority over the earth. Ecumenism was the zeitgeist.[103] The Āšïnà *khağans*, like pagan rulers before and after them, found themselves between these two ecumenisms vying for their subjects' allegiances, particularly in eighth-century wars with the Caliphate, and by the time these had subsided, the *khağans* found themselves increasingly drawn into the monotheistic world beyond the Caucasus (ostensibly via Judaism from Armenia). Islam constituted an alternative ecumenical mode of legitimacy to the Roman *oikoumene*: wherever the Roman/Byzantine imperial Orthodoxy

---

[98] Dunlop, *History of Jewish Khazars*, 167; DeWeese, *Islamization*, 304–5.
[99] Al-Dīmašqi, *Cosmography*, ed. and tr. Mehren, *Cosmographie*, 263; Sharf, *Byzantine Jewry*, 99; Olsson, 'Coup d'état', 503.
[100] Rabbi Yehuda ben Barzillai separately verified this portion of the *Schechter Text*, cited in Starr, *Jews in Byzantine Empire*, 166.
[101] Holo, 'Genizah Letter from Rhodes', 1–13.
[102] Sarris, *Empires of Faith*.
[103] I chose the term *ecumenism* instead of *universalism* since it more accurately describes not so much each respective state or identity as their ecumenical institutions, from which such identities are ultimately derived. See Haldon, *Empire that Would Not Die*, 120–1.

sought to proselytise was equally fair game for the Sunni Caliphate: ninth-century Khazaria being a case in point.[104]

The only historical consensus about Khazaria is the reason for choosing Judaism: to avoid ecclesiastical subjugation to the Caliphate's Islam or Rome's Christianity, and the figure of Bulan-Sabriel in *King Joseph's Reply* and the *Schechter Text* chose the third Abrahamic option. To wit, Judaism gave him the benefits of monotheism while ensuring political independence. Whereas this positioned Khazaria on an entirely separate path of political development, it also meant that the *khağans* could expect no support from either power and eventually, from Byzantium, open hostility.

The external Christian and Islamic pressures to adopt either form of monotheism were probably reflected internally by proselytisation efforts on the *khağans*' subjects within Khazaria. For example, the eighth-century *Notitia Episcopatuum* lists a metropolitanate of Gotthia meant to Christianise Khazarian-ruled towns in the Pontic-Caucasian region by preaching and/or settlement. Islamic sources document similar efforts to Islamise Khazarian-ruled towns in the Caspian-Caucasian region by conquest and/or settlement.[105] Fadlān reports that tenth-century hostility between the *khağans* and the caliphs continued to trouble the Khazar capital of Itīl', when the Khazar ruler ordered the destruction of a mosque's minaret and its muezzins' deaths in retaliation for a synagogue's destruction in a place named Dār al-Bābūnaj (the location is unknown).[106]

While the origin of Khazarian Judaism is ultimately unprovable, sources of Jewry possibly include age-old Caucasian and Persian communities,[107] the long-standing Pontic communities of the Crimean and Taman' peninsulas, which were incorporated into Khazarian administrations for nearly two centuries,[108] and itinerant Radanite Jewish

---

[104] Wasserstein, 'Khazars and Islam', 373–86; Zhivkov, *Khazaria*, 47; Golden, 'Conversion of Khazars to Judaism', 143; Vachkova, 'Danube Bulgaria and Khazaria', 339–62; Chekin, 'Jews in Early Russian Civilization', 386–9; Coene, *Caucasus*, 79; Kupoveckij, 'Анализ формирования коллективной памяти', 58–73.

[105] Dunlop, *History of Jewish Khazars*, 84–5; *Ḥudūd al-ʿĀlam*, tr. Minorsky, 162; ibn Rusta, *Kitāb al-Aʿlāk an-Nafīsa*; al-Masʿūdī, *Meadows of Gold*, tr. Lunde and Stone, *Ibn Fadlān*, 117, 133; ibn al-Athīr, tr. in Petrukhin, 'Khazaria and Rus', 263.

[106] Ibn Fadlān, *Risāla*, tr. Lunde and Stone, *Ibn Fadlān*, 58; tr. Montgomery, *Mission to Volga*, 85; Wasserstein, 'Khazars and Islam', 385.

[107] Magomedov, *Образование хазарского каганата*, 173; Coene, *Caucasus*, 78–9; Kupoveckij, 'Анализ формирования коллективной памяти', 70.

[108] Dunlop, *History of Jewish Khazars*, 45 n25; Schama, *Story of Jews*, 266; Brook, *Jews of Khazaria*, 79–80; Flërov and Flërova, 'Иудаизм в хазарии', 189; Vachkova, 'Danube Bulgaria and Khazaria', 353.

merchants.¹⁰⁹ The seventh- to ninth-century Radanite hypothesis is popular among certain scholars. According to Thomas, the Radanites and Khazars shared not only interests and Judaism, but 'shared destiny'.¹¹⁰ According to Gil, the Radanites dominated commerce throughout the entire Mediterranean and Black Seas.¹¹¹ Holo combines the Radanite hypothesis with other theories.¹¹² However, by the late ninth to tenth century, a time when al-Mas'ūdī reports fully fledged Khazarian Judaisation, Radanite commerce in Khazaria had already considerably declined.¹¹³ Yet it seems that the long-standing Crimean-Taman' Jewish communities, with their long incubation in Khazaria,¹¹⁴ along with Radanite merchants, probably as capable of trading as proselytising, are both likely avenues for Judaisation. Because the *Schechter Text* was written in Constantinople, the Crimean-Taman' origin of Khazar Judaism is likelier.¹¹⁵

Some have claimed that the Khazar conversion to Judaism completely brought about the advent of the legendary Khazarian diarchic kingship, or sacral kingship, wherein Judaism allowed the *beg/īšā* (king) to usurp institutional power from the *khağan*, who was relegated to an entirely sacral position.¹¹⁶ However, other scholars have clearly shown that Āšïnà sacral kingship predated Khazarian Judaisation and was therefore unconnected with the adoption of Judaism.¹¹⁷ The controversy pertains not so much to Judaism's effect on Khazarian rulership as to the extent that Judaism can be attested in Khazaria.

The problems of tracking Judaism in Khazaria

This section will examine three of the principal questions outlined at the beginning of the chapter: the dating of the conversion, the spread of the conversion, and the location of the Khazar capital city of Itīl'. I will employ

---

¹⁰⁹ Pritsak, 'Khazar Kingdom's Conversion to Judaism', 280; Asadov, 'Khazaria, Byzantium, and Arab Caliphate', 140–50.
¹¹⁰ Thomas, 'Râdhânites, Chinese Jews', 14–19.
¹¹¹ Gil, 'Râdhânite Merchants', 323.
¹¹² Holo, *Byzantine Jewry in Mediterranean Economy*, 169, 192–201.
¹¹³ Golden, 'Khazar Studies', 44; Novosel'cev, Хазарское государство, 10; Zhivkov, *Khazaria*, 164–5.
¹¹⁴ Petrukhin, 'Sacral Kingship and Judaism of Khazars', 292.
¹¹⁵ Holo, *Byzantine Jewry in Mediterranean Economy*, 169.
¹¹⁶ Artamonov, История хазар, 278–82; Olsson, 'Coup d'état', 496; Komar, Хазарское время, 146; Coene, *Caucasus*, 109.
¹¹⁷ Golden, 'Irano-Turcica', 161–94; Kwanten, *Imperial Nomads*, 44; Petrukhin, 'Sacral Kingship and Judaism of Khazars', 292; Klaniczay, 'Birth of New Europe', 120; Zhivkov, *Khazaria*, 54–5.

textual and archaeological evidence. Like other historians (although advocating different dates[118]), I suspect the conversion occurred gradually over three stages beginning in the early ninth century and concluding in the early 860s. As for the spread of Judaism, I suspect a very modest permeation of Judaism beyond the ruling elite in Itīl. Finally, I will conditionally support the archaeological site near Samosdel'ka in the Volga delta as Itīl's location. These three questions about Khazaria carry broad significance due to their larger relevance to the monotheisation of Pontic-Caspian Eurasia.

Dating: a three-stage conversion

While some have conceived the Khazarian adoption of Judaism as an anomalous historical event,[119] I infer that it should be contextualised with other Eurasian conversions. Other historians have stressed the gradual nature of the conversion, viewing it as a century-long process. For DeWeese, the *Schechter Text* narrates a gradual 'intrusion and displacement' involving, like other conversion stories, a 'sequence of summons, consent, test, and decisive affirmation'.[120] I will argue that these two developments, 'intrusion and displacement', are complementary, which explains why other authors, such as Pritsak and Olsson, argue for a three-stage conversion process. Pritsak's three-stage process begins in the 730s, whereas Olsson's begins in the 830s.[121] Because I find both arguments convincing, albeit imperfect, I will offer a three-stage conversion process partially based on other Eurasian conversions, to provide comparative evidence. This comparative model considers the conversion processes of the Rjurikids (Vladimir – Orthodox Christianity), the Árpáds (Stephen – Latin Christianity), the Almušids (Almuš – Sunni Islam) and others, when there are gaps in the sources of the Khazarian conversion process.

Because the entrance of Islam, Christianity and Judaism into Khazaria occurred primarily in an urban context,[122] the long-standing Jewish communities of the Crimean and Taman' peninsulas, which were acquainted with the Khazars in the eighth to ninth centuries,[123] and reinforced with

---

[118] Olsson, 'Coup d'état', 495–526; Zhivkov, *Khazaria*, 58–9.
[119] Novosel'cev, 'Хазария в системе международных отношений', 20–32; Bartha, *Hungarian Society*, 20–1.
[120] DeWeese, *Islamization*, 314–15; Golden, 'Conversion of Khazars to Judaism', 161; Olsson, 'Coup d'état', 505 n41.
[121] Pritsak, 'Khazar Kingdom's Conversion to Judaism', 261–81; Olsson, 'Coup d'état', 495–526.
[122] Kravčenko, 'Городища среднего течения северского донца', 268.
[123] Feldman, 'Autonomy and Rebellion in Cherson', 27–32.

Jews fleeing imperial persecutions, probably provided the first 'intrusion' until it became a critical mass, or 'displacement'. The *Schechter Text* clearly displays this interpretation. DeWeese and Golden both employ a staged conversion model based on Eaton's conversion process of *inclusion*, *identification* and *displacement*. The process involved an initial conversion, then a phase of falling away and pagan retrenchment (for example, Svjatoslav in the *PVL*) and finally a decisive commitment.[124] Based on the tenth-century Khazarian sources, we know this process began with Bulan-Sabriel and his 'return' to Judaism.

Stage 1: Bulan-Sabriel 'returns' to Judaism (early ninth century)

First, what would be the *terminus post quem* for Bulan-Sabriel's 'return' to Judaism in the Khazarian sources? Based on Judah HaLevi's twelfth-century *Kuzari*, some scholars have supposed that the Khazarian conversion process began c. 740, and they have dated the figure of Bulan-Sabriel accordingly.[125] For example, citing Dunlop's narration of the Khazars' defeat of a Muslim commander named Jarrāḥ and sack of Ardabīl (Erbil) in 730 and *King Joseph's Reply*, indicating war booty used for sacred purposes,[126] Pritsak argues that Bulan-Sabriel's conversion occurred in 730–1.[127] Yet Dunlop translates al-Athīr: 'Jarrāḥ fled from the polytheists [Khazars]' and calls the story 'legendary'. In other words, just because the Khazars' sack of Ardabīl in c. 730 was later celebrated by the building 'of a tabernacle on the biblical model',[128] this hardly proves that 730 marks the initial Khazar conversion to Judaism.

Other sources consider the eighth-century Khazars as pagans, casting further doubt on the commencement of a conversion process during this period.[129] The *Life of St. Abo* records that the Khazar *khagan* (named Bağatur according to ibn A'tham)[130] remained pagan in the mid-780s.[131] The *Kartlis Cxovreba* records that a certain Christian Georgian king, Ĵuanšer,

---

[124] DeWeese, *Islamization*, 312–15; Golden, 'Conversion of Khazars to Judaism', 127–8; Eaton, *Islam and Bengal Frontier*, 268–303.
[125] Coene, *Caucasus*, 109. Zhivkov (*Khazaria*, 58) assigns the 630s–640s as the period of Bulan's Judaisation, but does not explain his claim.
[126] *King Joseph's Reply*, ed. and tr. Kokovcov, Еврейско-хазарская переписка, 21–2.
[127] Pritsak, 'Khazar Kingdom's Conversion to Judaism', 274–5.
[128] Dunlop, *History of Jewish Khazars*, 71–6.
[129] Shapira, 'Armenian and Georgian Sources on Khazars', 349–51.
[130] Abo of Tiflis, *Vita*, tr. Lang, *Georgian Saints*, 117–19; al-A'tham, ed. Kurat, 'Muḥammad bin A'sam al-Kūfī'nin Kitāb al-Futūḥ'u', 272–3.
[131] Vernadsky, *History of Russia*, 292; Golden, *Khazar Studies* (1980), 65.

shortly after 786 sought his family's advice about whether to send his sister to wed the Khazar *khağan* who had sent his general Bluč'an to collect her.[132] He received the reply: 'it is better to go to Greece, to his fellow Christians, than to be polluted by heathens'.[133] Clearly, the *khağans* remained pagan into the late eighth century.[134]

According to the much more reliable al-Mas'ūdī, the king adopted Judaism during Hārūn al-Rašīd's reign (786–809), so the first stage of the conversion could not have occurred long after Abo's stay and baptism in Khazaria. While I agree with most of Olsson's argument for a three-stage conversion, although he references al-Mas'ūdī frequently, he neglects to explain his disregard of al-Mas'ūdī's dates for the conversion (around the turn of the ninth century[135]). So if 786 *is* the *terminus post quem* for the first stage of Bulan-Sabriel's conversion, and I believe we should include al-Mas'ūdī's dating (786–806),[136] then it seems we can begin with a *terminus post quem* at around the turn of the ninth century for a possible royal conversion (the earliest end of the time frame for the conversion process). As the rest of our sources relate that this was a private conversion, substantial Judaisation could only take noticeable root at a later date.

Stage 2: Obadiah and the Moses coins (late 830s)

Based on two main sources, namely *King Joseph's Reply* and several Khazarian coins, I suggest that this later date is possibly the late 830s. True, to discuss the reforms of a later Khazar *khağan*, Obadiah, is to tread on admittedly speculative terrain, since *King Joseph's Reply* alone mentions Obadiah. Yet Golden recognises that a reformist phase frequently characterises the previously mentioned *identification* phase, corresponding to other Eurasian monotheistic conversions.[137] According

---

[132] Minorsky ([tr.], *Sharvān and Darband*, 42, 106) and Pritsak ('Khazar Kingdom's Conversion to Judaism', 261, 272) connect this Bluč'an to Bulan in *King Joseph's Reply*. Yet Pritsak does not seem to notice the separation of these two dates (901 and 786) from two separate sources (*Kartlis Cxovreba* and *King Joseph's Reply*). Zuckerman ('Khazars' Conversion to Judaism', 251) sees the two names as entirely separate, assigning the episode to the eighth century.

[133] *Kartlis Cxovreba*, ed. Qauxčišvili, 249–50.

[134] Shapira, 'Armenian and Georgian Sources on Khazars', 350–1.

[135] Al-Mas'ūdī, *Meadows of Gold*, tr. Lunde and Stone, *Ibn Fadlān*, 131–3; Olsson, 'Coup d'état', 495–526.

[136] Ivik and Ključnikov, *Хазары*. Zhivkov (*Khazaria*, 58) correlates al-Mas'ūdī's dating for Judaisation (786–809) with Obadiah in *King Joseph's Reply*.

[137] Golden, 'Conversion of Khazars to Judaism', 147 n123.

to the *Reply*,[138] Obadiah was the reformer who instituted Jewish law and Hebrew literacy, and brought in Tanakh (the Old Testament), Mishnah and Talmud scholars from Israel, thereby strengthening rabbinical Khazarian Judaism.[139] But the *Reply* provides no dates for his reign.[140]

The *Reply* indicates that Obadiah succeeded Bulan-Sabriel by some indeterminate period. If we accept that Bulan-Sabriel adopted some rudimentary form of Judaism between 786 and 809,[141] the next stage for which we have reliable evidence of Khazarian Judaism is in the late 830s, and is perhaps the most persuasive.

In 1999, a coin hoard was found on the Spillings farm on the Swedish island of Gotland in the Baltic Sea. Now called the 'Spillings Hoard', it is the world's largest-yet find of Viking-era treasure. Along with copious silver and bronze bangles and coins, numerous Khazarian silver coins (dirhams) appeared which imitated contemporaneous Islamic dirhams, yet seven Khazarian dirhams curiously contained the Arabic inscription 'Moses is the messenger of God' (*Mūsā rasūl Allāh*) alongside the standard Islamic *Shahada*: 'Muhammed is the messenger of God.' This Khazarian *Moses* coinage was published by the numismatist Rispling and explained by the scholar Kovalev.[142] So far, these coins are the only archaeological evidence for an attempted Judaisation of Khazaria. They are reliably dated to the year 837/838, and were discontinued almost immediately afterwards.[143] While Kovalev argues this was due to the coins' transport northward,[144] if we consider Golden's 'backsliding' phase in Eurasian conversions, the coins were probably instead discontinued due to pagan (or Islamic) resistance against the accelerating top-down Judaisation.[145] Thereafter, it is unclear whether *khağans* derived legitimacy from both Judaism and traditional

---

[138] *King Joseph's Reply* ed. and tr. Kokovcov, Еврейско-хазарская переписка, 21–4, 28–31, 75–80, 92–7; tr. Kobler, *Letters of Jews*, 111.

[139] Zhivkov, *Khazaria*, 91; Shapira, 'Judaization of Central Asian Traditions', 507. It is also clear that Judaism practised in Khazaria without such supplementary scriptures, or Karaïsm, was therefore quite limited. So with some debate (Vachkova, 'Danube Bulgaria and Khazaria', 353; Szyszyman, 'Question des Khazars', 189–202), Khazarian elites probably adopted rabbinical Judaism (Ankori, *Karaites in Byzantium*, 64–79; Róna-Tas, *Hungarians and Europe*, 232; Golden, 'Judaism in Khazaria', 138–9).

[140] Komar, Хазарское время, 183–4.

[141] Ivik and Ključnikov, Хазары.

[142] Rispling, 'Khazar Coins'; Kovalev, 'Monetary History of Khazaria' 97–129; Kovalev, 'Khazar Identity through Coins', 220–52.

[143] Petrukhin, 'Sacral Kingship and Judaism of Khazars', 294.

[144] Kovalev, 'Khazar Identity through Coins', 237–40. On the dating of these coins, see Chapter 4.

[145] Golden, 'Conversion of Khazars to Judaism', 161.

Turkic rulership,[146] or Judaism rendered *khağans* powerless, resulting in a de facto *coup d'état*.[147]

In Khazaria, resistance against Judaisation has been conceived as the 'Qabar revolution' theory[148] based on the following passage in the mid-tenth-century *DAI*, written by the Byzantine/Roman emperor Konstantinos VII:

> The so-called Kabaroi were of the race of the Chazars. Now it fell out that a secession was made by them to their government, and when a civil war broke out their first government prevailed, and some of them [...] came and settled with the Turks in the land of the Pechenegs, [...] and were called 'Kabaroi'.[149]

Combining the *DAI* and Khazarian sources (and Judaic archaeological evidence from Čelarevo in Serbia[150]), many historians have theorised about this event. For Kristó, the Qabars were Onoğur-Bulğars, who revolted in the 810s and were linked to a 'Hungarian–Khazar alliance' c. 840–60.[151] For Pálóczi Horváth, they were Muslim Khwārazmians.[152] For Davidescu, they were Cumans.[153] Some historians speculate that they were Magyars

---

[146] Zhivkov, *Khazaria*, 55–6, 126.

[147] Petrukhin, 'Sacral Kingship and Judaism of Khazars', 298; Komar, *Хазарское время*, 146; Olsson, 'Coup d'état', 513–16.

[148] Ludwig, *Struktur und Gesellschaft des Chazaren-Reiches*, 168–75; Golden, 'Irano-Turcica', 184; Dunlop, *History of Jewish Khazars*, 203; Salmin, *Savirs – Bulgars – Chuvash*, 91.

[149] Konstantinos VII Porphyrogennetos, *De Administrando Imperio*, ed. Moravcsik, tr. Jenkins, §39:1–7: 'Ἰστέον, ὅτι οἱ λεγόμενοι Κάβαροι ἀπὸ τῆς τῶν Χαζάρων γενεᾶς ὑπῆρχον. Καὶ δὴ συμβάν τινα παρὰ αὐτῶν ἀποστασίαν γενέσθαι πρὸς τὴν ἀρχὴν αὐτῶν, καὶ πολέμου ἐμφυλίου καθιστάντος, ἡ πρώτη ἀρχὴ αὐτῶν ὑπερίσχυσεν, καὶ οἱ μὲν ἐξ αὐτῶν [...] ἦλθαν καὶ κατεσκήνωσαν μετὰ τῶν Τούρκων εἰς τὴν τῶν Πατζινακιτῶν γῆν, [...] καὶ Κάβαροί τινες ὠνομάσθησαν.'

[150] Erdélyi, 'Кабары', 174–81, claims that numerous Jewish motifs, (*menorot, shofarim, etrogim, lulavot* and a Hebrew inscription reading, 'Yehudah') found on seventy brick fragments in 1972 at a necropolis in Čelarevo (present Serbia) belonged to the Qabars, along with 'Avar' burials of human and horse skeletons (carbon-14 dated to the late tenth century). Although such a designation is inherently speculative, Golden ('Irano-Turcica', 185) accepts such archaeological evidence of the Qabars. The finds from Čelarevo are undeniably Judaic in nature, but I am unconvinced that they can be definitively attributed to the Qabars.

[151] Kristó, *Hungarian History*, 33.

[152] Pálóczi Horváth, *Pechenegs, Cumans, Iasians*, 27.

[153] Davidescu, *Lost Romans*, 114.

desiring greater autonomy and led by the Khazar-appointed Árpád clan.[154] Other historians suppose that, whoever they were, they attempted and failed to overthrow Obadiah, prompting their exodus.[155]

While I agree with Golden's suspicion of the inherent conjecture of the 'Qabar revolution theory',[156] I would support an amalgamation of the last two interpretations: namely, the Qabar story indicates resistance to Obadiah's Judaisation reforms and aspirational autonomy, although I doubt their ethnicity can be ascertained.

Pagan resistance to monotheisation attempts are common, regardless of time, place and form of monotheism.[157] In the Rus' case, Svjatoslav refused Christianity when his mother Olga urged him to baptism. According to the *PVL*, he responded, 'How shall I alone accept another faith? My followers will laugh at that.'[158] Similar resistance recalls the emperor Julian's apostasy in the 350s or the Bulgarian boyars' revolts against *khağan* Boris' Christianisation efforts during the 860s.[159] In the 920s, ibn Fadlān indicates pagan resistance to Islam among the Volga Bulgars,[160] and we know of similar pagan resistance to Stephen's late-tenth-century Christianisation among the Magyars.[161] Even in the thirteenth century, the '"apostasy" following Berke's [d. 1266] conversion, necessitated Özbek's conversion as the decisive event in the Islamisation of the Golden Horde'.[162]

Such comparative examples of Eurasian conversions anticipate a resistance or 'backsliding' phase. Therefore, despite the sagacity of his methodology for dating the *Moses* coins, Kovalev's proposition of a single-stage conversion in 837/838[163] is a highly unlikely conclusion for the Khazarian

---

[154] Hildinger, *Warriors of Steppe*, 84; Brutzkus, 'Khazar Origin of Kiev', 114; Róna-Tas, 'Khazars and Magyars', 274–5; Curta, *Southeastern Europe*, 189.
[155] Artamonov, *История хазар*, 278–80; 457–8; Olsson, 'Coup d'état', 513–16; Novosel'cev, *Хазарское государство*, 135; Pletnëva, *Хазары*, 63.
[156] Golden, 'Irano-Turcica', 184–5.
[157] Flërov and Flërova, 'Иудаизм в хазарии', 189.
[158] *Povest' Vremennÿkh Let*, tr. Cross and Sherbowitz-Wetzor, *Russian Primary Chronicle*, 84; Zhivkov, *Khazaria*, 20.
[159] Sullivan, 'Khan Boris', 55–139; Curta, 'Qagan, Khan, or King?', 18.
[160] Ibn Fadlān, *Risāla*, tr. Lunde and Stone, *Ibn Fadlān*, 16–17. According to Fadlān, 'The first of their kings and chiefs that we met was Ināl the Younger. He had converted to Islam. It was said to him: "If you become a Muslim, you will no longer be our leader." So he renounced Islam'.
[161] Klaniczay, 'Birth of New Europe', 113.
[162] DeWeese, *Islamization*, 90.
[163] Kovalev, 'Khazar Identity through Coins', 241.

conversion to Judaism.[164] Additionally, acknowledging Byzantine displeasure about Khazarian Judaisation,[165] why would imperial policy include constructing the fortress of Sarkel on the river Don for the *khağan* in 841,[166] three years after Kovalev's claimed fully fledged conversion? Furthermore, archaeological evidence suggests Khazarian pagan burial practices into the tenth century.[167] Therefore, 837/838 is too early for a fully fledged Khazarian Judaisation, especially as a single-stage event.[168]

So far, the basic outline of a three-stage Khazarian conversion process is visible, but distinct from other historians' suppositions. Combining the independent evidence of al-Mas'ūdī and the *Life of St. Abo*, the first phase is estimable between 786 and 809. Then, by combining *King Joseph's Reply* with the *Moses* coinage, the second phase is conceivable during the late 830s. But the process's final stage remains: the 'decisive affirmation'.[169]

Stage 3: the court debate (early 860s)

Many historians support a Khazarian conversion in the early 860s,[170] as the final 'decisive affirmation', precipitated by a theological court debate. Four sources provide a firm chronology: the Slavonic *Vita Constantini*, Christian of Stavelot's *Expositio*, the *Schechter Text* and the *Reply*. The first two are mutually independent, and all were written within living memory of the event. Chekin reliably dates the *Expositio* to c. 869.[171] The *Vita*

---

[164] Olsson, 'Coup d'état', 505.
[165] On Byzantine displeasure at Khazarian Judaisation, patriarch Nicholas Mystikos called Khazaria: 'that deluded nation' in 920, after the *khağans* rejected Byzantine Christianity (Nicholas Mystikos, Epistles, eds and tr. Jenkins and Westerink, *Letters*, 390–1). The *Schechter Text* also indicates this post-Judaisation turn of Byzantine–Khazarian relations: eds and tr. Golb and Pritsak, *Khazarian Hebrew Documents*, 130–42; Shepard, 'Khazars' Formal Adoption of Judaism', 9–34.
[166] Zuckerman, 'Early History of *thema* of Cherson', 210–22; Zhivkov, *Khazaria*, 243; Afanas'ev, 'Где археологические свидетельства хазарского государства', 47–51.
[167] Shepard, 'Khazar's Formal Adoption of Judaism', 16–17.
[168] Olsson, 'Coup d'état', 507.
[169] Golden, 'Conversion of Khazars to Judaism', 161.
[170] Olsson, 'Coup d'état', 520–3; Shepard, 'Khazars' Formal Adoption of Judaism', 9–34; Zuckerman, 'Khazars' Conversion to Judaism', 237–70; DeWeese, *Islamization*, 170.
[171] Christian of Stavelot, 'Expositio in Matthaeum Evangelistam', tr. Chekin, 'Judaism among Khazars', 13–34; Zuckerman, 'Khazars' Conversion to Judaism', 246; Zhivkov, *Khazaria*, 89–90.

Constantini (c. 870s–880s), *Schechter Text* and *Reply* (c. 940s–950s) each describe a theological court debate.[172]

According to the *Vita*, there were several Jews in the Khazar court even before the debates, implying that they were tilted in their favour.[173] The *Schechter Text* and *Reply* illustrate an episode during the debates when, after their respective arguments, the Christian and Islamic delegations acknowledged the comparative decency of the Judaic argument, leading to the *khağan*'s final decision.[174] Since the *Vita*, written not long after Konstantinos-Kyrillos' death in the early 860s, provides an accurate dating of the debates, when combined with the independently authored *Expositio*, which documents Khazarian Judaisation shortly before Boris' Christianisation in the late 860s, the story appears chronologically credible, especially given the advances that Judaism had already made within Khazaria by such a time. The sources' sheer variety and geographical separation ensure their mutual independence, even as they recorded a genuine historical event.[175]

This provides the early 860s as the *terminus ante quem* for the final conversion – the latest end of the time frame of conversion. To placate objections that this dating provides insufficient rulers from Bulan-Sabriel's time (786–809) to the court debates (early 860s), considering the problems inherent in the number of kings the *Reply* affords, and how this number would constitute too many generations, we cannot assume that each king lived long. Succession could be inherited by brothers as much as by sons.[176] Thus we arrive at a three-stage conversion, albeit conjectural, yet fitting

---

[172] *Vita Constantini*, eds Grivec and Tomišić, *Constantinus et Methodius*, 109–25; tr. Kantor, *Slavonic Lives*, 25–33, 65–81; Curta, *Southeastern Europe*, 122–8; Christian of Stavelot, 'Expositio in Matthaeum Evangelistam', tr. Chekin, 'Judaism among Khazars', 18–19; Butler, 'Oral Culture in *Vita Constantini*', 367–84; Ivik and Ključnikov, *Хазары*.

[173] *Vita Constantini*, eds Grivec and Tomišić, *Constantinus et Methodius*, 112: "'в'се равно глаголюѱе, ѡ семь тъкмо различь дрьжімь: вы бо троицѹ слвите, а мы бога ѥдиного, оулѹчше книгы". *Vita Constantini*, tr. Kantor, *Slavonic Lives*, 47: 'The Kagan [said to Konstantinos-Kyrillos]: "We [. . .] maintain the following difference: you glorify the Trinity, while we, having obtained the scriptures, the One God".' Huxley ('Byzantinochazarika', 80) rejects the *Vita Constantini* as acknowledging the Khazarian adoption of Judaism at the debate.

[174] *King Joseph's Reply*: tr. Kobler, *Letters of Jews*, 109–11; *Schechter Text*, eds and tr. Golb and Pritsak, *Khazarian Hebrew Documents*, 108–11. The *Vita Constantini* only mentions the *khağan*, never the *beg* (Petrukhin, 'Sacral Kingship and Judaism of Khazars', 297).

[175] DeWeese, *Islamization*, 171.

[176] Curta, *Southeastern Europe*, 217; Szyszman, 'Question des Khazars', 190.

with a common Eurasian conversion context and avoiding being dated too late[177] or too early,[178] thereby utilising sources befitting their historicity.[179]

Ultimately, I am suggesting a three-stage Khazar conversion to Judaism: the first stage beginning c. 786–809, the second stage in the late 830s and the final stage in the early 860s. The relevance of a Eurasian three-stage conversion process functions as a primary component in a model for the monotheisation of Pontic-Caspian Eurasia. The top-down monotheisation process, emanating from the ruling dynasty (here, the Āšĭnà *khağans*), serves as an archetype to contextualise the otherwise national histories of various modern countries in Pontic-Caspian Eurasia. The top-down social extent of Khazarian Judaisation, however, will define the subsequent discussion.

The social extent of conversion

Precisely estimating Judaism's permeation into Khazaria would be impossible, although this topic requires exploration. Therefore, we will discuss less the Jewish communities in Khazaria, and more the manner in which Judaism, functioning as Khazaria's official faith, is confidently ascertainable. Most historians analyse the Khazarian Judaisation process in two portions: among the ruling elite in Itīl' (and perhaps other urban centres such as Sarkel, Kiev, Samandar,[180] Balanjar[181] and in Crimea and Taman'), and then Judaisation among subject peoples. Judaism, like Islam and particularly Christianity, has been primarily, though not exclusively of course, an urban phenomenon. The term *paganus* originally referred to rustics while Christianity spread principally in cities. Accordingly, Khazarian urbanism and sedentarism would correlate with monotheism.[182] Since absolute chronology is less important

---

[177] Olsson, 'Coup d'état', 495–526.
[178] Zuckerman, 'Khazars' Conversion to Judaism', 237–70.
[179] Zhivkov, *Khazaria*, 268.
[180] On Samandar's location: Gadlo, Этническая история северного кавказа, 152–3; Bálint, 'Archaeological Addenda', 400; Golden, *Khazar Studies*, 234–7; Zhivkov, *Khazaria*, 234.
[181] On Balanjar's location: Magomedov, Образование хазарского каганата, 174–7; Pletnëva, Хазары, 28.
[182] Sixth- to eighth-century churches were found at Verkhnij Čir-jurt in Dagestan (Balanjar: the Khazar capital before Itīl') with graves of both nomadic-style kurgan-type burials and sedentary-style catacomb and pit-grave burials. For Bálint ('Archaeological Addenda', 399) and Magomedov (Образование хазарского каганата, 174–7), this archaeological evidence indicated social distinctions based on both faith and lifestyle. The following texts and analyses indicate urban-based Christian and Islamic proselytisation networks: Ioannes of Gotthia, tr. Huxley,

than for the dating of the conversion discussed in the preceding sections, in examining Khazarian sedentarism, I will therefore place a greater reliance on archaeological findings to interpret and then leverage my hypotheses in the next section.

Only the elites?

There were noticeable, if rudimentary, distinctions of rank (or class) in the urban centres under Khazarian rule. Khazarian elites and aristocrats are indicated by titles and military ranks such as *īšā*,[183] *tudun*,[184] *el'teber*[185] and *tarkhān*.[186] Golden conceives Khazarian elites as a quasi-*comitatus*, or military retinue,[187] and eighth- to eleventh-century archaeological material suggests considerable inequalities in Khazarian towns between the North Caucasus and the Black and Caspian Seas.

An archaeological culture spread across over 300 sites in this region dating to the Khazarian period (eighth to eleventh centuries) is termed by archaeologists the concurrent Saltovo-Majackij culture (hereafter, *SMC*) and has been ascribed to contemporaneous Khazaria. While there is debate

'Vita of St John of Gotthia', 161–9; *Notitiae Episcopatuum*, ed. Darrouzès, 241–2; Zuckerman, 'Byzantium's Pontic Policy in *Notitiae Episcopatuum*', 201–30; Ludwig, *Struktur und Gesellschaft des Chazaren-Reiches*, 318–25; Magomedov, *Образование хазарского каганата*, 158–72; Noonan, 'Byzantium and Khazars?', 120–1; Fletcher, *Barbarian Conversion*, 72–7; Carter and Mack, *Crimean Chersonesos*, 33–4; Shepard, 'Khazars' Formal Adoption of Judaism', 11–18; Golden, *Introduction to Turkic Peoples*, 239–42. Patriarch Photios remarked that the Black Sea was made 'pious' (Vachkova, 'Danube Bulgaria and Khazaria', 352). Archaeological evidence of Khazarian urban Christianity is manifested in white-clay liturgical cups for converts (Zalesskaya, 'Byzantine White-Clay Painted Bowls', 215–24) and tenth-century *enkolpion* crosses exported to Khazaria (Sarkel) from Cherson (Yashaeva et al., *Legacy of Byzantine Cherson*, nos 186–95; Feldman, 'Autonomy and Rebellion in Cherson', 65–71; Zhivkov, *Khazaria*, 162).

[183] Ibn Rusta, *Kitāb al-A'lāk an-Nafīsa*, tr. Lunde and Stone, *Ibn Fadlān*, 116–17.
[184] Theophanes, *Chronographia*, ed. de Boor, 377–9; Novosel'cev, *Хазарское государство*, 108; Zhivkov, *Khazaria*, 225.
[185] Ibn Fadlān, *Risāla*, tr. Togan, *Reisebericht*, 105–6; Semënov, 'Происхождение титула "хазар-эльтебер"', 160–3.
[186] Ibn Khurradādhbih, *Sallām the Interpreter*, tr. Lunde and Stone, *Ibn Fadlān*, 100; Curta, *Southeastern Europe*, 164; Olsson, 'Coup d'état', 517.
[187] Golden, '*Comitatus* in Eurasia', 154–5; Pálóczi Horváth, *Pechenegs, Cumans, Iasians*, 16; Pletnëva, *Славяно-хазарском пограничье*, 24; Vojnikov, *Първата българска държава*; Kulakov, 'Запад и Восток', 164–70.

about whether[188] or not[189] the *SMC* can be easily designated as 'Khazarian', it nevertheless organisationally constitutes a useful archaeological tool for examining Khazarian archaeology.

Finds ascribed to the *SMC*, for example, include glass and bead jewellery found at the Dimitrievskij Complex (30km southeast of Belgorod),[190] silver strap ornaments found in Taman',[191] and numerous finds from Sarkel including several silver and bronze belt buckles,[192] an entire ornamentally carved silver belt,[193] various glass and silver beaded jewellery,[194] a horn and iron mace-head with tamga symbols 'characteristic of a grand-prince'[195] and a silver and glass ring,[196] along with imported luxury goods: a Byzantine-made glazed serving plate,[197] a Byzantine-made elephant-ivory comb[198] and even an Indo-Persian-made elephant-ivory chess piece.[199] Titles like *īšā*, *tudun*, *el'teber* and *tarkhān* and material wealth also suggest considerable urbanism and regional governance, especially in contrast with many finds in Sarkel (beneath the Cimljansk reservoir in southern Russia) and elsewhere of much simpler clay wares, described as 'typical of tribal nomads'.[200]

---

[188] Pletnëva, *Кочевий к городам*, 185–7, fig. 50; Artamonov, *История хазар*, 235–424; Bálint, *Archäologie der Steppe*, 398–400.

[189] Werbart, 'Khazars or "Saltovo-Majaki Culture"?', 217; Erdélyi and Benkö, 'Problems of Khazar Archaeology', 1–3; Afanas'ev, 'Где археологические свидетельства хазарского государства', 43–55; Afanas'ev et al., 'Хазарские конфедераты дона', 146–53: these archaeologists have debated this supposition that the *SMC* can equate with the Khazars – due to the amount of typological variation within *SMC* finds. Pletnëva herself (*Очерки хазарской археологий*, 3–5; 207) was aware of the challenges her own conclusions led to and the doubt that *SMC* variation would shed on her analysis of a single *SMC* site as coefficient with the Khazars. However, the cohesiveness of the *SMC* was later demonstrated by the appearance of trephined skulls across geographic and 'ethnic' variations throughout the *SMC* by Rešetova ('Trephination Cases', 9–14), which Werbart later acknowledges ('Invisible Identities', 95).

[190] Zalesskaja et al., *Съкровище на хан Кубрат*, nos 198–203.

[191] Leskov, *Maikop Treasure*, no. 275.

[192] Zalesskaja et al., *Съкровище на хан Кубрат*, nos 230; 275.

[193] Pletnëva and Makarova, 'Пояс знатного воина из саркела', 62–77, fig. 3; Artamonov, *История хазар*, 340.

[194] Zalesskaja et al., *Съкровище на хан Кубрат*, nos 308–15.

[195] Ibid., no. 247.

[196] Ibid., no. 267.

[197] Ibid., no. 294.

[198] Ibid., no. 239; Artamonov, *История хазар*, 374.

[199] Artamonov, 'Саркел', 75.

[200] Zalesskaja et al., *Съкровище на хан Кубрат*, nos 251, 257, 293.

Notwithstanding the long-standing Jewish communities of Crimea and Taman' (and the previously discussed *Moses* coins), are there archaeological finds suggesting Jewish communities elsewhere or top-down Judaisaton? Considering that very few Judaic artefacts have been found, it would be easy to assume not. However, Judaic epigraphic discoveries within Khazaria, dating to the appropriate period, although such evidence is still scant, merit discussion.

Aside from the finds in Čelarevo (Serbia), images of *menorot* (Judaic candelabra) have been discovered in sites across Pontic-Caspian Eurasia. The archaeologist Pletnëva uncovered the image of a *menorah* on a locally produced bronze ring otherwise common to the SMC in the Dimitrievskij complex, which was debatably[201] interpreted as indicating Judaism's permeation into 'local culture'.[202] In 2005, a late-tenth- to eleventh-century Hebrew inscription with two *menorot* was discovered on a quartzite slab in the Don Delta's 'Erik' settlement near Tanais. Jewish presence near a northern Black Sea port like Tanais is hardly surprising.[203] A late-ninth- to tenth-century female burial in the Volgograd oblast' yielded a metallic mirror interpreted as 'Judaic' from the appearance of a *menorah*-like image on the reverse.[204] Another *menorah*-like engraving was found on a ceramic pot in a late-eighth-century burial near Mariupol.[205] It could also be suggested that a symbol found on a brick in Sarkel, interpreted by Artamonov as a tamga, appears like a five-branched *menorah* resembling earlier examples of five-branched *menorot* graffiti of undeniable Levantine Judaic provenance.[206]

Hebrew epigraphy has also been discovered. During the late-Soviet era, the archaeologist Turčaninov discovered Hebrew epigraphy on a fortress wall at the Majackij *gorodišče* (78km south of Voronež),[207] which he read as 'Ben-Atÿf' (Son-of-Gracious), and therefore postulated the presence of

---

[201] Ivik and Ključnikov, *Хазары*.
[202] Pletnëva, *Славяно-хазарском пограничье*, fig. 61, 116; Afanas'ev, 'Где археологические свидетельства хазарского государства', 46.
[203] Maslovskij, 'Археологические исследования в азовском районе', 124–5.
[204] Kruglov, 'О атрибуции кургана 27', 372.
[205] Kravčenko and Kul'baka, 'Погребение из мариуполя', 278–80; Flërov, 'Иудаизм, христианство, ислам в хазарском каганате', 140.
[206] A ninth-century tamga on a brick in Sarkel excavated by Artamonov (*История хазар*, 277, 302–3) parallels five-branched *menorah* graffiti on a stone found in Jerusalem (BAR, 'Temple Menorah?').
[207] Turčaninov, *Древние и средневековые памятники*, 89–90; Afanas'ev, 'Где археологические свидетельства хазарского государства', 46; Flërov and Flërova, 'Иудаизм в хазарии', 188.

a Jewish community there. Another Hebrew epigraphic find, consisting of the word 'Israel' repeated four times on a partially reconstructed glass vessel found in 1901 at the Moščevaja Balka necropolis in the Northern Caucasus (112km northeast of Sochi), has been interpreted as unequivocal evidence of Judaism and Jewish communities existing and thriving in the eighth- to ninth-century Khazarian northern Caucasus.[208] Other finds of Hebrew epigraphy have been mentioned, but their veracity is uncertain.[209]

In Sarkel, Pletnëva excavated a public, brick-built structure, which she interpreted as probably a synagogue on the basis of its costly construction, a rarity in the steppe context, and because it bore no inscriptions identifying it as a mosque, church or pagan sanctuary.[210] Others propose a caravanserai (a roadside inn) instead.[211] Flërov and Flërova, despite doubts, note that the building was probably not used for other less religious functions, since no tools were found and also no bones of specifically *unclean*, or *unkosher* animals.[212] It should go without saying that the absence of evidence is not the evidence of absence.

It is completely impossible to state that Jewish communities did *not* exist in various areas of Khazaria outside of Crimea, Taman' and the Caucasian-Caspian regions. Clearly there were Jews, and where there were Jews, there were presumably Jewish communities. The question becomes not so much whether archaeological evidence exists to support Khazarian Judaism, but whether we can presume that they constituted the elite in a region where other literate monotheistic groups (and pagans) resided. The adoption of an elite's liturgical script by which to recognise such epigraphic occurrences, albeit infrequent, hardly signifies top-down mass conversion.[213] If anything, the above-mentioned Hebrew epigraphy simply indicates some literacy.[214] Shepard suggests that the *Kievan Letter* indicates 'functional literacy and long-distance correspondence [...] among Judaist communities [...] of the Khazar dominions'.[215] Similar remarks could be

---

[208] Jerusalimskaja, *Кавказ на шелковом пути*, 30–31; Kovalevskaja, 'Производства стеклянных на кавказе', 266.
[209] Afanas'ev, 'Где археологические свидетельства хазарского государства', 46.
[210] Pletnëva, *Саркел и "шелковый" путь*, 28.
[211] Kovalev, 'Critica', 246–7; Zhivkov, *Khazaria*, 159–60, 202, 255.
[212] Flërov, 'Крепости хазарии', 155; Flërov and Flërova, 'Иудаизм в хазарии', 190–3. However, contemporaneously dated camel bones found in the nearby Cimljansko *gorodišče* would challenge this theory (Franklin and Shepard, *Emergence of Rus*, 83).
[213] Golden, 'Conversion of Khazars to Judaism', 159; Szyszman, 'Question des Khazars', 190.
[214] Afanas'ev, *Донские аланы*, 151–3.
[215] Shepard, 'Khazars' Formal Adoption of Judaism', 11.

made about the other two Khazarian sources. It seems that Jewish communities with functional literacy existed in urban centres such as Kiev, Sarkel, the Dimitrievskij, Moščevaja Balka and Majackij *gorodišči*, and continued to exist long afterwards in places such as Kiev and particularly those in Crimea and Taman'.

Yet literacy, Hebrew or otherwise, among the Khazarian elite was only ever rudimentary at best. According to the archaeologist Afanas'ev, specifically eighth- to ninth-century Khazarian (rather than of other groups such as Suwārs, Alans, Burtās, Adyges, etc.) burial kurgans had standardised red-lined square ditches.[216] Such burials, although recalling steppe-paganism, it is argued, indicate the existence of a specifically Khazarian elite.[217] Similar claims have been made about Khazarian elite ninth-century archaeological monuments in the middle Dniepr,[218] which would seemingly indicate Khazarian suzerainty extending at least as far as Kiev for much of the ninth century. Additionally, the following Khazar-era finds from Sarkel are describable as typical of a pagan elite: bronze mace-heads with tamgas,[219] bronze human figures carrying maces on horseback,[220] a horn fragment with a carved wolf-head motif[221] and, from the Majackij *gorodišče* and dating to the Khazarian era, a stone block with incised images of two warriors fighting.[222] Depictions of humans are traditionally prohibited in Judaism, which consequently calls into doubt its adoption even among the elite. So despite some archaeological indications of Judaism, it seems that Dunlop's words remain relevant: 'The character of the Khazars as Judaized Turks has constantly to be kept in mind. This

---

[216] Afanas'ev, 'Где археологические свидетельства хазарского государства', 53. However, such typologically determinative interpretation of archaeological material as belonging to particular cultural or 'ethnic' groupings (for example, Adyges, Burtās, Alans, Magyars, Suvars, Bulgars, Oğuz or Khazars) is methodologically dubious (Zhivkov, *Khazaria*, 253–4). That said, archaeological typologies are still used to determine 'ethnic identity' in funerary archaeology, especially in distinguishing Khazars from Pečenegs and Cuman-Qıpčaqs/Polovcÿ. Yet even Zhivkov (*Khazaria*, 260) and others (Afanas'ev and Atavin, *Что же такое хазарский погребальный обряд?*; Matyushko, 'Nomads of Steppe', 156) make deterministic suppositions that ethnic attributions can be gleaned from archaeological typologies in burials.

[217] Franklin and Shepard, *Emergence of Rus*, 80.

[218] Ambroz, 'Вознесенском комплексе', 204–21.

[219] Zalesskaja et al., *Съкровище на хан Кубрат*, no. 247.

[220] Pletnëva, *Кочевий к городам*, 178–9. For Pletnëva, the object might depict the sky-god Tengri, as deity over Khazaria.

[221] Zalesskaja et al., *Съкровище на хан Кубрат*, no. 263; Golden, 'Conversion of Khazars to Judaism', 158.

[222] Pletnëva, *Маяцкое городище*, 74.

probably means that their Judaism – limited no doubt in any case to a comparatively small group – was always superficial.'[223]

Beyond elites?

King Joseph's Reply declares that Judaism in Khazaria was a top-down affair, as Bulan allegedly converted 'the whole of his people'.[224] Several historians take this indication of extensive indoctrination at face value,[225] conceiving a Khazarian 'internalisation' of Judaism.[226]

Based on the accounts of al-Faqīh (c. 903)[227] and ibn Fadlān (c. 920–2),[228] Golden contends that Judaism had spread well beyond the elite by the late ninth to tenth century.[229] Other Islamic authors' accounts, albeit excluded by Golden, would further support his conclusion: for example, those of al-Mas'ūdī (mid-tenth century),[230] al-Muqaddasī (late tenth century)[231] and al-Hamdānī (mid-tenth century), importantly describing how 'the Khazars, as a collective', embraced all Judaic stricture, namely, observing Shabbat and all other holidays, adopting the kosher dietary laws, ritual washing and circumcision.[232] Yet to base an argument on textual sources alone means that their contradictions weaken the argument itself. According to Rusta (c. 903–13): 'Their [the Khazars'] supreme authority [the *khagan*] is Jewish, and so is the *īšā* and those commanding officers and important men who

---

[223] Dunlop, *History of Jewish Khazars*, 195.
[224] *King Joseph's Reply*, tr. Kobler, *Letters of Jews*, 110.
[225] Schama, *Story of Jews*, 266–7; Coene, *Caucasus*, 109; Brook, *Jews of Khazaria*, 107–108; Zuckerman, 'Khazars' Conversion to Judaism', 242; Kriwaczek, *Yiddish Civilization*, 46; Flërov and Flërova, 'Иудаизм в хазарии', 18.
[226] Golden, 'Conversion of Khazars to Judaism', 157–9.
[227] Al-Faqīh, *Kitâb al-Buldân*, ed. de Goeje, 298: 'All of the Khazars are Jews, but, they have been Judaised recently.'
[228] Ibn Fadlān, *Risāla*, tr. Lunde and Stone, *Ibn Fadlān*, 58: 'The Khazars and their king are all Jews.'
[229] Golden, 'Conversion of Khazars to Judaism', 159. Golden ('Khazaria and Judaism', 143) previously wrote: 'It seems probable that [...] Jews and Judaized elements constituted a minority.'
[230] Al-Mas'ūdī, *Meadows of Gold*, tr. Minorsky, *Sharvān and Darband*, 146: 'The Jews are: the king, his *entourage* and the Khazars of his tribe (*jins*). The king accepted Judaism during the Caliphate of Rashīd (786–814).'
[231] Al-Muqaddasī, *Ahsan al-Taqāsim fī Ma'rifat al-Aqālīm*, tr. Lunde and Stone, *Ibn Fadlān*, 171: 'Beyond the Caspian Sea is a large region called Khazar, a grim, forbidding place, full of herd animals, honey and Jews.'
[232] Al-Hamdānī, *Kitāb Tathbīt Dalā'il Nubuwwat Sayyidinā Muhammad*, tr. Pines, 'Conversion of Khazars to Judaism', 47; Brook, *Jews of Khazaria*, 85–6, 107–8.

support him. The rest follow a religion like the religion of the Turks.' According to al-Istakhrī (mid-tenth century): 'The Khazars are Muslims and Christians and Jews, and among them are a number of idol worshippers. The smallest number are Jews and the largest Muslims and Christians, but the king and his entourage are Jews.'[233] Relying on textual sources to support a claim of broad Judaisation is unfortunately confounded by other sources, which appear to refute such a thesis. Thus, if Golden's claim about a widespread 'internalisation' of Judaisation is true,[234] and if the accounts of al-Faqīh and Fadlān are worth more than those of Rusta and al-Istakhrī, then I would expect widespread Judaism among the ninth- to tenth-century Khazarian subjects to be better documented archaeologically, which it is not. Flërov and Flërova deem such a steppe-pagan adoption of Judaism improbable,[235] and I cannot contemplate an entire subject people, or even a large portion of one, becoming Jewish, because that would miss the depth, or lack of depth, with which Judaism could even possibly be comprehended by subjects without broad access to literacy, on which Judaism, as much as if not more than Christianity or Islam, unequivocally depends.

Shepard makes a convincing case for broad Judaisation by integrating archaeological evidence. Combining the accounts of Christian of Stavelot and al-Faqīh, who report a widespread Judaisation, Shepard surmises that since reliably pagan burials (kurgans raised over graves, outlined with square or circular trenches) throughout the rural steppe areas outside of the urban centres of Khazaria suddenly ceased by the mid-late-ninth century (c. 860s), it would be conceivable that the *khağans*' conversion relinquished 'the most flagrantly pagan features of their burial-ritual.'[236]

Yet this absence of 'flagrantly pagan' burials does not necessarily prove that the subject populations adopted Judaism en masse. Myriad pit and catacomb burials, both normally (although not always) associated with steppe-paganism, date at least to the tenth century.[237] These burials' commonness in the seventh- to tenth-century Pontic-Caspian steppe and forest-steppe (*SMC*) suggests mainly pagan populations.[238] Additionally, thirteen cases of trephination (boring into the skull's cranial cavity) appear in burial grounds across the *SMC*, and trephination is chiefly associated

---

[233] Ibn Rusta, *Kitāb al-A'lāk an-Nafīsa*, and al-Istakhrī, *Book of Roads and Kingdoms*, tr. Lunde and Stone, *Ibn Fadlān*, 116–17, 154.
[234] Golden, 'Conversion of Khazars to Judaism', 157–9.
[235] Flërov and Flërova, 'Иудаизм в хазарии', 186.
[236] Shepard, 'Khazars' Formal Adoption of Judaism', 16–18.
[237] Flërov and Flërova, 'Иудаизм в хазарии', 189.
[238] Stadnik and Stadnik, 'Могильник салтово-маяцкой культуры', 254–63.

with residual steppe-paganism.²³⁹ Such practices would have been especially forbidden by traditional Jewish strictures prohibiting body modifications. For the adoption of Judaism, to say nothing of Christianity or Islam, we would need to imagine whole populations of illiterate steppe-nomads abandoning their traditional lifestyles and settling down to urban lifestyles. Conversions are not difficult to believe on an individual basis. There is archaeological evidence, albeit slight, of individual conversions.²⁴⁰ However, due to the scarcity of archaeological evidence and the contradictions of textual evidence, it would be ill-advised to believe that subject populations essentially adopted Judaism in full.²⁴¹ According to the archaeologist of Khazaria, Evgenij Gončarov:

> There is very little archaeological evidence of the propagation of this faith among the population of the Khazar *khağanate*. Almost all of them are found in the large ancient cities on the shores of the sea, where the population was mixed, inhabited by people of different religious beliefs. But in the towns in the steppe and in the mountains, in the tombs, there are practically no Jewish artefacts. Their quantity does not allow us to think about the propagation of Judaism among the Khazars. Unfortunately, we do not know of the burials of the Khazar *khağan*-kings and we do not know by what rites they were buried, or if there is anything in their graves.²⁴²

Simply put, although Shepard uses the abandonment of ninth- to tenth-century pagan burials in the archaeological record to make a convincing

---

²³⁹ Rešetova, 'Трепанированными среди салтово-маяцкой культуры', 151–7; Zhivkov, *Khazaria*, 31; Bereczki and Marcsik, 'Trephined Skulls from Hungary', 65–69.

²⁴⁰ Rešetova, 'Трепанированными среди салтово-маяцкой культуры', 151–7; Vasil'ev, 'Итиль-мечта'.

²⁴¹ Brook (*Jews of Khazaria*, 107–8) believes that rabbinical Judaism was adopted by mid-ninth-century Khazarian subjects, and lists all Judaic strictures they adopted, including: circumcision, Hanukkah, Passover and Shabbat observance, kosher dietary laws, Jewish law (Halakha), ritual washing, Torah, Talmud and Mishnah study, Hebrew script, avoiding idol worship and kurgan construction ('simple burials'), imparting Hebrew names, synagogue construction and even constructing a tabernacle after that of Moses. There is little archaeological evidence for this, considering the persistence of pagan burials in Khazaria, undermining the belief that Khazarian Judaism was an affair involving a strict Jewish life-regimen (Afanas'ev, 'Где археологические свидетельства хазарского государства', 53; Zhivkov, *Khazaria*, 67). Others describe Khazarian beliefs, monotheistic or polytheistic, as 'complex and syncretistic', hardly a widespread strict Judaism (Róna-Tas, *Hungarians and Europe*, 349; Golden, 'Irano-Turcica', 185).

²⁴² Evgenij Gončarov, personal communication (author's translation), April 2015.

argument for Khazarian Judaism (despite the persistence of pit and catacomb burials), it does not necessarily signify a wide Judaisation of Khazarian subject populations. If anything, such data signal the precise opposite, but mostly, they signal very little at all. If we are still left asking where are more *menorot*, where are more Hebrew inscriptions and tombstone epitaphs outside of Crimea and Taman', where are easily recognisable synagogues, where is the tabernacle, we can only assume for the time being that they were never there. Certainly it is possible that once-purposed Hebrew tombstones were later used as spolia and once-purposed synagogues were later converted to churches or mosques, but the evidence remains negligible. In his *Tuḥfat al-Albāb*, the twelfth-century Islamic traveller from Granada Abu Ḥāmid al-Garnatī mentions mosques in Itīl'/Saksin. The Byzantine *NE* indicates a broad Christianisation effort in Khazaria.[243] The *Moses* coins and *King Joseph's Reply* hint at what the *khaǧans* wanted readers to believe, but do not necessarily offer the entire truth.

Judaism is hardly a faith, compared to Christianity or Islam, which leaves behind significant volumes of material traces. While it is possible that much of the ninth- to tenth-century Khazarian subject population adopted Judaism, we will never know for sure. We do know that the archaeological evidence is scanty and therefore suggests otherwise. We also know that Khazarian urbanism and sedentarism were much more limited than in Byzantium or the Caliphate, and any theory of strict steppe-nomadic monotheism at this time should invite scepticism.[244] So I believe Judaism in Khazaria should be connected to urban centres such as Kiev, Sarkel, Itīl' and particularly those of the Khazarian Crimea and Taman' peninsulas, for some of which (excluding Itīl' and Sarkel) the scanty archaeological evidence of Judaism we do possess at least exists at the appropriate times.[245] That said, such elite urbanism corresponds to the archaeologically confirmed luxury goods the elite possessed, containing Judaic symbols like *menorot*. That archaeological evidence exists confirming Judaism and literacy is now undeniable, and literacy was probably a significant marker of elite urbanism. But the problem with Judaism-as-elite-religion or even Judaism-as-official-religion is that they are archaeologically indistinguishable from simple urban

---

[243] Al-Garnatī, *Tuḥfat al-Albāb*, tr. Hamidullin, 'Ал-Гарнати', 98–9; tr. Dubler, *Granadino*, 50–2; Vasil'ev, *Самосдельское городище*, 160.

[244] Holo (*Byzantine Jewry in Mediterranean Economy*, 169) assumes that Khazarian Jews were 'semi-nomadic'.

[245] Pletnëva, *Саркел и "шелковый" путь*, 216; Petrukhin and Flërov, 'Иудаизм в Хазарии', 151–62.

Jewish communities. If we cannot distinguish Judaism-as-official-religion from simple urban Jewish communities such as those of the Crimean and Taman' peninsulas, then how can we interpret these finds as material evidence of Judaism-as-official-religion in Khazaria? They may well fit in with textual evidence that Judaism was the 'state' religion sanctioned by the *khağans* themselves, but to gauge how much of the subject populace in towns and cities, let alone in the open steppe, followed suit would be to implicitly base an argument on archaeological material for which there is little evidence.

Finally, there are other plausible conclusions regardless of the social extent of Judaisation. No matter when or how many converted to Judaism, the impact was time-limited to only a few centuries afterwards.[246] Khazarian Judaism was unlikely to have been a top-down affair.[247] It was not profound enough to internally root itself among the *khağans*' subjects by the late tenth century, when Byzantium, the Rus' and the commercial shifts between the Caliphate and Volga Bulgaria weakened Khazaria to the point of disintegration. Afterward, it is impossible to say how many Jews stayed or departed, and thus Khazarian Judaism disappeared.

The archaeology of Itīl'

Having considered the timing and propagation of Khazarian Judaism, the location of the Khazarian capital, Itīl' itself, remains to be examined. Can we identify the famed Jewish capital of Khazaria? Based on syntheses of ninth- to twelfth-century Islamic literature, several locations were proposed during the twentieth century.[248] Three sites have been put forward: Čistoj Banki, a site submerged in the rising levels of the Caspian Sea, Samosdel'ka and Semibugrÿ, the latter two located in the Volga delta. I will analyse the evidence and venture a contribution.

Lev Gumilëv was the first archaeologist to hypothesise that Itīl' must have become submerged due to the Caspian's water-level changes over the centuries: he called it a 'steppe Atlantis'. He claimed that the site of Itīl' lay near the largely submerged island of Čistoj Banki just offshore from the Volga delta.[249] There is some evidence, both archaeological and textual, for

---

[246] DeWeese (*Islamization*, 316–17) claims the impact lasted no more than four centuries.
[247] Schama, *Story of Jews*, 266–7.
[248] Pačkalov, *Города поволжья и кавказа*, 13.
[249] Gumilëv, 'Степная атлантида', 52–3.

the rise of the Caspian Sea since the late tenth century by about 15–16m.[250] This was used to support the theory of the submergence of either Itīl' or Saksin, as the city was called by the time of the arrival of the Andalusi author and traveller from Granada al-Garnatī (early twelfth century).[251] The site of Čistoj Banki as the legendary Itīl', however, was initially supported by scholars such as Magomedov[252] due to finds of seemingly medieval walls and ramparts. The 'rampart citadel walls' turned out to be poured concrete from the 1960s, confirmed by another geophysical survey.[253] Čistoj Banki has since fallen from consensus as Itīl's likely location.

In the late 1990s, the archaeologist Vasil'ev discovered ruins of a major settlement near a village named Samosdel'ka in the southwestern Volga delta. In the past twenty years, it has shown to have been a major eighth- to fifteenth-century city and has attracted a joint expedition from Astrakhan State University and Moscow State University, partially funded by the Russian Jewish Congress and led by Dimitrij Vasil'ev and Emma Zilivinskaja. The site comprises three settlement phases, roughly corresponding to the Khazarian period (Itīl': eighth to tenth century), the Oğuz period (Saksin: eleventh to twelfth century) and the Golden Horde period (Summerkent: thirteenth to fourteenth century). The excavators have had to excavate each habitation layer separately before claiming the site as Itīl's location in Khazaria.[254]

Samosdel'ka's identification with Itīl' has also recently received a limited consensus. The discovery of a fortress built in fired brick, the *khağans'* exclusive construction material,[255] persuaded some.[256] Furthermore, an ash destruction layer was discovered corresponding to the brick fortress at late-tenth-century levels, which have been associated with the conquest of Khazaria by Svjatoslav, father of Vladimir of Kiev, 965–9.[257] The finds are not altogether definitive, and some archaeologists remain unconvinced,[258]

---

[250] Gumilëv, 'New Data on Khazars', 61–103; Bulan, *Présence byzantine en Crimée*, 21.
[251] Al-Garnatī, *Tuḥfat al-Abāb*, tr. Hamidullin, 'Ал-Гарнати', 98–9.
[252] Magomedov et al., 'Каспийская атлантида', 51–60.
[253] Vasil'ev, *Самосдельское городище*, 162; Vasil'ev and Zilivinskaja, 'Городище в дельте волги', 43–4; Zhivkov, *Khazaria*, 205.
[254] Bulan, *Présence byzantine en Crimée*, 21.
[255] Dunlop, *History of Jewish Khazars*, 92.
[256] Ivik and Ključnikov, *Хазары*, 97; Zhivkov, *Khazaria*, 239; Ya'ari, 'Skeletons', 26.
[257] Bálint, 'Archaeological Addenda', 399; Aksënov, 'Форпост верхний салтов', 76.
[258] Erdélyi and Benkő, 'Problems of Khazar Archaeology'; Magomedov et al., 'Каспийская атлантида', 51–60; Afanas'ev, 'Хазарии и фурт-асии', 7–17; Curta, *Eastern Europe*, 139. Flërov and Flërova ('Иудаизм в хазарии', 186) disagree.

since neither specifically Judaic,²⁵⁹ numismatic, sigillographic nor epigraphic material has been uncovered from the site proving it to be Saksin or Itīl.

Yet both textual and archaeological evidence provides some support for Samosdel'ka as the site of Itīl. The significant changes in the Caspian Sea level that Gumilëv demonstrated, leading to settlement migration to higher ground, are a familiar phenomenon to archaeologists,²⁶⁰ which Vasil'ev and Zilivinskaja precisely detected in their excavations in Samosdel'ka.²⁶¹ According to Vasil'ev, many of the ceramic finds at the site correspond to typologically Oğuz ceramics, which corresponds to textual sources describing the nomadic Oğuz as 'formidable allies of the Khazars'.²⁶² However, ceramic attribution to the Oğuz with the *SMC* as an ethnic phenomenon is hardly verifiable and several archaeologists have doubted Samosdel'ka as Itīl's location for this reason.²⁶³ Numismatic evidence is also slim: no reliable coinage samples dated as early as the tenth century have yet been found.²⁶⁴ Dugout yurt-shaped dwellings have been found, which most archaeologists agree signifies the settlement and gradual sedentarisation of previously steppe-nomads. Yet the most convincing evidence linking textual and archaeological material is al-Garnatī's early-twelfth-century account from Saksin, embedded in his *Tuḥfat al-Albāb* (*Gift of Hearts*). He wrote that, in his time, the town was the only, albeit major city in the Volga delta, which is what Vasil'ev and his teams uncovered: a grandiose city dating back to the eighth century, and perhaps singular for the Volga delta.²⁶⁵

However, more recently, a new search for Itīl, led by the archaeologist Damir Solov'ov, has begun at another site where Gumilëv spent years searching: near the village of Semibugrÿ, (about 35km northeast of Samosdel'ka), also in the Volga delta. At Semibugrÿ, another settlement has been dated back to the eighth century based on the discovery of an eighth-century Tunisian coin. Brick buildings have also been uncovered

---

²⁵⁹ Flërov and Flërova, 'Иудаизм в хазарии', 188.
²⁶⁰ Archibald Dunn, personal communication, 22 March 2015.
²⁶¹ Vasil'ev, 'Итиль-мечта'; Gumilëv, 'Степная атлантида', 52–3.
²⁶² Zhivkov, *Khazaria*, 200; Vasil'ev, *Самосдельское городище*, 27–8; Curta, *Southeastern Europe*, 178.
²⁶³ Grečkina and Šnajdštejn, 'Археология астраханского края'; Ivik and Ključnikov, *Хазары*, 96–7.
²⁶⁴ Vasil'ev, *Самосдельское городище*, 4; Evgenij Gončarov, personal communication, April 2015.
²⁶⁵ Al-Garnatī, *Tuḥfat al-Albāb*, tr. Hamidullin, 'Ал-Гарнати', 98–9; Vasil'ev, *Самосдельское городище*, 48–59.

there, along with kurgans, vast amounts of ceramics, much of it dating back as early as the settlement in Samosdel'ka, and even some belt buckles and other coins.²⁶⁶ Whether or not the ceramics at Semibugrÿ can be attributed to the *SMC*, it seems that given such discoveries, there may be two archaeological sites as possible locations of Itīl'. Undoubtedly, more will be found in the coming years.

Nevertheless, the archaeological consensus is that there was one major city in the Volga delta that dated to the Khazar era, and before being called Saksin in the twelfth century, it was called Itīl'. Since three separate phases of a city have been found at Samosdel'ka, with the earliest layers dating to the eighth century, it seems possible that the site was once home to Itīl', even if the site itself has heretofore revealed nothing else archaeologically definitive for the questions of Judaism in Khazaria. Similarly, it seems that a substantial settlement has been found at Semibugrÿ dating to the eighth century. Either site, *or both*, could be revealed to have been the location of Itīl'. But this could easily change: both sites are vast and there is much material waiting to be discovered. Yet at the moment, it remains impossible to archaeologically prove that either Samosdel'ka or Semibugrÿ was even the Khazarian capital of Itīl', let alone the Judaic capital.

Monotheisation and Sedentarisation in Khazaria

While incompletely coefficient, monotheisation and sedentarisation are both processes characterising the settlement of peoples concluding their respective migrations (*völkerwanderungszeiten*).²⁶⁷ Viewed from the monotheistic and sedentary empires (Christian Byzantium/Rome and the Islamic Caliphate), such peoples, with their fluctuating ethnonyms, variously expressed or oversimplified in court historians' documents, all constituted *Scythians* for Atticising historians and others, and 'represented the universal threat of barbarism to civilization'.²⁶⁸ Only by becoming sedentary and monotheistic could they enter the Christian *oikoumene* or the Islamic *ummah*, or in Khazaria's case, avoiding acquiescence to either, maintain a separate Jewish civilisation.²⁶⁹ In ninth- to tenth-century Khazaria's case, both processes coalesce, involving pagans, Jews, Christians and Muslims practising horticulture, agriculture and pastoralism.²⁷⁰

---

[266] Golovina, 'Итиль найден?'.
[267] Kaldellis, *Ethnography after Antiquity*, 125.
[268] Stephenson, *Byzantium's Balkan Frontier*, 107–10.
[269] Eisenstadt, *Jewish Historical Experience*, 66–9.
[270] Noonan, 'Khazar Qaghanate and Early Rus", 79.

This section proceeds from subject-specific debates about the when, who and where of Khazarian Judaisation towards a broader consideration of monotheism and sedentarism as parallel processes according to textual and archaeological sources. The first part considers the partial monotheisation of Khazaria; the second, the partial sedentarisation of Khazaria.

Monotheisation

This subsection explores in detail the nature of not only Judaism, but also the other Abrahamic confessions in the urban areas of Khazaria as lived phenomena.

Internalisation

Syncretism between multiple monotheisms and indigenous paganism was typical for most steppe-nomads, and in Khazaria, strict observance of a single faith was uncommon. Steppe-paganism persisted after the initial Judaic proliferation. Yet nominal nomadic conversion to Judaism need not have *remained* nominal: I agree with Zhivkov and DeWeese that rabbinical Judaism could have been gradually adopted in the steppe context,[271] although this is hardly provable. Certainly Khazarian sources sought to present the Khazars as having internalised a Judaic identity, but this too, is hardly conclusive. The *Schechter Text* relates: 'Then returned Israel, with the people of Qazaria, (to Judaism) completely', which the translators Golb and Pritsak contrast with earlier contradictions in the text.[272] *King Joseph's Reply* claims that the 'the whole of the [*khaǧans*'] people' adopted Judaism. The sources contradict not only each other but also themselves: the *Reply* later acknowledges that King Joseph's subjects include Christians and Muslims.[273] The *Schechter Text* hints at a patchy process of Jewish identity internalisation. We also find the alleged Judaisation of Khazaria was predicated not so much on denying traditional steppe-paganism as incorporating it into a Judaic tradition,[274] hence Golden's application

---

[271] DeWeese, *Islamization*, 301–2; Zhivkov, *Khazaria*, 19.
[272] *Schechter Text*, ed and tr. Golb and Pritsak, *Khazarian Hebrew Documents*, 110–11. In the accompanying annotation, they write: 'The lack of strict consistency in the statements perhaps reflects the inability of the writer to decide on the appropriateness of the term "Jew" with reference to the early generations of Khazars.'
[273] *King Joseph's Reply*, tr. Kobler, *Letters of Jews*, 110–15.
[274] Curta, 'Introduction', 9.

of Eaton's model of conversion to Khazarian Judaisation: *inclusion, identification* and *displacement*.²⁷⁵ This is reflected in the absorption of the previously mentioned refugees from faraway Jewish communities,²⁷⁶ leading to the *Schechter Text*'s description that 'they became one people' and 'return[ed] to Judaism'.²⁷⁷ Yet ibn Rusta (c. 903–13) and al-Istakhrī (mid-tenth century) both remark that most of the *khağans*' subjects remained pagan.

Archaeological finds also imply vestigial nomadic pagan traditions in suggestively pagan burials and polytheistic artefacts. Khazar-era kurgans, pit and certain catacomb burials themselves attest to the retention of pagan traditions in eighth- to tenth-century Pontic-Caspian regions.²⁷⁸ Bronze sun discs and serpent-legged goddess amulets²⁷⁹ have been discovered in kurgans and other burial complexes linked to the *SMC* in *gorodišči* such as Saltovo, Sarkel or the Dimitrievskij Complex, or linked to north-Caucasian finds.²⁸⁰ Although one sun disc was thought to symbolise Judaism due to its six-pointed shape, the Magen-David symbol was adopted as 'Judaic' in much later and different circumstances – *not* as archaeological evidence of Judaism-as-official-religion.²⁸¹ These discs and amulets have frequently been interpreted as signifying paganism of the steppe and north-Caucasus (respectively, nomadic and semi-nomadic *SMC* and Alania). An artefact from the Majackij *gorodišče* displays imagery which would clearly have been sacrilegious in Judaism, such as warrior figures on horseback, one including what appears to be a phallus.²⁸² Additionally, tamga symbols found on Crimean tombstones, and bricks and mace-heads in Sarkel²⁸³ and

---

[275] Golden, 'Conversion of Khazars to Judaism', 127–8.
[276] DeWeese, *Islamization*, 311.
[277] *Schechter Text*, eds and tr. Golb and Pritsak, *Khazarian Hebrew Documents*, 107, 131; Golden, 'Conversion of Khazars to Judaism', 157–8.
[278] Flërov and Flërova, 'Иудаизм в хазарии', 189; Zhivkov, *Khazaria*, 113; Davis-Kimball, 'Excavations in Lower Don', 11–13; CSEN, '2001 Report'; CSEN, '2004 Report'. Curta makes an analogous argument for the ninth- to eleventh-century southern Balkans: 'Burials in Prehistoric Mounds', 269–85.
[279] Zhivkov, *Khazaria*, 118–119.
[280] Leskov, *Maikop Treasure*, nos 115–22; Zaleskaja et al., *Съкровище на хан Кубрат*, nos 181–204; Artamonov, *История хазар*, 291, 296–8; Ascherson, *Black Sea*, 118–19.
[281] Wyszomirska, 'Religion som enande politisk-social länk', 138–44; Pletnëva, *Кочевий к городам*, 179; Flërova, *Образы и сюжеты*, 23.
[282] Pletnëva, *Маяцкое городище*, 74; Zaleskaja et al., *Съкровище на хан Кубрат*, no. 209.
[283] Artamonov, *История хазар*, 302–3; Zaleskaja et al., *Съкровище на хан Кубрат*, no. 247.

in the Semikarakorsk *gorodišče*,[284] point to the continued use of indigenous pagan engravings, as opposed to the use of recognisably monotheistic alphabets such as Hebrew, Greek or Arabic.[285] A ninth- to tenth-century bone fragment with a carved wolf-head motif found in Sarkel corresponds to the Turkic descent-myth from 'a wolf ancestress'.[286] Pletnëva, who advocated archaeological proof of Khazarian Judaism, described a figure found in Sarkel as a depiction of the sky-god Tengri, lending further testimony to the continued presence of traditional steppe-paganism in eighth- to tenth-century urban Khazaria.[287]

In the light of textual and archaeological evidence for the retention of indigenous paganism in Khazaria, the analysis has tended towards some indigenous reaction against the Judaic reforms of Bulan-Sabriel or Obadiah, depending on whichever scholars' beliefs have been apparently vindicated by either archaeological or textual evidence. Pagan resistance to monotheism in Khazaria was less a historical anomaly than a religious adoption which shared many traits with other historical conversions elsewhere.[288] For example, despite the choice of Judaism, many processes in the Khazarian *khağans*' conversion(s) can be compared to the Christianisations of Danube Bulgaria, Hungary, Rus' or even Francia, Germania or Anglia, or the Islamisations of Volga Bulgaria or the Golden Horde. This is principally demonstrated by the numerous attempts to tie 'the Qabar revolt' mentioned in the *DAI* to nomadic reaction against Judaisation, although the archaeological evidence is weak.[289] Yet the *DAI*, a generally trustworthy source, clarifies that Khazaria was subject to internal strife.[290] Instability and pagan resistance are almost beyond doubt in the case of any monotheising process, and Judaisation would appear to be no exception.

The issue of pagan resistance is reflected in Khazar sources' allusion to Jewish internalisation, such as the 'return to Judaism', 'becoming one people', 'converting the whole of the people' and so on. I believe Golden's model of Khazaria's gradual 'internalisation' of Judaism is a helpful notion,[291]

---

[284] Flërov and Flërova, 'Иудаизм в хазарии', 191. Zhivkov (*Khazaria*, 194) and Pletnëva (*Очерки хазарской археологий*, 85) confirm that the entire eighth- to tenth-century Don valley was significantly populated and thoroughly sedentarised.

[285] Golden, *Introduction to Turkic Peoples*, 152.

[286] Zaleskaja et al., *Съкровище на хан Кубрат*, no. 263; Golden, 'Conversion of Khazars to Judaism', 158.

[287] Pletnëva, *Кочевий к городам*, 178–9.

[288] Vachkova, 'Danube Bulgaria and Khazaria', 353.

[289] Bálint, 'Archaeological Addenda', 412.

[290] Konstantinos VII Porphyrogennetos, *De Administrando Imperio*, ed. Moravcsik, tr. Jenkins, §39:1–7.

[291] Golden, 'Conversion of Khazars to Judaism', 157–8.

which can explain other monotheisations in Pontic-Caspian Eurasia we will discuss in the following chapters. Khazarian sources imply that Judaism became 'internalised' and that its adoption was as much a statement of identity as an adoption of a code of law, writing system and so on, but it is highly significant as a 'return' rather than a classic 'conversion'.[292] Such internalisation has also been overstated. For example, the historian Simon Schama suggests that the *Schechter Text* manifests a heavy identification with Judaism and an embracing of its ritual strictures. For Schama, although the *Schechter Text* contains numerous embellishments, as many conversion stories do, it conveys a sense of the internalisation of Judaism among some portion of the population subject to the *khağans*.[293] Some elements of the narrative reflect a blending of indigenous Khazarian Turkic characteristics such as the sacred 'cave in the plain of TYZWL' (תיזול), where the scripture was received, with Judaism.[294] Its copious references to Judaic literary tradition are certainly reflected by its *inclusion* of and *identification* with the sacred scripture, in effect signifying the ('returned to') religion.[295]

Golb and Pritsak have even claimed that the *Schechter Text* should be interpreted 'on the basis of local Jewish (not royal Khazar) traditions and other epic traditions'.[296] *King Joseph's Reply* can be read as implying that the *khağan's* sacred synagogue was little more than a convenient place to store treasure,[297] such as pagan warlords had sought for centuries. The apparent syncretism is a common trait of living faith; Judaism in Khazaria was never as monolithic as we might otherwise imagine. While I would certainly agree that the *Schechter Text* surely carries the flavour of initially steppe-pagan elements, we cannot forget that the documents are undeniably *retrospectively* Judaised.

Despite the mythologisation of the conversion story in the *Schechter Text*, the process of converting to Judaism nevertheless implied a confessional 'displacement' in the reality of the event. The mythologisation was retrospective and constituted the Judaisation of earlier pagan stories and traditions.[298] Still, it is doubtful that this epic narrative could have been produced by any other than a highly literate individual or community, which indicates some sort of literate Khazarian elite as a candidate for its

---

[292] DeWeese, *Islamization*, 305.
[293] Schama, *Story of Jews*, 266.
[294] *Schechter Text*, eds and tr. Golb and Pritsak, *Khazarian Hebrew Documents*, 110–11; Zhivkov, *Khazaria*, 75.
[295] *Schechter Text*, eds and tr. Golb and Pritsak, *Khazarian Hebrew Documents*, 131.
[296] Ibid., 129.
[297] *King Joseph's Reply*, tr. Kokovcov, Еврейско-хазарская переписка, 94; Flërov and Flërova, 'Иудаизм в хазарии', 192.
[298] DeWeese, *Islamization*, 305–6.

authorship. Authorship aside, the document clarifies that Judaism was the determining factor of Khazarian identity, or at least that of its elite. The question remains, then, what sort of religious syncretism, or lived religion, could have been appropriated alongside various versions of Judaism in Khazaria to make such an identity viable, particularly in the presence of not only steppe-paganism but also urban Christianity and Islam?

Homogeneity and heterogeneity in Khazaria

The heterogeneity of Khazaria's subject population(s) invites gratuitous debate. Was Khazaria a genuine ethnic 'melting pot', or was it more homogeneous due to the alleged top-down attempt to instil Judaism-as-official-religion? Or were there eighth- to tenth-century processes and counter-processes of Judaic homogenisation with simultaneous resistance and dogged heterogeneity? Both arguments have their advocates, but the heterogeneous model seems more probable.

Several historians, for example, extensively discuss the presumed ethnic diversity in Khazaria. Zhivkov spends copious pages on this.[299] Kaplan describes Khazaria as 'heterogeneous in composition'.[300] Mason went so far as to say that Khazarian diversity ensured 'a blossoming of [...] culture among the Khazars [forming] the basis for the remarkable symbiosis [...] and formed so unique a characteristic of the Khazar state'.[301] Such a starry-eyed treatment of Khazaria, while doubtlessly agreeable to recent multiculturalism advocacy, is fundamentally anachronistic and therefore invites scepticism.

Yet the structural argument for heterogeneity is sensible. Most historians readily acknowledge base-level fluidity of identity in early sedentary regions. Pálóczi Horváth claims that eighth- to tenth-century grave goods in the Lower Volga suggest 'a population of ethnically mixed origin [in] the Khazar Empire'.[302] Accounting for persistent traditional nomadism, Noonan advocated a similar position.[303] Franklin and Shepard make a characteristically measured, yet persuasive archaeological argument for heterogeneity.[304] Certainly a homogeneous population can hardly be defined let alone proven: diversity by default.

---

[299] Zhivkov, *Khazaria*, 221–67.
[300] Kaplan, 'Khazars and Varangians', 1–10.
[301] Mason, 'Religious Beliefs of Khazars', 387.
[302] Pálóczi Horváth, *Pechenegs, Cumans, Iasians*, 19.
[303] Noonan, 'Khazar Qaghanate and Early Rus'', 77.
[304] Franklin and Shepard, *Emergence of Rus*, 80.

However, it depends on how we define diversity and conformity. In regions undergoing sedentarisation and monotheisation processes, such as in Khazaria, top-down identity formation facilitated some level of homogeneity. Klaniczay, for example, describes monotheisation as causing homogeneity through top-down identity indoctrination.[305] Werbart, Bálint and Zhivkov make similar arguments from the relative homogeneity of SMC material culture.[306]

Yet a deterministic view of homogenisation as based on monotheisation betrays viewing the past through the resulting cultural vacuum, that is, via a sedentary or monotheistic teleology. DeWeese points out examples in Christian and Islamic sources retrospectively Christianising and Islamising earlier cultural heritage. It would also make sense for Khazarian Judaising sources.[307] Although Zhivkov enumerates different ethnicities in Khazaria ('Khazars, Bulgars and Alans'), he acknowledges that Judaisation was 'a deliberate attempt to unify into an ethnic whole the often multilingual and multi-ethnic population.'[308] Clearly, top-down conversions, in this case of Khazaria, attempt homogenisation[309] (for example: a communal, perhaps even an obligatory, Judaisation), at least to whatever extent they are successful, to the detriment or delight of the *khağans*' subjects.

This seems comparable with the seventh- to twelfth-century Islamisation of Persia, whose populations did not convert overnight, but took generations of top-down economic and social pressure to internalise Islam. In this 'conversion curve', according to Bulliet, the Persian population confessing Islam rose from roughly 40 per cent in the mid-ninth century to nearly 100 per cent by the twelfth century.[310] The 'Abbasids' top-down conversion process was eventually successful since Islam became central to Persian identity, and therefore conferred, when most Persians confessed Islam by the early twelfth century, a measure of homogeneity. Perhaps the measure of failure of top-down conversions, however, determines heterogeneity (that is, resistance to a communal, perhaps obligatory form of monotheism), which in the

---

[305] Klaniczay, 'Birth of New Europe', 119. He refers specifically to a Western/Central European milieu and to the 'homogenising' capabilities of the Catholic Cistercian monastic order.
[306] Werbart, 'Invisible Identities', 95; Bálint, 'Archaeological Addenda', 410; Zhivkov, *Khazaria*, 222–4, 249.
[307] DeWeese, *Islamization*, 309.
[308] Zhivkov, *Khazaria*, 17–20.
[309] Vachkova, 'Danube Bulgaria and Khazaria', 353; Semënov, 'Происхождение титула "хазар-эльтебер"', 162.
[310] Bulliet, *Conversion to Islam*. Referenced from Siebers, *Religion and Authority of Past*, 113–15.

Khazarian case was Judaism.³¹¹ This primarily top-down monotheisation process is what Russian scholars often term 'potestarian state formation'. It was top-down monotheisation, along with the respective creeds and laws, which later became confessional identities, and through confessional identities, eventually, current ethnicities. Or in other words, 'It is politics that define ethnicity, not vice versa.'³¹²

Nevertheless, we know from both the extant and absent archaeological material that Judaism failed to sufficiently root itself in the subject populations of Khazaria. So while the three-stage model (*inclusion, identification, displacement*³¹³) appears applicable to top-down Khazarian Judaism, such a scenario of long-term identity internalisation would be measurable only to the extent that it preserves itself, which it did not. In other words, Judaisation ultimately failed in Khazaria since the Khazarian Jewish identity eventually disappeared. Yet it nevertheless clearly existed.

Adopting a Judaic timeline

Khazarian sources display another aspect of the process of Khazaria's conversion to Judaism: the adoption of Jewish time. Although an absolute chronology is assignable to the events described in these sources, they also bear their own chronologies derived from biblical scripture, which is worth considering.³¹⁴

---

[311] Kaplan, 'Khazars and Varangians', 9; Vachkova, 'Danube Bulgaria and Khazaria', 359; Artamonov, *История хазар*, 262–4, 329–34; Pletnëva, *Хазары*, 61–2; Novosel'cev, *Хазарское государство*, 153–4; Zhivkov, *Khazaria*, 17; Golden, 'Khazaria and Judaism', 151.

[312] Derks and Roymans, *Ethnic Constructs in Antiquity*, 1. Quoted from Reher and Fernández-Götz, 'Archaeological Narratives in Ethnicity', 404.

[313] Golden, 'Conversion of Khazars to Judaism', 127–12

[314] This has been considered in the poem by Oswald Le Winter, 'Among Khazars':

> The great Khan, thick in skins,
> drowses and waits.
> Advisers juggle time away.
> Only the jester meditates.
> But meditates upon the God
> a Spanish rabbi makes
> wide though invisible, silent
> although his strange tongue quakes.
> No matter that in Granada sit
> young men with insect eyes,
> proving the one God by the rule
> of that Pythagoras who never lies.

The *Schechter Text* abundantly references the Torah and Israel.³¹⁵ The *Kievan Letter* alludes to the Tanakh (the Old Testament).³¹⁶ *King Joseph's Reply* also firmly attaches Khazarian identity to a timeline adapted from the Old Testament. I believe the *Khazar Correspondence*, between a Jew from an older community (Hasdai ibn Šaprut) and another Jew of a younger community (*khağan* Joseph or the anonymous Khazar author), reveals the most about Khazarian Jewish identity, basing itself on the Tanakh (the Old Testament), as this is the primary common denominator between the two men. In their adoption of Hebrew as an official writing system and Judaism as 'state-religion',³¹⁷ the Khazarian *khağans* also adopted a Jewish conception of linear time derived from the Old Testament. In *King Joseph's Reply*, Joseph explained his descent relative to famous passages of the Old Testament, namely the *Table of Nations* (Genesis 10):

> I hereby inform you that we are descendants of Yefeth [Japheth/Japhal], from the progeny of Togarma. This is what I have found in the family archives of my ancestors. Togarma had ten sons, and these were their names: The firstborn was Agyor, then Tiros, Ouvar, Ugin, Bisal, Tarna, Khazar, Zanor, Balnod, and Savir. We are from the seventh son, Khazar.³¹⁸

The epistle continues, noting Exodus, Malachi and Daniel to calculate a Judaic eschatology.³¹⁹

The retrospective monotheisation of previously pagan traditions is common. Similar instances occur in early literary traditions in Volga Bulgaria,³²⁰ in Rus'³²¹ and further West,³²² in Lombardy,³²³ Hungary,³²⁴ Lithuania,³²⁵

---

[315] *Schechter Text*, eds and tr. Golb and Pritsak, *Khazarian Hebrew Documents*, 110–11; 116–17.
[316] *Kievan Letter*, eds and tr. Golb and Pritsak, *Khazarian Hebrew Documents*, 10–15.
[317] Golden, *Introduction to Turkic Peoples*, 152.
[318] *King Joseph's Reply*, tr. Korobkin, *Kuzari*, 351; Yehuda HaLevi, 'Kuzari: King Joseph', Ben-Yehuda Project:

מוֹדִיעַ אֲנִי לְךָ שֶׁאָנוּ מִבְּנֵי יֶפֶת מִזֶּרַע תּוֹגַרְמָה, כָּךְ מָצָאתִי בְּסִפְרֵי יְחוּסִים שֶׁל אֲבוֹתַי, שֶׁהָיוּ לְתוֹגַרְמָה.
עֲשָׂרָה בָנִים, אֵלֶּה שְׁמוֹתָם: הַבְּכוֹר אוּיוּר, הַשֵּׁנִי תּוּרִיס, הַשְּׁלִישִׁי אֲוָור, הָרְבִיעִי אוּגוּז, הַחֲמִשִּׁי בִּיזָל
הַשִּׁשִּׁי תַּרְנָא, הַשְּׁבִיעִי כַּזַר, הַשְּׁמִינִי יָנוּר, הַתְּשִׁיעִי בֶּלְגָּר, הָעֲשִׂירִי סָאוִיר, אָנוּ מִבְּנֵי כַּזַר הַשְּׁבִיעִי.'

[319] *King Joseph's Reply*, tr. Korobkin, *Kuzari*, 356–7.
[320] See below Chapter 4, Monotheisation in Metal, Empires of Faith and their Finances.
[321] Franklin, 'Invention of Rus(sia)(s)', 180–95; Meyendorff, *Byzantium and Rise of Russia*; Martin, *Medieval Russia*; Raffensperger, *Reimagining Europe*.
[322] Collins, 'Law and Ethnic Identity', 1–23.
[323] Zancani, '"Lombard" and "Lombardy"', 217–32.
[324] Fodor, *New Homeland*; Stephenson, *Byzantium's Balkan Frontier*, 187.
[325] Meyendorff, *Byzantium and Rise of Russia*, 226–45.

Anglia[326] and Francia.[327] Such rulers' respective adoptions of Christian or Islamic timelines is revealed in Christian or Hijric calendars.[328] Because Joseph was adamant about his Jewishness to Hasdai, if only for appearance's sake, the former's adoption of Togarmah as his ancestor is revealing, especially since such information as a list of sons of Togarmah derives not from the Tanakh (Old Testament) but from the mid-tenth-century *Sefer Yosippon*, written in Sicily or southern Italy.[329] The sons enumerated in this document are obviously based on contemporaneous Khazarian tribal affiliations.[330] The fact that these peoples are referred to as descendants of Togarmah should not be interpreted literally, albeit this was Joseph's desire.[331] The patchiness of the *Reply*'s chronology must be considered when analysing contemporaneous understandings of extra-biblical chronology.

Clearly Joseph's acceptance of Judaic linear time derived from the Tanakh, inviting a theoretical framework for adoptions of a given monotheism's linear time structure. Historians distinguish between cyclical time and linear time, mostly to draw a separation between paganism and monotheism.[332] This is not to describe paganism as universally monolithic,[333] in the steppe or elsewhere.[334] In Khazaria, the transition from paganism to Judaism-as-official-religion can be seen, vis-à-vis Eliade's concepts of myth-time and the eternal return,[335] in terms of linear time received from the Tanakh. For Zhivkov, where there were gaps between text and practice, however, steppe-pagan traditions were recycled and imbued 'with new meaning'.[336] So as various Eurasian rulers adopted various monotheisms,

---

[326] Scherb, 'Assimilating Giants', 59–84; Smyth, 'English Identity', 24–52; Reuter, 'England and Germany', 53–70.

[327] MacMaster, 'Trojan Origins', 1–12; Brown, 'Trojan Origins of French', 135–79.

[328] Zhivkov, *Khazaria*, 41.

[329] *Sefer Yosippon*, ed. Flusser, vol. 2, 255.

[330] *Schechter Text*, eds and tr. Golb and Pritsak, *Khazarian Hebrew Documents*, 36–7.

[331] This contrasts with Zhivkov (*Khazaria*, 43), who concludes that Joseph's assertion of his own descent from Togarmah was ultimately adopted 'from the Caucasian Christian tradition'; although his evidence is quite considerable, I am unconvinced.

[332] Craig, 'Whitrow and Popper', 165–6. This concept of linear versus cyclical time, in a Byzantine perspective, is clearly visible in Anna Komnene's opening remark in her *Alexiad* (eds Reinsch and Kambylis, *Annae Comnenae Alexias*, I, 5): 'ὅ γε λόγος ὁ τῆς ἱστορίας ἔρυμα καρτερώτατον γίνεται τῷ τοῦ χρόνου ῥεύματι' (tr. Dawes, *Alexiad*, 1): 'The tale of history forms a very strong bulwark against the stream of time.'

[333] Kirk, *Nature of Greek Myths*, 64; Kirk, *Myth*, 255.

[334] Zhivkov, *Khazaria*, 268–83.

[335] Eliade, *Sacred and Profane*, 107; Eliade, *Myth of Eternal Return*.

[336] Zhivkov, *Khazaria*, 73–86.

Sedentarisation

Are similar patterns reflected in Khazarian sedentarisation? This subsection details the process of becoming sedentary and the emergence of fortified, urban areas in Khazaria as lived phenomena.

Settlement

Archaeological materials (ceramics, burials [kurgans, pit-graves, catacombs], epigraphy, mixed coin hoards, bronze figurines, horse bits, etc.) again provide most evidence for the retention of nomadic lifestyles. Many finds of kurgans and characteristically nomadic ceramic wares, primarily from ninth- to tenth-century Sarkel (crude clay bowls, cups and jugs described as 'typical of tribal nomads'), indicate the retention of nomadic lifestyles.[337] Artamonov discovered incised graffiti on bone and bronze fragments depicting horses and riders in Sarkel and the Majackij *gorodišče*, typical of steppe-nomadism.[338] Nevertheless, there are also archaeological indications of the settlement of previously nomadic populations.

Samosdel'ka revealed pit latrines, signifying a rudimentary urban sedentarisation of previously nomadic populations during the period in question.[339] Samosdel'ka's yurt-shaped dwellings with wattle-and-daub wall installations have also been interpreted as highly suggestive of the sedentarisation of former steppe-nomads.[340] In Sarkel, Artamonov described certain grave goods as typical of nomadic burials, although a cross appears on one object,[341] perhaps suggesting a rudimentary appropriation of Christian imagery.

Nomadic groups were seldom purely nomadic; they included farmers, blacksmiths, builders and so on. The Khazarian era was marked by large-scale nomadic settlement, deemed 'pastoral-urbanization'.[342] *SMC*

---

[337] Zaleskaja et al., *Съкровище на хан Кубрат*, nos 251, 257, 293.
[338] Artamonov, *История хазар*, 289, 304.
[339] Vasil'ev, *Самосдельское городище*, 26–7; Bulan, *Présence byzantine en Crimée*, 25–9.
[340] Vasil'ev, *Самосдельское городище*, 48–59.
[341] Artamonov, *История хазар*, 316.
[342] Kwanten, *Imperial Nomads*, 32.

70   THE MONOTHEISATION OF PONTIC-CASPIAN EURASIA

smithing and agricultural implements have been uncovered in Sarkel and the Cimljansk *gorodišče* (across from Sarkel on the river Don), which clearly indicate Khazar-era nomads gradually becoming sedentary or semi-sedentary.[343] Permanent and temporary dwellings existed concurrently in many areas of the *SMC*.[344] Steppe river valleys revealed contemporaneous traces of once-temporary yurts converted into permanent installations by the covering of the sides with turf for winter insulation.[345] Finally, an osteoarchaeological analysis of comparative dental abrasion of two eighth- to tenth-century Khazarian subject populations revealed fundamentally different lifestyles: agriculture, horticulture, semi-nomadic and nomadic pastoralism.[346] One population (comprising eleven skulls discovered near Červona Gusarivka, 80km southeast of Kharkiv) had a diet primarily based on hunting and fishing.[347] The other forest-steppe population (comprising fourteen skulls discovered near Volčansk, 43km east of Kharkiv) had a diet mainly based on agriculture and horticulture. The analysis of sets of teeth from skulls in both populations' burials shows that signs of abrasion in the agricultural population were due to ingesting primarily cereals, by contrast with those of the pastoral population, whose softer meat and fish diets were more typical of nomadic and semi-nomadic pastoralism. This is clear evidence of diverse livelihoods.[348]

Livelihoods shifted in close proximity. Khazar-era game animal bones found at the Cimljansk *gorodišče* suggest predominant hunting livelihoods,[349] while in Sarkel, contemporaneous finds of domestic livestock bones suggest the opposite: a gradual shift towards agriculture and semi-sedentary pastoralism.[350] Additionally, various seeds of wheat, barley,

---

[343] Zaleskaja et al., *Съкровище на хан Кубрат*, nos 217, 220, 224 (Cimljansk), 282 (Sarkel); Artamonov, *История хазар*, 319–20.
[344] Werbart, 'Khazars or "Saltovo-Majaki Culture"?', 213.
[345] Fodor, *New Homeland*, 215.
[346] Arnold et al., 'Tooth Wear', 52–62.
[347] Predominant reliance on game and fish as foodstuffs is attested archaeologically (Bálint, 'Archaeological Addenda', 407) and textually by al-Istakhrī (tr. in Dunlop, *History of Jewish Khazars*, 93) and *King Joseph's Reply* (tr. Kobler, *Letters of Jews*, 112). For Zhivkov (*Khazaria*, 174, 206–7), al-Istakhrī's account regarding an allegedly subsistence economy based on hunting and fishing contributed to a 'general presumption that the agricultural and handicraft products were not enough to ensure the self-sufficient existence of the Khazar economy'. Since the domains of the *khağans* varied by the decade during the tenth century, I doubt the degree of self-sufficiency of the Khazarian economy can be ascertained.
[348] Arnold et al., 'Tooth Wear', 52–62; Bartha, *Hungarian Society*, 54.
[349] Flërov and Flërova, 'Иудаизм в хазарии', 189.
[350] Matolcsy, 'A Kazár állattartás', 1589–92.

millet, hemp, melon and cucumber have been found throughout Khazar-era *SMC* sites, indicating gradual sedentarisation.[351] Finally, individuals buried in Khazar-era catacomb burials of the Majackij and Dmitrievskij *gorodišči* averaged longer life-expectancies than in concurrently sedentary Western Europe, leading archaeologists to suspect agricultural livelihoods.[352]

Such a Khazarian 'mass sedentarisation' inevitably provoked resistance from traditionally nomadic populations, somewhat mirroring resistance to monotheisation.[353] For example, skull trephination throughout the *SMC* (discussed above) attests not only to its ubiquity in Khazaria, but also the tenacity of nomadism.[354] Elsewhere, the late-ninth-century nomadic strife between the Pečenegs and Magyars has been archaeologically associated with the destruction of agricultural settlements between the Dniepr and the Don in the forest-steppe region.[355]

Clearly a mixture of horticulture, agriculture, hunting, fishing and pastoralism was practised across Khazaria, corresponding to the sedentarisation of local variants of the *SMC*[356] and the Caucasian-Crimean regions by the mid-ninth century.[357] Even Khazaria's nomads such as Pečenegs engaged in subsistence agriculture during wintertime. In the Don Basin, for example, *SMC* populations produced grain with 'advanced agricultural' practices until the tenth century.[358] Agricultural implements excavated from the Cimljansk *gorodišče*, for example, attest to such growing reliance on agriculture.[359] In the thoroughly sedentary Crimean and Taman' peninsulas, there was a long tradition of agriculture and viticulture,[360] which extended up the Don to Sarkel and the Cimljansk *gorodišče*.[361] Rivers like the Don, Volga and Dniepr gradually became rivers of sedentarisation. Like monotheisation, sedentarisation was not merely a top-down phenomenon, but also consisted of bottom-up proactivity and reactivity (resistance and

---

[351] Bálint, 'Archaeological Addenda', 407.
[352] Afanas'ev, *Донские аланы*, 14–50.
[353] Golden, 'Nomadic Economic Development of Rus", 79–87; Honeychurch, 'Alternative Complexities', 277–326; Popova, 'Blurring Boundaries', 296–320.
[354] Rešetova, 'Trephination Cases', 9–14. These thirteen cases of trephined skulls have not yet been calculated as a percentage of the total number of excavated skulls in the *SMC*.
[355] Pálóczi Horváth, *Pechenegs, Cumans, Iasians*, 20; Zhivkov, *Khazaria*, 127, 193.
[356] Brook, *Jews of Khazaria*, 58–60.
[357] Petrukhin, 'Sacral Kingship and Judaism of Khazars', 292.
[358] Pálóczi Horváth, *Pechenegs, Cumans, Iasians*, 18.
[359] Pletnëva, *Кочевий к городам*, 144–70; Artamonov, *История хазар*, 319–21.
[360] Feldman, 'Autonomy and Rebellion in Cherson', 66.
[361] Bartha, *Hungarian Society*, 52; Franklin and Shepard, *Emergence of Rus*, 83.

gradual adoption).³⁶² Variations in production inevitably led to inequalities vis-à-vis hunting and pastoral rights and land ownership, and the landed elite formed the *khağanate*'s main constituency.³⁶³ Such elites, urban or at least semi-sedentary, would have been directly loyal to the Khazar *khağan* and fundamental to the very *khağanate* itself.³⁶⁴ Regardless of Judaism, there was a gradual shift throughout the *SMC* towards sedentarism. For example, *King Joseph's Reply* refers not only to elite agrarianism and viticulture, but to his own semi-nomadism (living in Itīl' during the winter and at his hereditary estate during the summer). In his *Reply*, Joseph refers to 'each family [having] its own hereditary estate'.³⁶⁵ Some degree of sedentarism was clearly internalised by the ninth- to tenth-century Khazarian elite, which was effectively a conversion (of livelihood) of the tribal elite into a feudal aristocracy, and indirectly paralleled a conversion (of faith).³⁶⁶

Centre and periphery in Khazaria

Sedentarisation initiated urbanism, which produced a centre, which yielded peripheries. Khazarian sources indicate the Judaic sacralisation of the final Khazarian capital, Itīl'. To that effect, the *khağans* (Benjamin, Aaron or Joseph³⁶⁷) placed themselves in the biblical context, to consolidate vassals' power and to impose tribute on peripheral subject populations. Similar occurrences are visible in the establishment of other Eurasian capitals in Kiev (Rus'³⁶⁸), Bolgar (Volga Bulgars³⁶⁹), Kazan' (the Golden Horde³⁷⁰), Preslav (Danube Bulgars³⁷¹), Esztergom (Magyars³⁷²) and so forth.

The *khağans*' settlement in the brick palace of Itīl' was as symbolic as it was functional: a permanent, fortified structure in the nomadic and

---

³⁶² Zhivkov, *Khazaria*, 191.
³⁶³ Kwanten, *Imperial Nomads*, 43.
³⁶⁴ Golden, '*Comitatus* in Eurasia', 153–70.
³⁶⁵ *King Joseph's Reply*, tr. Kobler, *Letters of Jews*, 112–13; Noonan, 'Khazar Qaghanate and Early Rus'', 78.
³⁶⁶ Werbart, 'Invisible Identities', 95; Zhivkov, *Khazaria*,181–92.
³⁶⁷ *Schechter Text*, eds and tr. Golb and Pritsak, *Khazarian Hebrew Documents*, 132–42. Each ruler's regnal years are indeterminable.
³⁶⁸ Franklin and Shepard, *Emergence of Rus*, 169–80.
³⁶⁹ See below Chapter 3, Case Studies of Monotheisation in Eighth- to-Thirteenth-Century Pontic-Caspian Eurasia, Volga Bulgaria.
³⁷⁰ DeWeese, *Islamization*, 76–77; Golden, 'The Turks', 30.
³⁷¹ Nikolov, 'New Basileus', 101–8; Zhivkov, *Khazaria*, 227; Stephenson, *Byzantium's Balkan Frontier*, 320–1.
³⁷² Engel, *Realm of St. Stephen*, 40–4.

semi-nomadic context epitomised a sacred centre.³⁷³ *King Joseph's Reply* describes many peoples spread across a territory over which he claimed sovereignty and tribute.³⁷⁴ Yet his suzerainty over his vassals (namely, the Volga Bulgars, Magyars, Alans, Slavs, Pečenegs, Oğuz, etc.) was never absolute. Although they intuit a healthy scepticism of the document, some historians seek to concretely define Khazaria's borders based on the *Reply*, and nonetheless adhere to the notion of Khazaria's ninth- to tenth-century boundaries.³⁷⁵ Khazaria's boundaries are better thought of as *frontiers* which constantly fluctuated, based not on vaguely modern notions of ethnicity, linguistics or any other population marker along similar lines,³⁷⁶ but primarily on periodically declared loyalties, visible through tribute or confessional allegiances.

Yet natural boundaries did exist. They appear in sources like the *Ḥudūd al-ʿĀlam*.³⁷⁷ The Caucasus, the Carpathians and the Crimean Mountains easily separated the steppe from the Caliphate, Byzantium and the Carpathian Basin (Pannonia) respectively. River boundaries proliferate in the steppe, separating for example the dominions of various Pečeneg tribes.³⁷⁸ Yet natural boundaries such as rivers and mountains were not always sufficient to guarantee security, necessitating frontier fortifications not unlike the Roman *Limes*, or the Chinese Great Walls (there were several), which were in a sense the closest the preindustrial world came to defined borders. Like other concurrent rulers, the Khazar *khaǧans* erected artificial boundaries in earth and stone, whether directly or indirectly through vassalised elites and/or tribal communities.³⁷⁹

This explains the construction of Sarkel and twelve garrisoned *gorodišči* which have been discovered along the Upper Donec and between the Donec and Upper Don,³⁸⁰ which al-Masʿūdī debatably called the 'river of Khazaria.'³⁸¹ Sarkel and possibly Itīl' were not only significant fortified

---

[373] Ivik and Ključnikov, *Хазары*, 95–6; Dunlop, *History of Jewish Khazars*, 92; Zhivkov, *Khazaria*, 238–9.
[374] *King Joseph's Reply*, tr. Kokovcov, *Еврейско-хазарская переписка*, 81, 98.
[375] Galkina, 'Территория хазарского каганата', 132–45.
[376] Golden, *Introduction to Turkic Peoples*, 5.
[377] *Ḥudūd al-ʿĀlam*, tr. Minorsky, §1–8.
[378] Pálóczi Horváth, *Pechenegs, Cumans, Iasians*, 8–9.
[379] Marvakov, 'Първото българско царство и кримска хазария', 210; Zhivkov, *Khazaria*, 204; Afanasʾev, *Донские аланы*, 152; Pletnëva, *Саркел и "шелковый" путь*, 142.
[380] Zhivkov, *Khazaria*, 246–8.
[381] Franklin and Shepard, *Emergence of Rus*, 79; Zhivkov (*Khazaria*, 38, 193, 205) and Uspenskij ('Могильники', 96), refer to other 'rivers of Khazaria'.

urban centres, but vital links in the Silk Roads and therefore Khazarian commercial infrastructure.[382] It is impossible to say whom these fortresses were built to defend against. While there is little archaeological proof to support conjecture, these projects may have been planned in Itīl'.

Despite Joseph's admission that 'We are far away from Zion,'[383] it was from his capital in Itīl' that the *khağanate*, like all early political formations, was ruled and to where wealth flowed. A centralised administration in Khazaria enabled and/or demanded the integration of wealthy non-steppe peripheries, namely, Caucasian and Crimean cities. This raises the question: was the growth of wealth in peripheral cities caused by nomadic sedentarisation or were nomads attracted to cities already growing wealthy from sedentarisation? Both phenomena are attested. Regardless of whether wealth was generated by agriculture, pastoralism, commerce or warfare, it sustained the *khağanate*. Certainly Itīl' was the main vehicle and destination of wealth (bullion, furs, grain, wax, slaves, etc.), which was paid as tribute by peripheral subject populations in that their tribute assured their 'protection' by the *khağans*.[384]

Elite and subject; tribute and tax

Tribute collection was certainly not a Khazarian innovation. Eventually tribute collection became tax collection and subject tribes became homogenised subjects of the *khağan* – as in many other arrangements of the tributary mode of production.[385]

Yet not all subjects and vassals acquiesced. Some vassals who ruled their own subjects and paid tribute to the *khağan* chafed at their status. For example, Almuš, the early-tenth-century ruler of Volga Bulgaria, regularly paid tribute to the *khağan*. He claimed that he was 'enslaved' (according

---

[382] Pletnëva, *Саркел и "шелковый" путь*, 155; Zhivkov, *Khazaria*, 159; Kovalev, 'Khazar Identity through Coins', 55–105.

[383] *King Joseph's Reply*, tr. Korobkin, *Kuzari*, 356.

[384] Noonan, 'Economy of Khazar Khaganate', 207–44; Zhivkov, *Khazaria*, 212–24, 251; Pletnëva, 'Города в хазарском каганате', 117; Flërov, '"Хазарские города"', 66; Stepanov, 'Цивилизационно равнище на българите', 29.

[385] Although archaeological evidence cannot easily demonstrate the formation of a feudal structure of lords and peasant-serfs, it is accepted in both Western and post-Soviet historiography: Haldon, *State and Tributary Mode of Production*; Afanas'ev, *Донские аланы*, 151–3. *King Joseph's Reply* mentions: 'I and my princes and serfs [...] make the circuit of our country' (tr. in Zhivkov, *Khazaria*, 211). This 'circuit' is comparable to the early Rus' tribute collection, called 'round-making', or *'poljud'e'* (for example: Kobiščankov, *Полюдье*, 220–3; Petrukhin, *'Феодализм'*, 164).

to ibn Fadlān[386]) to the Khazar *khağan*. It could be suggested that Almuš and his own subjects were to some degree part of Khazaria.[387] A similar remark could be made about the Magyars.[388] However, this requires qualification, since Byzantine emperors frequently paid tribute to other rulers, yet Byzantium was never permanently absorbed by them (until the fifteenth century). Paying tribute was, vis-à-vis Almuš' case, largely a matter of exporting valuables, although it could be collected in different ways, based on the vassals' size and strength, as, for example, in the case of Almuš' disputed subjugation to the Khazar *khağans*. Therefore, conceiving the Volga Bulgars, Alans, Magyars and so on as 'external' ethnic communities of Khazaria is rather oversimplified based on recent arbitrary assumptions of ethnicity and externality. While Zhivkov earnestly seeks to separate 'internal' from 'external ethnic communities', he continues to assume distinct ethnicities and borders even as he tries to minimise or qualify these terms' usages.[389]

Nevertheless, Volga Bulgaria's Islamisation also coincided with sedentarisation.[390] That Almuš was addressed as 'King Yiltawār, King of the Bulgars'[391] indicated his subjection to Khazaria, since the title *Yiltawār* was a corruption of the subordinate princely title *el'teber*. Because of Almuš' subordination to Khazaria, al-Muqaddasī includes Bolgar and Suwār as among Khazarian towns.[392] Theophanes' *Chronographia* and the *Reply* indicate that tribute payments dated from the late-seventh-century Khazarian conquest

---

[386] Ibn Fadlān, *Risāla*, tr. Frye, *Journey to Russia*, 47.
[387] Zuckerman, 'Khazars and Byzantium', 426.
[388] Róna-Tas, 'Khazars and Magyars', 274–5.
[389] Zhivkov, *Khazaria*, 221–2, 268–83; Somogyi, 'Byzantine Coins in Avaria and Walachia', 141; Howard-Johnston, 'Byzantine Sources for Khazar History', 192. Economies of the period were based on the net assets a ruler could obtain by impounding, conquest, collection or importation, either from his own subjects or from rival rulers and their respective subjects. Self-sufficiency was typically the goal. Inter-kingdom 'trade', while referred to in many terms, was ultimately either booty or tribute, while assuming internal markets and production contributed to some imagined gross domestic product for an imagined pre-modern 'state' would amount to a gross oversimplification. Certainly, various rulers' subjects and/or vassals could be considered economic free agents, but their allegiances could be up for grabs as well. This was especially true for ninth- to tenth-century Khazaria.
[390] Noonan, 'Khazar Qaghanate and Early Rus'', 85; see Chapter 4 below, Monotheisation in Metal, Empires of Faith and their Finances.
[391] Ibn Fadlān, *Risāla*, tr. Lunde and Stone, *Ibn Fadlān*, 27.
[392] Dunlop, *History of Jewish Khazars*, 99; Semënov, 'Происхождение титула "хазар-эльтебер"', 160–163; Zhivkov, *Khazaria*, 233.

of Batbayan's Old Great Bulgaria.[393] This clearly explains Almuš's impetus to adopt Islam and cease paying the *khağans* tribute in the early 920s, according to Fadlān.[394] Almuš sought to distinguish himself and his subjects from the Khazars, resulting in another example of top-down confessional indoctrination and the Islamic identity internalisation of disparate pagan tribes subject to periodic tribute.

Although archaeologists have tried to distinguish pagan groups in this region based on funerary, ceramic and metallurgical typologies alone, various peoples (for example, Sabirs, Alans, Burtās, Kasogs, etc.) found themselves subject to the *khağans*. The Sabirs (alias Savirs, Suwārs[395]) are mentioned in the *Reply*[396] and *DAI*.[397] They are associated with 'proto-Hungarians', or Magyars perhaps,[398] and/or 'Huns',[399] although al-Mas'ūdī associated them with the Khazars.[400] That they are mentioned in the Khazarian Hebrew sources debatably[401] suggests some of them adopted Judaism.[402] A similar remark could possibly be made regarding the Don Alans, who have been connected to the Jas[403] and Burtās, via Rus' and Arabic sources.[404] *King Joseph's Reply* also lists as tributaries the Adyges, who have been connected with the Zichians and Kasogs[405] in the *DAI*.[406] The *PVL* describes

---

[393] Theophanes, *Chronographia*, tr. Mango et al., *Chronicle of Theophanes*, 498; *King Joseph's Reply*, tr. Kokovcov, Еврейско-хазарская переписка, 92.

[394] Ibn Fadlān, *Risāla*, tr. Lunde and Stone, *Ibn Fadlān*, 25–31.

[395] Golden, 'Etymology of *Sabir*', 49–55; Salmin, *Savirs – Bulgars – Chuvash*, 13–82.

[396] Galkina, 'Территория хазарского каганата', 133, 145.

[397] Konstantinos VII Porphyrogennetos, *De Administrando Imperio*, ed. Moravcsik, tr. Jenkins, §38.

[398] Golden, 'Khazar Studies', 13; Coene, *Caucasus*, 106; Kwanten, *Imperial Nomads*, 25; Artamonov, *История хазар*, 263; Brutzkus, 'Khazar Origin of Kiev', 114.

[399] Stoljarik, *Monetary Circulation*, 54.

[400] Golden, *Introduction to Turkic Peoples*, 236; Ludwig, *Struktur und Gesellschaft des Chazaren-Reiches*, 24; Magomedov, *Образование хазарского каганата*, 176–7; Novosel'cev, *Хазарское государство*, 85.

[401] Kulik, 'Judeo-Greek Legacy', 53.

[402] *Schechter Text*, eds and tr. Golb and Pritsak, *Khazarian Hebrew Documents*, 15, 35–8.

[403] Palóczi Horváth, *Pechenegs, Cumans, Iasians*, 64–5; Pletnëva, *Славяно-хазарском пограничье*, 269; Bubenok, *Ясы*, 37–44; Kravčenko, 'Городища среднего течения северского донца', 269.

[404] *Schechter Text*, eds and tr. Golb and Pritsak, *Khazarian Hebrew Documents*, 134; al-Mas'ūdī, tr. Lunde and Stone, *Ibn Fadlān*, 235 n43; Novosel'cev, *Хазарское государство*, 120; Afanas'ev, *Донские аланы*, 5–50; Kulik, 'Jewish Presence in Western Rus'', 17; Kovalev, 'Monetary History of Khazaria', 101.

[405] Hellie, 'Rewriting Pre-Mongol Russian History', 75; Arzhantseva, 'Zilgi', 211–50.

[406] Konstantinos VII Porphyrogennetos, *De Administrando Imperio*, ed. Moravcsik, tr. Jenkins, §42.

Khazars and Kasogs, linked to the Čerkess and Slavs east of the Dniepr, as comprising Mstislav's army in 1023.[407] Joseph claimed many peoples as tributaries, and their tribute ostensibly rendered them Khazarian, at least for as long as there was a Khazarian identity to bear.

The *PVL* also describes ninth- to tenth-century competition between Khazaria and the Rus' over tribute from Slavic tribes.[408] Conceivably, the *khağans*' attempt to impose a form of monotheism was occasioned by Rus' tribute competition.[409] While Kovalev and Noonan have provided explanations for the prevailing Khazarian and Rus' economic models,[410] the *PVL* describes tribute collection in kind, namely furs. Notwithstanding the *PVL*'s record that, until 885, the Radimichians paid a monetary tribute to Khazaria,[411] there was insufficient bullion to circulate across Rus' and Khazarian tributary areas, leading to hoarding and marginal monetary circulation.[412] Yet this entry also implies that these tribes temporarily accepted their place under Khazarian suzerainty. Khazarian coins found in Eastern European hoards suggest monetary diffusion: besides garnering more tributaries, northern suzerainty was extendable by increasing coin circulation.[413] In this way, the Rus' can be viewed as economic satellites of Khazaria before Svjatoslav's conquest in the 960s, which engendered a '*translatio-imperii*' from Itīl to Kiev.[414] Therefore

---

[407] *Povest' Vremennÿkh Let*, tr. Cross and Sherbowitz-Wetzor, *Russian Primary Chronicle*, 134, 256.

[408] Petrukhin, 'Normans and Khazars', 393–400; Kaplan, 'Khazars and Varangians', 1–10; Chekin, 'Jews in Early Russian Civilization', 379–94; Shepard, 'Viking Rus and Byzantium', 496–501; Schorkowitz, 'Cultural Contact and Transfer', 84–94. See also below Chapter 2, A Commonwealth Inchoate: Byzantium and Pontic-Caspian Eurasia in the Tenth Century, Khazaria's Decline and Disappearance; and Chapter 3, Case Studies of Monotheisation in Eighth- to Thirteenth-Century Pontic-Caspian Eurasia, Rus': Byzantine Christianisation.

[409] Kaplan, 'Khazars and Varangians', 1–10; Zuckerman, 'Khazars' Conversion to Judaism', 237–70; Noonan, 'Islamic Trade in Rus' Lands', 379–94.

[410] Noonan, 'Economy of Khazar Khaganate'; Kovalev, 'Khazar Identity through Coins'; Vinnikov, 'Контакты', 124–37.

[411] *Povest' Vremennÿkh Let*, tr. Cross and Sherbowitz-Wetzor, *Russian Primary Chronicle*, 59–61.

[412] Noonan, 'Did Khazars Possess Monetary Economy?', 219–67; Zhivkov, *Khazaria*, 207.

[413] Franklin and Shepard, *Emergence of Rus*, 78–82.

[414] Petrukhin, 'Normans and Khazars', 393–400; Kaplan, 'Khazars and Varangians', 1–10; Brutzkus, 'Khazar Origin of Kiev', 111, 122; Chekin, 'Jews in Early Russian Civilization', 379–94; Golden, 'Nomads in Sedentary World', 29–34; Noonan, 'Khazar Qaghanate and Early Rus'', 76–102; Shepard, 'Viking Rus and Byzantium', 496; Cherniavsky, 'Khan or Basileus', 459–76; Koptev, '"Chazar Tribute"', 189–212; Koptev, '"Khazar Prince"', 84–120. See also below Chapter 2, A Commonwealth Inchoate: Byzantium and Pontic-Caspian Eurasia in the Tenth Century, Reinterpreting Northern Peoples in the *DAI*.

the *Moses* coins' diffusion northward was unlikely to have been the reason for their discontinuation (more likely is pagan resistance), since according to Kovalev, this was their ultimate destination anyway. Ultimately, the *Moses* coins present a case for Judaic-Khazar diffusion through these special edition releases.[415] They also suggest Khazarian economic influence projected into better fur-producing regions further north.

Approximate Conclusions

Besides suggesting themes for future research on Khazaria, this part summarises two sets of conclusions: tentative hypotheses (dating, Itīl' and monotheisation's effects) and more certain deductions.

Less certain conclusions

The sources support the majority consensus for a three-stage conversion (the *inclusion, identification* and *displacement* model). A single-stage conversion would have been quite highly improbable, especially to Judaism, since it bore older literary and jurisprudential traditions than Christianity or Islam for newcomers' absorption. Adopting these traditions would have been a gradual process, unattainable in a single stage. A two-tiered conversion would have omitted the crucial stage of resistance. Certainly some may argue that there is no supporting evidence for this. In response: missing evidence necessitates comparative analyses. Many Eurasian conversions transpired in three-stage processes, and Khazarian sources themselves imply a conversion in three stages, beginning with a figure named Bulan-Sabriel, then Obadiah, and finally a court debate in which Judaism was decisively chosen.

For Khazaria, the first stage is unlikely to have been in the early-to-mid-eighth century, since combining the *Kartlis Cxovreba* with the *Life of St. Abo* confidently dates events occurring in the 780s under a still-pagan *khaǧan*. However, al-Mas'ūdī, a particularly trustworthy author, dated the *khaǧan's* conversion between 786 and 809 and there is no reason to doubt a *khaǧan*'s personal conversion could have occurred in the first decade of the ninth century.

The second stage is probably dated by the *Moses* coins. Khazarian-minted dirhams unequivocally dated to 837/838 correspond to other Khazarian dirhams proclaiming Moses as God's prophet: the only clear

---

[415] Kovalev, 'Khazar Identity through Coins', 237–40.

archaeological sign yet of Judaism-as-official-religion in Khazaria. Kovalev asserts that the coins suddenly disappeared because they were not circulating within Khazaria, although he also implies that this was the purpose of the coinage, that is, to be traded northward in exchange for furs. I infer that the coinage was discontinued due to traditional pagan resistance to monotheisation, common in many conversions, whereas a single-stage conversion model has few comparative parallels.

The final stage, the court debate, is likely to have occurred in the early 860s, based on Christian of Stavelot's *Expositio*, the *Vita Constantini* and the Khazarian sources, all independent. Therefore, we encounter three approximate stages for a three-stage conversion in the ninth century: around the turn of the ninth century, then the late 830s and finally in the early 860s.

As for Itīl's location, some historians' scepticism is justified regarding both Samosdel'ka and Semibugrÿ as Itīl's original location. No sign has been found at either site reading 'Welcome to Itīl" in Hebrew. To date, no undeniably Khazarian coins or seals containing Hebrew epigraphy have been found at either site. The major finds are largely generic (wattle-and-daub houses, dugouts, ceramics, etc.) and mostly from later periods (such as the Golden Horde era – thirteenth to fifteenth centuries). Vasil'ev's team excavates three urban layers, bypassing the thirteenth- to fourteenth-century Golden Horde era and the eleventh- to twelfth-century Cuman-Qıpčaq era.

Nevertheless, both Vasil'ev and Solov'ov have made important discoveries. At Samosdel'ka, an ash-lined destruction layer was carbon-dated to the late tenth century, possibly corroborating the *PVL* account of Svjatoslav's conquest in the 960s. The uncovered brick fortress persuades some other historians about Samosdel'ka as Itīl's location. I believe the best evidence is al-Garnatī's mid-twelfth-century testimony from Saksin, previously Itīl', which he remarks was the Volga delta's only city. Clearly, both Vasil'ev and Solov'ov have discovered parts of a major city in the Volga delta with layers dating to the eighth to ninth centuries. However, if a consensus is ever attainable about either Samosdel'ka or Semibugrÿ as Itīl's location, more excavation is required. Presently it appears possible that both could have formed nearby settlements relating to Itīl', although the relative size of each settlement during the ninth to tenth centuries has yet to be determined. Of course, more remains to be discovered.

Regardless, the relationship between monotheisation and sedentarisation remains imperfect; certainly there is no clear, processual link between them, but there are undeniable parallels, both spatial and temporal. Agrarian empires rose and fell for millennia long before the Abrahamic confessions. The difference, however, is that once these confessions were adopted as official religions by specifically urban and sedentary agrarian empires, they could be readily adopted and/or joined when pagan rulers encountered them. This process is visible beginning with the fourth- to sixth-century 'migration period' in Western Europe, and it has been argued as continuing through 'late antiquity', up to the Avaro-Slavic invasions of the Balkans or Charlemagne's coronation in 800. Yet further migrations continued much later than Slavic migrations into the Balkans, as we have noted Old Great Bulgaria's disintegration by the Khazars, resulting in the Bulgars' migrations to what later became Danube and Volga Bulgaria.[416] These migrations across the Pontic steppes continued with the Magyars, Pečenegs and Oğuz in the late ninth century, and nomadic Cuman-Qıpčaqs (also Polovcÿ) and Selčuqs continue this trend into the thirteenth century.[417] Each migration involved conversions and resistance. Rulers who successfully monotheised their subjects created lasting dynasties or identities, while those who failed were ultimately forgotten.

If successful, the elite ('conquering minority'[418]) gradually imposed their monotheism in a top-down indoctrination process, which internalised the monotheistic identity among the subject populations, laying the foundations of modern ethnicity. This process is also visible in the adoption of a liturgical language for preserving sacred texts and laws, and a linear conception of time in which successive rulers occupy the central role in an older narrative inherited from the sacred text and reflected back to the rulers in their own literary and historical traditions.

Kingdoms, empires and civilisations were forged primarily by the adoption of a brand of monotheism, as opposed to some amorphous concept of cultural or geographical 'worldview and ritual' indigenous to Europe, Asia or the steppe.[419] The ability of the dynasty to successfully disseminate its newfound monotheistic identity among its subjects, top-down, ultimately defined the survival, or success, of polities – what Russian scholars call 'potestarian state formation'.

Khazaria's adoption of Judaism coincided with partial sedentarisation, which presupposed a capital and periphery. The sedentary (or semi-sedentary) elite which ruled sedentary (or semi-sedentary) subjects via

---

[416] Vojnikov, *Първата българска държава*.
[417] See below Chapter 3, Case Studies of Monotheisation in Eighth- to-Thirteenth-Century Pontic-Caspian Eurasia, Magyars, Pečenegs and Cumans.
[418] Somogyi, 'Byzantine Coins in Avaria and Walachia', 110–11.
[419] In contrast to Zhivkov, *Khazaria*, 282.

tribute and then tax collection (in coin or kind) gradually sought to diffuse its Judaic identity among its subjects. But the Judaic identity was not preserved in its subjects: Judaism-as-official-religion ultimately failed and the Khazarian identity eventually disintegrated.

More certain conclusions

The vast majority of the *khağans*' subjects remained pagan or followed other faiths. Yet archaeological evidence of Judaism has been found throughout Khazaria, some corresponding to the *SMC* and apparently 'locally produced'. The *Moses* coins aside, such objects do not demonstrate Judaism-as-official-religion; they only offer tantalising clues without settling the question. Outside of the Jewish communities of Crimea and Taman', it remains improbable that Judaism diffused deep into rural Khazaria. The majority of uncovered steppe burials are characterised as pagan, not to mention prevalent and long-standing nomadic lifestyles in Khazaria into the tenth century and later. To suppose that the majority of the *khağans*' subject populations espoused Judaism would be inadvisable. Khazaria's diversity, described by Zhivkov,[420] was directly due to the failure to impose Judaism top-down as a 'state-religion' in the way other rulers imposed their chosen faiths top-down elsewhere. Although this did not cause Khazaria's demise, it precluded a minority Jewish identity from becoming a majority in later centuries.

This discussion will certainly continue. Coin hoards are always potentially discoverable. Excavations continue in Samosdel'ka and Semibugrÿ. Textual scholars continue making new interpretations. It is also reasonable to warn against hasty conclusions and false presumptions based on modern agendas. For example, some have made arguments *ex silentio* to disprove a model of Judaism-as-official-religion in Khazaria,[421] perhaps with current disputes about the origin of Ashkenazi Jews in mind. The Ashkenazi descent theory, however politically convenient, is unsupported by serious evidence, but that hardly means that the disparate accounts of Khazarian Judaism are categorically dismissible by arguments *ex silentio*, even though the scarcity of evidence renders conjecture unavoidable. By combining many kinds of evidence, future research on Khazaria should begin with comparative, interdisciplinary analysis rather than preformed conclusions. For a further discussion of the Ashkenazi descent theory, see Appendix 3.

---

[420] Zhivkov, *Khazaria*, 86–7.
[421] Gil, 'Did Khazars Convert to Judaism?', 429–41; Stampfer, 'Did Khazars Convert to Judaism?', 1–72.

The conversion to Judaism was not a historical anomaly. Monotheisation was a regular occurrence among previously non-sedentary and non-literate peoples. Khazaria was not the first to attempt a top-down Judaisation.[422] To view the histories of conversions in a binary between Christianity and Islam would be fundamentally unsound, especially given the relatively well-organised 'empires of faith' – Christian Rome and the Islamic Caliphate – in the seventh to tenth centuries. While Western European rulers and their subjects primarily encountered Christianity and settled themselves into jostling kingdoms within a single Latin church, Khazaria could choose Judaism from among three Abrahamic faiths and avoided subjugation to either Byzantium or Islam. Consequently, Khazaria represents an effective bonding of Western European and Eastern European history to a broader context of Eurasian history.

---

[422] Sand, *Invention of Jewish People*, 190–209.

2

A Commonwealth Inchoate: Byzantium and Pontic-Caspian Eurasia in the Tenth Century

"The crisis consists precisely in the fact that the old is dying and the new cannot be born; in this interregnum a great variety of morbid symptoms appear."

Antonio Gramsci, 1930, *Quaderni del carcere, Einaudi*

The story of the development of Christendom, specifically Byzantium's portion of it (the Byzantine *commonwealth*, or *oikoumene*), is a familiar one; it unfolds across Pontic-Caspian Eurasia. But like all great historical trajectories, it had an inchoate period subject to great debates. These discussions typically hinge on the question: how should we interpret the imperial relationship with the populations of Pontic-Caspian Eurasia throughout their respective ninth- to tenth-century monotheisations? Obolensky supposed the process of establishing the Orthodox *commonwealth* to have begun in about the sixth century, but was it exclusively Orthodox?[1] And did it actually begin c. 500 as Obolensky supposed, or could it be argued that it began instead with ninth- to tenth-century Byzantine Christianisation? This has major implications for our discussions of both ethnicity and sovereignty in the framework of top-down adoptions of monotheism – in this case, of Byzantine Christianity.

Yet the successful Rus' Christianisation was possible because of the failure of political détente between Byzantium and Khazaria following the latter's attempted Judaisation, since tenth- to eleventh-century Byzantine policy was able to expand its ecclesiastical administration in Pontic-Caspian Eurasia only by abandoning the attempts at Christianising Khazaria. Along with the Almušids' Islamisation, the late-tenth-century

---

[1] Fowden, *Empire to Commonwealth*.

Rjurikids' increasing embrace of Byzantine Orthodox Christianity contributed to Khazaria's isolation and decline, which is demonstrated in emperor Konstantinos VII Porphyrogennetos' mid-tenth-century *DAI*. Because Khazaria's disappearance was central to the monotheistic foundations of several other dynasties (Rjurikids, Almušids, Piasts, etc.), the topic is the last major debate about Khazaria concerning the larger themes of ethnicity and sovereignty amid the monotheisation of Pontic-Caspian Eurasia.

Khazaria's Decline and Disappearance

The word 'decline' is frequently, if contentiously used by historians. My advisor at the University of Birmingham was not fond of the word. Despite wide disagreement about the word's usage, it fulfils the vague function of defining certain periods, even if the word choice is seldom explained. One example is Gibbon's notorious characterisation of Byzantium, 'whose decline is almost coeval with her foundation [...] in the lapse of a thousand years,'[2] constituting a self-anathematising position for Byzantinists. While Khazaria generally receives less impassioned defence from historians regarding 'decline', the word's usage is perhaps merited since it separates a period of stability (ninth to tenth century) from a later period of non-existence, even if historians disagree on the exact dating of the disappearance. Nevertheless, there are probable causes of Khazaria's decline, which preceded its disappearance: the most commonly cited cause is the dissolution of Byzantium's traditionally decent relationship with Khazaria, probably due to the official adoption of Judaism instead of Christianity. But this is not the *only* cause of Khazaria's decline and disappearance.

Composed in the mid-eighth to mid-ninth century, the *NE* 3 records the Byzantine eparchy of Gotthia,[3] an ecclesiastical region which theoretically covered most of Khazaria, primarily the Crimean and Taman' peninsulas. However, the precise dating and possession of Crimea and Taman' by Byzantium, Khazaria or Rus' is debated.[4] Nevertheless, this was a time of détente between Byzantium and Khazaria. The question arises: what happened to the détente, and does it relate to Khazaria's disappearance?

---

[2] Gibbon, *Decline and Fall*, VI:LXIV:IV.
[3] Obolensky, *Byzantine Commonwealth*, 174; Vasiliev, *Goths in Crimea*, 97; *Notitiae Episcopatuum*, ed. Darrouzès, 42–5, 241–2; Komatina, 'Composition of Notitiae Episcopatuum', 204.
[4] Soročan, 'Византийско-хазарском кондоминиуме в крыму', 278–97; Čkhaidze, 'Византийская власть на боспоре', 721–30; Zuckerman, 'Byzantine Rule in North-Eastern Pontus', 311–36; Sljadz', 'Византийской аннексии приазовья', 161–74.

Two eighth- to ninth-century hagiographies provide useful information about Khazar tolerance for Christianity. The hagiography of Ioannes of Gotthia, compiled anonymously in the early-ninth century, tells the story of a certain Ioannes from Parthenitai (present Alušta) in Crimea who became the bishop of Crimean Gotthia. He led a failed rebellion against the Khazar domination of Doros (present Mangup, 22km east of Sevastopol') and died after returning to Amastris on the northern Anatolian coast in 791–2.[5] The hagiography presents the *khağan* as an oppressive figure, but not Jewish. Likewise, the hagiography of Abo of Tiflis, whose Christianity was still a work in progress by 786, presents a general Khazar tolerance of Christianity.[6] These hagiographies' significance is bound to Gotthia's status as an eparchy in the *NE* 3 during the iconoclast era.[7]

Concurrently, the *NE* 3 outlined a metropolitan list of sees which sought to Christianise Khazaria.[8] The suffragan list included the Chotzirs (Khazars) near Phoullon (Phoullai, present Crimean Koktebel'),[9] Astel/Itīl' (in the Volga delta), the Chouales/Chwalisians,[10] the Onogours of Reteg (river

---

[5] Vasiliev, *Goths in Crimea*, 89–97; Ioannes of Gotthia, *Vita*, tr. Mogaričev et al., Житие Иоанна Готского, 192–3; ed. and tr. Auzépy, 'Vie de Jean de Gothie', 80; Alf'orov, 'Seals from Kherson', 360–7.

[6] Ioannes of Gotthia, *Vita*, tr. Huxley, '*Vita* John of Gotthia', 161–9; Abo of Tiflis, *Vita*, tr. Lang, *Georgian Saints*, 115–133; Abo of Tiflis, *Vita*, tr. Peeters, 'Khazars dans Abo de Tiflis', 21–56; Howard-Johnston, 'Byzantine Sources for Khazar History', 169; Vasiliev, *Goths in Crimea*, 96.

[7] Obolensky, *Byzantine Commonwealth*, 174; Feldman, 'Autonomy and Rebellion in Cherson', 27 n56.

[8] *Notitiae Episcopatuum*, ed. Darrouzès, 32–3; Vasiliev, *Goths in Crimea*, 97–102; Obolensky, *Byzantine Commonwealth*, 174–5; Pritsak, 'Khazar Kingdom's Conversion to Judaism', 263–6; Naumenko, 'Византийско-хазарские отношения', 231–44; Shepard, 'Khazars' Formal Adoption of Judaism', 18–20; Howard-Johnston, 'Byzantine Sources for Khazar History', 171–2; Olsson, 'Coup d'état', 504–24; Zuckerman, 'Byzantium's Pontic Policy in *Notitiae Episcopatuum*', 203; Dudek, *Chazarowie*, map 4.

[9] Phoullai's exact location is debated. It is identified as either Sougdaia/Sudak (Soročan, '"Дело" епископа Иоанна Готского', 84), Čufut-kale (Vasiliev, *Goths in Crimea*, 98) or on the Tepsen Plateau in southeast Crimea close to Koktebel' (Mogaričev and Majko, 'Фулы и крымская хазария', 130–4; Brook, *Jews of Khazaria*, 36–7; Noonan, 'Khazar-Byzantine World of Crimea', 209–26). I am inclined to agree with the last of these locations.

[10] The location is uncertain; theories have been proposed from the Caspian coastline to Pannonia: Vasiliev, *Goths in Crimea*, 99–100; Çoban, 'Muslim Groups among Hungarians', 56; Türk, 'Khwarazmian-Hungarian Connections', 242–3; Berend, 'Islam in Hungary', 203–4; Dobrovits, 'Altaic World', 392.

Terek of the north Caucasus),[11] the Huns[12] and Tamatarcha/Tmutarakan.'[13] An imperial eparchy, covering much of Khazaria in Pontic-Caspian Eurasia, from the lower Volga to the Caucasus to Crimea, is visible. Yet it did not endure, ostensibly due to Byzantine disappointment with Khazaria's adoption of Judaism instead.[14] But when did relations sour? Regardless of the *NE* 3's dating, Byzantine collaboration with Khazaria continued as late as 841, since the *DAI* records that emperor Theophilos ensured the construction of the Khazarian Sarkel fortress on the Don, near today's Cimljansk in southern Russia.[15]

The Gotthia metropolitanate's disappearance demonstrated mutual estrangement due to the *khağan*'s Judaisation.[16] Further textual evidence appears in the ninth-century Slavonic *Vita Constantini*, which again hints at an imperial endeavour to restore ecclesiastical influence in Khazaria: Konstantinos-Kyrillos (that is, Cyril/Kyrillos and Methodios) was delegated to Khazaria for the religious debates (c. 860–1).[17] While this source presents the task as successful for the Christian delegation, the Khazarian sources are written in Hebrew.[18] Along with the *Vita Constantini*, an epistle of Patriarch Nicholas Mystikos (c. 920) reveals equal effort to Christianise Khazaria, although its ultimate failure is reflected by his description of Khazaria as 'that deluded nation.'[19] This demonstrates a begrudging Christian acknowledgment of Khazaria's Judaisation, although it omits naming Judaism specifically.

---

[11] Vasiliev, *Goths in Crimea*, 100; Obolensky, *Byzantine Commonwealth*, 174–5.

[12] The see of the Huns is also debated. It is identified with Black Bulgars and/or Magyars in the river Don region (Vasiliev, *Goths in Crimea*, 100–101; Zhivkov, *Khazaria*, 127–9), or in the river Kuban region of southern Russia (Obolensky, *Byzantine Commonwealth*, 175).

[13] Moravcsik, 'Byzantinische Mission des Schwarzen Meeres', 22–4; Čkhaidze, 'Зихская епархия', 47–68.

[14] Shepard, 'Khazars' Formal Adoption of Judaism', 19; Obolensky, *Byzantine Commonwealth*, 174–5; Howard-Johnston, 'Byzantine Sources for Khazar History', 172.

[15] Konstantinos VII Porphyrogennetos, *De Administrando Imperio*, ed. Moravcsik, tr. Jenkins, §42; Zuckerman, 'Early History of *thema* of Cherson', 210–22; Zhivkov, *Khazaria*, 243; Afanas'ev, 'Где археологические свидетельства хазарского государства', 47–51.

[16] Shepard, 'Khazars' Formal Adoption of Judaism', 20; Zhivkov, *Khazaria*, 210.

[17] *Vita Constantini*, tr. Kantor, *Slavonic Lives*, 43–63; Olsson, 'Coup d'état', 504–24.

[18] Preiser-Kapeller, 'Jewish Empire?'.

[19] Nicholas Mystikos, *Epistles*, eds. and tr. Jenkins and Westerink, *Letters*, 391. Line 14: 'τὸ ἐξηπατημένον ἔθνος'.

By the mid-tenth century, two sources credited to emperor Konstantinos VII reveal distinctly mixed Christian feelings about Khazaria. The *DAI* (c. 948–52[20]) indicates Khazarian potential vulnerability to the north-Caucasian Alans. Without specifically indicating a de facto 'breakdown of détente' with Byzantium,[21] the *DAI* suggests a Byzantine interest in Khazarian weakness.[22] However, later, judging from the three-*nomismata* gold seal used to address the *khaǧan* in his *De Ceremoniis* (c. 956–9[23]), Konstantinos recognises him as the foremost northern ruler.[24] Nevertheless, the *Schechter Text* (c. 949[25]) illustrates a more obvious degeneration of Byzantine–Khazarian relations.[26] Clearly this involved the *khaǧan*'s conversion to Judaism.

The ultimate reason for Khazaria's disappearance is typically drawn from the *PVL* under the year 965, when the Rus' prince Svjatoslav allegedly assaulted Sarkel and Itīl':

> Svyatoslav sallied forth against the Khazars. When they heard of his approach, they went out to meet him with their Prince, the Kagan, and

---

[20] Konstantinos VII Porphyrogennetos, *De Administrando Imperio Commentary*, eds Dvornik et al., 5–6.

[21] Konstantinos VII Porphyrogennetos, *De Administrando Imperio*, ed. Moravcsik, tr. Jenkins, §10–12; Stephenson, *Byzantium's Balkan Frontier*, 33; Zhivkov, *Khazaria*, 145–6; Huxley, 'Byzantinochazarika', 80; Howard-Johnston, 'Byzantine Sources for Khazar History', 181–3.

[22] Novosel'cev, Хазарское государство, 219.

[23] Konstantinos VII Porphyrogennetos, *De Ceremoniis*, tr. Moffatt and Tall, *Book of Ceremonies*, xxv.

[24] Konstantinos VII Porphyrogennetos, *De Ceremoniis*, ed. Reiske, *De Ceremoniis Aulae Byzantinae*, 690–1; Howard-Johnston, 'Byzantine Sources for Khazar History', 172; Zhivkov, *Khazaria*, 145–6.

[25] Zuckerman, 'Русь, византия и хазария', 68–80.

[26] Kralides, 'Χάζαροι καί τό Βυζάντιο', 142–58; *Schechter Text*, eds and tr. Golb and Pritsak, *Khazarian Hebrew Documents*, 112–15: '[But in the days of Benjamin] the king, all the nations were stirred up against [Qazar] *{Khazaria}*, and they besieged the[m with the aid of] the king of Maqedon *{Byzantium}*. Into battle went the king of 'SY' *{Burtās}* and TWRQ['. . .] *{Oǧuz}* [and] 'BM *{Black Bulgars}* and PYYNYL *{Pečenegs}* and Maqedon; *{. . .}* the king of Alan fought against Qazar, for the king of Greece enticed him. *{. . .}* Romanus [the evil o]ne sent great presents to HLGW *{Oleg}* king of RWSY' *{Rus'}* inciting him to (do) his evil.' The Byzantine–Rus' treaty of 944 probably allowed the Rus' to attack Khazaria with Byzantine support (*Povest' Vremennÿkh Let*, tr. Cross and Sherbowitz-Wetzor, *Russian Primary Chronicle*, 72–8; Sakharov, Дипломацията на древна русия, 227–8; Zhivkov, *Khazaria*, 141–62).

the armies came to blows. When battle thus took place, Svyatoslav defeated the Khazars and took their city of Bela Vezha [Sarkel]. He also conquered the Yasians and the Kasogians.[27]

However, the *PVL*'s tenth-century chronology is notoriously unreliable, which is compounded by an entirely different dating of the campaign in other sources: it is dated to 985 in the *Pamjat'* of Jakov the Monk,[28] and 969 by ibn Hauqal.[29] This conveyed confusion about exactly when and where Svjatoslav defeated the Khazars: c. 965–85 and in either Sarkel, Itīl' or both.[30] There is negligible present archaeological evidence that can confirm the time or location of Svjatoslav's assault(s) against the Khazars.[31] Yet Khazaria survived Svjatoslav's assault, since the *PVL* mentions eleventh- to twelfth-century Khazars as Rus' allies, captors and even kin.[32] Actually, Khazars allegedly captured Oleg Svjatoslavich and dispatched him in 1079 to Constantinople, where he married Theophano Mouzalonissa, known as a Rus' *archontissa* from her lead seal.[33] Byzantine (Leon Diakonos,[34] Ioannes Skylitzes[35]) and Islamic sources (al-Mas'ūdī,[36] al-Istakhrī,

---

[27] *Povest' Vremennÿkh Let*, tr. Cross and Sherbowitz-Wetzor, *Russian Primary Chronicle*, 84; Hanak, *Nature and Image of Power in Rus'*, 136; Baranov, Таврика в средневековья, 153; Tortika, Северо-западная хазария, 505–10; Vasiliev, *Goths in Crimea*, 119–31. The original Laurentian redaction (*Povest' Vremennÿkh Let'*, eds. Ostrowski and Birnbaum, Повість временних літ, 428–30), relates that Svjatoslav conquered two Khazar cities: Sarkel 'and their capital', ostensibly Itīl': 'Иде Стославъ на Козары. слышавше же Козари. изидша противу. съ кнѧземъ своимъ Каганомъ. и съступишас҇ бить. ѡ бивши брани. вдолѣ Стославъ Козаромъ и градъ ихъ и Бѣлу Вѣжю взѧ. [и] БѢсы побѣди и Касогы'.
[28] Jakov the Monk, *Pamjat' i Pokhvala*, tr. Hollingsworth, *Hagiography of Kievan Rus'*, 165–81; Golden, 'Nomads in Sedentary World', 60 n56.
[29] Ibn Hauqal, *Ṣūrat al-'Arḍ*, tr. Lunde and Stone, *Ibn Fadlān*, 175; Pletnëva, Хазары, 71.
[30] Al-Mas'ūdī, *Meadows of Gold*, tr. Minorsky, *Sharvān and Darband*, 113; Zuckerman, 'Khazars' Conversion to Judaism', 237–70; Petrukhin, 'Khazaria and Rus'', 261–2.
[31] Artamonov, История хазар, 426; Pletnëva and Makarova, 'Пояс знатного воина из саркела', 62–77; Flërov, 'Крепости хазарии'.
[32] *Povest' Vremennÿkh Let*, tr. Cross and Sherbowitz-Wetzor, *Russian Primary Chronicle*, 97, 134, 168, 203; Dunlop, *History of Jewish Khazars*, 353; Bubenok, 'Данные топонимии о миграциях адыгов', 31; Khotko, 'Концепции этнической истории', 181–9; Colarusso, 'Storehouse of History', 77.
[33] Čkhaidze, 'Феофано Музалон', 268–93.
[34] Leon Diakonos, *History*, tr. Talbot and Sullivan, *Leo the Deacon*, 153; ed. and tr. Karales, Λέων Διάκονος, 272–3.
[35] Ioannes Skylitzes, *Synopsis of Histories*, tr. Wortley, *Synopsis of Byzantine History*, 336; ed. Thurn, *Synopsis Historiarum*, 854–5.
[36] Al-Mas'ūdī, *Meadows of Gold*, tr. Minorsky, *Sharvān and Darband*, 51, 95, 106–7.

al-Muqaddasī, ibn Hauqal[37]) also mention Khazars long after Svjatoslav's tenth-century campaign. While the commonly held reason for Svjatoslav's campaign related to competition for tribute from nearby communities,[38] it may be rather due to gradual tenth-century silver shortages in Khazaria, from where the Rus' had previously accessed silver.[39] This was the result of restructured silver trade routes in the early tenth century, probably due to confessional alliances.

Numismatic evidence suggests that eighth- to ninth-century silver, slave, and fur trade routes between the Islamic Caliphate in the south and the emerging Rus' in the north benefitted Khazaria somewhat as a middleman, as the routes passed through the Caucasus, into Khazaria and then northward.[40] However, judging from both the work of al-Mas'ūdī[41] and finds of Islamic dirhams, the situation changed by the mid-tenth century, when the routes shifted to the east of the Caspian Sea, bypassing Khazaria towards Khwārazmia and Volga Bulgaria. Despite Svjatoslav's alleged campaign in 965 (inherited from the unreliable *PVL*), the underlying cause of Khazaria's decline was ultimately due to a loss of revenue, by about four fifths, from the early-tenth-century restructuring of Islamic trade routes.[42] Although there is no hard evidence for the primary reason for this early-tenth-century trade route restructuring, the *khağans'* endeavour to impose suzerainty on Volga Bulgaria in an effort to supplement their declining revenue coincided with Almuš's conversion to Islam in the 920s. It is possible this resulted in a brief period of cooperation between the Khazars and the Rus'.[43] Regardless, the reorientation of Islamic trade evidently reflected a greater interest in doing direct business with other Muslims in Volga Bulgaria instead of indirectly through Khazaria, where, according to ibn Fadlān, 'the Jews' had reduced Almuš, by then a Muslim, to 'slavery'.[44] Whether or not Khazaria conclusively collapsed in 965, 985 or 1016, regardless of

---

[37] Al-Istakhrī, *Book of Roads and Kingdoms*; al-Muqadassī, *Aḥsan al-Taqāsim fī Maʿrifat al-Aqālīm*; ibn Hauqal, *Ṣūrat al-'Arḍ*, tr. Lunde and Stone, *Ibn Fadlān*, 153–9, 171–8.
[38] Koptev, '"Chazar Tribute"', 189–212.
[39] Jankowiak, 'Two Systems of Trade', 137–48.
[40] Noonan, 'Why Dirhams Reached Russia', 151–282; Zhivkov, *Khazaria*, 147–70; Petrukhin, 'Русь и хазария', 76–8; Franklin and Shepard, *Emergence of Rus*, 87.
[41] Al-Mas'ūdī, *Meadows of Gold*, tr. Lunde and Stone, *Ibn Fadlān*, 137.
[42] Noonan, 'Economy of Khazar Khaganate', 234–8.
[43] Zhivkov, *Khazaria*, 154–6; Gumilëv, *Древняя русь и великая степь*, 215–19; Margoliouth, 'Seizure of Bardha-ah', 82–95.
[44] Ibn Fadlān, *Risāla*, tr. Lunde and Stone, *Ibn Fadlān*, 29.

how well developed were Khazaria's internal markets,[45] the reduction of customs revenues greatly contributed to Khazaria's decline.[46]

Nevertheless, Khazaria's memory survived as a toponym in the Crimean and Taman' peninsulas. This is not to say that the Khazarian *khağans*' rule had been geographically confined to these regions: Byzantine *themata* were often named for nearby frontiers, whose populations they often shared.[47] Whereas Khazarian Judaism gradually disappeared from textual sources, it was replaced with Christian topography in the northern Black Sea littoral previously subject to the Khazar *khağans*. For example, in the late eleventh century, the seal of a certain Michael, *archon* and *doux* of Tamtarcha (Tmutarakan'), Zichia and all Khazaria, appears to belong to a Rus' prince accentuating his dominion's heritage from an earlier Khazar topography, albeit in his time Christianised.[48] Additionally, the name 'Khazaria' in Crimea transformed into the Italianised name 'Gazaria' in thirteenth- to fifteenth-century Genoese documents.[49] When these Genoese Gazarian possessions became inaccessible after the Ottoman conquest of Constantinople in 1453, it galvanised Genoese sailors to seek an alternate route to the East, and one in particular proved successful in 1492. Finally, the name 'Khazaria' has long been associated with the Caspian Sea in many languages: 'Daryaye Khazar' in Persian, 'Bahr-ul-Khazar' in Arabic, 'Xæzær Dænizi' in Azeri and 'Hazar Denizi' in Turkish.[50]

When Christian emperors renounced Khazaria as an ally in tenth-century Pontic-Caspian Eurasia, emperor Konstantinos VII's *DAI* provides clues about possible proxies and replacements. However, the text is usually mined for information about the supposed ethnicities of northern peoples without a procedural interpretation of the literary qualities of the text itself. The following section attempts such a method.

Reinterpreting Northern Peoples in the *DAI*

As the Khazar–Byzantine détente dissolved in the mid-tenth century, several other groups, not only Rus', became more attractive as imperial allies in the Pontic-Caspian region. It cannot be assumed that such an alliance

---

[45] Zhivkov, *Khazaria*, 168–70; Huxley, 'Byzantinochazarika', 80.
[46] Golden, *Khazar Studies*, 111; Noonan, 'Economy of Khazar Khaganate', 243–4.
[47] Krsmanović, *Byzantine Province in Change*; Haldon, *Warfare, State and Society*, 243–5.
[48] Čkhaidze, 'Byzantine Seals Addressed to Matarcha', 61–70.
[49] King, *Black Sea*, 85; Bocharov and Sitdikov (eds.), *Genoese Gazaria*.
[50] Brook, *Jews of Khazaria*, 141.

naturally fell to the Rus', since the Rus' rulers, apart from Olga, were still pagans (*Tauroscythians*[51]). This is particularly apparent in emperor Konstantinos VII's *DAI*, which prefers the Pečenegs for a northern ally over any other people, although it nevertheless bundles them all together.[52] Before Vladimir's decisive baptism in 987–9,[53] the *DAI* carries the most considerable implications when examining how Byzantine concepts of northern 'peoples' are reconcilable with present notions of primordial ethnicity.[54]

Three principal words are used to describe northern (and other) peoples in the *DAI*: *ethnos*, *laos* and *genos*.[55] Although these terms hardly hint at the cohesiveness of the peoples they describe, they derive from much older ethnographic traditions. Used in the *DAI*, these terms have taken on an almost biblical quality for the ethnography of tenth-century Eurasia, especially given much preoccupation with primordial ethnicity, national genealogy and territorial custody (that is, blood-and-soil nationality). Many have scrutinised the text seeking clues about early ethnicity: for example, who exactly were the Narentines, where did they come from and what lands historically belonged to them? While the 'Narentine' ethnicity certainly does not exist today, though others undoubtedly do, can – or even should – present concepts of ethnicity be mapped onto antique ones? More simply, do these terms evoke a sense of geographical belonging (identity by constitution) or genealogical belonging (identity by putative descent)?

Words like *ethnos*, *laos* and *genos* are hardly used consistently even within the *DAI*. The 1967 edition and translation by Jenkins and Moravcsik usually renders derivatives of the word *ethnos* as *nation*, like the word *goy* in biblical Hebrew.[56] However, *ethnikos* is presented as referring to a

---

[51] Leon Diakonos, *History*, tr. Talbot and Sullivan, *Leo the Deacon*, 111; ed. Karales, Λέων Διάκονος, 202–3; *Povest' Vremennÿkh Let*, tr. Cross and Sherbowitz-Wetzor, *Russian Primary Chronicle*, 82–3, 239–40 nn62–3; Poppe, 'Baptism of Olga', 272–5.

[52] Konstantinos VII Porphyrogennetos, *De Administrando Imperio*, ed. Moravcsik, tr. Jenkins, §1, §13.25–6: 'εἴτε Χάζαροι, εἴτε Τοῦρκοι, εἴτε καὶ Ῥῶς, ἢ ἕτερόν τι ἔθνος τῶν βορείων καὶ Σκυθικῶν, οἷα πολλὰ συμβαίνει'.

[53] Feldman, 'Autonomy and Rebellion in Cherson'.

[54] Howard-Johnston, '*De Administrando Imperio*', 303.

[55] Magdalino, 'Constantine VII and Historical Geography of Empire', 23–41.

[56] Konstantinos VII Porphyrogennetos, *De Administrando Imperio*, ed. Moravcsik, tr. Jenkins, §προοίμιον: 8–19, 38; §1:17–25; §2:13–22; §4:7; §13:1–3, 25, 82–6, 106, 114–23, 175–9, 197; §15:5; §21:88; §23:5, 20; §24:10; §25:15; §29:2, 17, 56–75; §30:7–13; §38:1–3, 31–8, 62; §39:1; §41:3, 24–5; §45:21; §46:167; §48:22; §49:15; §53:100; Zernatto and Mistretta, 'Nation', 351–66; Greenfeld, 'Types of European Nationalism', 168; Connor, 'Nation Is a Nation', 43–6; Kaldellis, *Romanland*, 6.

foreigner or infidel,[57] matching *xenos* or *apistos* in Konstantinos VII's military treatises.[58] In one instance, Jenkins renders the use of the word *ethnos* as 'the ethnic term', regarding Iberians as a concrete ethnic group,[59] who might otherwise call themselves either Spanish or Portuguese, and/or Catalan, Basque, Extremaduran, Andalusian, Galician, Valencian and so on. In the *DAI* and military treatises, the term *laos* is usually rendered as 'common folk',[60] as opposed to outlining different 'peoples' in a national sense. Yet elsewhere Jenkins also translates *laos* as an 'army'[61] in quite a national sense, even though other terms (*stratos*, *phossatos*) are translated as 'army'.[62] The term *ochlos* ('crowd', 'mob', 'throng') is used to convey the same meaning.[63] While typically used in Byzantine literature to indicate shared ethnic identity,[64] the word *phylon* is similarly quite flexible; Jenkins renders it as 'tribe', 'men', 'foreigner' and 'race'.[65] It often overlaps with the term *genos*, which is perhaps the most elastic, translated by Jenkins as everything from 'nation', 'tribe', 'stock', 'kin', 'clan', 'race' and 'family' to 'party'.[66]

[57] Konstantinos VII Porphyrogennetos, *De Administrando Imperio*, ed. Moravcsik, tr. Jenkins, §13:96; §31:40; §48:5; Konstantinos VII Porphyrogennetos, *De Administrando Imperio Commentary*, eds Dvornik et al., 11.
[58] Konstantinos VII Porphyrogennetos, *De Administrando Imperio*, ed. Moravcsik, tr. Jenkins, §13:106–15, 143; §45:79; Konstantinos VII Porphyrogennetos, *Three Treatises*, ed. and tr. Haldon, *Imperial Military Expeditions*, C.224, 406.
[59] Konstantinos VII Porphyrogennetos, *De Administrando Imperio*, ed. Moravcsik, tr. Jenkins, §23:19.
[60] Ibid., §6:2; §8:5, 31 (Pečenegs); §26:23–6, 56–62 (Frankish folk); §28:44 (Venetian townsfolk); §29:2 (Romano-Dalmatian townsfolk); §30:65 (Croatians); §32:8, 124 (Serbs); §33:8 (Zachlumian Serbs); §37:69 (Pečenegs); §41:23 (Moravians); §47:4–7, 19 (Cypriot folk); Konstantinos VII Porphyrogennetos, *Three Treatises*, ed. and tr. Haldon, *Imperial Military Expeditions*, C:734 (Constantinopolitan townsfolk).
[61] Konstantinos VII Porphyrogennetos, *De Administrando Imperio*, ed. Moravcsik, tr. Jenkins, §21:104 (a Saracen army); §26:47 (Berengar's army); §28:27 (Pippin's army); §45:132, 168 (a Roman army); Konstantinos VII Porphyrogennetos, *Three Treatises*, ed. and tr. Haldon, *Imperial Military Expeditions*, B:18, 37 ('population'), 44, 88 ('host'), 92–9, 133.
[62] Konstantinos VII Porphyrogennetos, *De Administrando Imperio*, ed. Moravcsik, tr. Jenkins, §15:9; §30:49–55; §32:111–17 (*phossatos*); §21:120; §27:17; §29:106–8; §53:9–11, 194–218 (*stratos*).
[63] Ibid., §30:17; §53:197, 203, 342, 381.
[64] Leidholm, 'Political Families in Byzantium', 99–100.
[65] Konstantinos VII Porphyrogennetos, *De Administrando Imperio*, ed. Moravcsik, tr. Jenkins, §14:24; §15:13; §21:51 ('tribe'); §29:42, 43 ('men'); §15:13 ('foreigners'); §14:2; §37:57; ('race').
[66] Ibid., §13:178–80 ('nation'); §13:15; §15:1; §21:77; §22:38 ('tribe'); §13:152 ('stock'); §13:165; 21:105 ('kin'); §22:3; §37:34–9; §38:10; §39:11–13; §40:1, 4, 44, 50 ('clan'); §προοίμιον:46; §13:122, 178–80; §23:6; §39:2; §50:72 ('race'); §21:23, 50; §25:58–61, 81–5; §29:77–8; §32:32; §33:16; §38:55; §40:48; §45:113 ('family'); §21:25 ('party').

Each *ethnos* in the *DAI* is frequently introduced with an origin story, where ethnic distinctions are made via lineages from a common ancestor, for example, the Turk-Magyars, the Prophet Mohammed, and the Frankish king Hugh of Arles.[67] Yet in his *De Thematibus* (*DT*), Konstantinos equally uses the term *ethne* to describe various pre-monotheistic ethnicities of Anatolia and Ellas.[68] In juxtaposition, while present-day French, Hungarian, Serbian or Croatian readers might read their ethnicities in Konstantinos' *DAI*, who in present Greece or Turkey would refer to himself or herself as an Aeolian, Dorian, Lydian, Phrygian and so on? Such ancient Hellene or Anatolian peoples in the *DT*, may have each comprised an original *ethnos*, supposedly kin-related by putative common ancestry, but together their varyingly internalised Christianity in Konstantinos' time rendered them varyingly Roman, 'not true ethnic groups'.[69] But what is a 'true ethnic group'? If the term *ethnos* denoted foreignness, then for Konstantinos, Roman was the default setting. Unsurprisingly, the phrase *ethnos ton Romaion* ('*ethnos* of the Romans') appears exactly nowhere in the *DAI*, despite Konstantinos' many professions of the exclusivity of the Roman *genos*.[70] However, the ambiguity of one passage in the *DAI* has been interpreted as identifying Romans as one nation *(ethnos)* among others:

> For each nation has different customs and divergent laws and institutions, and should consolidate those things that are proper to it, and should form and activate the associations that it needs for the fusion of its life from within its own nation. For just as each animal species mates with its own race, so it is right that each nation also should marry and cohabit not with those of a different tribe and tongue but of the same tribe and speech.[71]

While clearly demonstrating imperial chauvinism, this passage reveals no more of a 'secular', 'modern definition of the nation' or 'modern ethnic sense'[72] than de Tocqueville's American exceptionalism necessarily reveals an attitude of American ethnicity, let alone American ethnocentrism.[73]

---

[67] Ibid., §38; §14; §26.
[68] Konstantinos VII Porphyrogennetos, *De Thematibus*, ed. Pertusi, I, 1:10, 39; 4:25; 5:12, 22; 6:7, 12, 23; 7:1; 17:10; II, 1:26, 34–5; 5:4 (*ethnos*); 2:6; 3:20–6; 7:6, 10–22; 12:25; 14:38–42; 15:23; II, 1:7; 6:19, 33; 8:15 (*genos*); 1:5–17; 5:6; II, 1:23 (*laos*).
[69] Vasiliev, *Goths in Crimea*, 68; Kaldellis, *Romanland*, 4–5, 117.
[70] Konstantinos VII Porphyrogennetos, *De Administrando Imperio*, ed. Moravcsik, tr. Jenkins, §13:15, 178–80; §15:1; §21:77; §22:38.
[71] Ibid., §13:175–86.
[72] Kaldellis, *Romanland*, 8, 67; Page, *Being Byzantine*, 42.
[73] de Tocqueville, *Democracy in America* II, 36.

Even in the closest place to referring to a Roman *ethnos* in the entire *DAI*, Konstantinos VII stops short. He avoids explicitly referring to a Roman *ethnos* precisely because for him, the word *ethnos* essentially referred to the foreign – questionably Christian, *never* Roman.[74] Nevertheless, his endeavours to project Roman homogeneity through his own genealogy are also reflected in his preoccupation with the supposed genealogical origins of various nations using biblical precedents.[75]

Konstantinos VII did not associate specific *ethne* with specific territories, which were understood as antique continental notions, such as the tripartite geographical division of the world into Asia, Europe and Africa.[76] Konstantinos relied on antique assumptions of ethnography derived both from biblical precedence and from geographer-ethnographers like Herodotus, Strabo, Ptolemy and Plutarch.[77] Ethnography was not so much preoccupied with the geographical spaces inhabited by varying primordial *ethne* as with what constituted their primary status as *ethne*: common foreignness and genealogical ancestries.[78] This is why Aeolians, Lydians, Phrygians and so on constituted *ethne* in the *DT* as much as Rus', Turk-Magyars, Pečenegs and so on did in the *DAI*. *Ethne* were those who had not yet been fully Christianised (or monotheised), frequently near or beyond the imperial frontier, and who could also be deemed barbarians, or perhaps *mixobarbaroi*.[79] Therefore, Konstantinos' ethnography cannot support current claims of territorial custody or primordial ethnicity, since it primarily describes pre-monotheistic groups, particularly the Turk-Magyars and Pečenegs.[80]

---

[74] Konstantinos VII Porphyrogennetos, *De Administrando Imperio*, ed. Moravcsik, tr. Jenkins, §προοίμιον:19, §13:197–200; Leidholm, 'Political Families in Byzantium', 117–18; Feldman, 'Autonomy and Rebellion in Cherson', 46; Obolensky, *Byzantine Commonwealth*, 196; Stephenson, *Byzantium's Balkan Frontier*, 26.

[75] Ian Wood, personal communication, March 2016; Toynbee, *Constantine Porphyrogenitus*, 587–8; Hanak, *Nature and Image of Power in Rus'*, 151–2; Stephenson, 'Byzantine Conceptions of Otherness', 245–58.

[76] Howard-Johnston, '*De Administrando Imperio*', 303; Dilke, 'Cartography in Byzantine Empire', 258–75; Lozovsky, 'Geography and Ethnography', 644–50; Angelov, 'Asia and Europe Called East and West', 43–68.

[77] Walter Pohl, personal communication, March 2016; Konstantinos VII Porphyrogennetos, *De Administrando Imperio*, ed. Moravcsik, tr. Jenkins, 336–9; Zhivkov, *Khazaria*, 41–7.

[78] Skinner, *Invention of Greek Ethnography*, 124–7; Magdalino, 'Constantine VII and Historical Geography of Empire', 23–41; Obolensky, *Byzantine Commonwealth*, 26–8.

[79] Stephenson, *Byzantium's Balkan Frontier*, 109–10.

[80] Ascherson, *Black Sea*, 103, Curta, *Southeastern Europe*, 137–8; Obolensky, *Byzantine Commonwealth*, 59–60; Stephenson, *Byzantium's Balkan Frontier*, 25–9, 117–18; Kaldellis, *Ethnography after Antiquity*, 88; Howard-Johnston, 'Byzantine Sources for Khazar History', 180.

The *DAI*'s 'limited ecumenism' presupposes its purpose as a foreign policy manual rather than ethnography.[81] Yet it never suggests that northern peoples comprised 'polities in their own right, with constitutions and defined territories.'[82] This is quite a broad assumption of primordial ethnicity.[83] First, although the *DAI* mentions peoples like the so-called 'Black Bulgars' and 'Qabars', they would hardly have comprised definitive 'polities' even by tenth-century standards.[84] Second, the supposition that such peoples had 'constitutions' is demographically indeterminable and judicially absurd. Finally, the assumption that such peoples had 'defined territories' is anachronistic, as if borders were arbitrarily assigned between peoples who knew only geographical frontiers at best.[85] Ultimately, this perspective assumes that the *ethnos* was a bottom-up phenomenon, as if all its members acted based on some imagined supra-awareness. Rather, the 'peoples' mentioned in the *DAI* are the *rulers* of various *ethne* with their own agency, but not the actual peoples themselves. Their top-down rule, what sociologists call 'potestarian state formations',[86] is truly what the *DAI* mentions when it mentions *ethne*: namely, the genealogy of the *rulers*, not the *ruled*.[87]

Ethnicity is hardly manifested clearly in the *DAI*, as either a geographical or a genealogical phenomenon in Konstantinos' mid-tenth-century Roman mind. The *DAI* no more contains an ultimate truth of ethnicity for present nations than does Genesis 10.[88] Furthermore, if primordial ethnicity would be rejected in Latin Christendom, why ought it continue as an arbitrary assumption elsewhere?[89] The methods by which Konstantinos

---

[81] Lougges, *Ιδεολογία της Βυζαντινής ιστοριογραφίας*, 106–12; Vasiliev, *Goths in Crimea*, 122; Kaldellis, *Ethnography after Antiquity*, 91; Stephenson, *Byzantium's Balkan Frontier*, 33.

[82] Howard-Johnston, '*De Administrando Imperio*', 305–6.

[83] Obolensky, *Byzantine Commonwealth*, 149–50; Curta, *Southeastern Europe*, 98.

[84] Konstantinos VII Porphyrogennetos, *De Administrando Imperio*, ed. Moravcsik, tr. Jenkins, §12; §39; Konstantinos VII Porphyrogennetos, *De Administrando Imperio Commentary*, eds Dvornik et al., 62, 149.

[85] Sorlin, 'Voies, villes et peuplement', 337–56; Berend, 'Notion of Frontier', 55–72; Melnikova, 'Mental Maps of Chronicle-Writer', 317–40; Stephenson, *Byzantium's Balkan Frontier*, 4–5.

[86] Popov, 'Этничность и потестарность', 13–20.

[87] Ibid.; Pálóczi Horváth, *Pechenegs, Cumans, Iasians*, 14; Curta, *Southeastern Europe*, 183; Kaldellis, *Ethnography after Antiquity*, 90–2.

[88] Dzino, *Becoming Slav, Becoming Croat*, 1–9; Boba, *Nomads, Northmen and Slavs*, 16; Huxley, 'Scholarship of Constantine Porphyrogenitus', 31–40; Toynbee, *Constantine Porphyrogenitus*, 578–82, 599–605.

[89] Anthony Kaldellis, personal communication, June 2018; Pohl and Heydemann, *Strategies of Identification*, 1–64.

VII conceived of the identities of northern peoples, inherited from both Herodotus and the Tanakh, came down to identity by constitution and/or by putative descent – and he might use either method as and when it suited him. For Konstantinos VII, various northern peoples could be different from his Romans due to putative descent from some imagined ancestor, without having anything to do with actual biological descent, a belief which was quite common. Failing that, then they could be constitutively different due to their language, appearance, varying adoptions of Christianity and so on. Both methods have had their rhetorical uses; neither can serve as the ultimate authority on ethnicity or ethnogenesis.[90] It is insufficient to dismiss primordial ethnicity as an arbitrary recent assumption without scrutinising the sources where it originated: primordial ethnicity was itself an arbitrary tenth-century assumption.

Collectively, tenth-century Byzantine and Rus' sources suggest that Byzantine Pontic policy involved indirect influence: economic incentivising and treaty-making, particularly in Crimea, instead of direct, top-down Christianisation. This was only achieved later, and aided by commercial encouragement.[91] Except for the Bulgar *khağan* Boris' baptism in 869, intermittently successful missionary efforts like those of Kyrillos and Methodios did not take root until after Vladimir's baptism in 987–9, corroborated in the *NE*.[92] Therefore, when defined by communion with Constantinople, the 'Byzantine commonwealth' truly began with ninth- to eleventh-century baptisms of northern rulers, instead of c. 500.[93]

---

[90] Geary, *Myth of Nations*, 46–62; Smith, *Ethnic Origins of Nations*, 21–68.
[91] Noonan and Kovalev, 'Prayer, Illumination, and Good Times', 73–96.
[92] Zuckerman, 'Byzantium's Pontic Policy in *Notitiae Episcopatuum*', 201–30; Angelov, 'Introduction of Christianity into Rus'', 29–35.
[93] Shepard, 'Byzantine Commonwealth, 1000–1550', 1–52.

3
Case Studies of Monotheisation in Eighth- to Thirteenth-Century Pontic-Caspian Eurasia

They say that the generation of mankind by means of one another is a more recent work of nature, but that the more original and ancient mode of their birth is out of the earth, since she both is and is considered the mother of all men. And they say that those men who are celebrated among the Greeks as having sprung from seed were produced and grew up as trees do now, being perfect and completely armed sons of the earth. But that this is a mere fiction of fable it is easy to see from many circumstances.

Philo of Alexandria, De Æternitate Mundi (57–8).

O mankind! Truly We created you from a male and a female, and We made you peoples and tribes that you may come to know one another. Surely the most noble of you before God are the most reverent of you. Truly God is Knowing, Aware.

Qur'an, sūrat al-Ḥujurāt (49:13).

Having analysed the monotheisation of Khazaria, this chapter embarks on similar analyses of other case studies in eighth- to eleventh-century Pontic-Caspian Eurasia. Considering nationalist, Soviet and other scholarship, we will re-examine the relationship between sedentarism and nomadism, monotheism and polytheism, and economic maturation from essentially looting, to collecting tribute, to taxation of local tribal populations in Pontic-Caspian Eurasia.

Can we assume local populations had inherent allegiances to one suzerain or another? Did these populations regard themselves as united just because they were all bound to the same suzerain, whether Khazar, Volga Bulgar, Magyar, Pečeneg or Rus'? Alternatively, was sharing an assumed common language with the suzerain, an imagined ethnolinguistic affiliation, an expression of loyalty to a given suzerain, as maintained by traditional scholarship?

It cannot be assumed that the local populations which had earlier paid tribute to Khazaria (Slavic-speaking or otherwise) would eventually *become* Russian, or that other populations in what later became Volgia Bulgaria or the kingdom of Hungary bore loyalty to a given leader from some ethnolinguistic allegiance imagined by modern scholarship.[1] The underlying question is, was there truly an original 'ethnicity', Rus', Magyar, Bulgar and so on, or just amorphous populations with no unifying characteristic besides paying tribute to the same overlord? Were migrations (for example, of the Volga Bulgars or Magyars) movements of entire peoples, or simply conquering minorities? This topic could renegotiate Eurasian nationalism in its fundamental nature: just as Stephenson 'rejects the notion that the various Balkan peoples were struggling constantly to cast off the despised "Byzantine Yoke",[2] this idea of falsely (or oversimplistically) projected peoplehood can be applicable to eighth- to eleventh-century Pontic-Caspian Eurasia, from the middle Volga to the lower Danube, the Carpathian Basin to the North Caucasus.

Volga Bulgaria

The emergence of Volga Bulgaria bears resemblance to the case of Khazaria, albeit in a different confessional context. Volga Bulgaria sprung from the efforts of successive tenth-century Almušid rulers to convert their subjects to their chosen faith, Sunni Islam, rather than Khazarian Judaism or Byzantine Christianity. Here, at the confluence of the river Kama with the middle Volga, which creates a vast inland waterway, Islam has successfully survived to the present, unlike Khazarian Judaism, in the form of Tatar ethnic identity in the Russian Federal Republic of Tatarstan.

From paganism to peoplehood

Why are there two Bulgarias? The Bulgars' conventional story (from Nikephoros[3]) begins with 'Old Great Bulgaria', ruled by *khağan* Kubrat and located around Crimea (Tauros) and the Sea of Azov (Lake Maeotis), along

---

[1] Zhivkov, *Khazaria*, 21.
[2] Stephenson, *Byzantium's Balkan Frontier*, 320–1.
[3] Nikephoros, *Brevarium*, ed. and tr. Mango, *Short History*, §35.

the rivers draining into the northern Black Sea. Old Great Bulgaria was probably dissolved by the incoming Khazars in the late-seventh century. After his death, Kubrat's sons led their respective clans in various directions. Asparukh's clan journeyed westward to the lower Danube, while Kotrag journeyed northward to the Volga–Kama confluence.[4] Theories about these events usually underpin ethnonationalistic interpretations.[5] Yet this story omits more prosaic realities derived from the earliest archaeological evidence of the sedentarisation and urbanisation of the populations of the Volga–Kama confluence. Ethnicities notwithstanding, nomadism prevailed until sedentarisation became widespread in the late ninth to tenth centuries. Therefore, questions of pre-Islamic ethnicity are irrelevant since Islam has traditionally defined the identity of the population of the Volga-Kama region since the religion's tenth-century adoption.

The pre-Islamic Volga-Kama region

Upon Aḥmad ibn Faḍlān's early-tenth-century arrival in the Volga-Kama region, he mentioned the 'Ṣaqāliba', presumably as the subjects of the ruler Almuš. Although scholars have long debated whether this term represents a garbled version of Slavs, the debate frequently assumes that Bulgars and Slavs constituted separate tribes and peoples before conversion to Islam. For example, ceramic typologies have been used to show that migrating Bulgars were the undisputed tribal leaders upon their original arrival in the middle Volga.[6] Clearly, knowledge about the pre-Islamic subject population of Volga Bulgaria depends on comparative surveys of linguistic and archaeological evidence for determining tribal affiliations.[7]

Linguistic evidence suggested that Khwārazmian Turkic became the dominant Volga Bulgarian liturgical language.[8] However, other nearby

---

[4] Ajbabin, 'Khazar Archaeological Monuments', 31; Gavrituhin, '"Trésor" de Pereščepina', 13–30; Leskov, *Maikop Treasure*, 259; Vachkova, 'Danube Bulgaria and Khazaria', 351; Hildinger, *Warriors of Steppe*, 134; Curta, *Southeastern Europe*, 79–81; Obolensky, *Byzantine Commonwealth*, 63; Zimonyi, *Origins of Volga Bulghars*, 63; Khalikov, Ранние болгары на волге, 74; Kovalev, 'Northern Silk Road', 77; Gagin, 'Волжская булгария', 131–2; Dimitrov, *Proto-Bulgarians*; Zhivkov, *Khazaria*, 192–3.

[5] Stephenson, *Byzantium's Balkan Frontier*, 13; Devletşin, *Törki-Tatar Ruḫi Mädäniyate Tariḫı*, 218.

[6] Gagin, 'Волжская булгария', 131; Stojanov, Другият Бог, 190.

[7] Mako, 'Islamization of Volga Bulghars', 201.

[8] Golden, 'Turks', 29; Grousset, *Empire of Steppes*, 159; Erdal, *Sprache der Wolgabolgarischen Inschriften*, 10–20; Khakimzjanov, Эпиграфические памятники волжской булгарии, 16–22; Tekin, *Volga Bulgar Kitabeleri*, 7–10.

tribes, like the Čuvaš[9] and Baškīrs[10] did not always entirely share Islam. Since the Baškīrs have been linguistically linked to the Magyars,[11] clearly linguistics cannot crisply define tribal identity. This then brings into question the efficacy of linguistics for determining the tribal affiliations of other known nearby groups: the Magyars,[12] Slavs, Balts, Mordvians/Finno-Ugrians[13] and so forth.

Similarly, archaeological typologies are used to identify various groups – with decidedly mixed results. For example, the typologies of ceramics have been used to delineate the territories of pre-Islamic tribal Bulgars and Čuvaš.[14] This assumes that current ethnicities, identities, ceramics and areas have existed unchanged since pre-Islamic, pre-Mongol times. One study identifies pre-Islamic Volga Bulgars specifically by 'Turkish' burial traits.[15] Another identifies the 'aṣ-Ṣaqāliba' as the pre-Islamic Bulgars themselves, not 'Slavs'.[16] Contrastingly, finds of the 'Imen'kov' archaeological culture are attributable to Slavs, according to one typological study; this was 'a higher' culture (mentioned in the *PVL*[17]). Accordingly, the study assumes that the Imen'kovs joined the population of Volga Bulgaria (a less advanced culture) and boosted late-seventh-century agriculture, judging from typological evidence alone.[18] Some archaeologists have even compared archaeological cultures to tenth-century economic scenarios of Volga Bulgaria and Khazaria.[19] Even for the Volga Rus', who have been imagined to deposit

[9] Al-Istakhrī, *Book of Roads and Kingdoms*, tr. Lunde and Stone, *Ibn Fadlān*, 237 n66; Kakhovskij, *Происхождение чувашского народа*; Zimonyi, *Origins of Volga Bulghars*, 84; Salmin, 'Iranian Chapter of Chuvash', 112–19; Salmin, *Savirs – Bulgars – Chuvash*, 83–125; Golden, 'Khazar Studies', 14.

[10] Frank, *Islamic Historiography and 'Bulgar Identity'*, 168.

[11] Al-Mas'ūdī, *Meadows of Gold*, tr. Lunde and Stone, 237 n56; Ananias of Širak, *Geography*, tr. Hewsen, *Geography of Ananias of Širak*, 55; Zuckerman, 'Khazars and Byzantium', 419–23; Golden, 'Migrations of Oğuz', 65; Artamonov, *История хазар*, 234–5; Semënov, 'Образование хазарского каганата', 118–27; Kristó, *Hungarian History*, 31–55; Róna-Tas, *Hungarians and Europe*, 104–14; Gyóni, 'Hungarian Traces in Bashkiria', 279–305; Fodor, 'Ungarischer Fund in Kasan', 303–13.

[12] Howard-Johnston, 'Byzantine Sources for Khazar History', 186.

[13] Klima, *Linguistic Affinity of Volgaic Finno-Ugrians*, 1–51; Franklin and Shepard, *Emergence of Rus*, 46–7; Zhivkov, *Khazaria*, 37–8.

[14] Kakhovskij and Kakhovskij, 'Булгарских памятников чувашии', 32–46.

[15] Koç, 'Bulgar boylarının orta idil bölgesine göçü', 37–58.

[16] Boba, *Nomads, Northmen and Slavs*, 59–63.

[17] *Povest' Vremennÿkh Let*, tr. Cross and Sherbowitz-Wetzor, *Russian Primary Chronicle*, 55.

[18] Galkina, 'Территория хазарского каганата', 135; Kovalev, 'Northern Silk Road', 73 n80; Zhivkov, *Khazaria*, 234 n42.

[19] Gagin, 'Волжская булгария', 132–3; Poddubnÿj, 'Гагин. Волжская булгария', 168–70.

uniform, 'Scandinavian-style' burials, such an assumption can no longer be made. Soviet-era archaeological methods re-emerge when archaeologists use levels of 'progress of ancient societies' to separate Bulgars from Slavs.[20]

Yet there are crucial differences in burial rituals not between supposed ancient ethnic groups but between pagan and Islamic Volga Bulgarian burial practices.[21] Therefore, it is Islam, not primordial ethnic classification, that proves the primary factor of identification between groups. Archaeological evidence alone can rarely distinguish suitably between pre-monotheistic groups on the basis of typologies alone. Yet for monotheistic groups, which typically leave recognisable traces in terms of urbanisation and sedentarisation, funerary archaeology proves much more convincing – in so far as Islamisation may be archaeologically detectable by the decreasing of noticeably pagan burials such as kurgans. That said, it remains doubtful that funerary archaeology can and ought to resolve all the issues binding Islamisation and urbanisation, but along with numismatic evidence and the archaeology of various settlements, these methodologies should together serve to elucidate the parallel phenomena of monotheisation and sedentarisation, thus implying an urban, top-down political structure.

So to refer to the pagan inhabitants of Volga Bulgaria, for example, as a single people, as 'Ṣaqāliba', is inherently problematic, since Volga Bulgaria itself did not exist until the adoption of Islam by the Almušids.[22] For ibn Fadlān, all the northern peoples were 'Ṣaqāliba', regardless of tribal distinctions.[23] Much like barbarians or Scythians in Roman eyes, any pagan group raided by their neighbours for slaves could be designated Ṣaqāliba.[24] Although primordial ethnicity remains a tempting attributive model, archaeologists of Volga Bulgaria acknowledge the assignment of 'ethnicity' to burial finds based on archaeological typologies alone is

---

[20] Goldina and Chernykh, 'Forest and Steppe', 41–52; Rudenko, 'Волжская булгария, русь и прикамье', 105–15; Smirnov, 'Этническом составе волжской булгары', 302–7; Belÿkh, *История народов волго-уральского*, 65; Sitdikov and Khuzin, 'Study of Kazan Kremlin', 66; Sedov, 'Этногенезу волжских болгар', 5–15; Khuzin, 'Sedentarization of Volga Bulgars', 68; Zhivkov, *Khazaria*, 26.
[21] Izmajlov, 'Ислам в волжской булгарии', 6; Kazakov, *Культура волжской болгарии*, 311–12; Khalikova, *Мусульманские некрополи волжской болгарии*, 43.
[22] *Ḥudūd al-ʿĀlam*, tr. Minorsky, 162; Smirnov, 'Вопросы истории волжских болгар', 173–4.
[23] Ibn Fadlān, *Risāla*, tr. Frye, *Journey to Russia*, 10.
[24] Noonan, 'Economy of Khazar Khaganate', 232–3; Shboul, *Al-Masʿūdī and his World*, 178–9; Golden, *Introduction to Turkic Peoples*, 253; Mako, 'Islamization of Volga Bulghars', 201.

a simplistic assumption. Therefore, the most archaeologically reliable evidence in Volga Bulgaria is sedentarisation and urbanisation.[25]

The first traces of sedentarisation in the Volga-Kama region have been attributed to the eighth-century 'Imen'kov culture', before the supposed Bulgar arrival,[26] although there is little evidence to support this hypothesis.[27] A growing archaeological consensus agrees that the process began in the early tenth century, and archaeologists indicate Islam as the main catalyst for sedentarisation.[28] Islam spread in the early towns of Volga Bulgaria (namely, Bolgar, Suwār, Biliar, Idnakar), directly correlating urbanism and Islam.[29] Several tenth- to eleventh-century dirhams suggest slaves and agricultural production being brought inside the early fortifications of Biliar and Bolgar in considerable quantities.[30] The fortifications were meant to secure the towns' commercial function: the town of Bolgar was primarily a slave market where coins, slaves and furs changed hands. That coinage can indicate so much in terms of not just urbanisation but Islamisation and economics is demonstrated by tenth-century official and imitative dirhams. Comparable to Sāmānid dirhams, these confirm the city of Bolgar used as a toponym and the Arabic *Shahada*.[31] They were probably minted by the Almušids as much for the sake of a circular tax system as for trade with Khwārazmian Sāmānids and other Muslim dynasties.[32] Besides exporting furs, Volga Bulgaria was famed for leather boots, as is commonly mentioned in Islamic sources.[33] These urban, economic and monetary developments were made possible by monotheisation: in this case, Islamisation.

The most unmistakable link between Islam and urbanisation in Volga Bulgaria is the mosque discovered in 1974 in Biliar, complete with a tenth-century dirham. The mosque had been destroyed in the Mongol conquest

[25] Mako, 'Islamization of Volga Bulghars', 217.
[26] Kovalev, 'Northern Silk Road', 73 n80.
[27] Goldina and Chernykh, 'Forest and Steppe', 42.
[28] Khuzin, 'Sedentarization of Volga Bulgars', 68–74; Khalikov, 'Ислам и урбанизм', 48.
[29] Starostin, 'Болгаре', 99–101; Smirnov, 'Труды государственного исторического музея', 150–61; Grekov and Kalinin, 'Булгарское государство', 147–50; Khalikov, 'История билиярского городища', 33–46; Khalikov, *Татарский народ*, 93; Ivanova et al., 'Fortifications at Idnakar', 108–19; Belÿkh, *История народов волго-уральского*, 66; Curta, 'Al-Andalus and Volga Bulghâria', 315–21.
[30] Tuganaev and Tuganaev, *Состав, структура и еволюция*, 79–83; Starostin, 'Болгаре', 100–1.
[31] Marek Jankowiak, personal communication, February 2017; Mukhamadiev, *Булгаро-татарская монетная система*, 22–40; Zhivkov, *Khazaria*, 150–8.
[32] Gagin, 'Волжская булгария', 134; Zhivkov, *Khazaria*, 241 nn75–6.
[33] Valiev, 'Leatherworking in Kazan Khanate', 73–95.

of the 1230s.³⁴ By one (perhaps overstated) estimate, the number of towns in Volga Bulgaria reached nearly two hundred by the early eleventh century.³⁵ Similar patterns occurred in the monotheisation and urbanisation of Khazaria. Nevertheless, although some of Almuš' subjects are likely to have continued nomadism upon his conversion in the early 920s, tenth-century sedentarisation and urbanisation increased quickly.³⁶ In the fortification of Idnakar (present-day Glazov, Udmurt Republic), archaeologists have reliably dated the beginnings of construction to the mid-tenth century.³⁷ The archaeologist Gubajdullin dates the beginnings of 124 of 167 Volga Bulgarian fortifications to later in the tenth century.³⁸ According to some archaeologists, Islam in Volga Bulgaria became both the primary vehicle for organising fortification and defense, and, by extension, the principal justification for war.³⁹ The overlap between monotheisation and sedentarisation in the case of Volga Bulgaria is clear.

Interpreting Islam in Volga Bulgaria

It is unsurprising that some historiography of Volga Bulgaria carries a distinctively ethnonational character.⁴⁰ Some Tatarstani historiography sees Volga Bulgaria, and specifically ibn Fadlān's depiction of Almuš' conversion, as the precursor to the current ethnonationality of Tatarstan's population.⁴¹ Much scholarship regarding the Islamisation of Volga Bulgaria portrays the process as unifying disparate tribes and strengthening the Almušid dynasty.⁴² For some historians, this overly politicises historiography, whereby ancient Rus' and Volga-Bulgarian identities are analysed with recent identities clearly considered.⁴³ Some scholarship has even used the correlation of Islamisation and urbanisation to depict Volga Bulgaria as a thoroughly Islamic theocracy, without citing primary or archaeological evidence, let alone interrogating it at all.⁴⁴ However, as the scholar Mako

---

[34] Khalikov, 'История билиярского городища', 33.
[35] Kol Gali, *Kyssa'i Yusuf*, tr. Beake et al., *Story of Joseph*, xii.
[36] Šarifullin, 'Жилищах волжских булгар', 63–76; Mako, 'Islamization of Volga Bulghars', 212–16; Deweese, *Islamization*, 292–9.
[37] Ivanova et al., 'Fortifications at Idnakar', 111, 119.
[38] Gubajdullin, *Фортификация волжской булгарии*, 77.
[39] Sitdikov et al., 'Weapons, Fortification and Military Art', 170–2.
[40] Abdullin, 'Islam of Volga Kama Bulgars and Tatars', 1; Miftakhov, 'First Islamic State'.
[41] Kol Gali, *Kyssa'i Yusuf*, tr. Beake et al., *Story of Joseph*, x.
[42] Abdullin, 'Islam of Volga Kama Bulgars and Tatars', 3.
[43] Devletşin, 'Russian–Volga Bulgarian Mutual Relations', 76–81.
[44] Halim et al., 'Volga Bulgaria and Baghdad', 21–30.

comments on the frequently anachronistic analyses of Islamisation in Volga Bulgaria, 'although ideas about unification resulting from the new religion are based on historical facts, their use to justify 10th century decisions in the East European steppe is far from historical'.[45] While analyses such as these may be heavily biased and often overstated, they are nevertheless significant perspectives to be considered.

Present ethnonationality aside, written history (including confessional identity) undoubtedly began with Almuš' early-tenth-century conversion, regardless of the imagined linguistic classifications of the middle Volga's inhabitants. Islam was adopted in a gradual top-down process similar to that for Judaism in Khazaria, although in Volga Bulgaria, Islamic identity was more successful in permeating into the broad subject population,[46] unlike the alleged Judaisation in Khazaria. Thus, Islam survives to the present in the populations of the middle Volga. This raises a question: do we regard the primary sources as legitimate textual bedrock on which to build history, or more as mythological fodder for current ethnonationality?

Primary sources or mythologies?

Written in Farsi and Arabic, the early-thirteenth-century *Kyssa'i Yusuf* of the poet Kol Gali is regarded as the foundation of Tatarstani literature. The poem recounts the biblical story of Joseph's prophecy bestowed through Islam as the inheritor of the Judaic tradition. This would undoubtedly have had special relevance in the historical memory of thirteenth-century Volga Bulgaria,[47] since Almuš had seceded from Khazarian Jewish suzerainty three centuries previously.

Considering the conspicuous Judaic narrative bequeathed to Islamic tradition, the work exhibits features of Taḥrīf, or Islamic supersessionism. Two translated verses read:

> Then the Messenger announced: 'Jews, sit yourselves down, toss your old religion away and convert openly to the true faith; and then only then you shall hear what happened to Joseph.' So he told the Jews what lay at the heart of that story and they were all delighted. The verbal skills of the Chosen One quite amazed them; they remarked: 'He tells it better than we can!'[48]

---

[45] Mako, 'Islamization of Volga Bulghars', 214.
[46] Izmajlov, 'Ислам в волжской булгарии', 5–6.
[47] Kol Gali, *Kyssa'i Yusuf*, tr. Beake et al., *Story of Joseph*, xxvii–xxix.
[48] Ibid., xxix; Keating, 'Revisiting Taḥrīf', 202–17.

Here, Islam is thoroughly built on a Judaic mythology, but is in turn shown in ascendance, assimilating the character Bustan the Jew, and incorporating Judaism into a new *Dar-al-Islam*. Theological considerations aside, the work reflects the cultural context which produced it instead of being a reliable source for the pre-Mongol era. The biblical Joseph story alone leans towards mythology; Kol Gali's work, written three centuries after Almuš' conversion, while typical for a literary tradition's beginnings, can hardly be conceived as reliable by most modern historians. This leaves the *Tārīkh-i-Bulghār*, written soon after Almuš' conversion but which has *not* survived, as the other primary example of pre-Mongol Volga Bulgarian literature.

The *Tārīkh-i-Bulghār*, or the *History of Bulgaria*, though lost, is condensed by Abu Hamid al-Garnatī, who claimed to have met the copyist in 1136 and read from the work itself, appropriating much into his own work.[49] These sources' overlaps are deemed early 'echoes' of the Bulgar conversion.[50] Later such 'echoes' in Tatarstani literature reverberate in eighteenth- to nineteenth-century works such as the *Tārīkh Nāma-yi Bulghār*, which presents an even more fantastic story wherein the city of Bulgar is founded by Alexander of Macedon.[51]

The original *Tārīkh-i-Bulghār* presents a conversion story comparable to ibn Rusta's and ibn Fadlān's early-tenth-century accounts.[52] Moreover, ibn Rusta mentioned Almuš accepting Islam nearly twenty years before ibn Fadlān arrived (920–2).[53] Chronological inconsistencies aside, ibn Fadlān's *Risāla* clearly has less fantastic elements than the *Tārīkh-i-Bulghār*.

In the story, the king and queen (unspecified names) were suffering from a severe sickness which none of their native remedies could heal. A Muslim merchant came and asked them to accept Islam if he could heal them; they agreed. When he cured them, they converted themselves and all their subjects. Later, the displeased Khazar king arrived with an army, a battle was fought and the Bulgars won, forcing the Khazar king to accept Islam as well.[54]

---

[49] Kol Gali, *Kyssa'i Yusuf*, tr. Beake et al., *Story of Joseph*, xviii; al-Garnatī, *Tuḥfat al-Albāb*, tr. Dubler, *Granadino*, 11–12, 54–5; DeWeese, *Islamization*, 76 n13; Izmajlov, 'Ислам в волжской булгарии', 7.

[50] DeWeese, *Islamization*, 75.

[51] Frank, *Islamic Historiography and 'Bulgar Identity'*, 95–115; Frank, 'Volga-Ural Muslims', 89–107; Usmanov, *Татарские источники*, 158–66; Izmajlov, 'Ислам в волжской булгарии', 7.

[52] Ibn Rusta, *Kitāb al-A'lāk an-Nafīsa*, tr. Wiet, *Atours précieux*, 159.

[53] Ibn Rusta, *Kitāb al-A'lāk an-Nafīsa*, ed. de Goeje, *Bibliothecarum Geographicorum Arabicorum*, 141.

[54] DeWeese, *Islamization*, 76–7.

The story's fantastic nature recalls the *Schechter Text*'s fanciful features.[55] Elsewhere, Vladimir's conversion story in the *PVL* is just as historically unreliable compared to the work of Byzantine authors like Leon Diakonos.[56] In comparing the utility of the *Tārīkh-i-Bulghār* and ibn Fadlān's *Risāla*, the latter offers more legitimate textual bedrock on which to build historical narratives.[57]

Therefore, we need not view the reliability of the historical narrative in the *Tārīkh-i-Bulghār* as an either/or paradigm as do later chroniclers and even some present historians. Although the source may not be entirely historically reliable, it served and continues to serve a meaningful literary and valuable religious purpose for Islamic identity on the middle Volga and should remain respected as such.[58] While ibn Fadlān's *Risāla* represents a more developed form of literature, the three primary reasons for Almuš' request for ibn Fadlān's journey remain: to teach masonry, medicine and monotheism.[59]

Islamisation, sedentarisation, centralisation, literisation

Once again we see monotheisation, and Islamisation in this case, coinciding with sedentarisation, literisation and centralisation. Archaeological evidence confirms the construction of mosques and the appearance of Islamic *necropoleis* (burial sites) far more easily than it distinguishes between various pagan tribes. With Islamisation came Islamic law and an imported literary tradition from the Islamic *ummah*.[60] With an imported literary tradition came a burgeoning native literature[61] beginning with a history of the Almušid Islamic dynasty in the *Tārīkh-i-Bulghār*. With sedentarisation, we encounter geographical centralisation around the principal fortified Bulgar cities, primarily Bolgar and Biliar.

Having considered archaeological and textual evidence, modern historiographies, and also the Islamisation process pertaining to sedentarisation in Volga Bulgaria, we may comfortably insert Volga Bulgaria into a similar

---

[55] Al-Garnatī, *Tuḥfat al-Albāb*, tr. Dubler, *Granadino*, 11–12, 54–5.
[56] Feldman, 'Autonomy and Rebellion in Cherson', 48–62.
[57] DeWeese, *Islamization*, 75.
[58] Frank, *Islamic Historiography and 'Bulgar Identity'*, 115; DeWeese, *Islamization*, 77–8.
[59] Feldman, 'Masonry, Medicine and Monotheism', 3–15.
[60] Izmajlov, 'Ислам в волжской булгарии', 11; Beliaev and Chernetsov, 'Eastern Contribution', 99.
[61] Golden, *Turks and Khazars*, 29 n124.

model to that in Khazaria. Namely, since Islam is the primary vehicle for ethnic identity in today's Tatarstan,[62] and both has been and continues to be widely seen as beginning with Almuš, we may conclude simply that. Essentially, Volga Bulgaria became Volga Bulgaria primarily because of Islam; the Bulgar migration is a secondary factor in the so-called ethnogenesis of the Tatar people, who may see themselves as descendants of the Volga Bulgars due to Islam as a tribal unifier, not as Bulgars as a specific tribe.[63] That said, this identity was created by Almuš and his descendants, who successfully imposed Islam on their subjects in a top-down conversion which ultimately spanned centuries, as opposed to the Khazarian *khağans* who did not successfully impose Judaism on their subjects, so that ultimately the Khazarian identity evaporated.

Magyars, Pečenegs and Cumans

If Volga Bulgaria's Islamisation represents a case where historiography congregates at one end of the ethnogenetic spectrum – namely as holding that peoplehood and therefore, history, begins with Islamisation, or broadly, monotheisation – then Hungarian historiography usually congregates at the spectrum's other end, with Christianisation as a comparatively minor event in the history of the Magyars, whose peoplehood is traditionally seen as stretching back farther. Consequently, the Magyars' late-ninth-century migration to Roman Pannonia (the Carpathian Basin) has been viewed as a more determinative event in Hungarian national history.[64]

The Magyar conquest of Pannonia, termed the *Honfoglalás* (or the 'Conquest of the Homeland'), is seldom challenged in most traditional historiographies within and beyond Hungary. The generally accepted story, with various modifications and caveats, derives primarily from accounts within the mid-tenth-century Byzantine *DAI*,[65] Latin authors such as Liudprand of Cremona (c. 920–72),[66] Regino of Prüm (late-ninth century),[67] St Gall (eighth

[62] Urazmanova, 'Симбиоз этнического и конфессионального', 69–83.
[63] Salmin, *Savirs – Bulgars – Chuvash*, 104–9.
[64] Szücs, 'Sur concept de nation', 53; Engel, *Realm of St. Stephen*, 5; Trencsényi, "Imposed Authenticity", 24.
[65] Konstantinos VII Porphyrogennetos, *De Administrando Imperio*, ed. Moravscik, tr. Jenkins, §38.
[66] Liudprand of Cremona, *Antapodosis*, ed. Pertz, *Liudprandi Episcopi Cremonensis*; tr. Squatriti, *Complete Works of Liudprand of Cremona*.
[67] Regino of Prüm, *Chronicon*, ed. Kurze, *Reginonis Abbaus Prumiensis*; tr. MacLean, *Chronicle*.

to eleventh century)[68] and the thirteenth-century *Gesta Hungarorum I* and *II* (hereafter, *GH*).[69] The Annales Fuldenses (ninth century) provide comparatively less detail than the former sources. Nevertheless, the events of the Conquest are typically ascribed to the years 895–6 (despite the mistaken dating in the late-thirteenth-century *GH II*), due to the Pečenegs' chasing of the routed Magyars to the Carpathians.[70] However, the story's archaeological evidence remains contentious. Therefore, although the Conquest is traditionally accepted in most historiographies, it is also subject to reinterpretation as historians have begun to question it as a foundation myth.[71]

But the question truly is, beyond the Conquest's textual sources, can we distinguish between ninth-century Magyars and other nomads? Can archaeological typologies, linguistics or toponymic evidence alone separate Magyars from Pečenegs or others, or are they even separable?[72] If not, what other archaeological methods can be used and what can they demonstrate about monotheisation (here, Christianisation) and ethnicity?

'Honfoglalás' and Christianisation: differing interpretations

The transition from Magyar nomadism and paganism to Hungarian sedentarism and monotheism c. 890s–1090s has long been mystified, often without serious historical context.[73] When it has been contextualised, it has come within a Christian framework.[74] The historian Berend, for example, envisions a continental conversion context, albeit without Volga Bulgaria or Khazaria, or other pagan-nomadic groups who resisted monotheisation such as most Pečenegs and Cuman-Qıpčaqs.[75]

Yet was the *Honfoglalás* really the Conquest of one nation by another nation,[76] or was it simply the victory of a conquering minority, like many

---

[68] St Gall, *Annales*, ed. Pertz, 'Annales Sangallenses Maiores'.
[69] *Gesta Hungarorum I*, tr. Rady, '*Gesta Hungarorum* of Anonymus' (*GH I*), 693–7; *Gesta Hungarorum II*, eds and tr. Veszprémy et al., *Simonis de Kéza* (*GH II*), 76–9. The *Gesta Hungarorum I* was written anonymously (c. 1200–30); the *Gesta Hungarorum II* is a continuation written by Simon de Kéza (c. 1282–5).
[70] Bowlus, *Battle of Lechfeld*, 165; Türk, 'Early Hungarian History', 5; Zhivkov, *Khazaria*, 128; Pálóczi Horváth, *Pechenegs, Cumans, Iasians*, 10; Golden, 'Nomadic Economic Development of Rus'', 91.
[71] Trencsényi, '"Imposed Authenticity"', 27.
[72] Berend, *Gate of Christendom*, 62; Todorov, 'Value of Empire', 317–18.
[73] Stephenson, *Byzantium's Balkan Frontier*, 187.
[74] Bartlett, 'Paganism to Christianity', 47–72.
[75] Berend, *Christianization and Monarchy*.
[76] Golden, 'Nomadic Economic Development of Rus'', 87.

other so-called barbarian conquests? Can current interpretations of the first Christian dynasty, the Árpáds, truly map a modern notion of Hungarian ethnicity and statehood onto an ancient one, or are archaeologists, believing they can conceive real differences between tribal ethnicities during the *Honfoglalás*, simply 'imagining communities'?[77] Ultimately, can the entire episode be described as a founding myth?[78]

Cross-examining the Gesta Hungarorum

Comparing events in the *GH* with synchronous texts generally confirms certain, albeit few elements, while other texts surpass its reliability. These belong to the era's more established Christian literary traditions, by the Latin-writing authors Liudprand of Cremona, Regino of Prüm and St Gall and the Greek-language *DAI*.

The *GH* directly presents a migration and 'Conquest' by the Hungarian 'people':

> 'how many realms and rulers the [Hungarians] conquered and why the people coming forth from the Scythian land are called Hungarians in the speech of foreigners but Magyars [Mogerii] in their own.'[79]

The *GH* mentions 108 original Hungarian clans, although this can hardly be substantiated.[80] While this depiction matches the concepts of Conquest and 'peoplehood' frequently imagined by nineteenth- to twentieth-century historians, contemporary Christian sources are more divided over the ninth- to tenth-century Hungarian Conquest and 'peoplehood'.[81]

For example, Liudprand writes:

> [New Rome] has to its north the Hungarians, the Pizaceni [Pečenegs] the Khazars, the Russians, whom we call Normans by another name, and the Bulgarians very close by.

He later records the conquest of 'the nation of Moravia' by 'the Hungarians',[82] matching the *GH*, although differing from Regino of Prüm regarding

---

[77] Anderson, *Imagined Communities*.
[78] Trencsényi, '"Imposed Authenticity"', 27; Coakley, 'Mobilizing Past', 544–7.
[79] *Gesta Hungarorum I*, tr. Rady, '*Gesta Hungarorum* of Anonymus', 683–5.
[80] *Gesta Hungarorum II*, eds and tr. Veszprémy et al., *Simonis de Kéza*, 22–5.
[81] Sinor, 'Outlines of Hungarian Prehistory', 513–40.
[82] Liudprand of Cremona, *Antapodosis*, tr. Squatriti, *Complete Works of Liudprand of Cremona*, 50–75.

Hungarian 'peoplehood'. Regino equates the Hungarians with other nomads: 'the Hungarian people [...] emerged from Scythian kingdoms'. Subsequent Christian Hungarian chroniclers derived the notion of Hungarian 'peoplehood' from this source.[83] Alternatively, the *DAI* is referenced by those wishing to discern the Magyars' origins; it mentions such mysterious places as *Levedia* and *Atelkouzou*, and such peoples as the *Sabartoi Asphaloi*.[84] Many historians have been tempted to theorise about who or where exactly these terms describe.

Presenting the *GH* as a dependable or untrustworthy source depending on their agendas, nineteenth- to twentieth-century historians have utilised it to imagine the primordial ethnic composition of ninth- to tenth-century Pannonia. Many have therefore seen the *GH* as the 'most misleading of all the early Hungarian texts'.[85] Others rely or discredit the *GH* whenever suitable,[86] particularly considering the 'original ethnicity' of Transylvania and southern Pannonia.[87] Although the *GH*'s twenty-first-century interpretations are less problematic, it remains somewhat contentious.[88] Nevertheless, the *GH II* is comparable to other early 'barbarian histories', like the *Russian Primary Chronicle (PVL)*, Jordanes and Priscus.[89]

Written with tribal considerations in mind, 'barbarian histories' have been mined for fragments of prehistoric founding mythology, and taken literally by a recent ethnic group seeking to map itself onto a perceived ancient counterpart.[90] The *GH* is comparable to the *PVL* regarding literary myth-making and fabrications in many places. Many historians agree

---

[83] Regino of Prüm, *Chronicon*, tr. MacLean, *Chronicle*, 202 n361; Silagi, 'Ungarnstürme', 245–72.

[84] Konstantinos VII Porphyrogennetos, *De Administrando Imperio*, ed. Moravscik, tr. Jenkins, §38; Konstantinos VII Porphyrogennetos, *De Administrando Imperio Commentary*, ed. Dvornik et al., 146–8; Zhivkov, *Khazaria*, 127.

[85] Macartney, *Medieval Hungarian Historians*, 59–60; Magosci, *Shaping a National Identity*, 107; Çoban, 'Muslim Groups among Hungarians', 57; Spinei, *Romanians and Turkic Nomads*, 70–5.

[86] *Gesta Hungarorum I*, tr. Rady, '*Gesta Hungarorum* of Anonymus', 682; Macartney, *Medieval Hungarian Historians*, 60.

[87] Madgearu, *Romanians in Anonymous Gesta Hungarorum*, 105; Djuvara, *Scurtă istorie a românilor*, 20; Boia, *Romanian Consciousness*, 124–5; Davidescu, *Lost Romans*, 124–33; Györffy, *Anonymus*; Csepeli and Örkény, 'Changing Hungarian Nationalism', 248; Köpeczi et al., *History of Transylvania*; Engel et al., *Korai magyar történeti lexikon*; Silagi, 'Gesta Hungarorum', 173–80.

[88] *Gesta Hungarorum I*, tr. Rady, '*Gesta Hungarorum* of Anonymus', 682.

[89] Macartney, *Medieval Hungarian Historians*, 101–5.

[90] Goffart, *Narrators of Barbarian History*, 436–7; Wood, 'Barbarians, Historians, and National Identities', 61–81; Coakley, 'Mobilizing Past', 544–7.

about the shaky reliability of the *PVL*[91] and Jordanes.[92] Others attribute similarly fabricated origin myths to the *GH*.[93] We may also recall the comparisons between Volga Bulgarian and Khazarian early sources alongside synchronous Judaic and Islamic sources. Biblical precedents are used in the *GH* as well, retrospectively Christianising older pagan elements of stories as in Judaisation in Khazaria and Islamisation in Volga Bulgaria; early Hungarian literature fits into the same context.[94]

Despite the consensus about the unreliability of the *GH*, the interpretation of Hungarian Conquest-era archaeological material remains far more debatable. There is a tradition of archaeological interpretation which frequently demonstrates a conception of pre-Christian Hungarian ethnicity, inherited from equally questionable textual material.

Archaeology: uses and misuses

Most Hungarian archaeology comprises the best knowledge garnered on ninth- to eleventh-century Pannonia. Whereas before 1990, common methodologies were skewed towards Marxist archaeology, now unfashionable,[95] a discernible tendency for nationalist archaeological methods has since replaced it.[96] Beginning with pre-Conquest Pannonia, for example, some studies label the population as 'Celtic', before conceding that typological evidence is 'unsuitable for distinguishing regional groups'.[97] Other archaeologists of the Pannonian 'Celts' distinguish between eighth- to eleventh-century Celts, Scordisci, Boii, Taurisci and Dacians by simply mapping typological finds of pots, beads and other material culture onto given cultures (like the Bjelo-Brdo culture) and from there, onto various groups mentioned in textual sources.[98] This approach, which typically assumes primordial ethnicity, is called 'culture-history'.

---

[91] Feldman, 'Autonomy and Rebellion in Cherson', 47–60.
[92] Goffart, *Narrators of Barbarian History*, 20–111.
[93] Trencsényi, '"Imposed Authenticity"', 27; Coakley, 'Mobilizing Past', 544–7; Szücs, 'Sur concept de nation', 54–62.
[94] *Gesta Hungarorum II*, tr. Veszprémy et al., *Simonis de Kéza*, xxv–cii; Veszprémy, 'Conversion in Chronicles', 144–5.
[95] Bartha, *Hungarian Society*, 56, 66; Laszlovszky, 'Social Stratification and Material Culture', 34–5; Gunszt, *A magyar polgári történetírás*; Vértes, 'Randbemerkungen', 427–62.
[96] Krekovič, 'Who Was First?', 60; Berend, *Gate of Christendom*, 22.
[97] Hellebrandt, *Celtic Finds*, 9; Sedov, *Sloveni*, 419–21; Barford, *Early Slavs*, 231.
[98] Szabó, *Celtes en Pannonie*, 11–48.

'Culture-history'[99] was once equated with the 'German school of archaeology'[100] before World War II, when archaeological cultures were methodologically assumed to carry the primordial ethnicities of modern national populations. This approach defined Nazi archaeology, which inherited nineteenth-century models of ethnolinguistic, racial and eugenicist pseudoscience. After World War II, these methodological assumptions gradually became discredited in Anglophone archaeology,[101] even as culture-historical assumptions continued in many Soviet archaeological literatures, and since 1990, remain a staple method in former Soviet states.[102] While certainly not all archaeology makes these assumptions, some studies undoubtedly do, and their evidence serves to substantiate a preformed conclusion.

In the most glaring example of the primordialist assumption of Magyar ethnicity, older histories commonly mapped Hungarians onto Attila's Huns based on a literal interpretation of the *GH II*,[103] although this notion is now rare.[104] Nevertheless, it is still often assumed that early Magyars comprised a distinct, exclusive 'nation.'[105] Although perpetually disavowed, this notion doggedly lingers in its application to both before and after the Conquest.[106] Therefore, unlike other national histories, Hungarian 'prehistory' has been extended much further back.[107] This greatly elongated ethnogenetic prehistory feeds into the assumption of a Magyar ethnolinguistic *urheimat*, or previous ancestral homeland. Many other theories have imagined its true location, but are inherently speculative and inconclusive.[108]

---

[99] Niculescu, 'Culture-Historical Archaeology', 5–24.
[100] Reher and Fernández-Götz, 'Archaeological Narratives in Ethnicity', 400–1.
[101] Rąszkowski, '"German School of Archaeology"', 197–214.
[102] Ghenghea, 'Review: *History of Central European Archaeology*', 179.
[103] *Gesta Hungarorum II*, tr. Veszprémy et al., *Simonis de Kéza*, 14–15, 76–7; Kosztolyik, 'Magyar Beginnings', 40–9; Moravcsik, 'Byzantine Christianity and Magyars', 29–45; Jaffrelot, 'Theory of Nationalism', 38–9; Krekovič, 'Who Was First?', 62; Trencsényi, '"Imposed Authenticity"', 27.
[104] Macartney, *Medieval Hungarian Historians*, 60.
[105] Berend, *Gate of Christendom*, 17; Trencsényi, '"Imposed Authenticity"', 21–2; Wood, 'Barbarians, Historians, and National Identities', 61–81.
[106] *Gesta Hungarorum II*, tr. Veszprémy et al., *Simonis de Kéza*, 28–9.
[107] Bartha, *Hungarian Society*, 47; Csepeli and Örkény, 'Changing Hungarian Nationalism', 247; Bóna, *Magyarok és Európa*, 9–13.
[108] Fodor, 'Östörténeti viták', 125–46; Bálint, 'Magyarság hagyatéka', 39–46; Langó, *Amit elrejt a föld*; Türk, 'Early Hungarian History', 1–3; Boba, *Nomads, Northmen and Slavs*, 74; Zhivkov, *Khazaria*, 21.

Based on linguistic affinities, the Magyar *urheimat* typically assumes some connection with the Volga Bulgars and/or Baškīrs.[109] Citing hints from al-Garnatī and the travel reports of two thirteenth-century Latin clerics who visited the middle Volga (Julianus and Petrus), subsequent theories postulate that any Muslims present among the conquering Magyars were not Magyars, but Baškīrs or Volga Bulgars,[110] since the Magyars, yet to adopt Christianity, remained nominally pagan at the time of the Conquest.[111] Yet speculation about the Magyar–Baškir connection is mostly based on material-typological or toponymic evidence.[112] This has led to the hypothesis of an ethnolinguistically exclusive homeland: a 'Finno-Ugric World'.[113]

The culture-historical approach to Hungarian prehistory therefore frequently makes two rudimentary assumptions based on inherently uncertain claims. It assumes, first, that Hungarian ethnicity drastically predates Christianisation, based on linguistic distinctiveness from surrounding populations,[114] and second, that other forms of evidence, (for example: toponymics[115] or archaeological typologies[116]) can substantiate that Hungarian populations have always been primordially exclusive.[117]

Nevertheless, there is some archaeological evidence which may apply to ninth- to tenth-century pre-Christian Magyars. Called 'Eastern find types', these finds, usually breastplates, pendants and weapons, are often typologically analysed and are few – only ever detectable at the elite level. They are characterised by palmette-ornamented leaf motifs, which distinguish them from earlier Bjelo-Brdo finds in Pannonia.[118] This has

---

[109] Türk, 'Early Hungarian History', 2; Sinor, 'Outlines of Hungarian Prehistory', 515; Klima, *Linguistic Affinity of Volgaic Finno-Ugrians*, 1–51; Róna-Tas, *Hungarians and Europe*, 315–25.

[110] Al-Garnatī, *Tuḥfat al-Albāb*, tr. Dubler, *Granadino*, 65; Julianus and Petrus, *Reports*, ed. and tr. Dörrie, *Texte zur Geschichte der Ungarn und Mongolen*; Macartney, *Medieval Hungarian Historians*, 84; Çoban, 'Muslim Groups among Hungarians', 55–75; Berend, 'Islam in Hungary', 203.

[111] Bierbrauer, 'Ethnischen', 69; Sinor, 'Outlines of Hungarian Prehistory', 515.

[112] Türk, 'Early Hungarian History', 4–5; Macartney, *Magyars*, 163, 173.

[113] Kazakov, 'Волжская булгария и финно-угорский мир', 33–53; Moór, 'Ungarn überschreiten die Wolga', 420–7; Klima, 'Ancestral Uralic Homeland', 15–24; Zhivkov, *Khazaria*, 172.

[114] Šabaev et al., '"Финно-угорский мир"', 147–55.

[115] Çoban, 'Muslim Groups among Hungarians', 66; Tóth, *Ethnics, Languages and Settlement Names*, 135–46.

[116] Horváth, 'Cemeteries and Grave Finds', 336.

[117] Laszlovszky, 'Social Stratification and Material Culture', 33.

[118] Fodor, *Verecke útján a magyar nép őstörténete*; Langó, *Amit elrejt a föld*.

spurred evolving interpretations of their presumed ethnic attribution.[119] Clearly, there is archaeological evidence of a change in typical material culture in ninth- to tenth-century Pannonia, but it is uncertain whether it can be ethnically attributable.

Commonly interpreted tenth-century Pannonian archaeological finds are weapons, particularly sabres and arrowheads. An elaborately gilded early-tenth-century sabre kept in Vienna exemplifies these so-called 'Hungarian sabres', traditionally attributed to ninth- to tenth-century Magyars.[120] Nevertheless, they have been found throughout Central and Eastern Europe and are hardly distinct from those of the Pečenegs.[121] Elsewhere, bows and arrowheads found in tenth-century Pannonian burials are typologically attributed to Magyars.[122] However, such Magyar arrowheads, some found as far from Pannonia as present Switzerland,[123] remain difficult to distinguish from so-called Pečeneg arrowheads, found near the river Dniestr.[124] What archaeological typology could definitively distinguish between ninth- to tenth-century Magyar and Pečeneg ethnicities? Does 'pots are not people' – the old archaeological adage warning against relying on material-typological assumptions about race and ethnicity – not apply to weapons?

Other archaeological literature, using ninth- to tenth-century Pannonian burial sites, identifies Conquest-era Magyar warriors as a nation of horse-mounted steppe-nomads.[125] Yet such ninth- to tenth-century 'horseman' burials are not exclusive to Pannonia and extend to the river Sava watershed.[126] Even skeletons and skulls have been recruited to identify primordial ethnicity. For example, Conquest-era skeletons stress-marked from compound bow usage are identified as ethnic Magyars, based on the assumption of primordial Magyar ethnicity and exclusive Magyar use of compound bows.[127] How can we confirm that ethnic Pečenegs did not also

---

[119] Laszlovszky, 'Social Stratification and Material Culture', 36; Bowlus, *Battle of Lechfeld*, 163.
[120] Fodor et al., *Ancient Hungarians*, 67–71.
[121] Iotov, '"Hungarian Sabers" of Bulgaria', 327–38; Pálóczi Horváth, *Pechenegs, Cumans, Iasians*, 11.
[122] Bíró, 'Weapons in Carpathian Basin', 519–39.
[123] Boschetti, 'Beginnings of Fortifications', 125.
[124] Pálóczi Horváth, *Pechenegs, Cumans, Iasians*, 18, 36–7.
[125] Hildinger, *Warriors of Steppe*, 84; Bowlus, *Battle of Lechfeld*, 164; Bubenok, 'Данные топонимии о миграциях адыгов', 17–20.
[126] Curta, *Southeastern Europe*, 190–1.
[127] Tihanyi et al., 'Hungarian Conquest Archery', 65–77.

use compound bows, or that these skeletons could not have belonged to Pečenegs? Recent craniometric studies continue the eugenicist tradition,[128] demonstrating primordial ethnicities based on various skull dimensions that purport to identify Conquest-era ethnic Magyars' 'racial type'. The assumption was that the comparison of skull dimensions would reveal ethnic differences between Pannonian populations before and after the Conquest.[129] Elsewhere, toponymic and typological evidence based on grave types is used to distinguish between Conquest-era Magyars and other populations.[130] There is always a preoccupation with the primordial ethnicity of the collective dead rather than a discussion of circumstantial identity or loyalty in larger regional contexts.[131]

Yet there are numerous popular archaeological works which narrate a homogeneous population of ancient ethnic Magyars for a broader audience, both present Hungarian and Western. Several publications laudably contribute to public appreciation of archaeology,[132] yet further the founding mythology of the Conquest and the assumption of primordial Magyar homogeneity. Similarly, allegedly Magyar runic writing also assumes primordial ethnolinguistic homogeneity,[133] although such 'Turkic' runes are known to have been carried all over the steppe 'from Mongolia to Hungary.'[134]

Some archaeologists insist that any theoretical dissociation from previous assumptions of imagined ethnolinguistic communities is unnecessary[135] and that problematic ethnonational interpretations no longer linger (they do[136]). This explains the residual archaeological presumption that ethnic groups are distinguishable in Pannonia before and after the Conquest, a belief reinforced by toponymic (that is, linguistic)

---

[128] The classic work of craniometry: Ripley, *Races of Europe*; revised by Coon, *Races of Europe, White Race and New World*. On the eugenicist methodology: de Lapouge, *L'Aryen*.
[129] Holló et al., 'Hungarian Plain: Craniometric View', 655–67.
[130] Horváth, 'Cemeteries and Grave Finds', 331–8; Révész, 'Cemeteries', 338–43.
[131] Chapman, *Tensions at Funerals*, 27–37, 161–3; Herold, 'Natural Environment', 109; Zhivkov, *Khazaria*, 254; Hofer, 'Ethnography and Hungarian Prehistory', 301.
[132] Siklódi, *Between East and West*; Sudár and Petkes, *A honfoglalók viselete*; Takács, 'Review: *Attire of Conquering Hungarians*', 1–3.
[133] Maxwell, 'Hungarian Rune-Writing', 161–75.
[134] Khazanov, 'Nomads in History of Sedentary World', 3.
[135] Bálint, 'Węgierska archeologia i nacjonalizm', 254–9.
[136] Hajnóczi et al., *Pannonia Hungarica Antiqua*, 12; Csepeli and Örkény, 'Changing Hungarian Nationalism', 248–9.

evidence.[137] The Bjelo-Brdo culture, for example, has been imagined to contain all Conquest-era ethnicities, the way the *SMC* was imagined to compose all the component ethnicities of Khazaria. Then, excavated Bjelo-Brdo artefacts were assigned to either the pre- or the post-Conquest, and the latter material would align with 'steppe' communities.[138] Such notions bear the impression of 'imagined communities',[139] especially when linguistic and toponymic evidence alone is hardly 'a reliable indicator of "ethnic" status'.[140]

Increasingly, historians and archaeologists contradict earlier works portraying the Magyars as distinct victors over the Slavic Moravians.[141] These scholars instead propose fluidity and 'peaceful integration'.[142] Clearly, these conclusions, albeit surpassing older theories, still illuminate recent events (EU integration) rather than ancient ones. All archaeological interpretation is politically and ideologically charged.[143] The debate is not the finding or the cataloguing of the so-called Conquest material, but what questions are asked of it.

The whole problem is predicated on the assumption that various ethnicities derive from primary sources, leading archaeology to begin with conclusions and search for evidence afterwards.[144] This has resulted in the idea of original ethnolinguistic homogeneity (*ursprache/urvolk*), an *urheimat*, a belief in either ethnolinguistic, toponymic or typological evidence for substantiation, and finally, an essentialist reading of textual sources (such as the *DAI* and *GH*).[145] Archaeological methods which attempt to substantiate the 'Qabar revolution' using the *DAI* exemplify this.[146] It is unfortunate to dismiss such speculation, but if we are to contextualise a pre-monotheistic landscape, whether its inhabitants later adopt Eastern (Rus') or Western (Magyars) Christianity, Islam (Volga Bulgars) or Judaism (Khazars), until this process, ethnicities can hardly be assigned.

---

[137] Tóth, *Ethnics, Languages and Settlement Names*, 135–46; Bökönyi, 'Hungarian Archaeology', 144; Türk, 'Early Hungarian History', 1–2.
[138] Szöke, *A honfoglaló*.
[139] Anderson, *Imagined Communities*; Boba, *Nomads, Northmen and Slavs*, 68.
[140] Berend, 'Islam in Hungary', 204.
[141] Krekovič, 'Who Was First?', 59–67; Deér, 'A honfoglaló Magyarság', 127.
[142] Langó, 'Carpathian Basin and South East Europe', 321–7.
[143] Ghenghea, 'Review: *History of Central European Archaeology*', 179; Krekovič, 'Who Was First?', 65.
[144] Laszlovszky, 'Social Stratification and Material Culture', 45.
[145] Niculescu, 'Culture-Historical Archaeology', 9; Zhivkov, *Khazaria*, 27.
[146] Bartha, *Hungarian Society*, 62–4; Erdélyi, 'Кабары', 174–81; Le Calloc'h, *Asiatiques en Hongrie*; Györffy, *Anonymus*, 111; Berend, *Gate of Christendom*, 68.

This 'mainly negative' approach to primordial ethnicity must demonstrate that present Hungarian nationality is as disconnected from ancient references to peoples known as 'Magyars' as current French or Italian nationalities are from ancient references to 'Franks' or 'Langobards'.[147] Ultimately, a conclusion about primordial ethnicity cannot be established, and then evidence sought retrospectively.[148]

Instead of attempting to prove primordial Hungarian ethnicity, a different question may be asked of the archaeological material: can the tenth- to eleventh-century monotheisation process be charted in Pannonia?[149] Unfastened from textual sources, although not oblivious to them, we may instead explore the archaeology of Christianisation, or rather any broad monotheisation in ninth- to tenth-century Pannonia.

There have been some archaeological indicators of demographic discontinuity in Conquest-era Pannonia, craniometry aside. Another study of skulls found that the rate of skull trephination on skeletons dated to the era of Christianisation (c. early eleventh-century) decreased around the traditional date of St Stephen's coronation (c. 1000–1[150]) despite the assumption of underlying pre-Christian Hungarian ethnicity.[151] This helps demonstrate that skull trephination was broadly common for nomadic paganism, surpassing assumptions of primordial ethnicity,[152] especially given that skull trephination is rare in pre-tenth-century Pannonia.[153]

The sedentarisation process is also demonstrated by dental archaeology. The rate of tooth decay due to growing cereal consumption in tenth-century Pannonian populations increased slightly.[154] The evidence overlaps with studies on tooth wear in populations corresponding to the *SMC* regarding a predominantly agricultural versus a mostly carnivorous diet.[155] Broadly speaking, although the populations on both sides of the Carpathian Mountains have as much in common after the Conquest as before it, the key distinguishing factor is increasing sedentarisation.

---

[147] Sinor, 'Outlines of Hungarian Prehistory', 540; Boba, *Nomads, Northmen and Slavs*, 74–6; Zancani, '"Lombard" and "Lombardy"', 217–32; Pohl, 'Deliberate Ambiguity', 47–58.
[148] Niculescu, 'Culture-Historical Archaeology', 10–14; Hofer, 'Ethnography and Hungarian Prehistory', 302.
[149] Berend et al., *Central Europe*, 125–38.
[150] Hartvic, *Life of Stephen*, tr. Berend, *Life of King Stephen*, 375–98.
[151] Grynaeus, 'Skull Trephination', 131–40.
[152] Rešetova, 'Trephination Cases', 9–14.
[153] Fodor et al., *Ancient Hungarians*, 294.
[154] Maczel et al., 'Dental Disease', 457–68.
[155] Arnold et al., 'Tooth Wear', 52–62.

Other archaeologists proposed that instead of an archaeological distinction based on the belief in the Conquest, funerary evidence of pagan–Christian change should be considered. For example, finds of coins of St Stephen in tenth- to eleventh-century graves in present eastern Hungary clearly indicate a gradual permeation of Christianity.[156] While finds of crosses or crucigram images in graves, however, do not necessarily 'indicate that the deceased was a convert to Christianity', Christianisation is easily evidenced by finds of crosses in graves nearby synchronously dated churches.[157]

There is also evidence of increasing average lifespan, indicating a 'growth in the living-standard from the 10th century to the 13th century, as well as calculable ingestion connected with the spread of a settled way of life'. This corroborates similar findings regarding sedentarisation in Volga Bulgaria and Khazaria during their respective monotheisations. Like these other cases, Magyar Christianisation was an urban, top-down affair, synchronous with and opposing residual paganism. Christianity existed among elites by the turn of the eleventh century[158] and only much later did the process of Christianisation become detectable among subject populations.[159] Although tenth- to eleventh-century funerary finds of reliquary crosses, Christian coins and other Christain motifs may imperfectly indicate top-down Christianisation, their analysis transcends the worn-out presumption of ethnic identification based on typological evidence.

Therefore, both textual and archaeological evidence of confessional affiliation clearly points towards the beginnings of actual differences between tenth- to eleventh-century Pannonian populations.[160]

Archaeological studies identify Muslim or Jewish burials based on the lack of pig bones and on burial orientation. Evidently these features should distinguish such cemeteries from others, although it is unclear whether this is certain.[161] Yet churches could be built near pre-existing pagan graves.[162] It is possible that pagan and Christian populations are identifiable by some aspects of funerary archaeology, such as orientation and the placement of the deceased, but material-typological evidence alone is

[156] János et al., 'Pagan–Christian Change', 305–17.
[157] Fodor et al., *Ancient Hungarians*, 98, 183–93, 230–47, 272–300, 330–45.
[158] János et al., 'Pagan–Christian Change', 305–10.
[159] Laszlovszky, 'Social Stratification and Material Culture', 39–43.
[160] Szathmáry, 'Anthropological Research', 98–9.
[161] Rózsa et al., 'Árpád Muslim Settlement', 1–7; Berend, 'Islam in Hungary', 206; Antalóczy, 'A nyíri izmaeliták központjának', 131–70; Nagy, *Islamic Art and Artefacts in Hungary*, 10–13.
[162] Bóna, 'Arpadenzeitliche Kirche und Kirchhof', 99–157.

CASE STUDIES OF MONOTHEISATION   119

insufficient. Therefore, separating pagans, Christians, Muslims and Jews based exclusively on typological distinctions from burial finds is inherently problematic.[163]

Textual sources also reveal Islamic communities in Transcarpathia. In particular, Islamic sources, especially al-Garnatī's works, are quite useful regarding the Magyars.[164] Al-Garnatī definitively indicated there were Muslim Magyars in the ninth to tenth century.[165] Aside from speculation about Islam-related toponymy in present Hungary,[166] there is a growing historical consensus about diversity even among Islamic communities amid the nebulous Conquest-era Pannonian population.[167]

Returning to archaeology, although the 'Eastern find types' indicate a ninth- to tenth-century demographic shift in Pannonia, they do not perfectly demonstrate an exclusive Magyar ethnic group, and are found alongside many other find types in Pannonia,[168] which ought to dispel preoccupations with ethnic 'culture-history'. Therefore, the Conquest was simply part of a centuries-long migration process, rather than a national renaissance as portrayed by traditional nationalist thought.[169] If the essential heterogeneity of the pre-Christianised Pannonian populations and their eventual assimilation into the Hungarian kingdom have been satisfactorily demonstrated, we are left with one final recourse for the primary vehicle of Hungarian ethnic identity: Christianity.

There was never any shared Magyar 'ethnicity' before Christianisation, and 'ethnically pure' Magyars never were. While there was certainly a ruling elite, as there was anywhere else, before written language, there is insufficient evidence to definitively reconstruct the spoken language(s) of their subject populations. Ethnicity was never a concern until quite recently and pre-monotheistic ethnicity can never successfully be equated with linguistic groupings.[170] After all, languages can be both learned and forgotten over time and in the course of the passing of generations. In a way analogous to

---

[163] Pálóczi Horváth, *Pechenegs, Cumans, Iasians*, 19.
[164] Zimonyi, *Muszlim Források*; Makk, *Mythischen Vogel Turul*, 51–81; Çoban, 'Muslim Groups among Hungarians', 56; Pauliny, *Arabské správy o Slovanoch*, 163; Türk, 'Khwarazmian–Hungarian Connections', 242.
[165] Çoban, 'Muslim Groups among Hungarians', 55–75.
[166] Berend, 'Islam in Hungary', 203–4.
[167] Štulrajterová, 'Convivenza, Convenienza and Conversion', 177–8; Berend, 'Islam in Hungary', 202.
[168] Pálóczi Horváth, *Pechenegs, Cumans, Iasians*, 8–9.
[169] Langó, 'Review: *Peoples of Eastern Origin*', 1; Postică and Tentiuc, 'Amulete-calareti de bronz', 45–72.
[170] Krekovič, 'Who Was First?', 62–4.

what happened in Volga Bulgaria, Magyars became Hungarians because of the top-down imposition of Christianity by a ruling dynasty, the Árpáds.

Christianisation, sedentarisation, centralisation, literisation

Having recognised the myth of Magyar primordial ethnicity, we arrive at a place similar to monotheisation among the Khazars and Volga Bulgars, that is, conversion, sedentarisation, centralisation and literisation: essentially, the creation of a top-down political formation. After the final defeat of the pagans at the 955 Battle of Lechfeld by Christian Frankish armies, under the first ruler to convert to Christianity, St Stephen, the Magyars 'integrated into [Latin] Christendom'.[171] By gathering textual and archaeological conclusions together and remaining detached from nationalist mythology, we can juxtapose the case of Magyar monotheisation with the case studies of the Khazars, Volga Bulgars, and then Pečenegs, Cuman-Qıpčaqs and Rus'.

Settlement archaeology has played a significant role in demonstrating the process of sedentarisation and urbanisation in ninth- to eleventh-century Pannonia. However, while most settlement archaeology has typically focused on early Neolithic, Bronze Age and Iron Age studies of Pannonia, ninth- to eleventh-century settlement archaeology was neglected because of earlier assumptions of synchronous Magyar nomadism.[172] While the nomadic model is no longer widely believed, the ninth- to eleventh-century settlement archaeology of Pannonia remains rather understudied compared with earlier epochs.

As for ninth- to eleventh-century Pannonian settlement archaeology, it is unclear how much vestigial Roman-era agriculture persisted among resident Pannonian populations (whatever their supposed ethnicities). For example, some archaeologists focus on the effects of gradual eleventh-century sedentarisation evident in Hungarian archaeology instead of assuming dichotomies between ethnicities.[173] Others insinuate that the pre-Conquest populations (termed 'Celts') must have been farmers due to few finds of ninth- to eleventh-century warrior graves and many spindle whorls.[174] But this neither proves nor disproves fully fledged sedentarisation and agriculture. By the tenth century, there is evidence for

---

[171] Bowlus, *Battle of Lechfeld*, 6.
[172] Wolf, '10th–11th Century Settlements', 326.
[173] Hofer, 'Ethnography and Hungarian Prehistory', 303.
[174] Hellebrandt, *Celtic Finds*, 102, 235.

the widespread use of subsistence kilns for small-scale ceramic production in rural settlements,[175] which implies subsistence agriculture, for grain storage in ceramic vessels.[176] Other archaeologists have assumed that the Magyars were already agriculturalists long before their 895 arrival in Pannonia,[177] while still others have stressed a more nuanced view. The archaeologist András Róna-Tas, for example, infers that populations of so-called Magyars and other peoples during the Conquest-era practised several economic lifestyles, from settled agriculturalists, to semi-nomadic horticulturalists and pastoralists, to full nomads.[178] Unsurprisingly, some writers are still more concerned with distinguishing the ethnic affiliation of various ninth- to eleventh-century settlements, and base their work exclusively on toponymies, rather than on considering the cumulative archaeological data of the settlements themselves.[179] While it remains difficult to accurately estimate the degree of tenth-century Pannonian urbanisation and sedentarisation,[180] it may be more helpful to utilise what we already understand about the process of monotheisation for Volga Bulgaria and Khazaria.

As in the sedentarisation of previously nomadic peoples via yurt and wattle-and-daub house-framing in Khazaria, such housing is archaeologically common in ninth- to eleventh-century Pannonia.[181] Although some pre-Conquest (eighth- to ninth-century) hill forts in Pannonia, exhibiting wattle-and-daub housing, have been labelled as 'Slavic', it is uncertain whether they demonstrate increasing urbanisation.[182] Palynological research in Pannonia has shown that since the early-ninth-century, the increase of cereal pollen and the decrease of tree pollen suggest forest clearances and intensifying agriculture.[183] In other words, there is reliable evidence for increasing sedentarisation in ninth- to tenth-century Pannonia.

But some distinguish between sedentarisation implied by increasing agriculture and the urbanisation attested by increasing fortifications. For

[175] Vágner, 'Pottery Kilns', 337.
[176] Wolf, '10th–11th Century Settlements', 327–8.
[177] Fodor, *A magyarság születése*, 106–11.
[178] Róna-Tas, *Hungarians and Europe*, 143–5, 360–4; Whittle, 'Fish, Faces and Fingers', 133–50.
[179] Engel, *Realm of St. Stephen*, 23–4.
[180] Berend, *Gate of Christendom*, 22.
[181] Wolf, '10th–11th Century Settlements', 326–7.
[182] Biermann, 'Slavic Strongholds', 85–94; Kouřil, 'Staří Maďaři a Morava z pohledu archeologie', 110–46.
[183] Herold, 'Natural Environment', 117–20.

example, semi-urbanised fortifications are attestable in Pannonia only by the eleventh century, which is associated with St Stephen's Christianisation.[184] Contextualised with centralisation in Volga Bulgaria (Biliar, Bolgar, etc.) and Khazaria (Itīl, Sarkel, etc.) amid top-down monotheisations, this suggests Stephen pursued the same objectives in eleventh-century Pannonia. For example, although third-century Roman coins have been found in Esztergom, indicating a much older semi-urbanised settlement,[185] Stephen's decision to establish his capital at Esztergom after his coronation there is evidenced by the fact that it became the see of the Latin archbishop of Hungary.[186] Similarly, his adoption of Latin Christianity, alphabet and jurisprudence demonstrates his adoption of Latin Christian literisation. This is most easily signified by concurrent Latin hagiographies such as bishop Hartvic's *Life of St. Stephen of Hungary*.[187] Briefly, it was top-down political centralisation which enabled large-scale urbanisation, not the reverse.[188]

Returning to the issue of ethnicity, while the precise ethnic labels of the inhabitants of tenth- to eleventh-century Pannonia may be ultimately indeterminable, we may rather make inferences about their identity based on their later assimilation into Christian Hungary. However, some national-minded historiography continues to attribute this assimilation to a linguistic phenomenon, still espousing a primordial ethnolinguistic model and *urheimat*.[189] These assumptions not only separate the Hungarian case from other case studies in which identities derive from the adoptions of various respective monotheisms (Khazaria–Judaism; Volga Bulgaria–Islam; Rus'–Orthodoxy), but also directly contradict the assumption of Latin Christianity as the original vehicle for Hungarian identity.

Nevertheless, nomadic assimilation into Christianising Hungary cannot be doubted. Such nomads (Pečenegs, Oğuz, Cuman-Qıpčaqs etc.) as did Christianise and assimilate have disappeared from the textual record after the eleventh century,[190] indicating that they ceased to exist as an identifiably independent group within the domain of the Árpád kings. By the eleventh to twelfth centuries, when the Cuman-Qıpčaqs dominated the relations between nomads and sedentary peoples in Pannonia, Christianity was the

---

[184] Wolf, '10th–11th Century Settlements', 330.
[185] Bakos, 'Römische Münzfunde im Esztergom', 52–64.
[186] Engel, *Realm of St. Stephen*, 40–4.
[187] Hartvic, *Life of Stephen*, ed. Szentpétery, *Scriptores Rerum Hungaricarum II*; tr. Berend, *Life of King Stephen*, 375–98.
[188] Urbańczyk, 'Strongholds in Polish Lands', 95–106.
[189] Róna-Tas, *Hungarians and Europe*, 385.
[190] Pálóczi Horváth, *Pechenegs, Cumans, Iasians*, 32–3.

defining factor for sedentarism, which led to strife between nomadic Cuman-Qıpčaq pagans and sedentary Christians.[191] Conversely, although the pagan assimilation into Christendom can partially explain the basis of Christian Hungarian identity, it cannot explain the ability of Jews to maintain their identity isolated from the majority Christianising Hungarian population. The same has been insinuated gradually for other non-Christian communities.[192] The very fact that Christianity was the defining and assimilating factor of later Pannonian populations should serve to place Hungary in the context of other early political formations such as Khazaria and Volga Bulgaria.

Whereas top-down Islamisation and Christianisation endured in Volga Bulgaria and Hungary respectively (and Judaisation evaporated in Khazaria), these attempted Eurasian monotheisation processes bore a striking resemblance to each other.[193] In Hungary's case, Hungarian identity was not some primordial ethnicity attached to a linguistic group, but specifically predicated on Latin Christianity.[194] There is little reason to insinuate that the nation existed before Christianisation, as some have.[195] Rather, Christianity laid the administrative groundwork that only many centuries later created the nation.[196] Ultimately, the Conquest was precipitated by a nomadic minority, in which subject populations were eventually subsumed into what would only much later become a kingdom in a loose sense, and later still, the kingdom of Hungary.

The eight themata of Patzinakia

The archaeological evidence of the late-ninth-century Conquest hardly allows for distinguishing between nomadic Pečenegs or Magyars. Yet these two groups differ in that the early-eleventh-century Magyars loyal to Stephen intermittently accepted Christianisation, whereas the majority of nomads, nominally Pečenegs remaining east of the Carpathian Mountains, did not. According to textual sources like the *DAI*, the Pečenegs allegedly inhabited eight separate regions corresponding to river frontiers running into the northern Black Sea littoral,[197] but how can we interpret this textual information

---

[191] Berend, *Gate of Christendom*, 56.
[192] Ibid., 269.
[193] Klaniczay, 'Birth of New Europe', 99–129; Bartlett, 'Paganism to Christianity', 47–72.
[194] Berend, 'Défense de la Chrétienté et naissance d'une identité', 1009–27.
[195] Macartney, *Medieval Hungarian Historians*, 109.
[196] Laszlovszky, 'Social Stratification and Material Culture', 39–43.
[197] Pálóczi Horváth, *Pechenegs, Cumans, Iasians*, 8–9.

relative to archaeological material? Despite the methodological problems of distinguishing ninth- to eleventh-century Magyars from Pečenegs and other pagan nomads, what do we know about the Pečenegs specifically, and what can we learn about them by examining their assigned archaeological material via-à-vis other ninth- to eleventh-century pagan nomads?

Linguistics, social organisation, tribute

Tenth- to eleventh-century sources such as the *DAI*, the *Ḥudūd al-ʿĀlam*, ibn Fadlān's *Risāla*, the *Russian Primary Chronicle (PVL)*, the *GH* and other Islamic geographies and Byzantine hagiographies indicate that the urbanised, sedentary populations of the Crimea and other settlements of Pontic-Caspian Eurasia often interacted with, traded with and paid tribute to Pečeneg groups. Yet accurately identifying Pečeneg groups has proven elusive. Therefore, historians and archaeologists have relied on Pečeneg linguistics, social organisation and tribute collection, which will permit taking a broader perspective on questions of Pečeneg ethnicity, identity and assimilation into other communities between the ninth and eleventh centuries.

Most linguistic and textual studies of the Pečenegs conclude they were originally a Turkic-speaking group inhabiting the eighth-century Syr Darya riverine region,[198] due to the records of contemporary Islamic geographers, most notably the compendium of Turkic languages (the *Dīwānu l-Luġat al-Turk*) by the scholar al-Kāšġarī, writing in the early 1070s.[199] He wrote that by his time, the Pečenegs lived near the Rūm (Romans), or Byzantium, whose frequent warfare with them in the 1030s–1050s is corroborated by authors like Michael Attaleiates, Ioannes Skylitzes and Michael Psellos.[200] Later linguists have employed evidence from al-Kāšġarī and the *DAI* to

---

[198] Golden, 'Imperial Ideology and Political Unity', 63; Karpat, *Turkish Politics and Society*, 441; Spinei, *Great Migrations*, 95; Spinei, *Romanians and Turkic Nomads*, 182; Zhivkov, *Khazaria*, 35.

[199] Al-Kāšġarī, *Dīwānu l-Luġat al-Turk*, eds Kelly and Dankoff, *Türk Şiveleri Lügatı, Dīvānü Luġāt-It-Türk*; ed. and tr. Auezova, *Махмуд ал-Кашгари*.

[200] Michael Attaleiates, *Historia*, ed. Tsolakis, *Michaelis Attaliatae Historia*, 24–35; tr. Kaldellis and Krallis, *History*, 53–77; Ioannes Skylitzes, *Synopsis of Histories*, ed. Thurn, *Synopsis Historiarum*, 454–74; tr. Wortley, *Synopsis of Byzantine History*, 426–42; Michael Psellos, *Chronographia*, ed. Reinsch, *Michaelis Pselli Chronographia*, 239–41; tr. Sewter, *Fourteen Byzantine Rulers*, 317; Curta, *Southeastern Europe*, 293–301; Stephenson, *Byzantium's Balkan Frontier*, 89–103; Obolensky, *Byzantine Commonwealth*, 213–14.

link the Pečeneg tongue to the sub-branches of the Oğuz²⁰¹ and Cuman-Qıpčaqs.²⁰² Yet despite a conjectural phonetic restoration,²⁰³ these classifications remain highly speculative, based on the meagre scraps of texts and onomastic and toponymic studies.²⁰⁴ That the Pečenegs specifically can be associated with a distinct branch of spoken 'Turkic' remains uncertain, although the general consensus is that the Pečenegs can be described as Turkic nomads.

Despite historians' justifications for using linguistics to classify the Pečenegs, we also know that ethnicity was of course quite fluid, and tribal identity could not neatly correspond with ethnicity. Therefore, it would be inaccurate to assume that Pečenegs could not be easily absorbed into other tribal groups of Oğuz, Cuman-Qıpčaqs or others and vice versa, which they often were.²⁰⁵ Effectively, like the Magyars and many other groups, Pečenegs can hardly be defined by their linguistic grouping, and Pečeneg tribal identities would not warrant consideration as primordial ethnicity. Can lateral inferences about their social organisation be made based on contemporaneous nomadic groups?

Like most coeval nomadic tribes, the Pečenegs did not form a kingdom in the steppe. Relative to Khazaria, there is uncertainty about the political status of the ninth- to tenth-century Pečenegs due to the *Ḥudūd al-ʿĀlam*, which mentions some Pečenegs allegedly subsumed into Khazaria, the so-called 'Khazarian Pečenegs', listed in *King Joseph's Reply* as B-c-ra (בזרא).²⁰⁶ While it cannot be proven that they were separate from the 'Turkic Pečenegs' during this period,²⁰⁷ any distinction would be made between the Khazar allegiances of some and others' erstwhile independence.²⁰⁸ Yet like the the *Ḥudūd al-ʿĀlam*, the *DAI* hints that those Pečenegs remaining in the

---

²⁰¹ Baskakov, *Тюркские языки*, 126–31; Wolf, *Abeceda národů*, 272; Golden, 'Migrations of Öguz', 58.
²⁰² Vörös, 'Relics of Pecheneg Language', 617–31.
²⁰³ Ščerbak, *Печенежский язык*, 107–10.
²⁰⁴ Györffy, 'Monuments du lexique petchénègue', 74; Németh, 'Petschenegischen Stammesnamen', 27–34; Madgearu, 'Periphery against Centre', 52–5.
²⁰⁵ Golden, *Nomads and their Neighbours*, 64.
²⁰⁶ *Ḥudūd al-ʿĀlam*, tr. Minorsky, §47, 160; *King Joseph's Reply*, ed. and tr. Kokovcov, *Еврейско-хазарская переписка*, 98–102; Zhivkov, *Khazaria*, 128–36; Howard-Johnston, 'Byzantine Sources for Khazar History', 188–90; Pletnëva, 'заселении славянами саркела-белой вежи', 82–98; Garkavy, *Еврейских писателей о хазарах*, 86–7; Artamonov, *История хазар*, 386.
²⁰⁷ Pritsak, *Pečenegs*, 214.
²⁰⁸ Spinei, *Great Migrations*, 113.

east among the Oğuz were different from those of the west in the Black Sea littoral.[209]

This indicates doubt about the extent and authority of centralised Pečeneg rulership. A mixture of rudimentary Pečeneg allegiances based on kinship structure is more likely.[210] Nevertheless, some have modelled a hierarchical socio-political structure for the Pečenegs based on an assumption of their higher organisation into chiefdoms in the *DAI*.[211] But this is difficult to prove, since the *DAI* also indicates Pečenegs' individual autonomy,[212] even while later implying a somewhat more hierarchical structure for 'Patzinakia', with *megalous archontas* (greater rulers) corresponding to each *thema* and *elattonas archontas* (lesser rulers) for each of forty *mere*, or sub-partitions.[213] The *DAI*'s vagueness regarding the Pečenegs is compounded by its tendency to apply these deeply hierarchical Roman/Byzantine political concepts to peoples who would neither recognise these concepts nor necessarily refer to themselves as Pečenegs.[214] Even the most centralised ninth- to tenth-century nomads were hardly comparable with sedentary political formations like Christian Rome/Byzantium or the Islamic Caliphate. Konstantinos VII does not mention a single Pečeneg ruler among the *megalous archontas*. By comparison, several Byzantine texts mention the similarities between the Pečenegs and Selčuqs when the latter group invaded and occupied Byzantine Anatolia. They even speculate about possible relations between the late-eleventh-century Selčuq Turks (who 'resembled in all respects' the Scythians/Pečenegs according to Byzantine sources) via the Qanglı-Oğuz tribes.[215] Both the Pečeneg and Selčuq ruling clans were highly decentralised and relied on indirect imperatives over local tribes, despite

---

[209] Konstantinos VII Porphyrogennetos, *De Administrando Imperio*, ed. Moravcsik, tr. Jenkins, §37.
[210] Konstantinos VII Porphyrogennetos, *De Administrando Imperio*, tr. Litavrin, Константин Багрянородный об управлении империей, 155.
[211] Marey, 'Socio-Political Structure of Pecheneg', 450–6.
[212] Konstantinos VII Porphyrogennetos, *De Administrando Imperio*, ed. Moravcsik, tr. Jenkins, §6; Vasjutin, 'Typology of Pre-States', 59.
[213] Konstantinos VII Porphyrogennetos, *De Administrando Imperio*, ed. Moravcsik, tr. Jenkins, §37.
[214] Konstantinos VII Porphyrogennetos, *De Administrando Imperio Commentary*, eds Dvornik et al., 145–6.
[215] Konstantinos VII Porphyrogennetos, *De Administrando Imperio*, ed. Moravcsik, tr. Jenkins §37; Michael Attaleiates, *Historia*, ed. Tsolakis, *Michaelis Attaliatae Historia*, 120–2; Leiser, *History of Seljuks*, 21–7; Golden, 'Migrations of Oğuz', 58, 79. Zhivkov, *Khazaria*, 32–6, 134 n34; Sinor, *History of Early Inner Asia*, 272; Harris, *Byzantium and Crusades*, 36.

the Selčuqs' gargantuan domains.²¹⁶ In fact, by 1091, Selčuqs and Pečenegs were considering a joint ultimate assault on Constantinople.²¹⁷ While we may examine a comparison with the Selčuq Turks, Vasjutin also compares Pečeneg decentralisation to that of the Cuman-Qıpčaqs and Oğuz.²¹⁸

Konstantinos VII's words regarding the Pečeneg *themata* and *mere* ruled by various *archontes* and *elattones archontes* can be reinterpreted, perhaps even to include the Pečeneg domains of Khazaria.²¹⁹ Like the Cuman-Qıpčaqs and Oğuz, the Pečenegs were merely one of many decentralised nomadic groups held together by kinship ties and 'lineage-tribal structures',²²⁰ as opposed to constituting a centralised, hierarchical political formation.²²¹ Nevertheless, such attempts to classify, schematise or define various nomadic groups or empires²²² misses the dynamism of nomadic existence, since varying degrees of centralisation and authority did coexist, but were never enshrined in native literary traditions.²²³ While some individual Pečenegs did embrace monotheism, bottom-up, there was no concerted effort towards top-down centralisation and literisation, linked to sedentarisation and monotheisation. Among the Pečenegs, the fluidity of political and social allegiance resulted in the fluidity of identity. Therefore, despite the *DAI*, we cannot be certain about the Pečenegs' self-identification. Perhaps one of the primary indicators of political and social allegiance was a willingness to pay tribute to a local tribal chief, as in the case of Khazaria.

Imposing tributary status on and guaranteeing plunder from sedentary communities were the essential actions for a nomadic tribal chief (whether Cuman-Qıpčaq, Oğuz, Pečeneg or Magyar) to ensure his dynasty's dominance and survival.²²⁴ Not only did tribute collection (conceivably extortion) imposed by nomads on sedentary communities measure tribal warlords' success, but nomads were partially economically dependent on it and their raiding or outright victory in war conferred the right to demand

---

[216] Klausner, *Seljuk Vezirate*, 9; Rice, *Seljuks in Asia Minor*, 29–31.
[217] Curta, *Southeastern Europe*, 301.
[218] Vasjutin, 'Typology of Pre-States', 59; Golden, 'Nomadic Economic Development of Rus", 86.
[219] Zhivkov, *Khazaria*, 208–9.
[220] Vasjutin, 'Typology of Pre-States', 59; Golden, 'Qıpčaqs of Eurasia', 132–57; Zhivkov, *Khazaria*, 132.
[221] Marey, 'Socio-Political Structure of Pecheneg', 455–6.
[222] Bondarenko et al., 'Introduction', 15; Kradin, *Кочевые общества*, 168.
[223] Rogers, 'Inner Asian States and Empires', 37–40; Holmes and Standen, 'Global Middle Ages', 111–12.
[224] Todorov, 'Value of Empire', 317; Zhivkov, *Khazaria*, 178–80.

and collect tribute.²²⁵ Even as tribute gradually became tax for the tribes under Kievan rule during eleventh- to thirteenth-century Rus' Christianisation (the *poljud'e*²²⁶), on the steppe and in Crimea, it remained more a method of exchange than of identification. For example, the exchange of commodities such as wax, honey, slaves and furs by the Pečenegs with the Chersonites of Crimea in return for luxury items such as silks, gold, salt and wines at times resembled trade and at other times tribute, but the Chersonites were hardly Pečeneg nomads.²²⁷ The Pečenegs themselves resembled earlier barbarian *foederati*: unreliable, unorthodox mercenaries, as prone to fighting against the empire as for it, in return for plunder.²²⁸ It is needless to over-schematise communities as either non-Pečeneg groups subjected to Pečenegs, or Pečenegs themselves.

Tribute gradually became tax; tributary communities became taxable subjects, regardless of imagined ethnolinguistic affiliation. Allegiance was manifested less as ethnic identity than to a local warlord due to his ability to deliver tribute from subject peoples.

Pečenegs and Cuman-Qıpčaqs: avoiding sedentarism and monotheism

For the Byzantine author Michael Attaleiates, who typified the Byzantine attitude towards the nomads, the Pečenegs who occupied the trans-Danube during the tumultuous 1030s–1050s were manageable by proselytising Christianity among them.²²⁹ Yet while Christianisation, sedentarisation and assimilation were achieved for some individual Pečeneg clans, which usually assimilated into the surrounding Christian communities, the policy was unsuccessful for the nomadic majority, as there was no single leader or centralised hierarchy.²³⁰ Nevertheless, some archaeologists assume that certain finds can be attributed to the Pečenegs.

---

²²⁵ Khazanov, 'Nomads in History of Sedentary World', 1; Zhivkov, *Khazaria*, 132–3.
²²⁶ Kobiščankov, *Полюдье*, 220–3; Petrukhin, '*Феодализм*', 164; Zhivkov, *Khazaria*, 211.
²²⁷ Feldman, 'Autonomy and Rebellion in Cherson', 104–5.
²²⁸ Madgearu, 'Pechenegs in Byzantine Army', 211.
²²⁹ Michael Attaleiates, *Historia*, ed. Tsolakis, *Michaelis Attaliatae Historia*, 24–35; tr. Kaldellis and Krallis, *History*, 53–77; Malamut, 'L'image byzantine des Petchénègues', 105–47; Mănucu-Adameșteanu, 'Invasions des Petchénègues', 87–112.
²³⁰ Anna Komnene, *Alexiad*, eds Reinsch and Kambylis, *Annae Comnenae Alexias*, 174–5; tr. Dawes, 143–4; Mako, *Nomadic Conversion*, 36–44; Krumova, 'Pecheneg Chieftains in Byzantine Administration', 210–12; Jordanov, 'Sceau d'archonte de PATZINAKIA', 79–82; Curta, 'Image and Archaeology', 151, 180; Cresci, 'Michele Attaliata e "ethnè" scitici', 203–5.

CASE STUDIES OF MONOTHEISATION 129

Archaeological attempts to identify Pečenegs, like similar efforts made for other groups, have commonly relied on toponymic[231] and typological evidence. For example, clay cauldrons found in late-eleventh-century occupation layers in Belgrade have been specifically attributed to Pečenegs[232] as opposed to Oğuz, Cuman-Qıpčaqs, Magyars or other nomadic 'ethnicities'. Kurgans near the village of Solodovka (76km east of Volgograd) revealed leaf-shaped pendant equestrian fittings, which have been designated as Pečeneg material culture.[233] Similar burials have been assigned to the Pečenegs across the Balkans.[234] But this evidence hardly proves the presence of Pečenegs.[235] As with assigning bows, arrowheads, sabres and harnesses to Magyars, these implements could easily have been used by others, perhaps Oğuz, Cuman-Qıpčaqs or Pečenegs. This 'culture-history' approach essentialises ethnicity by using typologies and toponyms to designate various ethnicities.[236]

While monotheistic identities gradually defined surrounding sedentary peoples (for instance: Hungarians, Volga Bulgars and Rus'ians), the Pečenegs disintegrated, and nomadic survivors were probably absorbed by the Cuman-Qıpčaqs.

The nomadic Cuman-Qıpčaqs (also 'Polovcy' in Rus' sources), arriving in the eleventh- to twelfth-century source material of Pontic-Caspian Eurasia, have been extensively discussed within the context of the Oğuz, Pečenegs and Magyars, and later the Mongols. The Cuman-Qıpčaqs are first mentioned in the *PVL*'s entry for the year 1061:

> The Polovcians invaded Rus' to make war for the first time. On February 2, Vsevolod went forth against them. When they met in battle, the Polovcians defeated Vsevolod, but after the combat they

---

[231] Pálóczi Horváth, *Pechenegs, Cumans, Iasians*, 18–37; Madgearu, 'Periphery against Centre', 52–5.
[232] Marjanović-Vujović, 'Pechenegs in Beograd Town', 183–8.
[233] Glukhov, 'Погребения'; Madgearu, 'Pechenegs in Byzantine Army', 212 n20.
[234] Doncheva-Petkova, 'Плиска и печенезите', 244–58; Doncheva-Petkova, 'Zur ethnischen Zugehörigkeit', 644–58; Mikhajlova, 'Късономадски гробове', 259–66; Krumova, 'Pecheneg Chieftains in Byzantine Administration', 207–21; Schmitt, 'Petschenegen auf dem Balkan', 473–90.
[235] Armarčuk, '"Татарская археология"', 134; Kazakov, *Взаимодействии волжских булгар с тюркоязычным*, 168; Curta, 'Image and Archaeology', 181.
[236] Pohl, 'Telling Difference', 120–67; Zhivkov, *Khazaria*, 135, 240; Werbart, 'Khazars or "Saltovo-Majaki Culture"?', 199–221; Oța, *Mortuary Archaeology of Banat*, 21; Honeychurch, 'Alternative Complexities', 278.

retired. This was the first evil done by these pagan and godless foes. Their prince was Iskal.[237]

The mid-eleventh-century steppe witnessed unusual instability among pagan nomads like the Pečenegs and Cuman-Qıpčaqs, commonly understood as a 'chain reaction' of displacement according to one twelfth-century Armenian source.[238] How did they initially interact and why did the Pečeneg confederacy soon dissipate? Is it possible that the Pečeneg confederacy, militarily exhausted by the Danubian wars against Byzantium in the 1040s, disintegrated, being partially absorbed by the Cuman-Qıpčaqs, a group which suddenly arose soon after? If so, what does this reveal about ethnogenesis? Ultimately, there are two basic models of Pečeneg–Cuman relations: annihilation and/or absorption.

Like the other cases, the Cuman-Qıpčaqs hardly constituted a primordial ethnic group. Nor did Cumania, which replaced Patzinakia, constitute some archaic state.[239] Much as Christian sources (*PVL*, Georgios Amartolos, Leon Diakonos, Michael Attaleiates, Michael Psellos, Anna Komnene, etc.) typically refer to many pagan nomads as *Scyths*, the Pečenegs are comparable to Cuman-Qıpčaqs, despite frequently fighting alongside Christian armies, according to the *PVL* or at the climactic Battle of Lebounion (29 April, 1091).[240]

---

[237] *Povest' Vremennÿkh Let*, tr. Cross and Sherbowitz-Wetzor, *Russian Primary Chronicle*, 143. These were nearly concurrent events when they were written, according to Šakhmatov (*Разыскания*, 285–8, 309–11): 'The Laurentian Redaction (Ostrowski and Birnbaum [eds], *Повість временних літ*, 1292–94): "Придоша Половци первое на Русьскую землю воєвать. Всеволодъ же изиде противу имъ. мс̃ца ѳевралѧ. въ. в̃. дн҃ь. И бившимъсѧ имъ. побѣдиша Всеволода. и воєвавше ж҃идоша. се быс̃ первоє зло ѿ поганъıх̃ и безбожнъıхъ врагъ. быс̃ же кнѧзь ихъ Искалъ."'

[238] Matthew of Edessa, *Chronicle*, tr. Dulaurier, *Chronique de Matthieu d'Edesse*, 8. Pálóczi Horváth, *Pechenegs, Cumans, Iasians*, 39: 'The Snake-people marched into the land of the Yellow-men, and they smashed and routed them; whereupon the Yellow men fell upon the Ghuzz and the Pechenegs; and all these peoples, united, irrupted with blood-curdling anger upon the Romans.' This was not, as has been claimed, 'the 'last wave of migrations' in Eastern Europe' (Curta, *Southeastern Europe*, 306 n113): Timur's sack of Tbilisi and capture of Bagrat V in 1386 certainly constitute later, thirteenth- to fifteenth-century 'waves of migration in Eastern Europe'.

[239] Vásáry, *Cumans and Tatars*, 7.

[240] *Povest' Vremennÿkh Let*, tr. Cross and Sherbowitz-Wetzor, *Russian Primary Chronicle*, 143, 146–50, 165–8, 174–205; Konjavskaja, 'Половцы в ранних летописях', 180–90; Mavrodina, *Киевская русь и кочевники*; Inkov, *Древняя русь и половцы*; Pletnëva, *Половцы*; Rasovskij, *Половцы. Черные клобуки*; Toločko, *Кочевые народы степей и киевская русь*; Skržinskaja, 'Половцы', 255–69; Chekin, 'Безбожные сыны измайловы', 691–716; Birkenmeier, *Komnenian Army*, 76–7.

Not having adopted a form of monotheism accompanied by literisation, they left no written records.

The Roman/Byzantine historian and princess Anna Komnene describes the Pečenegs and Cuman-Qıpčaqs at Lebounion:

> The Scythians, on their side, kept still in their position on the banks of the stream called 'Mavropotamos' and made secret overtures to the Comans, inviting their alliance; they likewise did not cease sending envoys to the Emperor to treat about peace. The latter had a fair idea of their double-dealings so gave them appropriate answers, as he wished to keep them in suspense until the arrival of the mercenary army which he expected from Rome. And as the Comans only received dubious promises from the Patzinaks, they did not at all go over to them, but sent the following communication to the Emperor in the evening: 'For how long are we to postpone the battle? Know therefore that we shall not wait any longer, but at sunrise we shall eat the flesh either of wolf or of lamb.' On hearing this the Emperor realized the keen spirit of the Comans, and was no longer for delaying the fight. He felt that the next day would be the solemn crisis of the war, and therefore promised the Comans to do battle with the Scythians on the morrow, and then he straightway summoned the generals and 'pentecontarchs' and other officers and bade them proclaim throughout the whole camp that the battle was reserved for the morrow. But in spite of all these preparations, he still dreaded the countless hosts of Patzinaks and Comans, fearing the two armies might coalesce.[241]

---

[241] Anna Komnene, *Alexiad*, tr. Dawes, 202. Anna Komnene, *Alexiad*, eds Reinsch and Kambylis, *Annae Comnenae Alexias*, 8.5.1–2: 'οἱ δέ γε Σκύθαι κατὰ τὸν ῥύακα τοῦ καλουμένου Μαυροποτάμου κείμενοι ὑπεποιοῦντο λαθραίως τοὺς Κομάνους συμμάχους προσκαλούμενοι. Ἀλλ᾽ οὐδὲ πρὸς τὸν βασιλέα πέμποντες ἠρέμουν τὰ περὶ εἰρή νης ἐρωτῶντες. Ὁ δὲ τοῦ δολεροῦ τῆς γνώμης αὐτῶν στο χαζόμενος προσηκούσας καὶ τὰς ἀποκρίσεις αὐτοῖς ἐπε ποίητο ἀπαιωρεῖν ἐθέλων τοὺς αὐτῶν λογισμούς, εἴ που καὶ τὸ ἐκ τῆς Ῥώμης προσδοκώμενον μισθοφορικὸν καταλάβοι. Οἱ δὲ Κόμανοι ἀμφιβόλους ἔχοντες τὰς τῶν Πατζινάκων ὑποσχέσεις οὐ πάνυ τι αὐτοῖς προσετίθεντο, ἀλλ᾽ ἑσπέρας μηνύουσι τῷ βασιλεῖ· "Μέχρι πόσου τὴν μάχην ἀναβαλώ μεθα; Ἴσθι τοίνυν ὡς ἐπὶ πλέον οὐκ ἐγκαρτερήσομεν ἀλλ᾽ ἡλίου ἀνατέλλοντος λύκου ἢ ἀρνειοῦ κρέας ἐδόμεθα". Ταῦτα ὁ βασιλεὺς ἀκούσας καὶ τὸ ὀξὺ τῆς τῶν Κομάνων γνώμης διαγνοὺς οὐκέτι ἐν ἀναβολαῖς τοῦ μάχεσθαι ἦν, ἀλλὰ τὴν ἡμέραν ἐκείνην κρίσιν τοῦ πολέμου δημοτελῆ θέμενος ἐκείνοις μὲν κατὰ τὴν ἐπιοῦσαν τὸν μετὰ τῶν Σκυθῶν ὑπέσχετο πόλεμον, αὐτὸς δὲ παραχρῆμα μετακα λεσάμενος τοὺς ἡγεμόνας καὶ πεντηκοντάρχας καὶ λοιποὺς προσέταξε διὰ παντὸς τοῦ φοσσάτου διακηρυκεύσαι τὸν ἐς τὴν αὔριον ταμιευθέντα πόλεμον. 8.5.2 Ἀλλὰ κἂν τοιαῦτα ἐσκέπτετο, ἐδεδίει ὅμως τὰ ἄπειρα πλήθη τῶν Πατζινάκων καὶ Κομάνων ὑποπτεύων τὴν ἀμφοτέρων σύμβασιν.'

The only difference between Anna Komnene's Pečenegs and Cuman-Qıpčaqs at Lebounion was an insufficient oath of loyalty; there is little reason to doubt her account. She distinguishes between Pečenegs and Cuman-Qıpčaqs using the terms *Skythoi* and *Patzinakoi* versus *Komanoi*. The *PVL* draws a similar dichotomy between Pečenegs and Polovcÿ. Therefore, this battle can also be viewed as a fight between rival nomadic tribes, similarly to the original formation of Khazaria or the Pečeneg confederacy: fluid loyalties and kinship ties.

On the basis of Anna Komnene's narrative, the watershed Battle of Lebounion is traditionally interpreted as the tribal annihilation of the vanquished Pečenegs by the victorious Cumans.[242] Yet this analysis is uncertain since the Pečenegs reappear in later Byzantine and Rus' sources.[243] The Cuman-Qıpčaq (Polovcÿ) threat was common in the late eleventh century in Rus' sources, yet the Cuman-Qıpčaqs only became prevalent in Byzantine sources by the 1090s, although they were more a concurrent danger for the Rus' and more an ally according to Byzantine sources. By 1036, the *PVL* describes the last major assault on Kiev by Pečenegs, which confirms that date as the beginning of the construction of Kiev's metropolitan cathedral of St Sophia. The *PVL* reports no further nomadic assaults on Rus' until 1061, right after Jaroslav's death and his sons' campaign against the Torks (Oğuz) in 1060.[244] Regardless, the Cuman-Qıpčaqs had much in common with the Oğuz and Pečenegs. For example, using biblical genealogical precedents, the *PVL* reports in 1096 that the Pečenegs, Polovcÿ and Torks are all putatively descended from Ishmael:

> But the Saracens descended from Ishmael became known as the sons of Sarah, and called themselves Sarakÿne, that is to say, 'We are descendants of Sarah.' Likewise the Caspians and the Bulgars are descended from the daughters of Lot, who conceived by their father, so that their race is unclean. Ishmael begot twelve sons, from whom are descended the Torkmens, the Pechenegs, the Torks, and the Cumans or Polovcians, who came from the desert.[245]

[242] Brătianu, *Mer Noire*, 162; Stoljarik, *Monetary Circulation*, 86; Stephenson, *Byzantium's Balkan Frontier*, 103.
[243] Birkenmeier, *Komnenian Army*, 77; Diaconu, *Coumans*, 41–71; Golden, 'Review: Coumans', 380.
[244] *Povest' Vremennÿkh Let*, tr. Cross and Sherbowitz-Wetzor, *Russian Primary Chronicle*, 136–7, 143, 257 n163, 263–5 nn197–205; Jakov the Monk, *Pamjat' i Pokhvala*, tr. Hollingsworth, *Hagiography of Kievan Rus'*, 128.
[245] *Povest' Vremennÿkh Let*, tr. Cross and Sherbowitz-Wetzor, *Russian Primary Chronicle*, 184. The Laurentian Redaction (Ostrowski and Birnbaum [eds], Повість

CASE STUDIES OF MONOTHEISATION   133

Like the Pečenegs, while some Cuman-Qıpčaqs intermittently allied with Christians (as at Lebounion), traded, converted and assimilated, according to the archives of Mt Athos,[246] others maintained the adversarial nomadic role with the eleventh- to twelfth-century sedentary *oikoumene* by raiding the nearby Christian communities. The distinction between 'wild' and 'non-wild' Polovcÿ/Cumans in Rus' sources reveals that there was no centralised Cuman 'state'.[247]

Also like the case of the Pečenegs, an impressive array of archaeological (and linguistic[248]) data has been compiled on the Cuman-Qıpčaqs across Romania, Moldova, Hungary and Ukraine. Yet given the gradual assimilation of autonomous Iasian and Cuman-Qıpčaq communities into nearby populations (Hungary, Bulgaria, Rus', etc.), Cumans are addressed differently in each country.[249] It remains unclear how such material necessarily separates Cuman-Qıpčaqs from Pečenegs (or Oğuz, etc.), beyond arbitrary assumptions. The most famous Cuman materials are painted sandstone carvings, found all over Pontic-Caspian Eurasia, which, based on William of Rubruck's thirteenth-century travel journal (*Itinerarium*), are often attributed to Cumans rather than Mongols, but not necessarily instead of Pečenegs.[250] Elsewhere, various arrowheads, stirrups and a 'Russian-style helmet' found in burial sites in present-day Ukraine, Moldova and Romania have been labelled as from Cuman graves.[251] Soviet-era finds of horse-bits,

временних літ, 1848–50): 'а Срацини ѿ Измаила. творѧтсѧ Сарини^ж и прозваша имена собѣ. Саракъıне. рекше Сарини єсмы. тѣмже Хвалиси и Болгаре суть ѿ дочерю Лютову. иже зачаста ѿ отца своєго. тѣмьже неч^ето єсть племѧ ихъ. а Измаиль роди. ві҃. сн҃а. ѿ ни^хже суть Тортмени и Печенѣзи. и Торци. и Кумани. рекше Половци. иже исходѧть ѿ пустынѣ.'

[246] *Acts of the Great Lavra Monastery* V, eds. Lemerle et al., *Actes de Lavra*, 339:44–52: in 1181, several imperially employed Cuman soldiers were expelled from *Chostianes* (Moglena); Bartusis, *Land and Privilege in Byzantium*, 50–8; Madgearu, *Byzantine Military Organization*, 159–60; Franklin and Shepard, *Emergence of Rus*, 271–2.

[247] Golden, 'Polovci Dikii', 296–309; Noonan, 'Rus', Pechenegs, and Polovtsy', 301–26; Raffensperger, *Reimagining Europe*, 77–8; Konjavskaja, 'Половцы в ранних летописях', 180–90.

[248] For example, the early-fourteenth-century *Codex Cumanicus*, eds Schmieder and Schreiner, *Codice Cumanico*; Golden, 'Cumanica IV', 99–122; Golden, 'Codex Cumanicus', 33–63; Poppe, 'Mongolischen Lehnwörter im Komanischen', 331–40.

[249] Kálnoky, 'Des scythes aux Iasses', 65–84; Pálóczi Horváth, *Pechenegs, Cumans, Iasians*, 54–95.

[250] William of Rubruck, *Itinerarium*, tr. Rockhill, *Journey of William of Rubruck*, 80; Pálóczi Horváth, *Pechenegs, Cumans, Iasians*, 98–102; Stoljarik, *Monetary Circulation*, 87; Pletnëva, *Кочевники южнорусских степей*, 157–60.

[251] Pálóczi Horváth, *Pechenegs, Cumans, Iasians*, 48–50.

belt buckles, arrowheads and spear points at nomadic burial sites on the lower Danube (Olteniţa, Tangîru, Moviliţa, Rîmnicelu, Lişcoteanca, Moscu and Holboca) have been labelled as either Cuman or Pečeneg. Meanwhile, the 'autochthonous Romanian population' over which Cumans ruled, rather than the Cumans' material culture itself, has been 'narrowly' emphasised.[252] Therefore, the assumption of Romanian primordial ethnicity is demonstrably common (the indigenous Romanian is sedentary, while the invading Pečeneg and/or Cuman is nomadic). Burial sites like Moscu, Holboca, Căuşeni, Cârnăţeni, Copanca, Corjova, Hâncăuţi, Roma, Săiţi, Tudora, Sărata and Ursoaia have been attributed to the Cumans based only on the dating of source chronology.[253] This methodology may be acceptable for distinguishing nomadic sites with horse and livestock skeletons, 'nomadic-ware' ceramics, spindle whorls and trephined skulls, but finds alone cannot separate Cumans from Pečenegs.[254] The Cumans hardly constituted some primordial ethnicity, as has been assumed.[255] Nomads' daily implements cannot be labelled as either Magyar, Pečeneg or Cuman: what would stop a self-identifying (if s/he would self-identify) Cuman from taking the arrowheads, sabres and bridle-bits formerly used by a Pečeneg? These are assumptions made by archaeologists a thousand years later based on textual sources. Other present-day assumptions about steppe-nomads have been inherited from centuries of stereotyping, which has in turn led to counter-narratives about the relationship between settled Christian communities (Orthodox, Latin, etc.) and the steppe-nomads. This has resulted in a present-day ideology of 'Eurasianism'.[256]

Nevertheless, Cumans are indistinguishable from Pečenegs because of their 'stateless adaptation'.[257] No source mentions a Cuman ruler's attempt at top-down monotheisation. Juxtaposed with Rus', Volga Bulgaria, Hungary, Patzinakia and Khazaria, Cumania eventually disappeared for the same reason as Khazaria and Patzinakia: because no dynasty succeeded

---

[252] Pletnëva, *Половцы*; Diaconu, *Coumans*, 14–22, 128; Golden, 'Review: *Coumans*', 380.
[253] Spinei, 'Cuman Bishopric', 440; Spinei, *Romanians and Turkic Nomads*, 296; Petkov, 'Review: *Romanians and Turkic Nomads*', 554–6; Davidescu, *Lost Romans*, 10; Wooster, 'Enlightenment to Genocide', 80–99.
[254] Pálóczi Horváth, *Pechenegs, Cumans, Iasians*, 102; Stoljarik, *Monetary Circulation*, 86; Curta, *Southeastern Europe*, 308–9.
[255] Pylypčuk and Sabitov, *Очерки истории кыпчаков*, 210–14; Pylypčuk, *Дешт-и-кыпчак на цивилизаций*.
[256] See the further discussion of Eurasianism in Appendix 2.
[257] Golden, 'Qipčaqs of Eurasia', 132–57.

in forcing its subjects to convert to a monotheistic faith and adhere to its laws en masse.²⁵⁸ The Cumans themselves were eventually subsumed into the Mongol hordes, as the Pečenegs and Khazars had been previously, via fluid ties of kinship and loyalty, by the Cumans and later nomadic confederations.²⁵⁹ This was not because they lacked some imagined primordial ethnicity, but because their paganism was itself the basis of their identity. The nomads, therefore, can fit into the same context of top-down monotheisation: Christianity, imposed by Stephen, created Hungary; Islam, imposed by Almuš, created Volga Bulgaria. In contrast, Joseph's Judaism, which was not imposed on his subjects, led to Khazaria's disintegration, and the same can be said for Patzinakia and Cumania.²⁶⁰

Rus': Byzantine Christianisation

Despite their separate developments, their distinct challenges and their divergent historical trajectories, the Volga Bulgars' Islamisation, the Magyars' Latin Christianisation, the Khazars' aborted Judaisation and the Pečenegs' disintegration (due to their rejection of monotheism) all contribute to a broader understanding of the process of monotheisation as it was experienced over the course of generations. St Vladimir's adoption of Byzantine Orthodox Christianity in Kiev c. 987–9 must be discussed commensurately.²⁶¹ While the story of Vladimir's baptism has long been subject to meticulous textual analysis,²⁶² Orthodox Christianity in Rus' (that is, *Kievan Rus'*) has often been viewed as a 'state' affair. Alternatively, the Rus' generally could describe a collection of towns and peoples which gradually constituted and contained the Rus' identity, united by many clans claiming descent from the house of Vladimir and Rjurik (the Rjurikid dynasty). Kiev may have once been a Rus' capital, but it was Byzantine Christianity, not exclusive to Kiev alone, which begat Rus'.²⁶³

Before Christianisation, nearly every archaeological pursuit has been covered regarding Rus', including settlement archaeology, numismatics,

---

[258] Konjavskaja, 'Половцы в ранних летописях', 183–4.
[259] Halperin, 'Kipchak Connection', 233; Martin, *Medieval Russia*, 48–9.
[260] Khazanov, *Nomads and Outside World*, 178–9; Golden, 'Imperial Ideology and Political Unity', 64–6; Pritsak, *Pečenegs*, 11–16; Zhivkov, *Khazaria*, 134.
[261] Berend, 'Introduction'; Bartlett, 'Paganism to Christianity'; Shepard, 'Rus''.
[262] Poppe, 'Political Background', 195–244; Obolensky, 'Cherson and Conversion of Rus'', 244–56; Pritsak, 'What Really Happened in 988?', 5–15; Feldman, 'Autonomy and Rebellion in Cherson'.
[263] Franklin, 'Invention of Rus(sia)(s)', 188.

ceramics, epigraphy and funerary archaeology.²⁶⁴ Yet similar 'culture-history' debates linger regarding the imagined primordial ethnicities of Slavs and Scandinavians (Varangians/Vikings/Normans) before the Rus' Christianisation – primarily coming down to whether Belarusians, Russians and Ukrainians are ethnically Scandinavian or Slavic. Referred to as the 'Normanist debates', which were common in post-World War II Soviet historiography, such misconceptions of primordial ethnicity remain in textual and archaeological analyses. Can we truly recognise ethnicity in archaeological finds? And if so, would it then mean that certain groups (for instance, Scandinavians, Slavs, Turkic groups) perceived their own distinct pre-monotheistic 'ethnicities'?

Pre-Christian ethnicities in Rus': Slav and Varangian culture-history

While primary sources indicate differences between groups, such as Slavs or Varangians, based on imagined cultural or linguistic traits, can we presume that such differences constitute different ethnicities that existed as 'facts and facets of self-definition'?²⁶⁵ While such assumptions, made in the context of the Normanist controversy, necessarily place the importance of language over monotheism in determining ethnic identity, it may be a false premise when applied to a pre-monotheistic context,²⁶⁶ especially given that languages change and populations absorb new languages over centuries.

Specifically, the Normanist controversy refers to the late-twentieth-century historiographical debate, quite common in Soviet and post-Soviet history and archaeology, about whether or not the Rus', as an

---

²⁶⁴ Franklin and Shepard, *Emergence of Rus*; Kazanski et al., *Centres proto-urbains russes*; Pritsak, *Old Rus' Weights and Monetary Systems*; Noonan, 'Khazar Qaghanate and Early Rus'', 76–102; Noonan, 'Islamic Trade in Rus' Lands', 379–94; Noonan and Kovalev, 'Prayer, Illumination, and Good Times', 73–96; Noonan, 'Monetary History of Kiev', 384–461; Toločko, *Древнерусский феодальный город*; Toločko, *Южная русь и византия*; Ioannisyan, 'Development and Urbanization of Kiev', 285–312; ŠČapov, *Государство и церковь древней руси*; Limonov, *Владимиро-суздальская русь*; Kolčin, *Древняя русь*; Sedov, '*Распространение христианства в древней руси*', 3–11; Mil'khov et al., *Древняя русь*; Danilova, *Сельская община в средневековой руси*.

²⁶⁵ Franklin, 'Invention of Rus(sia)(s)', 184.

²⁶⁶ Obolensky, *Byzantium and Slavs*, 51; Mošin, 'Варяго-русский вопрось', 109–36, 343–79, 501–37; Stender-Peterson, *Varangica*, 5–20; Paszkiewicz, *Origin of Russia*, 109–32; Thomsen, *Relations between Ancient Russia and Scandinavia*; Grekov, *Киевская русь*; Šušarin, 'Сущности норманизма', 65–93.

'ethnic people' (народ), were in fact descended from either the Slavs or Vikings/Varangians, described by the Russian expressions 'Норман' and 'Норманизм'. The reasons for this debate may arguably be more redolent of the era in which they took place than the era they sought to elucidate. In terms of primordial ethnic differences between Scandinavians, Slavs and so-called Turkic groups (such as within Volga Bulgaria), there is still very little evidence.[267] By now the 'Normanist debate' is largely settled in so far as old models of primordial ethnicity and culture-history are fading, although primordial ethnic paradigms occasionally appear in textual and archaeological analyses.

While Christian and Islamic sources may refer to different peoples among the Rus' surmised as either Varangians or Slavs, it is yet unclear who was who and exactly what distinguished Varangians from Slavs. According to the *PVL*, Varangians were specifically from 'beyond the sea' in the year 859. Yet Slavs and Varangians were both descendants of Japheth from the Table of Nations in the book of Genesis:

> The following nations also are a part of the race of Japheth: the Varangians, the Swedes, the Normans, the Gotlanders, the Russes, the English, the Spaniards, the Italians, the Romans, the Germans, the French, the Venetians, the Genoese, and so on. [...] The Slavic race is derived from the line of Japheth, since they are the Noricians, who are identical with the Slavs.[268]

It is unclear if the Varangians and the Slavs were equally 'Rus'' from this account. Generally, eleventh-century Byzantine historians (Skylitzes,[269] Diakonos[270] and Psellos[271]) dismissively refer to the Rus' collectively as 'Tauroscythians' without explaining differences between ninth- to eleventh-century Varangians or Slavs. However, Skylitzes defines Varangians as a

---

[267] Beliaev and Chernetsov, 'Eastern Contribution', 97–124; Franklin and Shepard, *Emergence of Rus*, 28 n26, 39 n46; Klejn, 'Russian Controversy over Varangians', 27–38; Callmer, 'West to East', 46–7.

[268] *Povest' Vremennÿkh Let*, tr. Cross and Sherbowitz-Wetzor, *Russian Primary Chronicle*, 52–7.

[269] Ioannes Skylitzes, *Synopsis of Histories*, tr. Wortley, *Synopsis of Byzantine History*, 107–8; ed. Thurn, *Synopsis Historiarum*, 107.

[270] Leon Diakonos, *History*, ed and tr. Karales, Λέων Διάκονος, 202–5; tr. Talbot and Sullivan, *Leo the Deacon*, 111–12; Terras, 'Diaconus and Ethnology of Rus', 395–406.

[271] Michael Psellos, *Chronographia*, ed. Reinsch, *Michaelis Pselli Chronographia*, 144–5; tr. Sewter, *Fourteen Byzantine Rulers*, 147–8.

'Celtic *genos*'.²⁷² The *DAI* contains the most thorough account juxtaposing the Rus' and the Slavs, depicting the Slavs as 'tributaries' (πακτιῶται) of the Rus' although with different speech, but makes no mention of Varangians.²⁷³ In Byzantine eyes, Slavs and Varangians were certainly ethnic labels, but their differentiation was from Byzantines themselves, not necessarily from each other.²⁷⁴

As the Islamic author most familiar with Slavs and Varangians, ibn Fadlān describes many aspects of the Rus' (as opposed to his 'aṣ-Ṣaqāliba') which correspond to generic Vikings (for example, ship burials, chieftain death rituals, etc.). While this certainly parallels contemporary portrayals of Scandinavians, it hardly proves that the Rus' were collectively Scandinavian by supposed primordial 'ethnic' origin. Since ibn Fadlān's 'aṣ-Ṣaqāliba' cannot be perfectly labelled as 'Slavs',²⁷⁵ we may also note that the *Ḥudūd al-ʿĀlam* describes Slavs as part of the Rus' even while conceding that the 'Ṣaqlāb resemble the Rus".²⁷⁶

Textual sources make abundant casual observations of ethnicity, but these sources also reveal imperfect snapshots of ethnicity *at a given time*. They do not provide grounds to assume that ethnicity was a primordial, almost biological phenomenon. Therefore, inquiring into primordial ethnicity, whether Rus', Varangian, Slavic or for any other group, is ultimately a flawed question to be asking of textual material, even if these ethnicities themselves are 'fluid [...] more like honey, tar, or glue, and less like water or blood'.²⁷⁷ Yet some still claim that pre-Christian groups hinted at in textual sources (like Varangians, Slavs, Balts, etc.) can be linked to archaeologically substantiated ethnicities.²⁷⁸

In archaeology, the Slav/Varangian dichotomy resembles the cultural-historical debates about the pre-monotheistic populations of Hungary (Magyars, Pečenegs, Celts, Huns, Slavs) and Volga Bulgaria (Čuvaš, Baškīrs, Magyars, Slavs, Mordvians). Historians who use the same model for Rus'²⁷⁹

---

²⁷² Ioannes Skylitzes, *Synopsis of Histories*, ed. Thurn, *Synopsis Historiarum*, 481; tr. Wortley, *Synopsis of Byzantine History*, 449.
²⁷³ Konstantinos VII Porphyrogennetos, *De Administrando Imperio*, ed. Moravcsik, tr. Jenkins, §9; eds Dvornik et al., *De Administrando Imperio Commentary*, 35–42.
²⁷⁴ Kaldellis, *Romanland*, 136–54, 259.
²⁷⁵ Ibn Fadlān, *Risāla*, tr. Lunde and Stone, *Ibn Fadlān*, 45–55; tr. Frye, *Journey to Russia*, 63–71; Montgomery, 'Faḍlān and Rūsiyyah', 1–25.
²⁷⁶ *Ḥudūd al-ʿĀlam*, tr. Minorsky, §43–4.
²⁷⁷ Kaldellis, *Romanland*, 273.
²⁷⁸ Callmer, 'West to East', 46; Dolukhanov, *Early Slavs*, 199; Birnbaum, 'Slavic Settlements', 1–14; Vryonis, 'Slavic Pottery from Olympia', 15–42.
²⁷⁹ Barford, *Early Slavs*, 268–85; Mocja, 'Rôle des élites guerrières', 267.

encounter the same problems: it rests on an assumption of primordial ethnicity which cannot be proven, especially in Rus'.[280] Analyses of archaeological typologies are certainly unavoidable, but they cannot be definitively assigned to given ethnicities.[281]

For example, burials found at Šestovica (14km southwest of Černigov) have been labelled as ethnically Scandinavian based on their swords, arrowheads, belt buckles, combs and equestrian equipment. But how such finds can be proven *not to have belonged* to Slavic, Mordvian or steppe peoples is not explained. The arrowheads are not easily distinguishable from Magyar or Pečeneg arrowheads found in Switzerland. Furthermore, the tenth-century stirrups and belt buckles of Šestovica are only slightly distinct from the coeval stirrups and belt buckles found in Pannonia.[282] These finds cannot be ethnically labelled – at most they can only belong to an assimilated group such as a *družina*, or a prince's entourage.[283] True, there are slightly different typologies of bridle-bits and styles of swords (the swords of tenth-century Pannonia are stylistically sabres while the swords of Šestovica are straight swords) may be ethnically attributable, but they *cannot* prove that a member of one ethnic group (like a Slav) avoided using the implements of another ethnic group. Simply put, even if it can hint at the nomadic or sedentary lifestyle of the deceased, the typology of funerary goods *cannot* prove the ethnicity of the deceased.

At the Rjurikovo *gorodišče* (2km south of Velikij Novgorod), ninth- to tenth-century bow fibulae were found and also labelled as 'Scandinavian,'[284] as opposed to earlier fibulae ethnically labelled as Slavic. Yet while Slavic fibulae *could* have been culturally relevant for those who produced and wore them, they *cannot* ultimately prove the ethnicity (primordial or circumstantial) of the producer and/or wearer. Therefore, they cannot be proven as exclusively Slavic; after all, what would stop a Slav from being buried with a Scandinavian fibula?[285] The same can be said about Rjurikovo's fibulae.

Classifying burial assemblages based on notions of primordial ethnicity (namely Scandinavians, Slavs, etc.) is a recent projection onto the

---

[280] Plokhy, *Origins of Slavic Nations*, 354–61; Bushkovitch, 'Review: *Origins of Slavic Nations*', 846–8; Halperin, 'Identity in Rus'. Review: *Origins of Slavic Nations*', 275–94; Makarov et al., 'Beginning of Rus' through Archaeology', 496–507; Shepard, 'Back in Old Rus and USSR', 384–405; Curta, 'Archaeology of Identities in Old Russia', 31–62.
[281] Curta, '"Hesitating Journey through Foreign Knowledge"', 302.
[282] Mocja, 'Rôle des élites guerrières', 273–82.
[283] Kovalenko, 'Scandinavians in East Europe', 287.
[284] Nosov, 'Rjurikovo Gorodišče et Novgorod', 156–65.
[285] Curta, '"Slavic" Bow Fibulae', 1–108.

distant past and has been dismissed as a 'fairy tale'.[286] Such finds cannot be compelled to produce 'ethnic markings'.[287] Did these individuals view themselves as Scandinavians or Slavs? Could they not opt to be buried with the others' arbitrarily assumed 'ethnic markings'? Either case is ultimately unprovable and archaeology alone cannot answer these questions.

The same can be said about asking the equivalent question of archaeological material. To ascribe material culture based on typologies to one group or another and call them 'ethnicities', based on some assumption of primordial ethnolinguistic continuity, would be just as anachronistic for the case of Rus' as for Khazaria, Volga Bulgaria and Hungary. If individuals and communities absorbed new languages, and they did, then a supposed linguistic basis for primordial ethnicity necessarily collapses. So even while some historians expose the central paradox of retrospectively trying to view Rus' through a lens which places oversized importance on pre-Christian identity (as has been normal in traditional historiography), it has not stopped them from referring to ethnicity as an essentially pre-monotheistic, 'ancient' identity, instead of as a synthetic idea applied centuries later via an imposed monotheism, such as Byzantine Christianity in Rus'.[288]

Tribute to tax, a Rus' 'khağan' and a 'translatio imperii'

The processes of centralising power (under either a *khağan* or a *knjaz'*) and subjugating nearby communities (regardless of primordial ethnicity) by the Rus' resemble the same processes by the Khazars, Volga Bulgars and Magyars. While during the tenth century the number of Christians in Kiev gradually increased, which played a bottom-up role in Vladimir's decision to adopt Christianity, Rus' identity was ultimately a top-down phenomenon reaching subject and tributary populations eventually via Byzantine Christianity, as were other cases of monotheisation. It was only much later that Rus' identity became also a bottom-up phenomenon, after the first pagan Rus' *khağans* accepted Christianity, becoming princes, or *knjaz'ja*.

Five ninth- to eleventh-century sources indicate the transposition of Khazar ruling structures (the *khağan*) to the Rus' – a Rus' *khağanate* long before Vladimir's conversion: metropolitan Ilarion's *Sermon on Law and*

---

[286] Curta, 'Four Questions', 286–303.
[287] Afanas'ev, *Донские аланы*; Uspenskij, 'Могильники', 94.
[288] Franklin, 'Invention of Rus(sia)(s)', 187.

Grace (mid-eleventh century),[289] the *Ḥudūd al-ʿĀlam* (982),[290] the *Annales Bertiniani* (mid-late-ninth century),[291] the *Kitāb al-Aʿlāk an-Nafīsa* of ibn Rusta (c. 903–13)[292] and the *Zayn al-akhbār* of al-Gardīzī (mid-eleventh century).[293] The concept of shifting the previous Khazar hegemony with the title of *khaǧan* to the Rus' has been termed a *translatio imperii* from Itīl' to Kiev, where the late-tenth-century Rus' prince Svjatoslav not so much destroyed Khazaria as subsumed it. This idea has required an adjustment of the traditional chronology, with several historians relying as much as on Khazarian sources as the *PVL*, if not more so.[294] Yet this ninth- to tenth-century translation of the *khaǧanate* from Itīl' to Kiev had less to do with warfare between the Khazars and the Caliphate at that time (there is no evidence of this) than with the presentation of power over nearby subject populations in the northern Black Sea region.[295] A few scattered Rus' seals referencing Khazarian heritage mention a certain Michael, *archon* and *doux* of Tamatarcha (Matracha/Tmutarakan'), Zichia and all Khazaria;[296] Michael could be the Christian name of Oleg, Jaroslav's grandson (r. 1078–93). Clearly, Rus' princes valued 'their Khazarian heritage'.[297]

The presentation of power is also evident on the first Christian Rus' coins, which contain the *tryzub*, or trident (or bident) symbol; this derives from Khazarian notions of rulership[298] and relates to the 'trident' tamga symbol on Khazarian coins. This tamga appears in the same numismatic context as the *Moses* coins previously discussed and may conceivably be

---

[289] Ilarion, *Sermon on Law and Grace*, tr. Franklin, *Sermons and Rhetoric of Kievan Rus'*, xxi, 3, 17–26.

[290] *Ḥudūd al-ʿĀlam*, tr. Minorsky, §44.

[291] Garipzanov, 'Annals of St. Bertin and *Chacanus* of *Rhos*', 7–11.

[292] Ibn Rusta, *Kitāb al-Aʿlāk an-Nafīsa*, tr. Lunde and Stone, *Ibn Fadlān*, 116–17.

[293] Al-Gardīzī, *Zayn al-akhbār*, tr. Martinez, 'Gardīzī's Two Chapters on Turks', 167.

[294] *Schechter Text*, eds and tr. Golb and Pritsak, *Khazarian Hebrew Documents*, 64–5; Zuckerman, 'Khazars' Conversion to Judaism', 237–70; Zuckerman, 'Formation de l'ancien état russe', 95–120; Garipzanov, 'Annals of St. Bertin and *Chacanus* of *Rhos*', 7–11; Petrukhin, 'Khazaria and Rus", 254–65; Artamonov, *История хазар*, 368–87; Boba, *Nomads, Northmen and Slavs*, 39–76; Nazarenko, 'Западноевропейские источники', 290–2; Franklin and Shepard, *Emergence of Rus*, 50–70; Golden, 'Question of Rus' Qaghanate', 77–94; Noonan, 'Khazar Qaghanate and Early Rus", 76–102.

[295] Noonan, 'Khazar Qaghanate and Early Rus", 90–4; Hanak, *Nature and Image of Power in Rus'*, 135–7; Christian, 'Khaganate of Rus", 3–26.

[296] Alf'orov, 'Archon and Doux of Matarcha and All Khazaria'; Bulgakova, *Byzantinische Bleisiegel*, 240; Janin, *Актове печати древней руси*, 29.

[297] Alf'orov, 'Archon and Doux of Matarcha and All Khazaria', 101.

[298] Pritsak, *Old Rus' Weights and Monetary Systems*, 81–6; Flërova, *Образы и сюжеты*, 43–67.

Figure 3.1 An image of the Khazar tamga, potentially one of the symbols of the Āšĭnà dynasty, which appears on certain Khazar dirhams.

one of the symbols of the Āšĭnà dynasty of Khazaria, hypothetically Joseph's household.[299] Trident and bident symbols, common dynastic emblems throughout Eurasia for centuries, were therefore easily transplanted as Rjurikid symbols from the Khazarian Āšĭnà dynasty.[300] This symbol even survives today as the emblem of Ukrainian nationality.

The ninth- to tenth-century Rus' *khağans* competed against the Khazar *khağans* for tribute among nearby subject communities.[301] These communities can hardly be labelled, however, since they left no sources defining themselves. Whether 'Slavic', 'Baltic', 'Mordvian' or otherwise, by paying tribute to the Rus', instead of to Khazaria,[302] eventually, they became Rus' themselves through Christianisation.[303] Rather than imagined 'proto-ethnic' identities like Slavs versus Normans/Varangians, Rus' identity became a monotheistic one, like other cases, imposed on subject peoples in a top-down conversion process.[304] As in Khazaria, Hungary and Volga Bulgaria, textual and archaeological data better exhibit monotheisation, in this case Christianisation, than primordial ethnicity.

---

[299] Kovalev, 'Khazar Identity through Coins', 228–30; Shake, *Coins of Khazar Empire*, 31–54; Býkov, 'Из истории денежного обращения хазарии', 36–7.
[300] Zhivkov, *Khazaria*, 119.
[301] Petrukhin, 'Феодализм', 161–70; Koptev, '"Chazar Tribute"', 189–212.
[302] Haldon, *State and Tributary Mode of Production*, 272.
[303] Franklin and Shepard, *Emergence of Rus*, 225; Zuckerman, 'Formation de l'ancien état russe', 117; Feldman, 'Autonomy and Rebellion in Cherson', 19 n43.
[304] Franklin, 'Invention of Rus(sia)(s)', 189.

Christianisation, sedentarisation, centralisation, literisation

Several classes of evidence illuminate the processes accompanying Christianisation following Vladimir's conversion in 987–9 (I have previously addressed the historical misconceptions surrounding the event itself[305]). Although numismatic evidence clearly shows Christianisation through imagery, there is also indication of increasing monotheistic coin circulation in tenth- to twelfth-century Rus'. Despite the lower numbers of Byzantine coins circulating in Rus' compared to Islamic dirhams, the number of emperor Basileios II Porphyrogennetos' silver coins (*miliaresia*) peaked in mixed hoards throughout tenth- to eleventh-century Rus'.[306] Over seven hundred Byzantine coins have been found in present Sweden, mostly on the island of Gotland, 9.67 per cent of which are imitations, while 32.57 per cent belong to the early reign of Basileios II Porphyrogennetos (977–89). The numbers peak again at 15.79 per cent as *miliaresia* dating to Konstantinos IX Monomachos' reign (1042–55), which characterise the tenth to eleventh century as an era of maximum flows of Byzantine coins northward through Rus' during Christianisation.[307] This should not be surprising: the first Christian Rus' generation was still just as interested in accumulating treasure as its pagan forebears.[308] In the Soviet Union's territory, 172 uncovered hoards were more mixed, including Byzantine, Islamic and Western coins, which attests to their undifferentiated usage.[309] This challenges assumptions about the 'foreignness' and 'domesticity' of Rus' coinage: if Kievan 'national' coinage disappeared c. 1130s–1380s, while 'foreign' *deniers* from Western Europe circulated in Rjurikid-ruled towns, then eleventh- to fourteenth-century silver coins indicate ecumenical, rather than national authority.[310]

Economics and law were always adjoined. The appointments of loyalists (retainers [*družinniki*] and noblemen [*bojarÿ*]) to rapidly urbanising fortifications (*goroda*) demonstrate that the choice of local representatives

---

[305] Feldman, 'Autonomy and Rebellion in Cherson'.
[306] Noonan, 'Byzantine Coins in Rus'', 143–81; Stoljarik, *Monetary Circulation*, 93–6.
[307] Malmer, 'Importation of Byzantine Coins to Scandinavia', 295–8; Androshchuk, 'Byzantium and Scandinavian World', 147–92.
[308] Feldman, 'First Christian Rus' Generation', 3–25.
[309] Thompson, 'Byzantine Coins in Russia', 145; Kropotkin, 'Находки византийских монет на СССР', 166–89; Stoljarik, *Monetary Circulation*, figs 234–5; Janin, *Денежно-весовые системы руси*, 153.
[310] Zguta, 'Kievan Coinage', 484–8; Sedykh, 'Function of Coins', 475; Malmer, 'Importation of Byzantine Coins to Scandinavia', 295–302; Pavlova, 'Coinless Period in Rus'', 375–92; Feldman, 'Bullion, Barter and Borders'.

with aligned political agendas has always been of utmost importance within the *oikoumene*.[311] Personnel has always been policy – across time and space. Taxation began as tribute, collected by a prince (*knjaz'*) who donated a tenth (*desjatinna*) of his income to the church, from his tax-collection district (*pogost*).[312] The metropolitanate was itself materially supported by the princes in return for the metropolitan's conferral of legitimacy. The imperially appointed metropolitan, in return for his tithe and loyalty, dispensed canon law (and sometimes legal favours[313]) via his suffragan appointments, which yielded similar top-down monotheisation processes to those elsewhere.[314] Although debates remain about when exactly the Kievan metropolitanate was established, of the undisputed twenty-six metropolitans of Kiev and all Rus' until 1299, when the metropolitan St Maximos moved the seat to the city of Vladimir (180km northeast of Moscow), only three metropolitans (Ilarion, Kliment Smoljatič and Petro Akerovič) were *not* directly appointed from Constantinople.[315] Gradually, Jaroslav's church of St Sophia in Kiev became a centre from which imperial authority emanated,[316] legitimised by imperial law (*zakon*).[317] This was meant to

---

[311] Tikhomirov, *Towns of Ancient Rus*, 66; Lind, 'Russo-Byzantine Treaties', 362–70; Langer, 'Preindustrial Russian City', 209–40; Mezentsev, 'Emergence of Podil', 48–70; Miller, 'Monumental Building and Patrons', 321–55; Morris, 'Emergence of Volga-Oka Region', 697–710; Kovalev, 'Zvenyhorod in Galicia', 7–36; Shaw, 'Nature of Russian City', 267–70; Makarov, 'Rural Settlement and Trade Networks', 443–61; Kazanski et al., *Centres proto-urbains russes*; Bushkovitch, 'Towns and Castles', 251–64; Grinberg, '"Is this City Yours or Mine?"', 895–921.

[312] Vernadsky, *Kievan Russia*, 191; Noonan, 'Monetary History of Kiev'.

[313] Tiguncev, 'Власть и церковь в киевской руси', 185–90; ŠČapov, *Государство и церковь древней руси*.

[314] *Russkaja Pravda*, ed. Juškov, *Памятники русского права*; tr. Kaiser, *Laws of Rus'*; tr. Vernadsky, *Medieval Russian Laws*; Solov'ev, *Властители и судьи*, 4–5; Franklin, *Writing, Society and Culture*, 136; Chadwick, *Beginnings of Russian History*, 109–10; ŠČapov, *Церковь и становление древнерусской государственности*, 61–3; Soloviev, 'Influence du droit byzantin dans les pays orthodoxes', 599–650.

[315] *Povest' Vremennÿkh Let*, tr. Cross and Sherbowitz-Wetzor, *Russian Primary Chronicle*, 137–8, 262 n183; Arrignon, *Chaire métropolitaine de Kiev*; Blažejovs'kij, *Hierarchy of Kyivan Church*, 64–5; Šakhmatov, *Разыскания*, 414–583; Toločko, *Очерки начальной руси*, 21–6; Poppe, *Państwo i Kosciol na Rusi*, 25–8; Franklin and Shepard, *Emergence of Rus*, 226–30; Černigovskij (Gumilevskij), *Избранные жития святых*, 722.

[316] Boeck, 'Simulating Hippodrome', 283–301; Simmons, 'Rus' Dynastic Ideology in St. Sophia', 207–25; Franklin and Shepard, *Emergence of Rus*, 356.

[317] Weickhardt, 'Russian Law and Byzantine Law', 1–22; Franklin, *Writing, Society and Culture*, 136; Chitwood, *Byzantine Legal Culture and Roman Legal Tradition*, 125; Kaiser, *Growth of Law in Russia*; Feldbrugge, *Law in Medieval Russia*.

transcend pagan tribal loyalties and move towards the overarching purpose of loyalty to prince and emperor, rather than appealing to assumptions of primordial ethnicity.[318] Therefore, Rus' functioned as an extension of the sovereign *oikoumene*, not its own national sovereignty.

This is best demonstrated by the *NE*, a periodically updated list of all eparchies, metropolitanates and bishoprics appointed by the ecumenical Patriarch. Christian emperors had already attempted to Christianise eighth- to ninth-century Khazaria, labelled the metropolitanate of Gotthia in the eighth- to ninth-centuries *NE* (nos 3, 8), which was later absorbed into the metropolitanate of Rosia (nos 11, 13), covering similar areas in Pontic-Caspian Eurasia.[319] By the twelfth-century *NE* 13, the Rus' metropolitanate appeared alongside older, more established eparchies, bishoprics and *themata* of the Anatolian and Balkan mainlands, although it ranked in sixtieth place, and was later reduced by the Palaiologan emperors.[320] The Byzantine sees encompassed by Great Rus'ia (*megale Rosia*) included Belgorod (Πελογράδων), Novgorod (Νευογράδων), Černigov (Τζερνιγόβων), Polock (Πολοτζίκων), Vladimir (τοῦ Βλαδιμοίρου), Perejaslavl' (Περισθλάβου), Suzdal' (τοῦ Σούσδαλι), Turov (Τουρόβου), Kanev (Κάνεβε), Smolensk (Σμολίσκον) and Galica (Γάλιτσα).[321]

---

[318] Carile, 'Byzantine Political Ideology and Rus'', 400–13; Marinich, 'Revitalization in Kievan Russia', 61–8; Miller, 'Kievan Principality on Eve of Mongol Invasion', 215–40; Hurwitz, 'Kievan Rus' and Medieval Myopia', 176–87; Birnbaum, 'Jewish Life and Anti-Jewish Sentiments in Medieval Russia', 225–55; Hurwitz, 'Metropolitan Hilarion's *Sermon on Law and Grace*', 322–33; Codeso, 'Crónicas Griegas y entrada de Rusos', 93–109; Stein-Wilkeshuis, 'Scandinavians Swearing Oaths in Russia', 155–68; Thomov, 'Scandinavian Ship Graffiti from Hagia Sofia', 168–84; Curta, 'Archaeology of Identities in Old Russia', 31–62; Shepard, 'Back in Old Rus and USSR', 384–405; Makarov et al., 'Beginning of Rus' through Archaeology', 496–507; Halperin, 'Identity in Rus''. Review: *Origins of Slavic Nations*, 275–94; Plokhy, *Origins of Slavic Nations*.

[319] *Notitiae Episcopatuum*, ed. Darrouzès, 122–7, 151, 241–2, 294, 343–6, 367; Shepard, 'Close Encounters with Byzantine World', 37–65; Shepard, '"Mists and Portals"', 424; Čkhaidze, 'Зихская епархия', 47–68; Franklin and Shepard, *Emergence of Rus*, 227. Gotthia was mentioned a second time (*NE* 11), as containing Sougdaia, Phoullai, Tamatarcha and Zichia in the Black Sea region.

[320] Meyendorff, *Byzantium and Rise of Russia*, 73–95.

[321] *Notitiae Episcopatuum*, ed. Darrouzès, 124–15, 367; Zuckerman, 'Byzantium's Pontic Policy in *Notitiae Episcopatuum*', 201–30; Mačinskij, 'Предпосылки, силы и контекст', 506; Nazarenko, 'Архиепископы в русской церкви', 67–76; Khaljavrin, 'Проблема становления новгородской архиепископии', 23–30; Nikulina and Kravčenko, 'Візантійські хроніки як джерело', 164–8; Bibikov, 'Byzantinorossica', 7–8; Kungurov, *Киевской руси не было*, 127–31; Kleščevskij, 'Россия – тысячелетнее имя руси', 12; Androshchuk, 'Byzantine Imperial Seals in Rus'', 44; Toločko, 'Киевская земля', 28.

Christianity is also discernible in sigillography via images on lead seals of particular saints like St Nicholas, which transcend retrospective ethnonational affiliations in Rus' and elsewhere in the Byzantine *oikoumene*.[322] Late-seventh-century Byzantine lead seals have been found in what later became the Rus' lands, indicating long-term Christian contacts.[323] A seal of emperor Basileios II Porphyrogennetos (r. 976–1025) was found in Belgorod (430km east of Kiev), attesting direct correspondence between the Rus' rulership and Basileios II Porphyrogennetos by the time of Vladimir's conversion.[324] Three other eleventh- to twelfth-century imperial seals have been found in Rus'. Two, found in the Černigov oblast', belonged to the emperors Nikephoros III Botaneiates (r. 1078–81) and Alexios I Komnenos (r. 1081–1118). The third, found near Kiev, belonged to emperor Manouel I Komnenos (r. 1143–80). Imperial seals, with images of Christ and the respective emperor, easily attest to the long-standing cooperation of Byzantine and Rus' rulers regarding Christian administration.[325] Elsewhere, eleventh- to twelfth-century finds of Byzantine seals of Crimean imperial officials (*spatharioi, protospatharioi, notarioi, strategoi, disypatoi*, etc.) in contemporaneous Volhynia attest to continued negotiation between imperial official families and aspirational Rus' autonomy.[326] Some imperial administrators themselves even identified as Rus': a nearly indecipherable late-eleventh-century seal records a certain *protovestiarios* (a Byzantine general or diplomat of high standing), Ioannes the Ros, with an image of the archangel Michael.[327] And eleventh-century ecclesiastical correspondence crossed the Black Sea from Byzantium and reached the northernmost regions of Rus'. For example, an early-eleventh-century seal of a certain Leon, metropolitan of Laodikeia, was found in Staraja Ladoga (120km east

---

[322] Ivakin et al., *Byzantine and Rus' Seals*; Cheynet, 'Sceaux byzantins de Londres', 85; Cotsonis, 'Saints and Cult Centers', 9–26; Stepanenko, 'Horseman in Sphragistics and Numismatics', 65–77; Stepanova, 'St. Nicholas on Byzantine Seals', 185–96.

[323] Wassiliou-Seibt, 'Kommerkiarios Seal from Constans II's Reign', 37–41.

[324] Androshchuk, 'Byzantine Imperial Seals in Rus'', 43–4; Bulgakova, *Byzantinische Bleisiegel*, 46; Poppe, 'Political Background', 230.

[325] Androshchuk, 'Byzantine Imperial Seals in Rus'', 46–51; Smolij et al., *1000 Years of Ukrainian Seal*, 43.

[326] Smÿčkov, 'Моливдовулов древней руси и херсонеса', 331–48; Smÿčkov, 'Византийских печатей с фамильными именами', 476–83; Haldon, 'Bureaucracies, Elites and Clans', 147–69; Feldman, 'Local Families, Local Allegiances', 202–18; Alekseenko, 'Relations entre Cherson et l'empire', 75–83; Alekseenko, 'Херсонская родовая знат в сфрагистики', 256–66.

[327] Laurent, *Collection Orghidan*, no. 69.

CASE STUDIES OF MONOTHEISATION   147

of St Petersburg).[328] Another early-eleventh-century seal, of a certain Damianos, was found in the Vologda region (400km north of Moscow).[329] Even twelfth-century Byzantine *boulloteria* (hand-held seal stamps) were found in 2011 in Novgorod, and these help identify Rus' princely seals using Greek-Christian baptismal names and imperial titles.[330]

Numerous, long-discussed ecclesiastical seals have been found referring to the Rus' as a land and people.[331] In some cases, seals identifying clerics like *proedroi* and metropolitans correspond to individuals mentioned in texts. Eleventh- to twelfth-century clerical lists mention a certain Konstantinos, *metropolites/proedros* of all Rus'ia; these match a mid-twelfth-century seal found in the village of Melnitsa, Bulgaria.[332] The Kiev excavations revealed the seal of a certain Theopemptos, metropolitan of Rus'ia, which was textually dated to the late 1030s.[333] A seal of Georgios, metropolitan of Kiev and *synkellos*, was dated precisely to his reign (1065–76) as he was the only Kievan metropolitan to bear this name.[334] Using texts, another seal of a certain Nikephoros, metropolitan of all Rus'ia, matched another seal of a metropolitan Nikephoros of Myra (present Demre in Turkey) in 1174.[335] A seal of a certain Michael, *poimenarches* (chief pastor) of Rus'ia (r. 1130–45), was found in Dinogetia, Romania, matching clerical records.[336] Even a seal of the well-known Rus' metropolitan St Maximos (r. 1286–1305) has been found.[337] Many more eleventh- to twelfth-century Rus' metropolitans' seals do not always match clerical records.[338] Eventually, ecclesiastical administration became

---

[328] Bulgakova, *Byzantinische Bleisiegel*, no. 1.3.4; Kirpičnikov and Kazanskij, 'Византийская митрополичья печать', 78–85.
[329] Šandrovskaja, 'Печати с изображениями анаргиров', 69–78.
[330] Alf'orov, 'Молівдовули київських князів', 8–37.
[331] Kamenceva and Ustjugov, *Русская сфрагистика и геральдика*, 70–3.
[332] Jordanov, 'Byzantine Seals from Melnitsa', 37–9, 57–9.
[333] Janin and Gajdukov, *Актове печати древней руси*, no. 41; Smolij et al., *1000 Years of Ukrainian Seal*, 45.
[334] Smolij et al., *1000 Years of Ukrainian Seal*, 45–6; Blažejovs'kij, *Hierarchy of Kyivan Church*, 77.
[335] Seibt, 'Interesting Byzantine Seals with Surnames', 87–9.
[336] Smolij et al., *1000 Years of Ukrainian Seal*, 48–9; Alf'orov, 'Молівдовули митрополита Михаїла', 151–8; Janin, *Актове печати древней руси*, cat. no. 48.
[337] Eidel, 'Seal of Maximos, Metropolitan of Kyiv and All Rus'', 231–4.
[338] Ephraim, *protoproedros* and metropolitan of Rus'ia, late eleventh century: Laurent, *Corpus des sceaux de l'empire byzantin I*, no. 783; Georgios: Bulgakova, 'Софийский корпус печатей', no. 5; Ioannes, late eleventh century, lake Beloozero: Laurent, *Corpus des sceaux de l'empire byzantin I*, no. 781; Ioannes, late eleventh century: Laurent, *Corpus des sceaux de l'empire byzantin II*, no. 1605; Konstantinos, late twelfth century: Laurent, *Corpus des sceaux de l'empire byzantin I*, no. 790; Kyrillos, early

routinised, prompting eleventh- to twelfth-century Rus' metropolitans to use seals anonymously evoking '*D'nislovo*', or 'everyday' type seals (1093–1113).[339]

Seals of specific Rus' rulers also survive, written in prototypical Cyrillic and clearly referring to the Rus' land and prince, yet saturated with Christian and Byzantine imperial imagery. These include lead seals of *archontes* (Vladimir Monomakh, r. 1112–25[340]) and *archontissai* (Theophano Mouzalonissa, late-eleventh century[341]). In eleventh- to twelfth-century Rus' seals, the Greek term *archon* was interchangeable with the Rus' term *knjaz'*, both carrying Christian symbolism.[342] The most notable example would be two seals of Vladimir's son, Jaroslav the Wise (r. 1019–54), found in Novgorod in 1994 and in 2008 in the Kiev oblast' respectively, which match his silver coinage. They display a bust of Jaroslav in typical Byzantine-appropriated regalia (*korzno* in Rus') and both bear the inscription 'ІѦРО-СЛАВЪ КНZ-Р8С-СКН' (Jaroslav, *knjaz'* of Rus').[343] Both seals also bear the bust of St George on the reverse, spelled in Cyrillo-Greek characters, Ⓐ ГЕѾРГНѼС, accompanying the inscription around the seal: 'ЯРОСЛАВЯ ПЕЧАТЬ' (Jaroslav's seal). Compared to Jaroslav's coins, both bear similar busts of St George whereas the image of Jaroslav himself on the seal is replaced by a trident on the coin, and instead of the inscription around the seal, 'ЯРОСЛАВЯ ПЕЧАТЬ', the coin reads instead 'ІѦРОСЛАВЯ СРЕБРО' (Jaroslav's silver).[344] These seals clearly show how

    thirteenth century, Cherson: Smolij et al., *1000 Years of Ukrainian Seal*, 49–50; Nikephoros, early twelfth century: Bulgakova, *Byzantinische Bleisiegel*, no. 3.2.3.5; Nikephoros, *poimenarches* (chief pastor) of Rus'ia, late twelfth century: Janin, *Актове печати древней руси*, no. 52; Niketas, bishop of Rus'ia, eleventh to twelfth century: Bulgakova, *Byzantinische Bleisiegel*, no. 3.2.3.6; Nikolaos, *proedros* of Rus'ia, late eleventh century, Constantinople: Laurent, *Corpus des sceaux de l'empire byzantin I*, no. 786.

[339] Smolij et al., *1000 Years of Ukrainian Seal*, 46–8; Kamencev and Ustjugov, *Русская сфрагистика и геральдика*, 72–3; Alf'orov, 'Молівдовули київських князів', 25–30; Eidel, 'Буллы князей Ярополка-Петра и Владимира-Василия', 53–68.

[340] *Povest' Vremennÿkh Let*, tr. Cross and Sherbowitz-Wetzor, *Russian Primary Chronicle*, 136–88; Janin and Gajdukov, *Актове печати древней руси*, nos 15–22; Bulgakova, *Byzantinische Bleisiegel*, no. 3.2.1.1; Raffensperger, *Reimagining Europe*, 63, 99.

[341] Janin, *Актове печати древней Руси*, no. 30; Bulgakova, *Byzantinische Bleisiegel*, no. 3.2.1.3; Ul'janovskij, 'булла Феофано Музалон "археонтессы Росии"', 54–87; Čkhaidze, 'Феофано Музалон', 268–93.

[342] Alf'orov, 'Молівдовули київських князів', 44–6.

[343] Stepanenko, '"Portraits of Princes in Sigillography of Rus"', 245–60; Alekseenko, 'Печать как иконографический источник', 23–31; Alf'orov, 'Інсигнії влади на давньоруських печатках', 32–46.

[344] Gajdukov and Kalinin, 'Древнейшие русские монеты', 402–35; Smolij et al., *1000 Years of Ukrainian Seal*, 30–2.

the Rus' land and its inhabitants were formed by the top-down imposition of Byzantine Christianity.[345]

Several classes of evidence show how Rus'ia, and by extension the Rus'ian Orthodox identity, came into existence through Byzantium. Namely, it was in the language of Byzantine Christianity that Rus' elites and potentates referred to themselves. This is especially evident in the seals of the Rus' *knjaz'* Jaroslav and in all seals referencing the *Russkaja Zemljÿ* (the Rus'ian land), such as metropolitans' seals in Greek referring to various metropolitans of all Rus'. But the term *archon* during this period could be used in a variety of ways, both *de jure* and *de facto*. While it was commonly used in concurrent Byzantine sources to refer to peripheral rulers, it could also describe otherwise local 'Byzantine' rulers as close as Crimea or Trebizond. Its appearance on eleventh- to twelfth-century seals should not warrant dividing Rus' seals from Byzantine seals; rather the elastic (and therefore universal) nature of terms such as *archon* bound Rus' and Byzantium into a common ecumenical framework at least up to the fifteenth century.[346]

Therefore, although Kievan Rus' is arbitrarily considered as a separate state solely during the reigns of its first major Christian rulers, Vladimir and Jaroslav (987–1054), it can also be conceived as subject to Byzantine law and administration. While it was undoubtedly part of Christendom from the turn of the eleventh century onwards, it was equally therefore part of the Byzantine *oikoumene*.[347] This is hardly to say that Rus' was *not* a 'proto-state,'[348] but only that sovereignty, whether Rus', Byzantine or any other case, was never absolute. After Jaroslav's death, historians refer to a fragmentation of Rus' principalities, thus insinuating an overemphasis on Rus' statehood during the previous half-century. Therefore, it is difficult to imagine Rus' as a single political entity after Jaroslav, since the only unifying factor in these towns, ruled as they were by alternating Rjurikid dynasts, was Byzantine Christianity. For this reason, it was Orthodoxy which eventually gave rise to the idea, centuries later, that there was still in fact a Rus' to be collected and unified (despite Orthodox outposts as far afield as the White Sea's Soloveckij monastery[349]), as was done by fifteenth-century Muscovite

---

[345] Sotnikova, 'Seal of Jaroslav the Wise', 221–9; Beletsky, 'Rus' Seals as Text', 235–44.
[346] Obolensky, *Byzantium and Slavs*, 84.
[347] Raffensperger, *Reimagining Europe*; Kovalev, 'Review: *Reimagining Kievan Rus'* [in Unimagined Europe]', 158–87.
[348] Franklin, 'Empire of "Romaioi" Viewed from Kievan Russia', 518–28.
[349] Wilk, *Journals of White Sea Wolf*, 9: 'On Solovki, you can see Russia like the sea in a drop of water. Because the Solovetsky Islands are at once the essence and the anticipation of Russia.'

rulers (and remains an animating principle in the Kremlin even into the twenty-first century, as attested by the Russia-Ukraine conflict since 2014).

Given the significance of the imperial establishment of the metropolitanates of Gotthia and Rus' for Pontic-Caspian Eurasia, we may come to understand the Rus' metropolitanate not so much as a 'proto-state', as frequently imagined, but as an imperial dominion in a broader Eurasian context, albeit a province ruled by local *archontes* (whom we now refer to as Rjurikid princes) and theoretically loyal to the imperial *oikoumene*.

Like other dynasties embarking on the processes involved in monotheisation (Āšĭnà of Khazaria, Almušids of Volga Bulgaria, Árpáds of Hungary), the Rjurikids' political formation of Rus' fell roughly into a few rudimentary and coinciding categories: Christianisation, sedentarisation, centralisation and literisation. While sedentarisation is most visible in archaeology, the other processes are more visible in texts, seals and coins, which reveal self-conscious references to a Rus' identity (as opposed to either Slav or Varangian/Norman identities) which, unlike Judaism in Khazaria, ultimately endured.

4

Monotheisation in Metal

לִי הַכֶּסֶף וְלִי הַזָּהָב נְאֻם יְהוָה צְבָאוֹת:

'The silver is mine and the gold is mine', declares the LORD Almighty.

Haggai 2:8 (*NIV*)

In the seventh to ninth centuries, the Islamic caliphs, Roman/Byzantine emperors and Khazarian *khağans* minted coins which proclaimed their respective monotheistic affiliations: Islam, Christianity and Judaism. This chapter explores how gold and silver coin reforms representing divinity were a major departure from previous coins which primarily represented rulers. The first section, 'Empires of Faith and their Finances', charts the confessional coin reforms of these three 'empires of faith' from the late seventh century to Khazaria's *Moses* coins of the late 830s. The second section, 'Coinage and "Commonwealth" (Ninth to Eleventh Century): the *Ummah* and the *Oikoumene*', expands to include the monotheistic coinages of some eleventh- to thirteenth-century peripheral dynasties within the Islamic *ummah* and the Christian *oikoumene* and explores hints of Judaic involvement in otherwise Islamic and Christian mints across the worlds of both Islam and Christendom.

Empires of Faith and their Finances

According to the mid-tenth-century *De Ceremoniis*, emperor Konstantinos VII ranked the Khazarian *khağan* after the Christian Roman emperor and the Islamic caliph in importance based on weight in gold on correspondence seals.[1] These *empires of faith* minted coins to display their respective

---

[1] Konstantinos VII Porphyrogennetos, *De Ceremoniis*, ed. Reiske, *De Ceremoniis Aulae Byzantinae*, 686–92.

official monotheisms as seventh- to ninth-century top-down political programmes.² As a 'third force',³ Khazarian coin reforms should be considered alongside the other two Abrahamic ecumenical empires.

Having conquered lands inhabited by erstwhile Roman subjects, early caliphs beginning with the Prophet Mohammed mostly avoided coin reforms.⁴ This changed in the years 696–7 under caliph 'Abd al-Malik, when the first purely Islamic coin,⁵ a gold dinar, appeared, manifesting the supremacy of the *Shahada* in Arabic, being the coins' only reference. This coinage initiated a period of expressly Islamic reforms for coinage and other domestic policies.⁶ Along with the coin reforms, these Islamisation policies were primarily reflected in the adoption of Arabic as the ruling language, dislodging 'Greek, Latin, Coptic, and Pehlevi'.⁷ While 'Abd al-Malik was not the first to attempt coin reform, historians still debate whether his policies influenced Byzantine iconoclasm.⁸ Numismatists also debate when, where and in what metrics⁹ reforms were implemented on caliphal mints in silver and base denominations,¹⁰ but few would argue that ecumenical supremacy was *not* contested on the Islamic coin reforms of al-Malik and his successors, especially regarding Christian coinage.

---

[2] Sarris, *Empires of Faith*; Crossley, *Hammer and Anvil*, 65–75.

[3] Shapira, 'Judaization of Central Asian Traditions', 505.

[4] Exceptions include the 'standing caliph coinage': Grierson, *Byzantine Coins*, 144–9; Album and Goodwin, *Islamic Coins in Ashmolean*, 91–8, nos 608–731; University of Birmingham's Barber Institute: A-B34–A-B39.

[5] Walker, *Arab-Byzantine and Post-Reform Coins*, nos 186–959; Broome, *Islamic Coins*, 6–19; Grierson, *Byzantine Coinage in International Setting*, 6; Goussous, *Bilad al-Sham*, 50–3; Foss, *Arab-Byzantine Coins*, 109–11; Robinson, 'Abd al-Malik, 72–80.

[6] Sarris, *Empires of Faith*, 299; Sears, *Monetary History of Iraq and Iran*; Treadwell, "Abd al-Malik's Coinage Reforms', 357–81; King, 'Islam, Iconoclasm, and Doctrine', 267–77; Ilisch, "Abd al-Malik's Monetary Reform', 125–46; Humphreys, '"War of Images" Revisited', 229–44; Grierson, 'Monetary Reforms of 'Abd al-Malik', 241–64; Bacharach, 'Signs of Sovereignty', 1–30.

[7] Walker, *Catalogue of Arab-Sassanian Coins*, xxxviii–xl; Treadwell, 'Byzantium and Islam', 145–55; Broome, *Islamic Coins*, 10–19.

[8] Sarris, *Empires of Faith*, 300; Brubaker and Haldon, *Byzantium in Iconoclast Era*, 1–68.

[9] Grierson, 'Monetary Reforms of 'Abd al-Malik', 248–64; Ilisch, "Abd al-Malik's Monetary Reform', 125–46; Treadwell, "Abd al-Malik's Coinage Reforms', 357–81; Kunkova, 'Торговые отношения арабов до династии Аббасидов', 57–60; Sears, *Monetary History of Iraq and Iran*, 188–320, 403–29.

[10] Nicol, *Sylloge of Islamic Coins in Ashmolean*, nos 1–1364; Shams-Eshragh, *Silver Coinage of Caliphs*, nos 224–803.

Perhaps al-Malik provoked the Christian emperor Justinian II by sending his new Islamic coinage as tribute, which was answered by a new Roman coin exhibiting Christ's portrait on the obverse,[11] and Justinian himself on the reverse (c. 689–91).[12] Conversely, it is also possible that Justinian II's Christ-type coinage may portend the earliest post-reform Islamic silver coinage.[13] Although numismatists debate this interpretation of conflict over coin iconography between Justinian and al-Malik, there is nevertheless textual evidence from Theophanes Omologetes (the Confessor) and al-Baladhuri that such conflict did exist in some form.[14] The contemporary Trullan Council's canon 82 perhaps also contributed to Justinian's coin reforms with Christ's depiction.[15] Regardless, Christ's appearance on Justinian II's coinage represents a break from precedent – a Christian coin reform.

Unlike al-Malik's coin reforms, which appeared rapidly in various metal denominations and mints, Justinian's monetary depiction of Christ appears in two distinct styles, corresponding to his two reigns,[16] and they only appeared from the mints of Sardinia and Constantinople. Christ's depiction on imperial coinage was discontinued after Justinian II's death (711) until Michael III's reign.[17] The Christ-type coinage appears only in gold and silver from Constantinople and in gold from Sardinian mints. There are no known base-metal Christ-type coins during Justinian's reign, and none whatsoever from Carthage, Syracuse, Rome or Ravenna. Because the era

[11] Sarris, *Empires of Faith*, 299; Grierson, *Byzantine Coinage in International Setting*, 7–8.
[12] Grierson, *Byzantine Coins in Dumbarton Oaks*, 568–70; Olster, 'Imperial Presentation in Islam's Victory', 45–72; Brubaker, *Inventing Byzantine Iconoclasm*, 18–19; Grabar, 'Islamic Art and Byzantium', 274–5.
[13] Shams-Eshragh, *Silver Coinage of Caliphs*, nos 224–803; Treadwell, "Abd al-Malik's Coinage Reforms', 357–81; Montinaro, 'Premiers commerciaires byzantins', 351–538.
[14] Theophanes, *Chronographia*, ed. de Boor, 365; tr. Mango et al., *Chronicle of Theophanes*, 509–11; al-Baladhuri, *Futuh al-Buldân*, ed. de Goeje, 240; Treadwell, 'Byzantium and Islam', 146–52.
[15] Breckinridge, *Numismatic Iconography of Justinian II*, 57; Grierson, *Byzantine Coins in Dumbarton Oaks*, 570; Hahn, *Moneta Imperii Byzantini von Heraclius bis Leo III*, 166; Morrisson, *Catalogue des Monnaies Byzantines de Bibliothèque Nationale*, 397; Humphreys, '"War of Images" Revisited', 233; Whitting, *Byzantine Coins*, 153–8; Haldon, *Empire that Would Not Die*, 48.
[16] Goodacre, *Coinage of Byzantine Empire*, 114–24; Vrij, 'Numismatic Iconography of Iconomachy', 85–97.
[17] Kent, *Byzantine Coins in Barber Institute*, nos 52–8; Sear, *Byzantine Coins and Values*, nos 1413–44; Sabatier, *Description générale des monnaies byzantines*, 19–35; Tolstoï, Византійскія Монеты, nos 27–39.

of iconoclasm (or *eikonomachia*) began decades into the eighth century, the disappearance of Christ's image from Byzantine gold coins immediately after 711 cannot evince immediate iconoclasm. While the reason for the temporary abandonment of Christ's depiction on Byzantine coinage remains unclear,[18] it is undeniable that Justinian II's coin reforms (689–711), featuring the expressly ecclesiastical *loros* along with a depiction of Christ, were meant to evoke allegiance to the Christian *oikoumene*, rather than to the Islamic *ummah*.

The eighth-century Christian and Muslim coin reforms contesting the Mediterranean may at first glance appear remote from Khazaria in the Pontic-Caspian steppe. Yet we recall from the previous chapter the extensive relations (war, commerce and diplomacy) between Khazaria and both Christian Rome and the Islamic Caliphate not only during the time of al-Malik and Justinian II, but throughout the eighth to tenth centuries. Both groups of rulers (Islamic caliphs and Roman/Byzantine emperors) sought to emulate the biblical king David.[19] Eventually, the Khazarian *khağans*, according to the *Khazar Correspondence*, followed suit. The *khağans* also sought to emulate contemporary 'Abbasid and other Islamic dynasties' coinages in their *Moses* coins, as previously discussed.[20] While there is less scholarship on the Khazarian Judaic coinage than on the two monotheistic coin reforms outlined above, I will discuss the Khazarian *Moses* coins, found in the Spillings 2 Hoard (and Ralswiek Hoard) on Gotland, and dated precisely to the year 837/838.

Understandably, this is the year that the scholar Roman Kovalev hypothesises a Khazar conversion, by juxtaposing the Khazarian Judaisation with Volga Bulgaria's Islamisation and Rus' Christianisation. Analysing three separate Khazarian coin types corresponding to the same die chain, all minted in Khazaria, the correctly dated (837–8) *Arḍ al-Khazar* ('land of Khazaria') dirhams, the *Moses* dirhams and the *Jalīl*/*Khalīl* dirhams (the latter two types bearing fictitious dates and mint marks[21]), Kovalev and Rispling determined that all shared the same dating (837–8) since they all shared the same die link (#108). Additionally, samples of each Khazarian dirham type have all been found alongside correctly dated 'Abbasid dirhams presumably having been deposited in cloth or leather sacks or wooden boxes.[22]

[18] Vrij, 'Numismatic Iconography of Iconomachy', 89–93.
[19] Sarris, *Empires of Faith*, 300; Magdalino and Nelson, 'Introduction', 1–38.
[20] Vachkova, 'Danube Bulgaria and Khazaria', 359.
[21] Rispling, 'Khazar Coins'; Kovalev, 'Khazar Identity through Coins', 226–7.
[22] Kovalev, 'Monetary History of Khazaria', 112–25; Pettersson (ed.), *Spillings Hoard*, 16.

Since Kovalev's dating methodology is numismatically sound, such numismatic evidence could suggest a Judaic attribution,[23] but ought not be overstated.[24] And while his research undoubtedly has far broader implications for Khazar studies, such a numismatic (and by extension archaeological) confirmation of Judaism-as-state-religion in Khazaria in 837/838 underscores the *Khazar Correspondence* and the *Schechter Text*.

With the same metrology as common Islamic dirhams, the *Moses* dirhams read: '*Mūsā rasūl Allāh*' alongside '*Mohammed rasūl Allāh*' (Moses/Mohammed is/are the messenger[s] of God).

As previously discussed (Chapter 2, the Monotheisation of Khazaria, the Advent of Khazarian Judaism), the second stage of the Khazarian *khağans*' conversion to Judaism may be cautiously attributed to 837/838. The *Moses* dirhams were possibly minted by a Jew, somewhere in Khazaria,[25] in clear imitation of Islamic dirhams, and that this was sanctioned by the rulership of Khazaria is confirmed by the text and dating of the *Arḍ al-Khazar* dirhams: 'the land of Khazaria'. These *Arḍ al-Khazar* dirhams also bear the same 'trident' tamga symbol, and Kovalev claims they symbolise the Khazarian ruling dynasty. Whether or not this connotes the Āšĭnà dynasty is speculative, but it would nevertheless imply that if the tamga appeared in reference to the Āšĭnà dynasty, then the coins would have been minted in Itīl. Kovalev also links this symbol with the Saltovo culture,[26] although this would be difficult to prove.[27] However, one of the tamgas found on a brick excavated by Artamonov from Sarkel appears almost exactly the same as this trident symbol found on the reverse of the *Arḍ al-Khazar* dirhams.[28] If this were to be verified, it could be that the coins of die chain #108 were struck in Sarkel, not Itīl.

Kovalev posits that the *Moses* dirhams were discontinued due to their ephemerality within Khazaria and their endemic disappearance northward to the lands of Rus'; yet, judging from these coins' imitation of Islamic coins, they were minted expressly to be traded northward in exchange for furs, honey, slaves and other goods valued in the Islamic world.[29] This raises the

---

[23] Golden, 'Khazar Studies', 43; Golden, 'Conversion of Khazars to Judaism', 156; Brook, *Jews of Khazaria*, 74–6.

[24] Wyszomirska, 'Religion som enande politisk-social länk', 140–1; Kulešov, 'Средиземноморье, балканы и восточная европа', 89.

[25] Shake, *Coins of Khazar Empire*, 31–55.

[26] Kovalev, 'Khazar Identity through Coins', 228–30; Brook, *Jews of Khazaria*, 74–6; Zhivkov, *Khazaria*, 59–65; Fomin, 'Рунические знаки и тамги', 187.

[27] Afanas'ev, 'Где археологические свидетельства хазарского государства', 43–55.

[28] Artamonov, *История Хазар*, 303.

[29] Kovalev, 'Khazar Identity through Coins', 237–40.

question: why would the Khazars discontinue their own coinage within one year when its sole purpose to be traded northward was being achieved?

Several theories have been proposed; all have merits. One possibility is that the *Moses* coins were minted and then traded northward as a means of extending Khazarian dominion to the north.[30] Another surmises that the purpose was to facilitate trade more than anything.[31] For example, such Khazarian (and Volga Bulgarian) imitation Islamic coinage made up 10 per cent of all ninth- to tenth-century silver coinage exported northward to the Baltic.[32] In fact, according to the scholar Marek Jankowiak, a mere 0.0007 per cent of all ninth- to tenth-century silver coins traded northward were such Khazarian *Moses* issues, suggesting it mattered little whether the coins themselves are classed as *miliaresia*, 'Mohammed' or 'Moses'. Jankowiak's database records only about 500 coins (dirhams) classed as Khazarian by origin, out of 10,000 such imitations in northern hoards. Of those roughly 500 Khazarian imitative dirhams, only 7 are *Moses* dirhams. Therefore, the Judaic nature of these coins ought not be overstated. Furthermore, given that only one die out of about 200 Khazar imitative dies mentions Moses, it is still uncertain whether there was any involvement of so-called 'state' power in its production.[33]

Yet the mention of Moses on these coins and the inherent reference to Judaism is indisputable. Judaisation would not have been easy for pagans to accept immediately,[34] a case which is quite similar to the difficulties al-Malik's predecessors encountered in their attempted reforms. Therefore, reflecting a schematic monotheisation template common to most Eurasian conversions (including a 'backsliding' phase[35]), the *Moses* dirhams may also have been discontinued due to a pagan reaction against top-down Judaisation,[36] since the Khazar *khağan* sought legitimacy via both Judaism and traditional Turkic sacral rulership.[37]

---

[30] Petrukhin, 'Sacral Kingship and Judaism of Khazars', 291.

[31] Shake, *Coins of Khazar Empire*, 75.

[32] Rispling, 'Nachahmungen islamischer Münzen', 172–220; Jankowiak, 'Two Systems of Trade', 137–48.

[33] Marek Jankowiak, personal communication, February 2017. His database forms part of the *Dirhams for Slaves* project at the Khalili Research Centre at the University of Oxford.

[34] Olsson, 'Coup d'état', 517.

[35] See above Chapter 2, the Monotheisation of Khazaria, the Advent of Khazarian Judaism.

[36] Petrukhin, 'Sacral Kingship and Judaism of Khazars', 298. A de facto *coup d'état* seems unlikely (cf. Komar, *Хазарское время*, 146; Olsson, 'Coup d'état', 513–16).

[37] Zhivkov, *Khazaria*, 55–65; above Chapter 2, the Monotheisation of Khazaria, the Advent of Khazarian Judaism.

The endurance (or lack) of confessional coin reforms of these three 'empires of faith' will be reflected politically and geographically in their respective peripheries, as each empire evolved into a 'commonwealth' of the *ummah* and the *oikoumene*, as local dynasties adopted various symbols on their own coinages to demonstrate their monotheistic allegiances.

Coinage and 'Commonwealth' (Eighth to Thirteenth Century): the *Ummah* and the *Oikoumene*

While much conventional scholarship has regarded history as the province of a given 'nation', this study of comparative numismatics first surveys the coinage of a number of ninth- to eleventh-century Christian and Muslim dynasties across Pontic-Caspian Eurasia. Numismatics can help refine our understanding of the top-down beginnings of ethnicity and sovereignty on which dynastic lineage has been predicated.[38] First we will examine the coinage of some ninth- to eleventh-century Islamic dynasties of Central Asia (Ṭāhirids, Ṣaffārids, Sāmānids, Volga-Bulgar Almušids) and next some synchronous Christian dynasties of Central/Eastern Europe (Piasts, Rjurikids, Árpáds, Danube-Bulgar Asenids). We frequently consider these Christian families the forerunners of the modern nations of Poland, Russia, Hungary and Bulgaria respectively, yet we would hardly make such an inference for the Ṭāhirids, Ṣaffārids, Sāmānids and Almušids respectively. In other words, juxtaposing these numismatic cases suggests that nationhood originally stemmed from loyalty to a given dynasty – not the product of an otherwise mystified medieval nebula of nations.

The final subsection, 'Hidden communities and coins across "Islamo-Christian civilisation"', addresses eighth- to thirteenth-century Judaic-related coins beyond Khazaria.

Coins of the ummah dynasties

Coins tell the story of how the initially centralised Islamic Caliphate evolved into a constellation of ninth- to eleventh-century Islamic dynasties in Eurasia. Four main Eurasian Islamic dynasties illustrate local autonomy within the Islamic Caliphate and with relevance to Khazaria: the Ṭāhirids, Ṣaffārids, Sāmānids and Volga-Bulgar Almušids. This analytical order demonstrates the continuity of religious evocation on Islamic coinage from Ṭāhir ibn Hussein's appointment as governor of eastern Khwārazmia (essentially the

---

[38] March, 'Genealogies of Sovereignty', 293–322; Escalona, 'Endings of Medieval Kingdoms', 5–6. For precisely this reason, I use the word 'polities' instead of 'states'.

northeastern regions of greater Persia) by the 'Abbasid caliphs (c. 821), and his family's (the Ṭāhirids') rivalry with the Ṣaffār family, who were later accommodated by the 'Abbasid Caliphate in the 870s.[39] The importance of local dynasties, while they were not necessarily appointed by the caliph, but nevertheless loyal to Sunni doctrine, underscores the importance of both loyalty and autonomy as predicated on the sovereignty of religious doctrine[40] – as has been exhibited on many Islamic coins.[41]

The mid-eighth-century 'Abbasid revolution preserved the basic Umayyad Islamic coinage and local provincial governors were appointed, who at first were customarily replaced, but by the ninth century began to foster their own dynasties.[42] Soon, powerful regional families exhibited aspirational autonomy. In the east, c. 821, Tāhir ibn Hussein's appointment as governor of Khwārazmia from Merv and Nishapur (present eastern Turkmenistan and northeastern Iran) engendered coins which were scarcely distinguishable from central 'Abbasid coins – regional autonomy is hardly detectable on these coins.[43] Such coins typically exhibit the ruling caliph's name and often even omit the Ṭāhirid ruler's name.[44] By the second half of the ninth century, the local Ṣaffārid dynasty began to usurp other urban centres in Khwārazmia at the expense of the Ṭāhirids from their bases in Sīstān and Zaranj (present eastern Iran and western Afghanistan). Ṣaffārid coins, like those of the Ṭāhirids, feature the ruling caliph's name, and are hardly distinguishable from those of the Ṭāhirids before them due to official recognition from the 'Abbasid Caliphate.[45] Yet the situation deteriorated, and by the early tenth century, the Ṣaffārid family was subdued by another clan, the Sāmānids, ruling from Samarqand and Tashkent (present

---

[39] Donner, 'Muhammad and Caliphate', 38. With the eventual 'Abbasid accommodation of the Sāmānid dynasty in Khwārazmia at the turn of the tenth century and the increasing flow of Central Asian silver dirhams towards northern Eurasia and Scandinavia – presumably in return for slaves amongst other commodities (see above Chapter 2, the Monotheisation of Khazaria, the Advent of Khazarian Judaism) – we can see genuine numismatic continuity from the Sāmānid coinage through the Khazarian and Volga Bulgarian coinages as well.
[40] Bosworth, *New Islamic Dynasties*, 4; March, 'Genealogies of Sovereignty', 293–322.
[41] Martín and Martín, 'Hallazgo de monedas almohades', 73–8; Noonan and Kovalev, 'Output of Spanish Umayyad Emirate', 253–60; Lowick, *Coinage and History of Islamic World*; Insoll, *Archaeology of Islam*, 149–65.
[42] Shams-Eshragh, *Silver Coinage of Caliphs*, 43.
[43] Bosworth, 'Ṭāhirids and Ṣaffārids', 90–106; Bosworth, 'Tahirids and Arabic Culture', 45.
[44] Shams-Eshragh, *Silver Coinage of Caliphs*, nos 998, 1119, 1136; Bosworth, 'Ṭāhirids and Ṣaffārids', 104; Broome, *Islamic Coins*, 62–3.
[45] Broome, *Islamic Coins*, 63–4.

eastern and northeastern Uzbekistan), who then granted autonomy to the Ṣaffārids for their nominal allegiance.⁴⁶ The coins produced in Sīstān during this period have accordingly been described as 'rebel issues'.⁴⁷

The best exhibition of local autonomy in ninth- to tenth-century Khwārazmia, therefore, is on Sāmānid dirhams. Although these were still based on standard 'Abbasid caliphal coins, the Sāmānids insisted their patronym appear on their coins alongside that of the 'Abbasid caliphs, a major innovation that continued well into the tenth century.⁴⁸ As silver production expanded and dirhams were increasingly traded northward in return for amber, wax, honey, furs and, primarily, slaves, the coinage attracted the attention of other rulers further north, who desired the benefits of monotheism while retaining their autonomy.

The best example of this exchange is arguably Almuš, the early-tenth-century convert to Islam, and ruler of the Volga Bulgars on the middle Volga, whose dynasty may be conveniently termed 'Almušids'.⁴⁹ After Almuš' adoption of Islam in the early 920s, early dirhams attributed to his dynasty have been described as 'imitative' of Sāmānid coinage, while later issues, by about 950, have been described as 'official' dirhams.⁵⁰ In other words, early Volga-Bulgar issues seldom evoke Volga Bulgaria itself, preferring instead to directly copy Sāmānid dirhams.⁵¹ But by the mid-tenth century, Volga-Bulgar dirhams reached an 'official' status, whereby Almušid dirhams commonly include Volga-Bulgar mint marks such as Suwār or Bolgar and the names of Almušid rulers, alongside the names of Sāmānid emirs and 'Abbasid caliphs in Baghdad.

Nevertheless, the importance of the information on an Islamic coin was secondary to its ultimate purpose: to be traded northward for slaves and other goods.⁵² When coins are juxtaposed, a pattern is discernible. Initially,

---

⁴⁶ Bosworth, 'Islam to Afghanistan', 17–19.
⁴⁷ Bosworth and Rispling, 'Ayyār Coin from Sīstān', 215–17.
⁴⁸ Broome, *Islamic Coins*, 66; Stern, 'Coins of Āmul', 213–25.
⁴⁹ Tor, 'Islamization of Central Asia', 279–99; Noonan, 'Trade of Volga Bulghāria with Sāmānid Asia', 140–219; Noonan, 'Output and Circulation of Sāmānid Mint', 163–74; Kovalev, 'Output in Bukhārā', 245–271; Kovalev, 'Output of Sāmānid Samarqand', 197–216; Gagin, 'Волжская булгария', 132–40.
⁵⁰ Marek Jankowiak, personal communication, February 2017; Kovalev, '"Official" Volga Bulġār Coins', 193–207.
⁵¹ Mako, 'Islamization of Volga Bulghars', 200; Mukhamadiev, *Булгаро-татарская монетная система*, 22–40.
⁵² Kazakov, 'Nature and Chronology of Volga Bulgar Trade'; Izmajlov, 'Ислам в волжской булгарии', 5–12; Curta, 'al-Andalus and Volga Bulghâria', 305–30; Mako, 'Islamization of Volga Bulghars', 199–223; Mukhamadiev, *Булгаро-татарская монетная система*, 22–40; Zhivkov, *Khazaria*, 157–8.

coin issues imitate those of older, established Islamic dynasties such as the 'Abbasid caliphs, then Ṭāhirids and Sāmānids. Later, they bear the marks of a distinct dynastic minting tradition, with inscriptions identifying the ruler, year and mint mark. All bear the traditional *Shahada*, signifying each dynasty's respective monotheistic allegiance to the Islamic *ummah* (and caliph) and reflect top-down Islamisation by the rulers. In theory, this would imply the centrality of the caliphal dynasty and doctrine and the remoteness of peripheral dynasties. In practice, however, peripheral dynasties gradually asserted their own autonomies on their coins.[53]

Similar patterns appear in the coinages of the ninth- to eleventh-century peripheral dynasties of the Christian *oikoumene* as well.

Coins of the oikoumene *dynasties*

The dynasties of the Piasts, Rjurikids, Árpáds and Asenids are normally considered the progenitors of the modern nations of Poland, Russia, Hungary and Bulgaria respectively. Yet they can also be seen as peripheral dynasties of the ninth- to eleventh-century Christian *oikoumene*. We can observe autonomous tendencies appearing in their respective Christian coinages, similarly to the cases of the Islamic dynasties in the previous subsection.

Beginning chronologically, the Piast family, based in tenth-century Gniezno and Poznań,[54] is best known as the first Christian Polish dynasty. Although Mieszko I is commonly thought to have converted to Christianity in 966, his son Bolesław minted the first Piast coins, and his grandson Mieszko II minted his own silver coinage inscribed with his name, *Misico*.[55] Bolesław's silver coins bore the Latin inscriptions PRINCE[P]S POLONIE, GNEZDUN CIVITAS and BOLIZLAUS REX,[56] thereby evoking his stronghold (Gniezno), name and titulature.[57] While these coins contrast with the Ṭāhirids' coins (in that they proclaim the peripheral ruler and his possessions), they recall the Sāmānids' dynastic nomenclature appearing alongside their own mint marks on their coins. Furthermore, these Piast coins

---

[53] Kristó-Nagy, 'Arab Rulers and Persian Administrators', 54–80.
[54] Urbańczyk, 'Strongholds in Polish Lands', 95–106.
[55] Suchodolski, 'Początki rodzimego mennictwa', 351–60; Urbańczyk and Rosik, 'Kingdom of Poland', 290.
[56] Suchodolski, *Moneta polska*; Szczesniak, 'Dependency of Kievan Rus on Bolesław', 31–43.
[57] Kiernowski, 'Teksty pisane na polskich monetach', 4–22; Berend et al., *Central Europe*, 146 n122.

exhibit Christian iconography such as the cross and peacock, symbolising Christ's resurrection and eternal life,[58] and consequently, Piast membership in the *oikoumene*. The coins are also comparable to concurrent Rjurikid coins, especially given the overlaps of their intended audiences.[59]

The first three Christian Rjurikid rulers, Vladimir (converted 988[60]), Svjatopolk (r. 1015–19) and Jaroslav (r. 1019–54), minted their own silver (*srebreniki*) and gold (*zlatniki*) coins, although few survive. These coins were frequently used symbolically in a tenth- to eleventh-century burial context, in a way that is opposed to traditional assumptions of monolithic usage in trade.[61] That they were also based on Byzantine coinage indicates their preferred mode of legitimacy: ecumenical[62] rather than 'national' coinage.[63] For example, Jaroslav's coins bear the Byzantine iconography of his Christian namesake with Greek-Cyrillic inscriptions: ЯРОСЛАВЛЕ СРЕБРО (Jaroslav's silver) and АГ. ГЕѠРГНѠ (St George). Jaroslav's matching of his Christian iconography on both his coins and seals accentuates the centrality of ecumenical Christianity by which he sought legitimacy.[64] But like Khazarian currency, these coins too were traded northward, and the relative absence of coinage between c. the 1130s and 1380s suggests that taxes were still paid in kind, especially because Jaroslav is the last Kievan ruler known to have minted coinage before this period.[65] While Rus' statehood has been accepted uncritically based on the tenth- to eleventh-century coinage, it may equally be challenged by the disappearance of so-called 'national' coinage during the twelfth to fourteenth centuries. This notion, however, may be harder to challenge regarding the Árpáds.

Having converted to Christianity c. 1000, Stephen, the Magyar ruler, began minting silver coins. The bullion was probably mined near present

---

[58] Urbańczyk and Rosik, 'Kingdom of Poland', 291; Pleszczynski, *Birth of Stereotype*, 146; Suchodolski, 'Czy orzeł polski ma tysiąc lat?', 1–12; Berend et al., *Central Europe*, 146–7.
[59] Szczesniak, 'Dependency of Kievan Rus on Bolesław', 31–43; Hleboniek, 'Herb Ziemi Kijowskiej na pieczęciach', 82–98.
[60] Feldman, 'How and Why Vladimir Besieged Cherson', 145–70.
[61] Pavlova, 'Coinless Period in Rus'', 375–6; Sedykh, 'Function of Coins', 471–8.
[62] Spassky, *Russian Monetary System*, 50–1; Gajdukov and Kalinin, 'Древнейшие русские монеты', 402–35.
[63] Zguta, 'Kievan Coinage', 488.
[64] See above Chapter 3, Case Studies of Monotheisation in Eighth- to-Thirteenth-Century Pontic-Caspian Eurasia, Rus': Byzantine Christianisation.
[65] Pavlova, 'Coinless Period in Rus'', 375–92; Zguta, 'Kievan Coinage', 484; Feldman, 'Bullion, Barter and Borders', 1–12; Pritsak, *Old Rus' Weights and Monetary Systems*, 115; Noonan, 'Monetary History of Kiev', 401–2.

Banská Štiavnica (central Slovakia). That his coinage survives in a moderate quantity indicates the extent to which he monopolised the mining of new bullion for his mintage; unlike neighbouring dynasties, the Árpáds had ready access to productive silver mines.[66] Similar in metrology to Piast coins, most Árpád coins bear ecumenical symbols such as crosses and Latin inscriptions: LANCEA REGIS (with a lance), REGIA CIVITAS and STEPHANUS REX with either a church or a crown on the reverse.[67]

Notably, some coins of Stephen's successors, Peter I (r. 1038–41, 1044–6) and Andreas I (r. 1046–60), also bear the geographical name PANNONIA/PANONEIA, which, like the Piasts' PRINCE[P]S POLONIE coins, may indicate an emerging geographical focus on such coins.[68] Perhaps this suggests a general trend towards peripheral dynastic differences between the tenth- to eleventh-century Latin West and Orthodox East.

The twelfth- to thirteenth-century coinage of the Asen family of the lower Danube may also contribute to improving our understanding of antique 'statehood' and 'national' coinage in the Christian *oikoumene*. First, we note that numismatic evidence cannot substantiate the traditional, national narrative of Bulgarian sovereignty (the first and second Bulgarian Empires), because no coins of the first Christian Bulgarian monarchs after Boris' conversion in the 860s are known. The earliest known coins described as Bulgarian belong to the Asenids around the turn of the thirteenth century.[69] Numismatists debate whether this coinage can be considered 'tsarist' minting by the Asenids or simply local counterfeiting, since it is hardly distinguishable from concurrent Byzantine base-metal coinage and seals.[70] It is primarily documented from the Northern Thracian Plain and the Sredna

---

[66] Ödön, 'Magyarország barbárpénzeinek áttekintése', 59–63; Gedai, *A magyar pénzverés kezdete*, 9–25; Csiky, *Magyar Pénzek*; Unger, *Magyar éremhatározó I-IV*; Fejér and Huszár, *Bibliographia Numismaticae Hungaricae*; Engel, *Realm of St. Stephen*, 62–3.

[67] Berend et al., *Central Europe*, 156; Szentgáli, 'Az "Árpádok" specializálása', 20–3; Szentgáli, 'Bizanc pénzei', 187–209; Gedai, 'Pénzverés', 541–2; Kovács, 'Coinage and Other Currency in Hungary', 125–6; Jeszensky, 'Az első Magyar rézpénzek', 3–46.

[68] Réthy and Probszt, *Corpus Nummorum Hungariae*, nos 171–96; Huszár, *Münzkatalog Ungarn*, nos 1–30; Hóman, *Magyar Pénztörténet*; Gedai, *A magyar pénzverés kezdete*, 26–55.

[69] Metcalf, *Coinage in South-Eastern Europe*, 127; Hendy, *Coinage and Money in Byzantine Empire*, 221. This analysis is derived from the examples in the University of Birmingham's Barber Institute (nos B6560 ADD–B6565 ADD; B6049–B6062).

[70] Atanasov, 'Durostorum–Dorostol(os)–Drastar/Dristra–Silistra', 565–71; Jordanov, 'Взаимоотношения киевской руси, византии и болгарии', 368–75; Thomson, 'Bulgarian Contribution to Byzantine Culture in Rus'', 214–61; Alf'orov, 'Княжі знаки на печатках київської русі', 102–34.

Gora, and bears the iconography of three contemporary emperors: Manouel I Komnenos, Isaakios II Angelos and Alexios III Angelos.

However, these Bulgarian imitations can be distinguished from Byzantine originals by the jewelling on the imperial *loros* – the imperial vestment. Additionally, few Komnenian imperial coins were found in contemporaneously Asenid-ruled areas mentioned above, while the majority of these 'imitative' coins are found in such areas. Yet base-metal coinage was far more subject to questions of authenticity[71] and so Kalojan Asen received papal permission to mint coins in his own name (1203–4); this comprised a different coinage altogether.[72] But it should be noted here that no coins of Kalojan Asen himself are known. The first known coins of his dynasty belonged to his grandson, Ivan II Asen (r. 1218–41), whose gold coins have engendered much numismatic debate.[73] Still, despite minor differences between concurrent Byzantine base-metal coins (*folleis*) and the 'Bulgarian imitative coinage', due to the invocation of imperial authority, these need not be referred to exclusively as Bulgarian national coinage – these coins are equally conceivable as imperial coins minted by local representatives.[74]

From a comparison of the coins of the Islamic caliphs and peripheral Eurasian dynasties of the *ummah* to those of the Christian emperors and peripheral Eurasian dynasties of the *oikoumene*, broader numismatic developments are conceivable in greater context rather than as isolated coinage traditions within various national histories.[75] The differences in coin metrology and iconography between peripheral dynasties of the *oikoumene* and *ummah* and the imperial/caliphal mints themselves may be attributable to their respective capacities to acquire precious metals. Since gold and silver were obtained primarily by war or mining, taxation represented a relatively inelastic circuit. Rulers therefore had a limited supply of bullion for minting coins, reflecting a relatively inelastic amount of bullion available. This explains the lack of 'Rus' national' coins in circulation during much of the twelfth to fourteenth centuries.[76] Therefore, for most rulers, the predominant form of political economy was to acquire more bullion, which along with rulers' protectionist policies, like capital controls

[71] Maria Vrij, personal communication, November 2016.
[72] Hendy, *Coinage and Money in Byzantine Empire*, 219–22.
[73] Hendy, *Byzantine Coins in Dumbarton Oaks*, 82, 135–6; Gălăbov, 'Златна ли е златната монета на Йоан Асен II', 23–40.
[74] Metcalf, *Coinage in South-Eastern Europe*, 127; Jordanov, *Монетни в средновековна България*, 59–66; Avdev, *Монетната система в средновековна българия*, 21–9.
[75] Berend, *Christianization and Monarchy*.
[76] Feldman, 'Bullion, Barter and Borders', 1–12.

and other interventions to ensure a suitable balance of trade, effectively amounted to early versions of the political economy of mercantilism.[77] Yet at such an early stage, the circulation of coinage at this time was therefore not meant as its supreme function; the purpose of minting coins was political: to exhibit a ruler's wealth, power and legitimacy to his subjects.

Hidden communities and coins across 'Islamo-Christian civilisation'

Certain coins in the eighth- to thirteenth-century *ummah* and *oikoumene* reveal an otherwise hidden Eurasian community across 'Islamo-Christian civilisation'.[78] Building on textual research,[79] recent coin circulation research exposes long-range and local eighth- to thirteenth-century Jewish merchant communities (primarily Radanites) traversing both the *ummah* and the *oikoumene*; this research includes, but is not limited to, Khazarian coinage.[80] While long-range and local Jewish merchant communities were certainly not the only merchant communities,[81] important distinctions between long-range and local commerce suggest that local buying power proves a better measurement of economic vitality than the existence of long-range traders willing to exploit such a market.[82]

Many disparate Eurasian single finds and coin hoards suggest Jewish (perhaps Radanite) merchants. For example, finds of mixed eighth- to tenth-century Byzantine-Islamic coin hoards found in the northern Black Sea littoral and southern Rus'[83] can be contextualised alongside the ostensibly Judaic-related hoards of eighth- to ninth-century Byzantine and Islamic gold coins found in Khazaria,[84] particularly in Crimea and

---

[77] Soročan, 'Случайность или система?', 122–32; Feldman, 'Mercantilist Thought in Byzantium'.
[78] Bulliet, *Islamo-Christian Civilization*, 15–32.
[79] Goitein, *Mediterranean Society*; Holo, *Byzantine Jewry in Mediterranean Economy*; Starr, *Jews in Byzantine Empire*; Sharf, *Byzantine Jewry*.
[80] Kulešov, 'Средиземноморье, балканы и восточная европа', 89–92.
[81] Golovnëv, *Антропология движения*, 469–70.
[82] Wickham, 'Donkey and Boat'; Holmes and Standen, 'Global Middle Ages', 112.
[83] Noonan, 'Byzantine Coins in Rus'', 143–81; Stoljarik, *Monetary Circulation*, 93–6; Malmer, 'Importation of Byzantine Coins to Scandinavia', 295–8; Androshchuk, 'Byzantium and Scandinavian World', 147–92; Thompson, 'Byzantine Coins in Russia', 145; Kropotkin, 'Клады византийских монет', 1–89; Kropotkin, 'Находки византийских монет', 166–89; Janin, *Денежновесовые системы*.
[84] Semenov, 'Slavyansk (Anastasiyevka) Hoard', 82–5; Gurulëva et al., 'Славянского (Анастасиевского) клада', 136–86.

Taman'. Egyptian, northern Italian, Sicilian and Sardinian coins have also been found in Khazaria, and these can be associated with Judaic mints and merchants according to the numismatist Kulešov.[85] Corresponding finds include: eleventh-century Barcelonan *mancúsii* found in the middle Dniepr,[86] twelfth- to thirteenth-century Selčuq *fals* found in Crimea and the middle Dniepr,[87] twelfth-century European silver *bracteates*[88] found in the middle Dniestr[89] and, finally, twelfth- to thirteenth-century Byzantine *tracheai* (and Bulgar 'imitative' coins) found in northern Rus'.[90] All correspond to well-known trade routes connecting known Jewish urban communities across the *ummah* and *oikoumene*. Individually, these hoard finds and single finds say little, but alongside undeniable Judaic mintings (like Khazarian *Moses* dirhams) and textual documentation,[91] while not excluding Christian or Muslim merchants, a Judaic attribution of these eighth- to thirteenth-century finds across both *ummah* and *oikoumene* is easily conceivable.

Lead seals also link the Jewish communities of Constantinople and Trebizond to those of Crimea, Taman' and elsewhere in Khazaria. One twelfth-century lead seal (possibly Georgian or southern Italian) references a silversmith named 'Theudatos Kurkutes' (תוי־טוס קורק־טיס), a Greek name, with a four-line metrical inscription in Hebrew. This seal is similar to contemporaneous Byzantine lead seals, and might even relate to Khazaria.[92] Another example, a fifth- to seventh-century rectangular bronze sealing device from Trebizond, contains the otherwise misspelled Christian Greek

---

[85] Kulešov, 'Средиземноморье, балканы и восточная европа', 93; Gončarov and Čkhaidze, 'Находки монет на таманского полуострова', 343–7; Čkhaidze, 'Таманские монеты – Original or Fake?', 113–19.

[86] Kulešov, 'Манкус барселонского графства', 211–17; Martínez, 'Mancús de Ramon Berenguer', 47–53; Archibald, 'Coins from Spanish Mints in England', 377–96; Bensch, *Barcelona and Its Rulers*.

[87] Gončarov, 'Восточная нумизматика херсона', 118–32; Khromov, 'Находки исламских монет', 1–11.

[88] *Bracteates* are coins or simple ingots which have been struck on only one side, leaving the reverse as a thin, sheet-like blank; see for example Friedenberg, *Medieval Jewish Seals*, 244, 270.

[89] On the potential misattribution to 'Western' and 'Eastern' Christendom in the coins of the eleventh to twelfth century, see Kulešov, 'Средиземноморье, балканы и восточная европа', 94–5 nn49–51.

[90] Gurulëva and Fëdorova, 'Шелонский клад', 63–99.

[91] Kulešov, 'Средиземноморье, балканы и восточная европа', 89–92; Goitein, *Mediterranean Society* I, 359–61; Mell, 'Money in Medieval Ashkenaz', 125–58; Schiffman, 'Coins in Jewish Jurisprudence', 141–60.

[92] Friedenberg, *Medieval Jewish Seals*, no. 177.

name Εφθυ|μίου (of Euthymios) along with unquestionably Jewish symbols: a large seven-branched *menorah*, an *etrog* (a ceremonial citrus) and a *shofar* (a ram's horn).[93] These lead seals undoubtedly indicate trans-Black Sea Byzantine Jewish communities.

These coinages reveal the interrelationship between minting and monotheisation. Monotheistic iconography and alphabet confirm each dynasty's ecumenical allegiance, as opposed to showing 'national' coinages. Comparative numismatics demonstrates such anachronisms, while maintaining the concept of monotheism as more than simply a given creed; rather it is a mode of legitimisation and a top-down process of identity formation.

Therefore, we can better conceive the developing peripheral autonomy on the coins of the eighth- to eleventh-century Islamic *ummah* dynasties of the Ṭāhirids, Ṣaffārids, Sāmānids and Almušids contrasting to the peripheral autonomy on the coins of the eighth- to eleventh-century Christian *oikoumene* dynasties.[94] In this manner, numismatic evidence may insinuate a stronger centralised nature of the Islamic Caliphate than that of the concurrent Christian Roman empire. Similarly, by contextualising the coins of the Ṣaffārid and Sāmānid dynasties alongside those of the Piasts and Árpáds, we take Poland and Hungary as nations at face value, but where are the equivalent present nations for the former Islamic dynasties? We might even reconsider the idea of the Piasts as founding Poland or the Árpáds Hungary. Comparatively, would we imagine that the Ṣaffārids or Sāmānids founded Uzbekistan or Tajikistan? Assuming that nationality or sovereignty can be projected backwards as early as possible is frequently anachronistic. And few classes of evidence demonstrate that better than coins.

---

[93] Feissel et al., *Trois donations byzantines*, 13.
[94] Haldon, *Warfare, State and Society*, 276–7.

A Reassessment of Civilisation in Pontic-Caspian Eurasia

His eyes are staring, his mouth is open, his wings are spread. This is how one pictures the Angel of History. His face is turned towards the past. Where we perceive a chain of events, he sees one single catastrophe which keeps piling wreckage upon wreckage and hurls it in front of his feet. The angel would like to stay, awaken the dead, and make whole what has been smashed. But a storm is blowing in from Paradise; it has got caught in his wings with such violence that the angel can no longer close them. This storm irresistibly propels him into the future to which his back is turned, while the pile of debris before him grows skyward. This storm is what we call progress.[1]

A nation is born stoic, and dies epicurean. At its cradle (to repeat a thoughtful adage) religion stands, and philosophy accompanies it to the grave.

Will Durant, Our Oriental Heritage

Дурак завяжет – и умный не развяжет.
A fool ties a knot even the wise can't untie.

Russian proverb

Regardless of time or place, the monotheisation process has occurred at the frontiers of each monotheistic empire (*oikoumene/ummah*) and involved

---

[1] Benjamin, *Illuminations*; cited in Anderson, *Imagined Communities*, 161–2. Anderson's footnote reveals more: 'The angel's eye is that of *Weekend*'s back-turned moving camera, before which wreck after wreck looms up momentarily on an endless highway before vanishing over the horizon.' The highway seems endless because it is a möbius strip.

top-down indoctrination and the imposition of monotheistic laws, through which norms and identities were later internalised. Understanding religious identity this way, as a base-layer of current national identity rather than a simple milestone in a national history, necessarily challenges the way history is typically understood – not as a national story, but as an ecumenical story, in which it is a given *oikoumene*, or monotheistic civilisation, that originates present identities, instead of primordial ethnicity. This requires the untying of the Gordian knot of tribalism, ethnicity and nationalism, which have been long conflated. In distinguishing between these perplexing categorisations (ethnicities, empires, civilisations), we will turn towards the dangers of separating the 'ancient' from the 'medieval', which have long perpetuated lazy assumptions about the tripartite division (ancient, medieval, modern) of history. Without these loaded terms, we can view Pontic-Caspian Eurasia as part of a template binding Western History to Global History.

Original inquiry and historiographical evaluation should be simultaneous endeavours, not separate affairs. As demand increases for both *relevant* and *original* research, to eschew one for the other would be to verge on either irrelevance or conformity. This inquiry originally proposed to assess both the short- and long-term consequences of monotheisation. The monotheisation of Pontic-Caspian Eurasia also demonstrates that periodisations like 'antiquity' and 'Middle Ages', commonly used as shorthand in Western historiography, cannot apply globally. At best these arbitrarily assigned periodisations obfuscate authentic civilisational analysis and at worst they lay grievous historical misconceptions as foundations of myopic political agendas. Rather than re-narrating current national histories, this inquiry seeks to view these stories backwards, knowing that the past can only be a province of the present, despite the preference for conceiving history without present interpretation. Thus, these broadly drawn, comparative conclusions will make a brisk, if conditional, case for monotheisation as a method of civilisational analysis in a world decreasingly defined by nations and increasingly defined by civilisations.

Monotheisation Revisited

Monotheisation until the thirteenth century

The early-thirteenth century saw twin crises gripping the Orthodox and Islamic worlds: the ascendancy of the Latin West and the pagan Mongols. The *Novgorod First Chronicle* records the Battle of the River Kalka, when the Mongol armies of Subutai and Jebe squared off against a combined Rus'–Cuman alliance near present-day Mariupol' beside Lake Maeotis (the Sea of Azov) on 31 May, 1223.[2] It was the crushing first of many Mongol victories in their devastating drive westward and would not be the last time an eastern army commenced a campaign westwards from Mariupol'. The Cuman-Qıpčaqs, as a distinct force, were already spent and, except for their soon-to-be deposed (and baptised) *khağan* Köten, were effectively absorbed by their conquerors, like the Pečenegs previously.[3] Pagan refugees were eventually absorbed by monotheistic populations.[4] Collectively, however, the Rus', throughout centuries of Mongol rule, did not assimilate into paganism. The eleventh- to fifteenth-century Rus' lands are commonly described as fragmented, which overstates Rus' unity beforehand, yet the interpretation lingers, since Rus' identity was predicated on Orthodoxy, supposedly waiting to be 'collected' later by Muscovite rulers such as Ivan III.

When the Fourth set of Crusaders and their Venetian sponsors pillaged Constantinople in early April 1204, the resulting *partitio imperii* split the contiguous empire apart, not on supposedly ethnic lines, but on confessional lines. The splinter dynasties from Nikaea to Epiros fought over much, but they nevertheless shared Orthodox identities. When viewed at comparative scale, the underlying logic is clear.

Despite the overarching difference between the Mongols, Selčuqs and Crusaders as opposite invading forces due to their respective monotheistic subscriptions (or none at all), the confessional aspect of loyalty can hardly be overstated. Despite the 'usual cocktail of political expediency',[5] the final lodestar of loyalty remained confessional affiliation, not retrospectively assigned ethnicity or sedentarism versus nomadism.[6] As for nomadism, the thirteenth-century Mongol invasions are the last recorded nomadic incursions of the sedentary Balkans.[7] Afterwards, nomads remained in the

---

[2] *Novgorod First Chronicle*, tr. Michell and Forbes, *Chronicle of Novgorod*, 64–7.
[3] Al-Mas'ūdī, *Meadows of Gold*, tr. Minorsky, *Sharvān and Darband*, 107, 130; Golden, 'Khazar Sacral Kingship', 91; Korobeinikov, 'Broken Mirror', 406; Toločko, *Кочевые народы степей и киевская русь*, 123; Woodfin et al., 'Foreign Vesture and Nomadic Identity', 155–86.
[4] Al-Mas'ūdī, *Meadows of Gold*, tr. Minorsky, *Sharvān and Darband*, 130; Golev, 'Edge of Another World', 89–126; Sardelić, 'Kumani-Kipčaci između Azije i Europe', 247–74; Golden, *Nomads and their Neighbours*, 132–57.
[5] Stephenson, *Byzantium's Balkan Frontier*, 313.
[6] Konjavskaja, 'Половцы в ранних летописях', 187–8; Zhivkov, *Khazaria*, 268–83; Anievas and Nişancioğlu, *How West Came to Rule*, 70–1; Neumann and Wigen, *Steppe Tradition in International Relations*, 178–94.
[7] Vásáry, *Cuman and Tatars*, xi.

steppe, but they increasingly adopted monotheism (as Christian Cossacks, Islamic Kazakhs, etc.) in later centuries – despite arbitrary diachronic distinctions between steppe and sedentary peoples.[8]

The thirteenth-century Orthodox communities of Eastern Europe are a case in point. Those who adhered to Orthodoxy instead of adopting their respective conquerors' faith (Latin Christian, Sunni Muslim) defined the subsequent populations as Romans, Rus'ians and other Orthodox peoples.[9] There is little evidence of reversion to paganism, despite widespread cooperation with the Mongols. But what made them Orthodox in the first place was not primordial ethnicity; it was generations of monotheisation: top-down identity internalisation, or what Russian sociologists deem the *potestarian process*.[10]

Monotheisation: a global perspective

The process of top-down monotheisation is a long and ubiquitous one. It is not confined to Europe, Asia, Africa or the Americas. Nor is it confined to so-called 'antiquity' or the 'Middle Ages'. It permeates these regions and transcends these periodisations. Yet it amalgamates the attendant processes of the adoption of a given monotheism by a given ruler and usually his dynasty's gradual, top-down coercion and indoctrination of their subjects into their chosen faith. This is not to say that bottom-up monotheism was not a factor; it certainly was. Top-down monotheisation was only possible after a critical mass of bottom-up conversion had already occurred. Usually monotheisation includes one or more of the following processes: a dynasty's adoption of a sacred text, its liturgical script, version of history and its laws, the sacralisation of a capital city, the sedentarisation (typically along rivers or coastlines) of the dynasty's subjects and the transformation of tribute into tax. Monotheisation can describe the legal adoption of many faiths: Judaism, Christianity, Islam and so on. The Rjurikids adopted Orthodox Christianity and imposed it on their subjects; the Almušids, Sunni Islam; the Piasts, Latin Christianity. This process can be seen everywhere

---

[8] Zhivkov, *Khazaria*, 281–3; Anthony, *Horse, Wheel and Language*; Paroń, 'Nomadic State of Early Medieval Europe', 163–82; Paroń, 'Power and Social Structures', 357-c. 90362; Paroń et al., *Potestas et Communitas*; Neumann and Wigen, *Steppe Tradition in International Relations*, 13.

[9] Papageorgiou, *Από το γένος στο έθνος*, 31–78.

[10] Popov, *Потестарность*; Popov, 'Этничность и потестарность', 13–20; Jakhšijan, 'Общинное самоуправление и государственное управление', 285–91; Šmurÿgina, 'Концепта потестарности', 34–7.

from the Tanakh's (Old Testament's) Davidic dynasty to Persia's Safavids to England's Tudors (respectively: Judaism, Shi'ism, Anglicanism). It may even apply to non-Abrahamic and Vedic faiths due to their sacred laws (for instance, *Dharmaśāstra* in Hinduism and Buddhism[11]) or Protestant-influenced American civil religion. Nevertheless, top-down monotheisation is common across time and space, although the choice of monotheism is initially a practical, political choice, later mythologised – for example: Brumidi's *Apotheosis of Washington*.

Therefore, Europe, as a geographical region, need not necessarily have evolved into Christendom, nor the Middle East necessarily have become Islamic; this shallow interpretation of history views historical processes as they have resulted, instead of as they could have unfolded but failed to do so (teleological history). For example: Khazaria, in Pontic-Caspian Eurasia, was neither fully Christian nor Islamic, and yet both European and Asian; the Khazars failed to fully Judaise their subjects as other dynasties respectively Christianised or Islamised theirs.

Monotheisation presupposes the joining of an ecumenical club (a civilisation): Orthodox, Latin, Sunni and so on. This aspect of monotheisation explains why, removed from the centres of each faith (Constantinople, Rome, Baghdad, etc.), peripheral dynasties (Rjurikids, Piasts, Almušids, etc.) cannot be described as constituting sovereign states (called 'Westphalian sovereignty' after the 1648 Peace of Westphalia) as one would describe current nation-states. How can Westphalian sovereignty precede 1648?[12] Instead, peripheral dynasties were preoccupied with shifting confessional allegiances.

Ultimately, many recent identifications of ethnic origins (*origo gentis*/ ethnogenesis) may be attributable to top-down monotheisation exemplified in Byzantium: by the top-down imposition of the ruling faith on subjects.[13] Unlike sovereignty, the Westphalian axiom *cuius regio, eius religio* (whoever rules, his religion) undoubtedly arose from earlier precedents. Without presuming to reject all ethnic classifications categorically, this is what makes today's ethnicity *seem* primordial even if it is not, despite pre-monotheistic *ethne* being thus described.[14] Therefore, ethnicity may be described as both situational (or circumstantial) and as seemingly primordial, but not

[11] Mauss, *Gift*, 176–7 n52.
[12] Morgenthau, *Politics among Nations*, 243–63; Marx, *Faith in Nation*; Jaffrelot, 'Theory of Nationalism', 1–51.
[13] Derks and Roymans, *Ethnic Constructs in Antiquity*, 1; Dzino, '"Becoming Slav", "Becoming Croat"', 196.
[14] Golovnëv, 'О традициях и новациях', 84.

simultaneously so. It is situational until, through generations-long top-down monotheisation, it finally *seems* primordial, due to the internalisation of confessional identity, laws, traditions and so on, even if it is not.

Tribalism, ethnicity and nationalism: renegotiating historical identity

If present ethnic identities can be viewed as the surviving residue of generations of monotheisation attempts, this idea does not explain why some monotheisations failed (such as Khazarian Judaisation). However, as the exception, Khazaria proves the rule: whatever other identities came and went on the Volga, the Danube, the Pannonian plain (or elsewhere in Eurasia), each region still today retains the residue (the confessional identity) of a previous dynasty, respectively Sunni Islamic, Orthodox Christian and Latin Christian; hence many nationalists' preoccupation with primordial ethnicity (or autochthonousness). Khazaria is an excellent case study of ethnogenesis because the Khazarian identity, except for some thoroughly debunked anti-Semitic theories, remains unclaimed today.[15] Yet it would be quite contentious to suppose that Khazarian identity, however indeterminable, could exemplify both pagan and monotheistic ethnicities. Zhivkov's inconsistent descriptions of Khazarian identity are a telltale case in point.

Like many ambiguous reviews of historical identity (especially in Eastern Europe[16]), Zhivkov's analysis distinguishes little between pre-monotheistic tribe and monotheised ethnicity, thereby conflating ethnicity with pagan tribalism. Both are cited without identifying a difference:

> Usually, the Khazar elite's conversion to Judaism is interpreted in light of the practice, widespread in the contemporary Khazaria 'barbarian' lands, whose nobility imposed Christianity or Islam on its subjects. This practice is viewed as a deliberate attempt to unify into an ethnic whole the often multilingual and multi-ethnic population that professed different cults. The adoption of a common religion is thus considered one

---

[15] Soteri, 'Khazaria', 12.
[16] Shnirelman, 'Story of Euphemism', 353–72; Shnirelman, 'Ancestral Wisdom and Ethnic Nationalism', 41–60; Shnirelman, *Myth of Khazars and Intellectual Antisemitism*; Klier, 'Review: *Myth of Khazars and Intellectual Antisemitism*', 779–81; Ivakhiv, 'Nature and Ethnicity', 194–225; Malinova, 'Status and Ressentiment', 291–303; Rossman, 'Lev Gumilev, Eurasianism and Khazaria', 30–51; Werbart, 'Khazars or "Saltovo-Majaki Culture"?', 199–221.

of the important conditions for the formation of a nation, and for the blurring of tribal and ethnic differences.[17]

Three pages later, Khazaria's population is defined:

> as all the ethnic groups that defined the appearance of the material culture and which most likely had a direct participation in the establishment and functioning of the state – the Khazars, the Bulgars and the Alans. In other words, these three ethnic groups' notions of power should be the leading issue in the process of defining the nature of the Khazar Khaganate in the tenth century.[18]

Is the entire population multi-ethnic, with the various tribes therein constituting distinct ethnicities, or is the ethnicity defined by a common faith imposed, top-down, by the ruler?[19] In other words, is ethnicity the raw, tribal material or the finished, monotheised product?[20]

If we consider it the former, then by the same logic, would that equally render today's Spaniards as *Celtiberians, Vandals* or *Visigoths*, French as *Franks* or *Gauls*,[21] Italians as *Lombards* or *Etruscans*,[22] English (or Germanic-language speakers[23]) as *Romano-Celtic*,[24] or even *Anglo-Saxon*,[25] Albanians as *Illyrians*, Russians, Poles, Ukrainians and other Slavic speakers as variously

---

[17] Zhivkov, *Khazaria*, 17.
[18] Ibid., 20. Similar questions could be asked of Dudek's treatment of ethnicity in Khazaria: Dudek, *Chazarowie*.
[19] Halsall, 'Review: *Barbarian Identity*', 1349–50.
[20] Pohl, 'Telling Difference', 120–67; ter Haar Romeny, *Religious Origins of Nations?* 341.
[21] Wood, 'Defining Franks', 110–119; MacMaster, 'Trojan Origins', 1–12; Garipzanov, 'Frontier Identities', 113–43; Nelson, 'Frankish Identity in Charlemagne's Empire', 70–83; Reimitz, '*Omnes Franci*', 51–69; Brown, 'Trojan Origins of French', 135–79; Coulson, '"National" Requisitioning', 119–34; Escalona, 'Endings of Medieval Kingdoms', 7.
[22] Pohl, 'Deliberate Ambiguity', 47–58; Zancani, '"Lombard" and "Lombardy"', 217–32; Hankey, 'Civic Pride versus Feelings for Italy', 196–216.
[23] Reuter, 'England and Germany', 53–70; Goffart, 'Distant Past', 91–109; Wolfram, 'Gothic History as Ethnography', 43–69; Wolfram, '*Origo et Religio*', 70–90; Brink, 'People and *Land* in Early Scandinavia', 87–111; Bagge, 'Division and Unity', 145–66.
[24] Richter, 'National Identity in Medieval Wales', 71–84; Webster, 'John of Fordun', 85–102.
[25] Smyth, 'English Identity', 24–52; Pappas, *English Refugees in Byzantine Armed Forces*; Shepard, 'Another New England?', 18–39; Brown, 'Higden's Britain', 103–18.

174   THE MONOTHEISATION OF PONTIC-CASPIAN EURASIA

Derevlians, Poljanians, Antes and so on?[26] The fact that swastikas are still attributed to this or that primordial ethnicity, residual from the blood-and-soil Nazi era, is a mind-boggling case of historical amnesia which should put these ideas to bed.[27] It was the form of monotheism that created the *nation*, not the *nation* which converted to the monotheism.[28]

Ethnicity may be compared to a layer cake: monotheism is not the only ingredient, but it comprises the basic recipe for the base layer of the cake. Although comparative implications are easily overburdened,[29] today's nations cannot be conflated with pre-monotheistic tribes or races. Ethnic cleansing has been (and remains) the result.[30] But tribalism ('otherisation',

[26] Plokhy, *Origins of Slavic Nations*, 354–61, and his mostly favorable reviews by Bushkovitch, 'Review: *Origins of Slavic Nations*', 846–8; Halperin, 'Identity in Rus'. Review: *Origins of Slavic Nations*', 275–94; Toločko, '*Primary Chronicle*'s "Ethnography"', 169–88; Franklin, 'Invention of Rus(sia)(s)', 180–95; Geary, 'Slovenian Gentile Identity', 243–57; Urbańczyk, 'Slavic and Christian Identities', 205–22; Lübke, 'Christianity and Paganism as Gentile Identities', 189–203; Budak, 'Identities in Medieval Dalmatia', 223–42; Dzino, '"Becoming Slav", "Becoming Croat"', 195–206; Curta, 'Four Questions', 286–303; Barford (*Early Slavs*, 268–85) gives a somewhat contradictory discussion.

[27] For example, Odnorоženko ('Зображення щитів на руських печатках', 150–267), who researches Rus' heraldry, is a well-known Ukrainian fascist affiliated with the Azov Battalion (itself riddled with Nazi-sympathisers), which, as of the time of writing, has been resisting the inexcusable 2022 Russian invasion of Ukraine. Elsewhere, Šelekhan', 'Свастика в культурі ранніх слов'ян та київської русі', 69–88, argues that swastikas distinguish ethnically primordial Slavs (the typologically determined 'Slavic Černjakhov culture') from other groups. Härke ('Archaeology and Nazism', 32–43) refers directly to the swastika symbols of the Černjakhov culture (attributed to the Crimean Goths) as an example which Nazi archaeologists, led by the infamous Herbert Jankuhn, sought to utilise as propaganda for conquering Crimea in World War II and repopulating it with ethnic Germans to replace the Goths as Crimea's original ethnolinguistic populace. Similar concerns over the abuse of history for campaigns of ethnic cleansing sadly continue to fuel animosity between Ukrainians and Russians in the twenty-first century.

[28] Sneath, *Headless State*, 176–9; Turchin, 'Formation of Agrarian Empires', 191–217; Holmes and Standen, 'Global Middle Ages', 108–13.

[29] Holmes and Standen, 'Global Middle Ages', 107; Escalona, 'Endings of Medieval Kingdoms', 8–10.

[30] Maxwell, 'Multiple Nationalism', 385–414; Wooster, 'Enlightenment to Genocide', 80–99; Coakley, 'Mobilizing Past', 531–60; Niculescu, 'Culture-Historical Archaeology', 5–24; Gillett, 'Ethnogenesis', 241–60; Gillett, *Barbarian Identity*; Brubaker, *Ethnicity without Groups*; James, *Globalism, Nationalism, Tribalism*; Geary, 'Crisis of European Identity', 33–42; Wimmer, *Ethnic Boundary Making*; Anderson, *Imagined Communities*; Gellner, *Nations and Nationalism*; Hobsbawm, *Nations and Nationalism since 1780*; Hutchinson and Smith, *Nationalism*.

'us versus them', etc.), as an ineradicable human trait and endemic to warfare,[31] is overall different.[32] Based on exclusion, tribalism takes many forms and transcends time and confessional identity. Although ecumenism sought to surpass pagan tribalism via collective subjection to common law and authority, it nevertheless resulted in rival faiths and dynasties.[33]

Moreover, why would primordial ethnicity only apply to post-Roman Europe (where 'late antiquity', coefficient with the end of the 'migration period', betokens a stable, if debatable, date[34]), while primordial ethnicity would not apply, counterfactually, to post-Mauryan India or post-Han China? Were the eighth- to fifteenth-century Viking, Mongol or Timurid invasions not also migrations?[35] By implication, if Eurasian pagan nomadism defines migration, then assuming the 'migration period' or 'late antiquity' ended in the sixth to ninth centuries reveals a sharp Western-centrism;[36] the 'period' otherwise arguably endured to the eighteenth- to nineteenth-century Kalmyk *khağanate*.[37] Therefore, periodisations based on 'Roman' and 'post-Roman', arbitrarily epitomising 'late antiquity' and 'early medieval', are equally outdated and/or Western-centric.

---

[31] Stouraitis, '"Just War" and "Holy War"', 227–64; Popper, *Open Society and Its Enemies*, 163–4.

[32] Typical human brains can only be familiar with a limited number of other individuals ('Dunbar's number' – normally about 150 acquaintances at maximum). Past this limit, the brain typically resorts to some amalgamation of stereotypes, hierarchical schematics and other simplistic structures in order to epitomise so many other people. The natural reaction is to resort to stereotypes in order to conceptualise 'we' and 'they'. Therefore, conceptions of 'us versus them', however manifested, may be a natural feature of human cognition. See for example Dunbar, *How Many Friends Does One Person Need?*; Bernard et al., 'How Much Does GSS and RSW Dredge Up?', 49–63; McCarthy et al., 'Methods for Estimating Network Size', 28–39; Killworth and Bernard, 'Pseudomodel of Small World Problem', 477–505; Killworth et al., 'Measuring Patterns of Acquaintanceship', 381–97.

[33] Crossley, *Hammer and Anvil*, 71; Neumann and Wigen, *Steppe Tradition in International Relations*, 165–78.

[34] Harper, *Fate of Rome*; Haldon et al., 'Plagues, Climate Change, and End of Empire'; Heather, *Empires and Barbarians*, 577–618; Heather, *Restoration of Rome*, 270–95; Curta, *Eastern Europe*, 11–14; Izdebski et al., 'Evidence for Climatic Changes', 1–20; Halsall, *Barbarian Migrations and Roman West*; Goffart, *Narrators of Barbarian History*; Collins, 'Law and Ethnic Identity', 1–23; Heather, '*Foedera* and *Foederati*', 292–308; Goffart, 'Barbarians in Late Antiquity', 235–61; Heather, 'Ethnicity, Group Identity, and Social Status', 17–49; Halsall, 'Movers and Shakers', 277–91.

[35] Beckwith, *Empires of Silk Road*, 165–6; Holmes and Standen, 'Global Middle Ages', 114; Faruqui, 'Forgotten Prince', 487–523.

[36] Wells, *Barbarians to Angels*, 30.

[37] Sneath, *Headless State*, 36–37.

Periodisation and Civilisation

Separating the 'late antique' from the 'medieval'

No 'medieval' source describes itself as such; not even Edward Gibbon used the word. Describing monotheistic principles, the word 'mediæval' was first published in English in 1817,[38] at the same time that John Darby's dispensational theology was beginning to strongly influence English-language philosophies of history (historiosophy).

The periodisations we commonly use as chronological shorthand can have nefarious consequences which obfuscate the real processes (namely, monotheisation) taking place. Ignoring them only further consolidates their stranglehold over our historical memory, for example the tripartite separation of history into 'ancient', 'medieval' and 'modern', which is taken for granted even in the otherwise most sober-minded historiography.[39] These lingering periodisations are seldom empirically challenged, since many historians and archaeologists prefer to bypass the issue altogether and work within prefabricated boundaries of time without interrogating them. Like separating one pre-monotheistic tribe from another,[40] attempts at separating the 'late antique' from the 'medieval' implies teleology, since ultimately such notions are retrospectively assigned instead of synchronously contrived.[41] When today's nations define their own histories within this tripartite formula (the 'ancient' nation, then the 'medieval' nation, etc.), this presupposes an inherently Western view of world history wherein 'antiquity' followed by the 'Middle Ages' descends from periodisations based on 'Roman' and 'post-Roman' formats. The example rhetorical

---

[38] Fosbroke, *British Monachism*, 10.

[39] Harper, *Fate of Rome*.

[40] Reher and Fernández-Götz, 'Archaeological Narratives in Ethnicity', 400–16; Effros, 'Grave Goods and Ritual Expression of Identity', 189–232; Härke, 'Archaeologists and Migrations', 262–6; Härke, 'Archaeology and Nazism', 32–43; Werbart, 'Khazars or "Saltovo-Majaki Culture"?', 199–221; Werbart, 'Invisible Identities', 83–99; Wołoszyn, 'Byzantine Archaeology', 259–92; Rąszkowski, '"German School of Archaeology"', 197–214; Aržanceva, 'Terenozhkin and Tolstov', 44–56; Kristiansen, 'Should Archaeology Service "Popular Culture"?', 488–90; Holtorf, 'Academic Critique', 490–2; Niculescu, 'Culture-Historical Archaeology', 5–24; Curta, 'Pots, Slavs and "Imagined Communities"', 367–84; Curta, '"Hesitating Journey through Foreign Knowledge"', 299–306.

[41] Holmes and Standen, 'Global Middle Ages', 110; Whittow, 'Byzantium and End of Ancient World', 134–53; Davis, *Periodization and Sovereignty*, 1–20; Haldon et al., 'Plagues, Climate Change and End of Empire'.

question arises: when is the chronological line between ancient Siberia and medieval Siberia? Or does this distinction only apply in Europe?

If historians cannot satisfactorily provide parameters for ancient ethnicity, and primary sources have too long been mined for imagined ancient ethnicities for dubious reasons (for instance, recasting 'barbarians' as 'us' versus the 'Romans' as 'them'[42]) then why should historians bother with such outdated delineations of 'late antique' and 'medieval' in the first place?[43] Convenient shorthand is an excuse; these categories have long taken on lives of their own amid recent ethnonational political agendas, some of which are still being contested on twenty-first-century battlefields. Furthermore, such a distinction ought to lead us to intuit a Western-centrism, which prevents expanding comparative historical interpretations, or perhaps a return to universal history. Hence, many historians have begun to transcend national or tripartite histories with an archetypical 'global Middle Ages'[44] or an elongated 'axial age'.[45]

While the term 'global Middle Ages' has yet to be critically defined, it has been conditionally assigned the chronological range of about 300 to 1600, leaving room for debate about the meaning of 'medieval' beyond Europe.[46] The term 'Middle Ages' seems troublesome to apply on a global scale as it implies a 'global antiquity' and a 'global modernity'. Similar remarks could describe the term 'pre-modernity'. Personally I prefer the

---

[42] Jones and Ereira, *Barbarians*, 288.

[43] Bachrach, 'Review: *Barbarian Identity* and *Medieval Frontiers*', 866–70; Derks and Roymans, *Ethnic Constructs in Antiquity*; Gillett, 'Ethnogenesis', 241–60; Gillett, *Barbarian Identity*; Halsall, 'Review: *Barbarian Identity*', 1349–50; Wood, 'Barbarians, Historians, and National Identities', 61–81; Wood, 'Introduction', ix–x; Pohl, *Suche nach den Ursprüngen*; Pohl, 'Telling Difference', 120–67; Pohl, 'Gender and Ethnicity', 168–88; Anderson, *Antiquity to Feudalism*; Wolfram, 'Origo et Religio', 70–90; Klaniczay, 'Birth of New Europe', 99–129; Geary, *Myth of Nations*, 151–74.

[44] Wells, *Barbarians to Angels*, 200; Holmes and Standen, 'Global Middle Ages', 110–11; Bell-Fialkoff, *Migration in Eurasian Steppe*; Golovnëv, Антропология движения; Anthony, 'Migration in Archaeology', 895–914; Härke, 'Archaeologists and Migrations', 262–76.

[45] Jaspers, *Origin and Goal of History*, 58–75, 245; Armstrong, *Great Transformation*; Arnason et al., 'Introduction', 287–93; Arnason, 'Rehistoricizing Axial Age', 337–65; Eisenstadt, 'Breakthrough in Israelite Civilization', 227–40; Eisenstadt, 'Axial Civilizations and Axial Age Reconsidered', 531–64; Eisenstadt, 'Axial Conundrum', 280; Joas, 'Axial Age Debate as Religious Discourse', 18–19; Wittrock, 'Meaning of Axial Age', 51–85; Wittrock, 'Axial Age in Global History', 102–25; Voegelin, *Order and History*, 79; Christian, *Maps of Time*, 319.

[46] Holmes and Standen, 'Global Middle Ages', 107.

'axial age', coined by Karl Jaspers to describe global historical intellectual developments. But regardless of the term used, we must acknowledge where we are today.

Many present nations have been presented, if mistakenly, as primordial, and so, likewise, has Western civilisation, which, as it has been supposed and taught for generations of Westerners, ascends from 'ancient' Greece and Rome, rather than 'medieval' Roman Catholic Christendom, or the Orthodox *oikoumene*. In other words, as long as Western civilisation is construed as having primordial (that is, pre-Christian) origins, then so will be current nations that define themselves as Western.[47] But if we invert this paradigm, which we already know to be misguided, then we are left with a major loose end. That is, if current nations cannot be primordial (pre-monotheistic), then neither can Western civilisation.

Instead of attempting yet another definition of 'Western Civilisation' (itself an eternal debate), it would be more helpful to rhetorically juxtapose 'the West' as a developmental framework alongside other monotheistic civilisations – via comparative scale.

Framing civilisation

The importance of monotheism when analysing civilisation cannot be ignored.[48] Yet this idea directly opposes the old notion of (at least Western) civilisation as some abstraction, completely detached from monotheistic identity, stretching back to the remote antiquity of Mycenaean Greece (or debatably Sumer). Two entangled ouroboroses define the Gordian knot of Western civilisation: a narrow, confessional definition and an abstract, allegedly secular definition (usually couched in terms of freedom, prosperity and so on), which has fuelled secularised, institutional counter-processes elsewhere (such as the Tanzimat or Meiji Reformation). When Western civilisation is framed alongside other confessionally predicated civilisations at scale (namely, the Orthodox *oikoumene*, Islamic *ummah*), we must understand history as it was understood by the confessional

---

[47] Härke, 'Archaeology and Nazism', 33, discusses the German 'national prehistorian' Gustaf Kossinna (1858–1931), whose ideas about the equivalence of civilisational prehistory to national prehistory paved the way for his *Siedlungsarchäologie* (1911), a forerunning concept of using the distribution of archaeological typologies to construct ethnic 'culture-history'. Using this archaeological method, finds of swastikas were enough to justify Nazi conquests in the 1930s–1940s, popularised in the Indiana Jones film franchise.

[48] Vásáry, *Cumans and Tatars*, xiii.

affiliations of contemporaries,[49] rather than as it has been teleologically explained by the present, supposedly secular aspirations of contortionists. Therefore, we arrive at a dichotomous basis for civilisational analysis: via formal, abstract and purportedly secular definitions versus confessional definitions.

In a summary of previous theorists' definitions of civilisation, the historian Niall Ferguson offers a six-point summary distinguishing 'the West' from 'the Rest', based on an abstract set of institutional principles, which transcend monotheism (for 'the West', read: Latin Christendom) and derive wholly from Graeco-Roman antiquity. His discussion of the time of the origin of 'Western civilisation' centres on an arbitrary distinction between what he terms 'Western civilisation 1.0' and 'Western civilisation 2.0', in which the centre is traditionally cut out between the fifth-century deposition of Romulus Augustulus and the fifteenth-century Italian Renaissance, thereby following the conventional, tripartite scheme.[50] He lists temporary 'stewards' of Western civilisation, until it was repossessed in the fifteenth-century: Byzantium, Ireland and the 'Abbasid Caliphate.[51]

Ferguson appropriately critiques the scholar Samuel Huntington's necessarily narrow, confessional definition of Western civilisation.[52] However, in perhaps his best logical demystification, Ferguson references the geographer Jared Diamond's geographical-deterministic argument,[53] distinguishing between 'politically consolidated', 'monolithic Oriental empires' and

---

[49] Escalona, 'Endings of Medieval Kingdoms', 8–10; Wilkinson, 'Cities, Civilizations and Oikumenes: I–II', 51–87, 41–72; Bulliet, *Islamo-Christian Civilization*.

[50] Ferguson, *Civilization*, 3–17.

[51] Brownsworth, *Lost to West*; Cahill, *How Irish Saved Civilization*, (known more for its profitability than its rigour); Dawson, *Making of Europe* (quite outdated); similarly, Freeman, *Closing of Western Mind*, xix.

[52] Huntington, *Clash of Civilizations*. I cannot claim to be able to take apart Huntington's argument point by point, and besides, this has already been done abundantly (that is, the ubiquitous Fukuyama–Huntington debates). But without advocating Fukuyama's ideas either, the most glaring problem with Huntington's argument is that he does not include Catholic Latin America as 'Western', even though the Catholic *oikoumene* which Christianised the space for generations is the same historical force which rulers from Charlemagne to Franz Joseph II purported to represent. Where does his 'Western civilisation' end and 'Latin American civilisation' begin? The dubiousness of some (though not all) of Huntington's ideas, specifically that the United States of America must be defined as an Anglo-Protestant ethnonational state, has been latched on to by many who still believe in primordial ethnicity, and I will leave it to the reader's imagination where that particular branch of inquiry will eventually lead.

[53] Diamond, *Guns, Germs and Steel*.

'the mountainous, river-divided Western Eurasia'. Yet there is no mention that China has been just as mountainous and river-divided, and frequently politically divided, while Europe has seen several intermittent periods of political unity by various ecumenical empires. While his criticism of Diamond's *Guns, Germs and Steel* is appropriate, the weakness of Ferguson's own counterargument is typified by his avoidance of Diamond's later work (*Collapse*), in which Diamond lays out how history, as a series of forces, could have unfolded differently and did not, although it could yet change.[54]

Victor Hanson makes a similarly romantic argument, treating 'the West' as some monolithic, value-defined institution, based on abstract notions of *'Europe'* and *'freedom'* transcending time and space, stretching back to the Battle of Salamis.[55] One might ask Hanson if 'freedom' enabled Tariq ibn Ziyād to win the field at Guadalete (712), or if Byzantine armies lost at Manzikert (1071) because they had forgotten their primordial Hellenic 'freedom'. Similar mystifications of Western civilisation have long been common.[56]

When 'the West' is contemporarily contrasted with another civilisation, usually Russia or the ubiquitously termed 'Arab World' (itself an egregious ethnological oversimplification[57]), one might ask, why do Plato and Ovid belong exclusively to the West, instead of Russia or Islam? Why do we pay lip service to valuing 'Byzantine studies' while 'the Classics' still lay claim to the foundation of 'the West'? Why does 'antiquity', however 'late' it goes, still end wherever the 'medieval' begins?[58]

---

[54] Diamond, *Collapse*. Escalona ('Endings of Medieval Kingdoms', 1–3) thoughtfully critiques Diamond's overschematic environmental ideas of societal collapse.

[55] Hanson, *Carnage and Culture*, 54: 'Western ideas of freedom, originating from the early Hellenic concept of politics as consensual government [. . .] were to play a role in nearly every engagement in which Western soldiers fought. [. . .] It is easy to identify the role of freedom among the ranks of Europeans at Salamis, less so at Mexico City, Lepanto – or among the intramural Western fights such as Agincourt, Waterloo, and the Somme. Yet whatever differences there were between the French and the English of the Middle Ages, [. . .] their shared measure of freedom on both sides of the battle line was not even remotely present in armies outside of Europe.'

[56] Morris, *Why West Rules – for Now*; Jaspers, *Origin and Goal of History*, 63–4: 'Western man [is] capable of experiencing the reality of the world in such a way as to know disaster in the profound sense that reaches beyond all interpretation. The tragic spirit becomes simultaneously reality and consciousness. Tragedy is known only to the West.'

[57] Eisenstadt, *Comparative Civilizations*, 457–65.

[58] Frankopan, *Silk Roads*, 213; Arnason, *Civilizations in Dispute*, 323–59.

Answers to these questions have been attempted based on the Russian experience, but they still validate a point of view in which Russian thinkers could not historically involve themselves with 'the Classics', a view which is simply false: criticism of Western arrogance hardly alters non-Westerners' abilities to engage with 'the Classics', historically or presently.[59] Russian civilisation, derived directly from Byzantium, undoubtedly shares a common Christian heritage with the West; therefore, bouts of Western–Russian conflict can equally be viewed as internal struggles within Christian civilisation.[60] Similarly, the preoccupation with 'statehood' in Eurasianist historiography is quite comparable with the Western preoccupation with the 'ancient–medieval–modern' paradigm.[61]

Without advocating either deterministic or alternative histories, I propose that the whole problem with these arguments is that they interpret history perhaps as written by the victors, as the saying goes, but ultimately *as it has turned out* and explain it forwards from some random era (like the fifteenth century), rather than viewing history backwards *as it could have turned out, but did not*. But this assumption is arbitrary, forcing historians into explaining how the past *succeeded* in becoming the present instead of explaining what forces *persevered* or *crumbled*[62] (exemplified by Khazaria), thereby leaving history, and our immediate ability to learn from it, all the shallower.[63]

Finally, if the historical borders of present nations have been anachronistically defined based on ethnonationalist theorising, whose proponents often seek answers to their questions in the remotest past, then in such vacuums without comparative scale, entire civilisations may be as well. Namely, the further back historians reach for answers to questions of present identities, the more teleological their conclusions will be.[64] Therefore, we must

---

[59] Thomson, 'Distorted Mediaeval Russian Perception of Antiquity', 303–64.
[60] Niebuhr, *Faith and History*, 110–11; Dragadze, 'Meeting of Minds', 119–128; Garagozov, 'Collective Memory', 55–89.
[61] Eisenstadt, *Comparative Civilizations*, 485–8.
[62] Escalona, 'Endings of Medieval Kingdoms', 1–11.
[63] In the words of Neal Ascherson (*Black Sea*, 237):

> History – the product, not the raw material – is a bottle with a label. For many years now, the emphasis of historical discussion has been laid upon the label (its iconography, its target group of customers) and upon the interesting problems of manufacturing bottle-glass. The contents, on the other hand, are tasted in a knowing, perfunctory way and then spat out again. Only amateurs swallow them.

[64] In the words of Gwynne Dyer (*War*, 176), "Our gravest error [...] is to overestimate our distance and our difference from the past.

fundamentally alter the questions we are asking of textual and archaeological materials. But while I am not advocating defining 'civilisation' as narrowly predicated on confessional affiliation, I suggest that the common definition of Western civilisation in the past two (or five) centuries has been critically mistaken when it assumes that it begins with Odysseus or Gilgamesh, and not with Cardinal Humbert, Urban II or Martin Luther.[65] The developments of civilisations resemble more an evolutionary family tree than a set of primordially distinct petri dishes. After all, it ought to be self-explanatory that the Islamic and Russian civilisations spring from the same Abrahamic fountainhead.[66] In other words, Abrahamic civilisation frequently proves a more relevant frame of reference than Western civilisation, since it is inclusive of the Islamic and Russian civilisations as well.

Personally, I prefer not to use a term like 'global Middle Ages', which implies both a 'global antiquity' and 'global modernity', as the lines between each epoch and in each region would vary inordinately and invariably evoke colossal anachronisms. Instead, as in the concept of 'Big History'[67] or the 'Axial age',[68] I would prefer no such delineations, save for the notion that monotheism functions as one of the base layers of ethnicities, sovereignties and civilisations. This follows the thought of the sociologists Durkheim and his nephew Mauss,[69] which distinguishes pre-monotheism (paganism) from monotheism anywhere, that is, top-down monotheisation: the imposition of sacred laws deriving from sacred texts, since this is how contemporaries contrived the world in which they lived. In this way, I would propose that so-called 'antiquity' ended wherever and whenever paganism was finally extinguished, and some common set of written laws, in whatever form, was adopted and/or imposed.

The goal of this inquiry is not to change the world; it is simply to interrogate our notions of 'ethnicity' and 'sovereignty' as well as the simplistic differences between 'antiquity' and 'the Middle Ages' as they apply to

---

[65] Holland, *Millennium*.
[66] Arnason, *Civilizations in Dispute*, 244.
[67] Christian, *History of Russia, Central Asia and Mongolia*.
[68] Hann, 'Anthropology, Eurasia, and Global History', 339–54; Kradin, 'Nomads and Theory of Civilizations', 303–22; Prozorova, 'Civilizational Analysis and Archaeology', 53–74; Arnason et al., 'Introduction', 287–93; Arnason, 'Making Contact and Mapping Terrain', xiii–xlii; Benovska-Sabkova, '"Orthodox", "Eurasian", or "Russian Orthodox" Civilization?', 323–38; Eisenstadt, 'Breakthrough in Israelite Civilization', 227–20; Eisenstadt, 'Axial Civilizations and Axial Age Reconsidered', 531–64; Eisenstadt, 'Axial Conundrum', 277–93; Joas, 'Axial Age Debate as Religious Discourse', 9–29; Wittrock, 'Meaning of Axial Age', 51–85; Wittrock, 'Axial Age in Global History', 102–25.
[69] Arnason, 'Mauss Revisited', 10–18.

Pontic-Caspian Eurasia, a part of the world which equally straddles the blurred lines between Europe and Asia. The utility of this region lies in its proximity to the same historical forces which generated the Islamic *ummah* and Christian *oikoumene*: it is sufficiently immense to transcend national, climatic and geographic confines, without being universal, while the time and place, at the fringes of 'ancient' and 'early medieval' Western civilisation, demonstrate its limits. Similarly, the conclusions about our (mis-)conceptions of historical identities (ethnicity, sovereignty, etc.) are not meant for specialists alone.[70] Sovereignty could never be absolute, despite claims to the contrary in myriad sources.

Byzantium makes for the greatest case in point, bearing two equally valid conceptions of what it represented: the Byzantium of the *themata* (*ton thematon*) and the Byzantium of the *oikoumene* (*tes oikoumenes*). Namely, Byzantium is conceivable in the traditional manner, as representing a pre-modern 'state', with varying limits of enforceable jurisdiction surrounding a self-contained unit,[71] and we can also simultaneously conceive Byzantium as an ecumenical empire, a civilisation, even if it was sometimes only an empire of the mind.[72] But Byzantium's universalist purpose reminds us to consider on a grand scale that subjective assumptions of identity and sovereignty have been fundamentally misunderstood ever since 'Western civilisation' has been arbitrarily conceived as beginning with classical Greece and Rome.

Viewed from Pontic-Caspian Eurasia, this is best demonstrated by considering the monotheisation process as it moved eastward, blurring the arbitrary (and Western-centric) lines dividing the so-called 'late antique' and 'medieval' worlds. What is the line between the ancient world and the medieval world? Is it 476? Is it 330? 632? 800? I believe there truly is no line and they are in fact much the same world, with the crucial exception of the pervading influence of one flavour of monotheism or another.

This inquiry has endeavoured to study tribal conversions to various monotheisms and their respective mythologisations (using examples from Pontic-Caspian Eurasia in the eighth to thirteenth centuries), interpreted through both textual and archaeological evidence. These processes serve as a primary factor for tribal unification and the early developments of what we might call 'statecraft' – and in many cases, much modern nationalism, however haphazard it may be. Monotheistic proselytisation efforts around

---

[70] Escalona, 'Endings of Medieval Kingdoms', 7; Tilly, *Identities, Boundaries and Social Ties*, 71–90.
[71] Yiannis Stouraitis, personal communication, May 2021; Kaldellis, *Romanland*, 92.
[72] Haldon, *Warfare, State and Society*, 258–9; Arnason, 'Mauss Revisited', 7–8.

the Black and Caspian Seas reveal how what we today call the 'age of migrations' (for example, the so-called 'Germanic' invasions of the third- to seventh-century Roman empire, the Khazars, Bulgars, 'proto-Hungarians', Rus', Pečenegs, Cuman-Qıpčaqs, etc.) was perpetuated up to the Mongolian invasions and even later. Different dynasties may have adopted differing religions, but eventually, it was the varying religions that defined the foundational layers of group identities, not blood, soil, language or the ever-abstract 'culture'. Viewed from Byzantium, the same Roman empire as always, any peripheral ruler won to the Christian faith was a newly admitted part of Rome – the *oikoumene* itself, and at least until 1054 (or perhaps 1204 or 1453), it was Byzantium which defined 'the West', even if we have forgotten these lessons today.

Western history and global history can be effectively bound together in the context of global monotheisation: the top-down implementations of various sacred laws. If notions of periodisation and civilisation are defined not by arbitrary primordial or abstract definitions, but by confessional, later national, loyalty, which is as pertinent today as centuries ago (especially in Eastern Europe), the question may be worth considering: why ought we continue to suppose the Middle Ages are over?

Appendices

Appendix 1

Gog and Magog's 's Association with Khazaria

Man was born to turn the world into a paradise, but tragically, he was born flawed. And so his paradise has always been soiled by stupidity, greed, destructiveness, and shortsightedness.[1]

The long, complicated and toxically disjointed story of Gog and Magog, from the Old Testament to current anti-Semitic narratives, is fraught with misleading ethnonational, conspiracy and prophetic theorising. It began with the Book of Ezekiel and continued in Christian and Islamic sources which attributed the legend of Gog and Magog to Khazaria.

Magog originates in the Table of Nations (Genesis 10), where he is listed as a son of Japheth, son of Noah, brother of Gomer, Meshech and Tubal and uncle of Togarmah, among others. The name Gog first appears in 1 Chronicles 1:5 in a repetition of the Table of Nations. Ezekiel 38–9 explains that a certain Gog, in the land of Magog, presumably descended from Noah's grandson, came with a large army, including the descendants of Gomer and Togarmah, against Israel from the vague far north. In Ezekiel, Gog is merely a single inhabitant (or perhaps a tribe) of the land of Magog whose name derives from the original Magog in Genesis 10 (possibly an adaptation of the seventh-century-BCE Lydian king Gyges). Whereas the original Hebrew mentioned 'Gog *from* Magog', the Septuagint rendered the wording 'Gog *and* Magog'.[2]

Gog *and* Magog feature heavily in Judaic, Christian and Islamic eschatologies. In Judaic and Christian eschatologies, they are last mentioned in Revelation 20:8, an eschatological tract about their release from the four

---

[1] Quinn, *Ishmael*, 83.
[2] Scherb, 'Assimilating Giants', 60; van der Toorn et al., *Dictionary of Deities and Demons in the Bible*, 536.

corners of the earth by Satan after Christ's thousand-year reign (the end of time). In his *Antiquities of the Jews*, Josephus equates Gog and Magog with the Scythians.[3] In Islamic eschatology, Gog and Magog surface in the Qur'an 21:96 (as Ya'juj and Ma'juj), which relates that these two evil tribes will break out of their imprisonment by Dul-Qarnayn (meaning 'the double-horned'; usually identified as Alexander of Macedon [the Great]) at the end of time and ravage the earth before being wiped out by divine disease.[4] Gog and Magog's identification with the Scythians is auspicious and ironic given their later association with Khazaria on the Volga.

Thereafter, Gog and Magog appear in many Christian and Islamic works discussing the pagan nomads of the steppe. The prevailing myth was that Gog and Magog had been enclosed by Alexander of Macedon (the Great) behind a legendary wall of incredible dimensions between mighty mountains lest they should escape and overrun the known world. The theme of attributing incredible deeds to Dul-Qarnayn (in the Alexander Romances) was prevalent in Christian sources like pseudo-Kallisthenes' *Letter of Alexander to Olympias*[5] and in Islamic sources from the Qur'an onwards.

Gog and Magog next appear in ibn Khurradādhbih's late-ninth-century (debatably reliable[6]) story of *Sallām the Interpreter*, which explicitly dissociates the Khazars from Gog and Magog, since the Khazar king assisted Sallām the Interpreter in his journey to the Wall, thereby hinting at Khazaria's conversion. Because Khazaria is not presented as allied with Gog and Magog but cooperative, rather, with the monotheistic Caliphate, it is conceivable that the original author thought of Khazaria as within the Islamic *ummah*.[7] His story contains 'chiasmus', a well-known rhetorical technique used by countless chroniclers, polemicists and panegyrists as a parabolic device.[8] In the story, the narrator finally reaches the nearest

---

[3] Josephus, *Antiquities of the Jews*, tr. Whiston, *Works of Flavius Josephus*, 1.123; 18.9.
[4] van Donzel et al., *Gog and Magog in Syriac and Islamic Sources*.
[5] Pseudo-Kallisthenes, *Letter of Alexander to Olympias*, tr. Wolohojian, *Romance of Alexander the Great*; Anderson, *Alexander's Gate, Gog and Magog, and Inclosed Nations*, 3–43.
[6] Ibn Khurradādhbih, *Sallām the Interpreter*, tr. Lunde and Stone, *Ibn Fadlān*, 99–104; Ibn Khurradādhbih, *Livre des routes et provinces*, ed. de Goeje, 132. Khurradādhbih's original source for *Sallām the Interpreter* was perhaps a traveller named ibn Isḥaq who had allegedly lived in Cambodia for two years, according to Barthold's preface to the *Ḥudūd al-'Ālam* (tr. Minorsky, 27); van Donzel et al., *Gog and Magog in Syriac and Islamic Sources*, 153.
[7] Wasserstein, 'Khazars and Islam', 382–3; Zhivkov, *Khazaria*, 87–8.
[8] Chiasmus is a common Abrahamic literary technique, like parallelism, where a plot line's passages criss-cross each other (rhetorically or thematically), creating an effect similar to JFK's famous quote, 'Ask not what your country can do for you; ask what

fortified city to the Wall (Īkah), which Lunde and Stone identify with the city of Hami – quite peculiar given the town's proximity, compared to the entire breadth of Asia, to the westernmost abutment of China's 'Great Wall' and particularly for the original reason the Han emperors extended the fortification system so far west.[9] Yet there is no definitive proof of where this city was located.

Nevertheless, Khurradādhbih's reference to Gog and Magog was taken literally by subsequent Islamic chroniclers. Unsurprisingly, other chroniclers distorted his ideas about Gog and Magog. Ibn Qutayba (c. 880[10]) claimed that the Khazars descended from the biblical Japheth and thus tied Khazaria to the notion of Gog and Magog.[11] This is the beginning of the Islamic association of Khazaria with Gog and Magog, which continued up to al-Nuwayri (fourteenth century).[12] The reason for this preoccupation with enclosure by mountains, walls or whatever barriers happen to be available is given by DeWeese, who asserts that the 'the theme of "enclosure" and "emergence" [comprises] the pivotal features of legends of origin and conversion myths.'[13]

Truly, Gog and Magog only represent scriptural bogeymen, albeit with countless variations stretching back to the remotest past. Despite Khazaria's attempted Judaisation, the legend represents a common Abrahamic form of 'otherisation' deployed for 'us' (Jews, Christians, Muslims, etc.) against 'them' (pagans, often nomads), which ironically manifests as a polemic on *behalf* of Jews rather than *against* them. Regardless of their Abrahamic form of monotheism, those faced with Gog and Magog could be brought together in opposition to a common pagan enemy. Therefore, Gog and Magog might not only function as agents of destruction but could also create unity among peoples.[14]

---

you can do for your country' (*Povest' Vremennÿkh Let*, tr. Cross and Sherbowitz-Wetzor, *Russian Primary Chronicle*, 110–19; Lund, 'Chiasmus in Old Testament', 104–26; Ostrowski, 'Volodimer's Conversion in "Povest' vremennykh let"', 567–80; Garnier, '"ṣifat sadd Yāǧūǧ wa-Māǧūǧ"', 605–7; von Grunebaum, *Medieval Islam*, 26.

[9] Ibn Khurradādhbih, *Sallām the Interpreter*, tr. Lunde and Stone, *Ibn Fadlān*, 99–109.
[10] Gil, 'Did Khazars Convert to Judaism?', 431.
[11] Ibn Qutayba, *Kitâb al-ma'ârif*, ed. 'Ukāsha, 26.
[12] van Donzel et al., *Gog and Magog in Syriac and Islamic Sources*, 152.
[13] DeWeese, *Islamization*, 273
[14] Ibid.; Scherb, 'Assimilating Giants', 59–76.

Appendix 2
Steppe-Nomadism and Gumilëv's Eurasian Ideology

The feeling of affinity, the participation in a common culture and tradition, the awareness of a common destiny, which are of the essence of national sentiment and patriotism, are transformed by nationalism into a political mysticism in which the national community and the state become superhuman entities, apart from, and superior to, their individual members, entitled to absolute loyalty and, like the idols of old, deserving of the sacrifice of men and goods.[1]

Across historiography, Pečenegs, Oğuz, Cuman-Qıpčaqs and other nomads have been cast within a binary: as either enemies of civilisation or manifesting cooperation between Rus' and the Eurasian steppe.[2] The former interpretation, common in Russian literature for centuries, plays into the standard Christian-versus-pagan dichotomy.[3] The latter interpretation is newer, and became an essential component of the Eurasianist school of Soviet and post-Soviet historiography led by Lev Gumilëv, which has reflected recent ethnonational geopolitics.

The commonly accepted interpretation of steppe-nomads in traditional Russian historiography derives from the *PVL*, which depicts the Polovcÿ (Cuman-Qıpčaqs) in the entries for the years 1068, 1093 and 1096[4] as a 'hostile force' bent on invasion.[5] Similarly, the sedentary and Christianised Russian narrative is presented by the compilers as demonstrating

[1] Morgenthau, *Politics among Nations*, 119.
[2] Golden, 'Nomadic Economic Development of Rus'', 58–62.
[3] Mavrodina, *Киевская русь и кочевники*, 11–45.
[4] *Povest' Vremennÿkh Let*, tr. Cross and Sherbowitz-Wetzor, *Russian Primary Chronicle*, 146–9, 174–9, 181–7.
[5] Garagozov, 'Collective Memory', 61.

supremacy over steppe-nomads.⁶ When inserted into the Orthodox Christian template to explain pagan-nomad victories against Christians, it became a divine punishment, resembling Jordanes' interpretation of Attila's Huns.⁷ Regarded as the 'Mongol yoke', this interpretation survived into the Soviet period.⁸ So deeply held was this interpretation, that Gumilëv called it the 'black legend'.⁹ Gumilëv's concept of 'Eurasianism' advocates a primordial ethnic alliance between the ancient Rus' and the steppe-nomads (Pečenegs, Cuman-Qıpčaqs, Oğuz, etc.). The traditional interpretation receded in the late Soviet period.¹⁰

Gumilëv's Eurasianism and theories of primordial ethnicity have become well established in current geopolitical relations within the post-Soviet Commonwealth of Independent States (Kazakhstan's Gumilëv Eurasian National University was refounded in 1996). Gumilëv reinterpreted the image of the alien steppe as a predominantly Western one and developed dual concepts of 'ethnic chimera' and 'passionarity' with the intention of fostering current transnational amity based on primordial ethnic identities.¹¹ Gumilëv's concept of 'passionarity' (пассионарность) rests on identifying ancient ethnicities based on their collective drive, or passion, which theoretically summarises groups based on their collective tendencies, although practically slips into simple stereotypes. The so-called 'ethnic chimera' for Gumilëv meant foreigners contaminating an otherwise pure ethnic host, acting as parasites.

This notion of parasitism went far in Soviet historiography to describe Jewish Khazaria, in contrast to 'a Russo-Turanian union' of Rus' and Pečenegs.¹² This thinly veiled anti-Semitism sought to create an imagined common parasitic enemy (Jews) to unite the ancient Rus' and Pečenegs,¹³

---

⁶ Koptev, '"Chazar Tribute"', 195.

⁷ Jordanes, *Getica*, tr. Mierow, *Jordanes: Origins and Deeds of Goths*, 57.

⁸ Golubovskij, *Печенеги, торки и половцы*; Solev'ëv, *История россии с древнейших времён*; Kostomarov, *Исторические монографии и исследования*, 112; Iwanus, *Democracy, Federalism, and Nationality*; Mavrodina, *Киевская русь и кочевники*, 11–45; Halperin, *Russia and Golden Horde*; Anderson, *Antiquity to Feudalism*, 218–28.

⁹ Gumilëv, *Древняя русь и великая степь*, 210–16.

¹⁰ Mavrodina, *Киевская русь и кочевники*, 76–8; Hurwitz, 'Review: *Kievskaia Rus' i kochevniki*', 102–3.

¹¹ Mjusse, *Варварские нашествия на западную европу*; Garagozov, 'Collective Memory', 78–9.

¹² Gumilëv, *Этногенез и биосфера земли*, 42, 302; Zhivkov, *Khazaria*, 166–7, 212–15.

¹³ Rossman, 'Lev Gumilev, Eurasian and Khazaria', 30–51; Hurwitz, 'Review: *Kievskaia Rus' i kochevniki*', 103; Klier, 'Review: *Myth of Khazars and Intellectual Antisemitism*', 779–81; Yasmann, 'Rise of Eurasians'; Shnirelman, 'Story of Euphemism', 353–72.

resembling traditional anti-Semitic conspiracy theories like the *Protocols of the Elders of Zion*.[14] Gumilëv portrays Jews as causing ethnic decay among Christians, Muslims and pagans, while simultaneously assuming that ethnicity is a primordial, biological phenomenon, unrelated to monotheism.[15]

Nevertheless, while Gumilëv rightly recognised the false dichotomy of steppe-paganism versus Rus'ian Christianity, his theories of ethnogenesis, 'passionarity' and 'ethnic chimera' have little else to commend them.[16] The Pečenegs and other nomadic pagan groups should be viewed as reflections of their contact with monotheistic and/or sedentary political formations.[17] Most of the ninth- to eleventh-century Oğuz, Cuman-Qıpčaqs, Magyars and Pečenegs were pagan nomads, but just because primary sources like the *DAI* refer to them as distinct groups does not mean we ought to accept such distinctions as primordial ethnicities. The major difference between such groups was whether a ruler adopted a form of monotheism and successfully imposed it on his subjects. Before Stephen's Christianisation, for example, we have little recourse to archaeological evidence confirming ethnic differences between Magyars and Pečenegs. After St Stephen, a gradual top-down process of Christianisation in Pannonia is visible, but there is nothing comparable for those eleventh-century nomads who remained in the Pontic-Caspian steppe.

---

[14] Ben-Itto, *Lie that Wouldn't Die*; Ignác, 'Egy miniszter a tévesztett úton', 966.
[15] Gumilëv, Древняя русь и великая степь, 282.
[16] Jakubovskij, 'Феодальное общество азии', 24.
[17] Khazanov, 'Nomads in History of Sedentary World', 2; Honeychurch, 'Alternative Complexities', 279; Todorov, 'Value of Empire', 320.

Appendix 3
The Khazar-Ashkenazi Descent Theory

Plato introduces his Myth of Blood and Soil with the blunt admission that it is a fraud. 'Well then', says the Socrates of the Republic, 'could we perhaps fabricate one of those very handy lies which indeed we mentioned just recently? With the help of one single lordly lie we may, if we are lucky, persuade even the rulers themselves – but at any rate the rest of the city.'[1]

A nation is a society united by a delusion about its ancestry and by a common hatred of its neighbours.[2]

L'oubli, et je dirai même l'erreur historique, sont un facteur essentiel de la formation d'une nation.[3]

There are many strands, subcategories and highly debated taxonomies within Judaism – governed by theology, doxology, jurisprudence, language and descent. The differences between the two main branches of Judaic communities, Sephardim (and Mizrahim) and Ashkenazim, are well known: they emerged from Judaic communities in the Islamic *ummah* and Christian *oikoumene*, respectively – with attendant geographical subcategories. Judaic communities also survived for centuries further south, east and beyond the Abrahamic worlds, such as Beta Israel and the Teimanim (Eastern Africa and Southern Arabia), Kaifeng Jews (western China) and Kochinim (southern India). All these communities date back centuries and

---

[1] Popper, *Open Society and Its Enemies*, 132.
[2] Inge, *End of an Age*, 127.
[3] Renan, *Qu'est-ce qu'une nation?*, 7: 'Forgetting, and I would even say historical error, are an essential factor in the formation of a nation.'

their origins remain the subject of many discussions. However, one of the most contentious debates is about the origin of the Ashkenazim – or as typically described, the Jewish populations of Central and Eastern Europe.

There are two schematic theories about the origin of the Ashkenazim: that they settled in Central and Eastern Europe via a western route through Western Europe and/or via an eastern route through Caucasia and Khazaria. The former, termed the 'Rhineland hypothesis', is the most commonly accepted theory for Ashkenazi origins: according to this theory, following the diaspora in the wake of the Roman suppression of the second-century Bar Kokhba Revolt, Jewish communities emerged in second- to fifth-century Western Roman imperial provinces like Hispania, Gaul, Britannia and Italy, which remained until various thirteenth- to fourteenth-century anti-Jewish expulsions and Crusader violence, leading to eastward migrations towards Piast-ruled lands due to simultaneous legal protections granted by Piast kings.[4] Yet the latter theory, via Caucasia and Khazaria, cannot be completely dismissed. Therefore, this has led to duelling misconceptions about the extent of Khazarian Judaism and Ashkenazi origins. The profoundly anti-Semitic and anti-Jewish implications are unmistakable,[5] as the Khazar-Ashkenazi descent theory has recently filled in for the *Protocols* theory – if a century ago, Jews controlled the world, now, for those who traffic in the Khazarian theory, Jews are not even truly Jews.[6]

Lacking nuance, both theories are overly schematic and simplistic – assuming a single layer of Ashkenazi ethnogenesis. Yet this has not stopped some from speculating about the possibility of Khazarian Jews as the forerunners of Ashkenazim.

This theory was most clearly promoted by Arthur Koestler's *Thirteenth Tribe*,[7] which compensated for little hard evidence with mostly innuendo

---

[4] Chazan, *European Jewry and First Crusade*, 16–27; Chazan, *Jews of Medieval Western Christendom*, 202–3.

[5] Soteri, 'Khazaria', 10–12; Ya'ari, 'Skeletons', 29–30; Weinryb, 'Solving "Khazar Problem"', 431–43; Roth, *Chasaren*, 204–5; Schirrmacher, 'Osteuropäischen Juden', 3–7; Preiser-Kapeller, 'Jewish Empire?'.

[6] Perhaps one of the most egregious examples of anti-Semitic and/or anti-Jewish literature regarding the abuse of the Khazar-Ashkenazi descent theory for political purposes was Soratroi's *Attilas Enkel auf Davids Thron*, which was banned in Germany. For example, he claims that 'currently the Semitic Jews are only 10 percent, but the eastern Jewish Khazar descendants make up 90 percent of the world's Jewish population and also in what is now Israel' (p. 56). Similar positions are staked by Texe Marrs' *DNA Science and Jewish Bloodline*. Regardless of their political agendas, these suppositions are not only unsupported by evidence, they are outrageous.

[7] Koestler, *Thirteenth Tribe*.

and conjecture, causing 'much confusion in discussion on cultural history and religion.'[8] According to Koestler, who employed the primordial assumption of ethnicity (still common in the 1960s–70s), Ashkenazim, recently Yiddish-speaking, were originally Turkic-speaking, and came to Central and Eastern Europe through the Caucasus and Khazaria. This theory, termed the 'Khazarian hypothesis', has garnered a small but devoted following who reject the Rhineland hypothesis because it unsatisfactorily explains a dramatic expansion of the fourteenth- to sixteenth-century Ashkenazi populations. Yet a confluence of Jews from Byzantine Eastern and Latin Western Europe would most probably explain the fourteenth- to sixteenth-century Ashkenazi population growth in Polish-Lithuanian lands, along with favourable judicial-economic conditions there.[9] Nevertheless, proponents of the Khazarian hypothesis have employed dubious linguistic and genetic methods to support their conclusions.[10]

Yiddish, the common Ashkenazi language (as Ladino for Sephardim), has been claimed to bear traces of Turkic speech and grammar, which may indicate a Khazarian basis for later Ashkenazi communities. Tracing the etymologies of various Yiddish words to Slavic roots, for example, the linguist Paul Wexler concluded that Yiddish contained linguistic evidence of Turkic elements – making a Khazarian connection possible.[11] This is not difficult to imagine: speakers of Slavic-Judaic dialects, known as Knaanic, are acknowledged to have intermingled with Yiddish speakers during the tenth to fifteenth centuries; Knaanic Jews certainly intermingled with concurrent Sephardic communities.[12] Jewish communities, presumably Slavic (Knaanic) speaking, are known to have existed in Kiev and nearby towns as early as the mid-tenth century and possibly earlier in the late ninth century, based on the *Kievan Letter*, which has been used as evidence of Khazarian converts to Judaism due to extra-biblical names and an inscription in Turkic runes meaning 'I have read it.'[13] However, the *Kievan Letter*'s extra-biblical names such as Sinai and Hanukkah are at most possibly Hebrew

---

[8] Werbart, 'Invisible Identities', 93.
[9] Faber and King, 'Yiddish and Settlement of Ashkenazic Jews', 409; Kulik, 'Jewish Presence in Western Rus'', 13–24.
[10] Elhaik, 'Missing Link of Jewish Ancestry', 61–74; Kriwaczek, *Yiddish Civilization*, 46–51; Wexler, *Ashkenazic Jews*; Sand, *Invention of Jewish People*, 210–49.
[11] Wexler, *Two-Tiered Relexification of Yiddish*, 513–518; Wexler, 'Yiddish Evidence for Khazar Ashkenazic Ethnogenesis', 387–98.
[12] Kulik, 'Jewish Presence in Western Rus'', 13–24.
[13] Chekin, 'Jews in Early Russian Civilization', 383–9; Taube, 'Scientific Texts in Eastern Knaan', 315–53.

names adopted by converts (as Greek Christian names were adopted by Rus' princes), but this alone does not prove Turkic descent.[14] Nevertheless, long-time Greek-speaking Byzantine Jewish communities in the Crimean and Taman' peninsulas contributed to later populations in Kiev and elsewhere in Rus' lands, which gradually became Knaanic-speaking.[15] Therefore, whether or not Turkic words in Yiddish indicate Khazarian linguistic residue, the Yiddish language preserves very few such Turkic words,[16] which are otherwise far better represented in languages spoken by Karaite Jewish communities claiming descent from Khazar Jews.

Yet a few loanwords have little bearing on a supposed Khazar-Karaite descent, let alone the Ashkenazim specifically.[17] According to Peter Golden, the 'Turkic speech of the East European Karaites is an adopted language, not one "inherited" from Turkic ancestors'.[18] Furthermore, due to the theological differences between Ashkenazim and Karaim (rabbinical and non-rabbinical practice, respectively), compounded by linguistic differences, it is unlikely that Khazar Jews were non-rabbinical, based on references to the Talmud and Mishnah in *King Joseph's Reply*.[19] However, it is also possible that although Joseph's Judaism was rabbinical (observing the Talmud, Mishnah, etc.), subsequent converts became Karaites (without recognising the Talmud, Mishnah, etc.).[20] Therefore, rabbinical Judaism suggested by *King Joseph's Reply* hardly proves that Karaim *cannot* claim Khazarian descent, and therefore non-Semitic status, which led to different racial legislation applied to each community in the World War II era, and eventually, Koestler's attempt to deny Ashkenazi Semitism. Ultimately, spoken languages have never been permanent; they have always changed,

---

[14] *Kievan Letter*, eds and tr. Golb and Pritsak, *Khazarian Hebrew Documents*, 14–15, 21–29; Kulik, 'Judeo-Greek Legacy', 53–4.

[15] Kulik, 'Judeo-Greek Legacy', 55–64; Kulik, 'Jews of *Slavia Graeca*', 297–314.

[16] Brook, 'Origins of East European Jews', 18.

[17] Faber and King, 'Yiddish and Settlement of Ashkenazic Jews', 411–12; Gold, 'Origins of Yiddish and Ashkenazic Jewry', 356–7.

[18] Peter B. Golden, personal communication, December 2020.

[19] *King Joseph's Reply*, ed. and tr. Kokovcov, Еврейско-хазарская переписка, 31.

[20] Peter B. Golden, personal communication, December 2020. However, it is also true that mid-tenth-century Karaite scholars like Japhet b. 'Āli harboured hostility towards the Khazars, whom Japhet b. 'Āli termed *mamzerim* (ממזרים) – illegitimate. On the original relationship between Khazars and Karaites, two points are most important: first, the Karaites were aware of Khazar Judaism (and most probably not from reading Arabic geographical accounts or ibn Fadlān) and second, Khazarian Judaism was not Karaite and there was little mutual interest: cf. Dunlop, *History of Jewish Khazars*, 221; Ankori, *Karaites in Byzantium*, 64–79.

sometimes rapidly, and sometimes even inside the same household within two generations.[21]

Because linguistic, toponymic and onomastic evidence is insufficient to prove Ashkenazi descent, the geneticist Elhaik and others have joined Wexler, instead attempting to supplement the slim linguistic evidence for the Khazar-Ashkenazi descent theory with genetic evidence. Beginning with the assumption that genetic evidence indicates primordial ethnicity (a patently misleading assumption), Elhaik fashioned a genetic methodology of using 'surrogate' present populations as substitutes for historical populations. According to his assumptions, 'Palestinians were considered proto-Judeans [...] Caucasus Georgians and Armenians were considered proto-Khazars', expecting that Ashkenazim would 'cluster with native Middle Eastern or Caucasus populations according to the Rhineland of Khazarian hypotheses, respectively'. One might ask: what is the determinative factor for defining 'Khazarian populations'? Can current Armenians, Georgians, Čečens and Ukrainians realistically be substituted as Khazars by genetics? How would this model *not* presuppose primordial ethnicity? How does this model account for historical processes like monotheisation and sedentarisation? Unsurprisingly, Elhaik found that neither hypothesis was entirely accurate and instead that 'the genome of European Jews is a tapestry of ancient populations'.[22] Elhaik subsequently joined Wexler and others in combining methods of ethnogenetic surrogacy and ethnolinguistic continuity. Unsurprisingly, they begin again with the same primordialist assumptions of Ashkenazi ethnogenesis. First, deeming their method 'GPS – (genetic population structure)', they attempt to link to several seventh- to tenth-century 'primeval' villages in the Byzantine Pontic region of Chaldia (northeastern Anatolia), due to similarities between the ethnonym 'Ashkenaz' and the names of these villages: İşkenaz, Eşkenez, Aşhanas and Aschuz. Then, they postulate a 'common Irano-Turkic-Slavic culture' as the Ashkenazi origin (even though this area was firmly within the Byzantine Pontic region for centuries) and categorically reject the Rhineland hypothesis as 'major migrations from Germany to Poland which did not take place'. Furthermore, they contradict themselves, claiming that Ashkenazim 'comprised a mostly homogeneous group in terms of genetic admixture', even though 'the broader Ashkenazic Jewish community [...] is likely more genetically heterogenous'. They conclude that although the GPS methodology is imperfect (but not current population genetic surrogacy), Yiddish

---

[21] Gold, 'Origins of Yiddish and Ashkenazic Jewry', 340, 354–5, 363.
[22] Elhaik, 'Missing Link of Jewish Ancestry', 64–6, 73.

ethnolinguistic origins indicate a broad confluence of Ashkenazi roots, probably related to the eighth- to eleventh-century Radanite presence in long-range Eurasian Silk Roads and trade networks.[23] None of this should be mistaken for rigorous historical methodology.

Yet without deploying models of ethnogenesis grounded in historical methodological research, these narrow linguistic and genetic approaches often prove misleading and easily misguided, assuming over-schematic models of Ashkenazi ethnogenesis and instead intentionally indicating misleading evidence 'for those with a political agenda for which the Khazar hypothesis is far more useful'.[24] It must be said that there is too much variance to prove beyond a shadow of doubt primordial ethnic identity using genetic markers alone.[25] For the most part, the DNA of those who identify as Ashkenazim is so disparate that even among the stratum of Levites alone, there are several different origins. However, they mostly coincide with Western European and Levantine provenances,[26] although the Levantine origin is more strongly indicated.[27] Nevertheless, the works of Costa, Nebel and their respective teams have demonstrated evidence suggesting a 'founder effect' as the foundation of later Ashkenazi populations.[28] This means that Ashkenazi communities probably emerged from founders who moved to Western Europe bearing Levantine genetic traces – although this is not yet conclusive. As for the Caucasian-Khazarian origin, there simply is no hard evidence to support it.[29] Studies of DNA cannot even be satisfactorily tied to specifically 'Turkic' peoples, let alone specifically Khazars.[30] A recent study has confirmed that 'no significant Ashkenazi genetic affinity was detected in any of the sequenced individuals' found in seemingly 'Khazar burials'.[31] Yet, as previously noted, funerary archaeology can hardly prove the ethnic status of the deceased – especially in the case of

---

[23] Das et al., 'Primeval Villages in Ancient Iranian Lands of Ashkenaz', 1140, 1144–6.
[24] Efron, 'Jewish Genetic Origins', 916.
[25] Carmi et al., 'Identity-by-Descent Sharing in Wright-Fisher Model', 911–28.
[26] Behar et al., 'Multiple Origins of Ashkenazi Levites', 768–79.
[27] Rootsi et al., 'Phylogenetic Y-Chromosome Sequences', 1–9.
[28] Costa et al., 'European Ancestry Amongst Ashkenazi Lineages', 1–10; Nebel et al., 'Founder Effect in Ashkenazi Jews', 388–91.
[29] Behar et al., 'No Evidence of Khazar Origin for Ashkenazi Jews', 859–900; Behar, 'Origins of Ashkenazi Levites'.
[30] Pilipenko et al., 'Генофонд днк древнетюркского населения алтая', 267–9; Afanas'ev and Korobov, 'Северокавказские аланы по палеогенетики', 180–91; Klyosov and Faleeva, 'DNA from Khazar Burials', 17–21; Werbart, 'Khazars or "Saltovo-Majaki Culture"?', 199–221; Werbart, 'Invisible Identities', 83–99.
[31] Mikheyev et al., 'Genetic Origins of Medieval Steppe Nomad Conquerors'.

the Khazars. It is far too simplistic to assume primordial ethnicity without first considering the effect of monotheism on ethnicity. Even though a similar point was made in response,[32] it seems that a new twenty-first-century Normanist debate has sadly emerged in Khazar studies, where two sides argue about whether Khazarian and Ashkenazi DNA can be linked, even though the whole debate is largely perpetuated for the sake of misguided current political and ideological agendas. Ultimately the entire edifice about applying genetics to understanding demographic history over a thousand years ago rests on ill-advised assumptions of continuous and primordial ethnicity – even though monotheistic identity is a far more crucial factor of ethnicity than genetics.[33]

The most pivotal debate about the Khazar-Ashkenazi descent theory concerns not toponymy and haplotypes but source evidence. This has contributed to some scholars' denial of Khazaria's conversion to Judaism at all. Two historians, Moshe Gil and Shaul Stampfer, have argued that the source evidence is insufficient to prove that the Khazars converted to Judaism in the first place.

Beginning with his shorter, earlier article, Gil argues that the entire conversion never happened because the first Islamic author to mention it, ibn Fadlān, from whom later authors derived this story of the Khazarian *khağan*'s Judaism, was evidently mistaken because he supposedly never visited Khazaria at all (*he did*).[34] Nevertheless, according to Gil's reasoning, subsequent Islamic geographers never believed the story at all, and if they did, their sources are 'devoid of real historical value'. For Gil, ibn Fadlān's characterisation of the Khazars as Jewish was meant purely as generic invective instead of an accurate portrayal of early–920s events between the Volga Bulgar king Almuš and the Khazar *khağan*. Interpreting ibn Fadlān's story as a literary trope may not be an entirely erroneous assumption, but the main problem with Gil's argument is its oversimplification of sources which *ignore* or *are silent about* Khazarian Judaism: arguments *ad ignorantiam* or *ex silentio*. Additionally, the *DAI* is the only non-Islamic source which Gil's article addresses and he categorically dismisses Khazarian sources. In presenting ibn Fadlān's *Risāla* as the original source of misinformation about Khazarian Judaisation, he neglects to

---

[32] Elhaik, 'Response to Mikheyev et al. (2019)'.
[33] Geary, 'Rethinking Barbarian Invasions through Genomic History', 1–8.
[34] This is misleading: Almuš paid tribute to the Khazarian *khağan* at the time of ibn Fadlān's visit. Therefore, by visiting Almuš, Fadlān entered the domain of the Khazarian *khağan*.

mention al-Muqaddasī's and ibn Rusta's assertions of the Khazars' Judaism, as well as ibn al-Faqīh, in his *Kitâb al-Buldân* (written a generation before ibn Fadlān's *Risāla* – c. 903), who reports, 'all of the Khazars are Jews. But, they have been Judaized recently.' This is puzzling, since Gil devotes a paragraph to the study of de Goeje's 1885 edition of al-Faqīh's *Kitâb al-Buldân* and cites no fewer than six pages of the source in his thirteenth note, yet never once refers to page 298 of de Goeje's edition, on which al-Faqīh writes that the Khazars had converted to Judaism. This raises questions about Gil's political agenda; he writes:

> This topic, the Khazars, their nature, their origin, and their assumed Jewish connection, preoccupied during several generations important historians, beginning with Harkavy, and some of our contemporaries, continuing it. Nothing in this is a wonder. It brought about some peacefulness in the self-hatred, which took hold of many Jews. Here is information, clear and enthusiastic, on the existence of a Jewish state in the Middle Ages. Most importantly: the Ashkenazi Jews, part of them or their majority, were shown to be not descendants of Abraham, Isaac and Jacob, but of Khazars who converted to Judaism.

Clearly, the argument was meant to address the Khazar-Ashkenazi descent theory, rather than engaging with Khazaria on its own terms. The article's final words are also noteworthy: 'all historical discussions, or assumptions on conversion of the Khazars to Judaism, inclusive of Jewish medieaval [sic] texts, are totally baseless. It never happened.'[35] Two years later in a similar argument with the same title, Shaul Stampfer, although broadly agreeing with Gil's conclusions, chose to include the statement: 'His article was translated into English, but it seems never to have been cited by any researcher.'

Nevertheless, Stampfer's subsequent publication is quite worthy of its own assessment, given its exploration of the sources Gil ignores.[36] These sources include the tenth-century Khazarian Hebrew documents, Christian of Stavelot, ibn al-Faqīh, the *PVL*, and archaeological evidence like the Khazarian *Moses* coins. However, as with Gil's article, Stampfer's arguments of textual interpretation begin with the preformed conclusion that any source confirming the *khağans'* conversion to Judaism must be doubted. This approach unfortunately implies that these sources ought to be rejected by other historians who use them to assess other aspects of Khazaria or even Pontic-Caspian Eurasia broadly. For example, are we to

[35] Gil, 'Did Khazars Convert to Judaism?', 429–41.
[36] Stampfer, 'Did Khazars Convert to Judaism?', 1–72.

accept Christian of Stavelot's late-ninth-century reference to the Bulgarian *khaǧans*' adoption of Christianity while we dismiss his simultaneous reference to the Khazarian *khaǧans*' adoption of Judaism? It may be easier to accept the former while doubting the latter if only due to the teleological assumptions of incautious historians. For another example, ought historians to doubt the reports of al-Faqīh and Rusta only when it comes to Khazarian Judaism, but accept their historicity regarding everything else? Stampfer's dismissal of the historical reliability of so many sources is worth evaluating, in terms of first the Islamic sources, then the Christian sources (Byzantine, Rus' and Latin), then the Khazarian sources and finally the archaeological material (including the *Moses* coins).

Stampfer begins by enumerating many seemingly permanent political and ideological agendas and counter-agendas in the field, from anti-Zionism and anti-Semitism to Stalinism, Turanism, Finno-Ugrism and so forth, which are also visible in genetic and linguistic studies. He rejects the model of gradual Judaisation in Khazaria as having 'little logic' and as indicative of 'ties, imagined or real, between Jews and Khazars'. Instead, Stampfer describes his criticism of many historians' assessments of the attempted Judaisation of Khazaria as 'long overdue' due to 'political and ideological repercussions, [though] such readings have little if any place in academic discourse'. He claims the voice of objectivity: 'I will deal here as much as possible with the simple question of what did or did not happen.' Unfortunately, separating evidence from agenda is never a simple question. Before commencing his treatment of the relevant sources, he remarks, 'if even one source can be proven reliable, then the question of Khazar conversion is decided.'[37] Rather, if many sources, from vastly different geographical regions and in different

---

[37] Ibid., 3–7. It is also notable that Stampfer disputes the idea that the Khazars chose Judaism over either Islam or Christianity as indicative of taking 'a neutral stance' 'in the conflict between Christianity and Islam'. He problematises the 'neutral stance' although he does not acknowledge that it could be viewed differently: namely that the Khazars could have chosen Judaism to avoid being ecclesiastically (and therefore politically) subjugated by either the Islamic caliph or the Christian emperor. In other words, Stampfer characterises the claim that the Khazars took a 'neutral stance' 'in the conflict between Christianity and Islam' as some kind of eternal conflict in which Judaism had no part (plainly a teleological trope when viewed from the eighth to tenth centuries), instead of as remaining *independent* from either Islam or Christianity. He is certainly correct that the logic of monotheistic independence is inherently speculative, but his claim that 'there is also no evidence [for choosing] a religion as a result of political calculation' is a bit simplistic when juxtaposed with the vast majority of contemporaneous rulers' conversions, in which the monotheism and politics were inseparable.

languages, all point towards the same thing, then it is instead the straw-man arguments rejecting them, *ex silentio* and *ad ignorantiam*, which are 'indirect and circumstantial'.

Three tenth-century Khazarian Hebrew documents, for example, *King Joseph's Reply*, the *Schechter Text* and the *Kievan Letter*, all point towards Judaisation, even if they separately narrate different versions of it or illuminate different aspects of it (in the case of the *Kievan Letter*). These sources ought not to be mined for imagined truths and fallacies to suit current ideological and political agendas. Whether they are deemed 'epic narratives' or 'official contemporary accounts', these categories are irrelevant since the sources are written in Hebrew.[38] As Marshall McLuhan famously said: 'The medium *is* the message'.

Much the same can be said about addressing the context surrounding contemporaneous Christian Greek and Latin sources. Simply put, the historian seeks to shift the burden of proof onto the sources, rather than his own argument. The opposite should be the case. For example, admittedly, neither the ninth- to tenth-century Slavonic *Vita Constantini*, nor the letter of Anastasius Bibliothecarius (the Librarian), nor the letters of the patriarch Nicholas Mystikos (to the bishop of Cherson regarding the Khazars, dating to the years 914 and 920) overtly reference the *khağans'* Judaisation.[39] Yet the context is unmistakable. Knowing these sources to be full of pro-Christian embellishments, and combining them with the Khazarian Hebrew sources which refer explicitly to the *khağans'* Judaisation, it is clear that Judaism was concurrently quite influential in Khazaria. To deny this would be to engage in logical fallacies and arguments from ignorance: the second letter of patriarch Nicholas Mystikos does not prove that the Khazars were *not* Jewish just because it refers to an effort to Christianise Khazaria without previously referring to Judaism among the Khazars. As the old saying goes, the absence of evidence does not prove the evidence of absence. Additionally, the second letter, dated 920, clearly refers to Khazaria as 'that deluded nation', testifying to the context of proselytic competition between Judaism, Christianity and Islam in ninth- to tenth-century Khazaria, which is clearly attested in the Slavonic *Vita Constantini*. The urge not to give one's competitors free publicity is timeless.

Considering Islamic sources such as ibn Fadlān's *Risāla*, which alleges both Khazarian Judaism and Khazarian practices that would have been 'in clear violation of Jewish law', certain reductive arguments can be evinced

---

[38] Pritsak, 'Khazar Kingdom's Conversion to Judaism', 261–81.
[39] Stampfer, 'Did Khazars Convert to Judaism?', 12–13.

based on normative, perhaps even Halakhic, strains of Judaism, which I find difficult to suppose was practised in Khazaria. Therefore, discrediting Fadlān's *Risāla* 'as a reliable source for Khazar conversion to Judaism' is ill-advised.[40] Ought Fadlān's *Risāla* be dismissed only when it comes to Khazarian Judaism, but not for many other topics, for which it is studied by historians? The same can be said about arguments from the silence of the sources. Just because ninth- to tenth-century Christian and Islamic authors like ibn Khurradādhbih, ibn Ja'far and Konstantinos VII Porphyrogennetos mention Khazaria yet ignore the Judaism therein, this does not mean that it was absent. Relying on arguments from silence in a few sources in order to prove Judaism *did not exist* among the Khazarian *khağans* distorts the overwhelming evidence that Judaism in Khazaria *did exist* in a variety of other sources – independently composed and largely confirmed. Ultimately, abductive reasoning is more straightforward than reductive reasoning; the former is expressed as the duck test: if it looks like a duck, walks like a duck and quacks like a duck, then it is probably a duck.

There is nothing 'false [about] statements'[41] which plainly accept the overwhelming textual and archaeological evidence of ninth- to tenth-century Khazarian Judaism, which was neither monolithic nor necessarily liturgically coefficient with present strands of Judaism. But equally, this statement does not endorse the position that the Ashkenazim are descended from Khazarian Jews either. There is a middle ground which can simultaneously accept Khazarian Judaism and doubt the Khazar-Ashkenazi descent theory advanced in dubious genetic studies. By making arguments about textual sources *ex silentio* and *ad ignorantiam*, and by intentionally discrediting numerous sources which otherwise confirm Khazarian Judaism, we are left with a deliberately hobbled view of Khazaria. Why should arguments from silence only apply to Khazarian Judaism and not elsewhere? Who ought to decide where and to what extent arguments from silence are acceptable and when they would establish or impinge on historical veracity?

Nevertheless, Stampfer makes an excellent point in discussing the veracity of the tenth-century Khazarian documents relating to the conversion when he calls attention to the deliberate mythologisation of conversion stories, and casts doubt on their historical reliability in conjunction with other Christian, Muslim and Jewish sources as well. Yet, by the same token, how can we justify rejecting one part of one source for one purpose

---

[40] Ibid., 13–14.
[41] Ibid., 37.

while accepting another part of the same source for a different purpose? For instance, if the historical utility of the *PVL* is rejected, which deliberately mythologises Vladimir's acceptance of Byzantine Christianity, what makes it a useful source in other instances such as Svjatoslav's conquest of Khazaria in 965–9? Stampfer rightly acknowledges that despite the absence of an abundance of texts referring to Jews themselves in Khazaria, 'this absence does not mean that there were no Jews in Khazaria in the medieval period'.[42] The extent to which Byzantine-Khazarian Jewish communities in places like the Crimean and Taman' peninsulas can be linked to later Jewish communities in Central and Eastern Europe may be debatable, but this possible linkage cannot ultimately be disproven.

The lands of Ashkenaz also developed their own cohesion – and were probably not formed exclusively from migration from Western Europe.[43] Many Jewish communities who later formed Ashkenazi Jewry could be traced back to Byzantium.[44] They could equally share common descent from the Karaite communities, but there is no evidence that either group claimed any affinity with the Khazars in the tenth to eleventh centuries.[45] The most likely scenario is that these Byzantine Jewish communities intermingled with Western Jewish communities as well as Sephardic and Mizrahi communities.[46] After all, there is ample evidence of conversion to Judaism followed by intermingling of previously distinct communities in many other times and places for centuries – it may have been uncommon but it was not *beyond the pale*.[47] This does not confirm the Khazar-Ashkenazi descent theory either – the thirteenth- to sixteenth-century migrations of Jewish populations eastward mostly likely dwarfed the smaller Byzantine Jewish communities in the northern Black Sea region.[48] Ultimately, wherever exactly the communities came from who later

---

[42] Ibid., 45 n48.
[43] Visi, *Peripheries of Ashkenaz*.
[44] Sivertsev, *Judaism and Imperial Ideology in Late Antiquity*; Kohen, *History of Byzantine Jews*; Kulik, 'Judeo-Greek Legacy', 51–64; Kulik, 'Jews of *Slavia Graeca*', 297–314; Dunlop, *History of Jewish Khazars*; Shepard, 'Khazars' Formal Adoption of Judaism', 9–34.
[45] Ankori, *Karaites in Byzantium*, 58–86.
[46] Chekin, 'Jews in Early Russian Civilization', 379–94; Brook, 'Origins of East European Jews', 1–22; Kulik, 'Jewish Presence in Western Rus', 13–24; Ioffe, 'Jews, Khazars and Slavic Cultural History', 385–405; van Straten, 'Origin of Ashkenazim via Southern Route', 239–70.
[47] Forster and Tabachnik, *Jews by Choice*, 32–3; Goodman, *Mission and Conversion*, 152–3; Epstein, *Welcoming Converts to Judaism*, 72–5; Seidel, 'Cases and Converts in Jewish History', 103–28.
[48] Brook, 'Origins of East European Jews', 22.

formed the Ashkenazi Jewish populations, there is insufficient evidence to categorically *dismiss* a tiny element drawn from Khazaria – yet this does not mean that Ashkenazim are Khazars – Khazar Jews were always a tiny portion of the subjects of the *khağans*. They were mostly residents of the Crimean and Taman' peninsulas, had resided there long before the Khazars appeared in the literature, and continued to reside there up to the nineteenth to twentieth centuries – even to this day. Yet the presence of Black Sea Jewish communities does not change the fact that the Ashkenazim have just as much claim to their Judaism as do the Sephardim and Mizrahim.

Whether or not we believe in a primordial or a circumstantial (or both) Jewish connection to Spain, Eastern Europe, or the Levant does not change the fact that Jews have always been Jews, and have also had to defend Judaism.[49] This is no more a comment on Khazaria than it is on Israel or other Jews worldwide today.[50] Ultimately, Judaism has been a scriptural tradition before being a genetic tradition. Two seemingly opposite concepts can be held in one's mind simultaneously; one can respect ancestors while simultaneously recognising that ancestry is never a simple story.[51]

---

[49] Weiss, 'Fortress Forever at Ready', 287–344.
[50] Asadov, 'Khazar Studies between Scarcity of Sources and Policy Concerns', 1–11; Kizilov and Mikhaylova, 'Khazars in Nationalist Ideologies and Scholarship', 31–53; in the words of Soteri ('Khazaria', 12),

> "There is a lesson to be learned from such an ironic twist of history. Whether one considers themselves Russian, Bosnian, Serbian, Albanian, Croatian, or Macedonian there is no valid criterion for establishing such nationalisms. Just as the Jews of Central and Eastern Europe (using the Khazar example) are more or less of the same 'racial stock' as the peoples they find themselves among, so too are the Muslims of the Balkans, Croats, Bosnians and Serbs. When one speaks of Bosnian Croats/Serbs this becomes a contradiction in terms (highlighting the futility of racial categorisations). Both are Bosnians, yet due to their religious bent, i.e. Orthodox or Catholic Christianity, identify, or are identified, with Serbian or Croat nationalisms. To add fuel to the fire, why do we in the West refer to 'Bosnian Muslims'? Using religion as an indication of ethnicity for the latter group but not for their Christian counterparts. The problems of nationalism in Eastern Europe are much more complex than a simple explanation of religious difference. However, using the example of the Khazars and their descendants, it can be exemplified that nationalist movements, with their tenacious convictions about race, can affect the perceptions of both aggressor and victim alike which, when one probes deeper into the espoused ideologies, seem to be based on false premises and, ultimately, contradictory theories."

[51] Levy-Coffman, 'We Are Not Our Ancestors', 40–50.

Bibliography

Primary Sources

Abo of Tiflis, *Vita*, tr. D. Lang, *Lives and Legends of the Georgian Saints*, 2nd edn (New York, 1976), 115–33.

Abo of Tiflis, *Vita*, tr. P. Peeters, 'Les Khazars dans la passion de s. Abo de Tiflis', *Analecta Bollandiana* 52 (1934), 21–56.

Acts of the Great Lavra Monastery, eds P. Lemerle, A. Guillou, N. Svoronos and D. Papachryssanthou, *Actes de Lavra. Première partie: Des origines à 1204, Archives de l'Athos* V (Paris, 1970).

Ahima'az, *Chronicle*, tr. M. Salzman, *The Chronicle of Ahimaaz* (New York, 1924).

Ananias of Širak, *Geography*, tr. R. Hewsen, *The Geography of Ananias of Širak (Ašxarhac'oyc')* (Wiesbaden, 1992).

Anna Komnene, *Alexiad*, eds D. Reinsch and A. Kambylis, *Annae Comnenae Alexias*, CFHB XL (Berlin, 2001).

Anna Komnene, *Alexiad*, tr. E. Dawes, *The Alexiad of Anna Comnena* (New York, 1928).

Anna Komnene, *Alexiad*, tr. E. Sewter, *The Alexiad of Anna Comnena* (New York, 1969).

Ibn al-A'tham, ed. A. Kurat, 'Muḥammad bin A'sam al- Kūfī'nin Kitāb al-Futūḥ'u and its Importance Concerning the Arab Conquest in Central Asia and the Khazars', *Ankara Üniversitesi Dil ve Tarih-Coğrafya Fakültesi Dergisi* VII (1949), 274–82.

Al-Baladhuri, *Futuh al-Buldân*, ed. M. de Goeje, *Futuh al-Buldân* (Leiden, 1886).

Christian of Stavelot, 'Expositio in Matthaeum Evangelistam', ed. J. Migne, Christian Druthmar, 'Expositio in Matthaeum Evangelistam', *Patrologiae Cursus Completus*, series Latina, vol. 106, col. 1456 A–B (Paris, 1864).

Christian of Stavelot, 'Expositio in Matthaeum Evangelistam', tr. L. Chekin, 'Christian of Stavelot and the Conversion of Gog and Magog: A Study of Ninth-Century References to Judaism among the Khazars', *Russia Mediaevalis* 9/1 (1997), 13–34.
Codex Cumanicus, eds F. Schmieder and P. Schreiner, *Il Codice Cumanico e il suo mondo* (Rome, 2005).
Al-Dīmašqi, *Cosmography*, ed. and tr. A. Mehren, *Cosmographie de Dimischqi* (St Petersburg, 1866).
Ibn Faḍlān, *Risāla*, tr. R. Frye, *Ibn Fadlan's Journey to Russia* (Princeton, 2005).
Ibn Faḍlān, *Risāla*, tr. P. Lunde and C. Stone, *Ibn Faḍlān and the Land of Darkness: Arab Travellers in the Far North* (New York, 2012).
Ibn Faḍlān, *Risāla*, tr. J. Montgomery, *Mission to the Volga by Aḥmad ibn Faḍlān* (New York, 2017).
Ibn Faḍlān, *Risāla*, tr. Z. Togan, *Ibn Faḍlān's Reisebericht* (Leipzig, 1939).
Ibn al-Faqīh, *Kitâb al-Buldân*, ed. M. de Goeje, *Kitâb al-Buldân* (Leiden, 1885).
Ibn al-Faqīh, *Kitâb al-Buldân*, tr. P. Lunde and C. Stone, *Ibn Faḍlān and the Land of Darkness* (New York, 2012).
St Gall, *Annales*, ed. G. Pertz, 'Annales Sangallenses Maiores', *MGH* (Hanover, 1826).
Al-Gardīzī, *Zayn al-aḵbār*, tr. A. Martinez, 'Gardīzī's Two Chapters on the Turks', *AEMA* 2 (1983), 109–218.
Al-Garnatī, *Tuḥfat al-Albāb*, tr. C. Dubler, *Abū Ḥāmid el Granadino y su relación de viaje por tierras euroasiáticas* (Madrid, 1953).
Al-Garnatī, *Tuḥfat al-Albāb*, tr. B. Hamidullin, 'Ал-Гарнати о гузах, печенегах, хазарах и булгарах', *Из глубины столетий* (Kazan', 2000), 98–9.
Gesta Hungarorum I, tr. M. Rady, 'The *Gesta Hungarorum* of Anonymus, the Anonymous Notary of King Béla: A Translation', *SEER* 87/4 (2009), 681–727.
Gesta Hungarorum II, eds and tr. L. Veszprémy, F. Schaer and J. Szűcs, *Simonis de Kéza: Gesta Hungarorum / Simon of Kéza: The Deeds of the Hungarians* (New York, 1999).
Al-Hamdānī, *Kitāb Tathbīt Dalā'il Nubuwwat Sayyidinā Muḥammad*, ed. M. de Goeje, *Kitâb al-Buldân* (Leiden, 1885).
Al-Hamdānī, *Kitāb Tathbīt Dalā'il Nubuwwat Sayyidinā Muḥammad*, tr. S. Pines, 'A Moslem Text Concerning the Conversion of the Khazars to Judaism', *Journal of Jewish Studies* 13 (1962), 42–55.
Hartvic, *The Life of St. Stephen of Hungary*, ed. E. Szentpétery, *Scriptores Rerum Hungaricarum II* (Budapest, 1999).

Hartvic, *The Life of St. Stephen of Hungary*, tr. N. Berend, 'Hartvic, *Life of King Stephen of Hungary*', in T. Head (ed.), *Medieval Hagiography: An Anthology* (New York, 2000), 375–98.

Hasdai ibn Šaprut, *Letter to Joseph*, ed. and tr. P. Kokovcov, *Еврейско-хазарская переписка в X веке* (Leningrad, 1932), http://gumilevica.kulichki.net/Rest/rest0503.htm, accessed 24 November 2020.

Hasdai ibn Šaprut, *Letter to Joseph*, tr. F. Kobler, *Letters of Jews through the Ages* I, 2nd edn (London, 1953), 97–115.

Hasdai ibn Šaprut, *Letter to Joseph*, cited in Yehuda HaLevi, *Kuzari*, tr. N. Korobkin, *The Kuzari: In Defense of the Despised Faith* (Northvale, NJ, 1998).

Ibn Hauqal, *Ṣūrat al-'Arḍ*, tr. P. Lunde and C. Stone, *Ibn Fadlān and the Land of Darkness* (New York, 2012).

Ḥudūd al-'Ālam, tr. V. Minorsky, *Ḥudūd al-'Ālam. The Regions of the World: A Persian Geography, 372 A.H.–982 A.D.*, 2nd edn (London, 1970), http://www.kroraina.com/hudud/index.html, accessed 24 November 2020.

Ilarion, *Sermon on Law and Grace*, tr. S. Franklin, *Sermons and Rhetoric of Kievan Rus'* (Cambridge, MA, 1991), 3–26.

Ioannes of Gotthia, *Vita*, tr. G. Huxley, 'On the *Vita* of St John of Gotthia', *Greek, Roman and Byzantine Studies* 19 (1978), 161–9.

Ioannes of Gotthia, *Vita*, ed. and tr. M-F. Auzépy, 'La vie de Jean de Gothie (BHG 891)', in C. Zuckerman (ed.), *La Crimée entre Byzance et le Khaganat Khazar* (Paris, 2006), 69–92.

Ioannes of Gotthia, *Vita*, tr. Ju. Mogaričev, A. Sazanov and A. Šapošnikov, *Житие Иоанна Готского в контексте истории крыма 'хазарского периода'* (Simferopol', 2007), http://samlib.ru/a/aspar/ioann.shtml, accessed 24 November 2020.

Ioannes Skylitzes, *Synopsis of Histories*, ed. J. Thurn, *Ioannis Skylitzes Synopsis Historiarum*, CFHB V (New York, 1973).

Ioannes Skylitzes, *Synopsis of Histories*, tr. J. Wortley, *John Skylitzes' A Synopsis of Byzantine History: 811–1057* (Cambridge, 2010).

Al-Istakhrī, *Book of Roads and Kingdoms*, tr. P. Lunde and C. Stone, *Ibn Fadlān and the Land of Darkness* (New York, 2012).

Jakov the Monk, *Pamjat' i Pokhvala Iakova Mnikha i Žitie Knjazja Vladimira*, tr. P. Hollingsworth, *The Hagiography of Kievan Rus'* (Cambridge, MA, 1992).

Jordanes, *Getica*, tr. C. Mierow, *Jordanes: The Origins and Deeds of the Goths* (Princeton, 1908).

Josephus, Flavius, *Antiquities of the Jews*, tr. W. Whiston, *The Works of Flavius Josephus, Complete and Unabridged* (Peabody, MA, repr. 1987).

Yehuda HaLevi, *Kuzari*, eds Ben-Yehuda Project, 'The Book of the Kuzari: Letter of King Joseph', https://benyehuda.org/read/3704, accessed 24 November 2020.

רזחוא. הדוהי-ןב טקיורפ. 'דלמה ףסוי בתכ :ירזוכה רפס'.ןבא הדוהי / יולה הדוהי (תיבוז, יהודה הדוהי (דיראתב)

Yehuda HaLevi, *Kuzari*, tr. H. Hirschfield, *Kuzari* (New York, 1946).
Yehuda HaLevi, *Kuzari*, tr. N. Korobkin, *The Kuzari: In Defense of the Despised Faith* (Northvale, NJ, 1998).
Julianus and Petrus, *Reports*, ed. and tr. H. Dörrie, *Drei Texte zur Geschichte der Ungarn und Mongolen: Die Missionreisen des fr. Julianus O.P. ins Uralgebiet (1234/5) und nach Rußland (1237) und Bericht der Erzbiscofs Peter uber die Tartaren* (Göttingen, 1956).
Pseudo-Kallisthenes, *Letter of Alexander to Olympias*, tr. A. Wolohojian, *The Romance of Alexander the Great by Pseudo Callisthenes* (New York, 1969).
Kartlis Cxovreba, ed. S. Qauxčišvili, *Kartlis Cxovreba* (Tbilisi, 1973).
Al-Kāšgarī, *Dīwānu l-Luġat al-Turk*, eds J. Kelly and R. Dankoff, *Türk Şiveleri Lügatı. Dīvānü Luġāt-It-Türk* [Compendium of Turkic Dialects of Maḥmūd Kāshgarī] (Cambridge, MA, 1982–5).
Al-Kāšgarī, *Dīwānu l-Luġat al-Turk*, ed and tr. Z-A. Auezova, *Махмуд ал-Кашгари: Диван Лугат ат-Турк* (Alma-Ata, 2005).
Ibn Khurradādhbih, *Livre des routes et provinces*, ed. M. de Goeje, *Bibliothecarum Geographicorum Arabicorum* VII (Leiden, 1892).
Ibn Khurradādhbih, *Livre des routes et provinces*, ed and tr. C. de Meynard, *Le livre des routes et des provinces* (Paris, 1865).
Ibn Khurradādhbih, *Sallām the Interpreter*, tr. P. Lunde and C. Stone, *Ibn Fadlān and the Land of Darkness* (New York, 2012).
The *Kievan Letter*, eds and tr. N. Golb and O. Pritsak, *Khazarian Hebrew Documents of the Tenth Century* (Ithaca, 1982).
King Joseph's Reply, ed. and tr. P. Kokovcov, *Еврейско-хазарская переписка в X веке* (Leningrad, 1932), http://gumilevica.kulichki.net/Rest/rest0503.htm, accessed 24 November 2020.
King Joseph's Reply, tr. F. Kobler, *Letters of Jews through the Ages* I, 2nd edn (London, 1953), 97–115.
King Joseph's Reply, tr. N. Korobkin, *The Kuzari: In Defense of the Despised Faith* (Northvale, NJ, 1998).
Kol Gali, *Kyssa'i Yusuf*, tr. F. Beake, R. Bukharaev and A. Minnekaev, *The Story of Joseph: Kyssa'i Yusuf by Kol Gali* (Leiden, 2010).
Konstantinos VII Porphyrogennetos, *De Administrando Imperio*, ed. G. Litavrin, *Константин Багрянородный об управлении империей*, 2nd edn (Moscow, 1991).

Konstantinos VII Porphyrogennetos, *De Administrando Imperio*, ed. Gy. Moravcsik, tr. R. Jenkins, *De Administrando Imperio of Constantine VII Porphyrogenitus*, 2nd edn (Washington, DC, 1967).

Konstantinos VII Porphyrogennetos, *De Administrando Imperio Commentary*, eds F. Dvornik, R. Jenkins, B. Lewis, Gy. Moravcsik, D. Obolensky and S. Runciman, *Constantine Porphyrogenitus: De Administrando Imperio, Volume II, A Commentary* (London, 1962).

Konstantinos VII Porphyrogennetos, *De Ceremoniis*, ed. J. Reiske, *Constantini Porphyrogeniti Imperatoris De Ceremoniis Aulae Byzantinae*, *CSHB* I (Bonn, 1829–30).

Konstantinos VII Porphyrogennetos, *De Ceremoniis*, tr. A. Moffatt and M. Tall, *Konstantinos Porphyrogennetos: The Book of Ceremonies in 2 Volumes* (Canberra, 2012).

Konstantinos VII Porphyrogennetos, *De Thematibus*, ed. A. Pertusi, *Constantino Porfirogenito: De Thematibus* (Rome, 1952).

Konstantinos VII Porphyrogennetos, *Three Treatises*, ed. and tr. J. Haldon, *Constantine Porphyrogenitus: Three Treatises on Imperial Military Expeditions*, *CFHB* XXVIII (Vienna, 1990).

Leon Diakonos, *History*, ed and tr. V. Karales, *Λέων Διάκονος, Ἱστορία* (Athens, 2000).

Leon Diakonos, *History*, tr. A-M. Talbot and D. Sullivan, *The History of Leo the Deacon: Byzantine Military Expansion in the Tenth Century* (Washington, DC, 2005).

Liudprand of Cremona, *Antapodosis*, ed. G. Pertz, *Liudprandi Episcopi Cremonensis Opera Omnia*, *MGH* (Hanover, 1839).

Liudprand of Cremona, *Antapodosis*, tr. P. Squatriti, *The Complete Works of Liudprand of Cremona* (Washington, DC, 2007).

Marwazī, *Sharaf al-Zamân Pâhir Marvazî*, tr. V. Minorsky, *Sharaf al-Zamân Pâhir Marvazî on China, the Turks and India*, (London, 1942).

Al-Mas'ūdī, *Meadows of Gold*, tr. P. Lunde and C. Stone, *Ibn Fadlān and the Land of Darkness* (New York, 2012).

Al-Mas'ūdī, *Meadows of Gold*, tr. V. Minorsky, *A History of Sharvân and Darband in the 10th–11th Centuries* (Cambridge, 1958).

Matthew of Edessa, *Chronicle*, tr. E. Dulaurier, *Chronique de Matthieu d'Edesse (962–1136)* (Paris, 1858).

Michael Attaleiates, *Historia*, ed. E. Th. Tsolakis, *Michaelis Attaliatae Historia*, *CFHB* L (Athens, 2011).

Michael Attaleiates, *Historia*, tr. A. Kaldellis and D. Krallis, *The History of Michael Attaleiates* (Cambridge, 2012).

Michael Psellos, *Chronographia*, ed. D. Reinsch, *Michaelis Pselli Chronographia* (Berlin, 2014).
Michael Psellos, *Chronographia*, tr. E. Sewter, *Fourteen Byzantine Rulers: The Chronographia of Michael Psellos* (New York, 1966).
Michael the Syrian, *Chronicle*, ed. and tr. J.-B. Chabot, *Chronique de Michel le Syrien, Patriarche Jacobite d'Antioche (1166–1199)* (Paris, 1901).
Al-Muqaddasī, *Aḥsan al-Taqāsim fī Ma'rifat al-Aqālīm*, tr. B. Collins, *The Best Divisions for Knowledge of the Regions. Ahasan al-Taqasim fi Ma'rifat al-Aqalim* (Reading, 1994).
Al-Muqaddasī, *Aḥsan al-Taqāsim fī Ma'rifat al-Aqālīm*, tr. P. Lunde. and C. Stone, *Ibn Fadlān and the Land of Darkness* (New York, 2012).
Ibn al-Nadim, *Fihrist of al-Nadim*, ed. and tr. B. Dodge, *The Fihrist of al-Nadim, A Tenth-Century Survey of Muslim Culture* (New York, 1970).
Nicholas Mystikos, *Epistles*, eds and tr. R. Jenkins and L. Westerink, *Nicholas I, Patriarch of Constantinople: Letters*, CFHB VI (Washington, DC, 1973).
Nikephoros, *Brevarium*, ed and tr. C. Mango, *Short History* (Washington, DC, 1990).
Notitiae Episcopatuum, ed. J. Darrouzès, *Notitiae Episcopatuum Ecclesiae Constantinopolitanae* (Paris, 1981).
Novgorod First Chronicle, tr. R. Michell and N. Forbes, *The Chronicle of Novgorod, 1016–1471* (London, 1914).
Origen, *Contra Celsum*, ed. P. Koetschau, *Origenes Werke, V–VIII Gegen Celsus* (Leipzig, 1899).
Origen, *Contra Celsum*, tr. H. Chadwick, *Origen: Contra Celsum* (New York, 1953).
Peter, *Letters*, ed. G. Pertz, Peter, Doge of Venice, 'Epistola', MGH (Hanover, 1839).
Povest' Vremennykh Let, eds D. Ostrowski and D. Birnbaum, *Повість временних літ: міжрядкове співставлення і парадосис* (Cambridge, MA, 2003).
Povest' Vremennykh Let, tr. S. Cross and O. Sherbowitz-Wetzor, *The Russian Primary Chronicle, Laurentian Text*, 1st paperback edn (Cambridge, 1953).
Ibn Qutayba, *Kitâb al-ma'ârif*, ed. T. 'Ukâsha, *Kitâb al-ma'ârif*, vol. 44 of *Dhakha'ir al-'arab* (Cairo, 1969).
Regino of Prüm, *Chronicon*, ed. F. Kurze, *Reginonis Abbaus Prumiensis Chronicon cum continuatone*, MGH (Hanover, 1890).

Regino of Prüm, *Chronicon*, tr. S. MacLean, *History and Politics in Late Carolingian and Ottonian Europe: The Chronicle of Regino of Prüm and Adalbert of Magdeburg* (Manchester, 2009).
Ibn Rusta, *Kitāb al-A'lāk an-Nafīsa*, ed. M. de Goeje, *Bibliothecarum Geographicorum Arabicorum* VII (Leiden, 1892).
Ibn Rusta, *Kitāb al-A'lāk an-Nafīsa*, tr. P. Lunde and C. Stone, *Ibn Fadlān and the Land of Darkness* (New York, 2012).
Ibn Rusta, *Kitāb al-A'lāk an-Nafīsa*, tr. G. Wiet, *Les atours précieux* (Cairo, 1955).
Russkaja Pravda, ed. S. Juškov, Памятники русского права (Moscow, 1952–63).
Russkaja Pravda, tr. D. Kaiser, *The Laws of Rus': Tenth to Fifteenth Centuries* (Salt Lake City, 1992).
Russkaja Pravda, tr. G. Vernadsky, *Medieval Russian Laws* (New York, 1947).
Schechter Text, eds and tr. N. Golb and O. Pritsak, *Khazarian Hebrew Documents of the Tenth Century* (Ithaca, 1982).
Sefer Yosippon, ed. D. Flusser, *Sefer Yôsippôn* (Jerusalem, 1978–80).
(דוד פלוסר, ספר יוסיפון, מוסד ביאליק, ירושלים)
Sefer Yuḥasin, ed. A. Niebuhr, *Sefer Yuḥasin, Medieval Jewish Chronicles* II (Oxford, 1895).
Theophanes Omologetes (the Confessor), *Chronographia*, ed. C. de Boor, *Theophanes Chronographia* (Hildesheim, repr. 1963).
Theophanes Omologetes (the Confessor), *Chronographia*, tr. C. Mango, R. Scott and G. Greatrex, *The Chronicle of Theophanes Confessor: Byzantine and Near Eastern History, AD 284–813* (New York, 1997).
Theophilos of Edessa, *Chronicle*, tr. R. Hoyland, *Theophilus of Edessa's Chronicle and the Circulation of Historical Knowledge in Late Antiquity and Early Islam* (Liverpool, 2001).
Vita Constantini (Slavonic *Life of Constantine*), eds F. Grivec and F. Tomišić, *Constantinus et Methodius Thessalonicenses, Fontes, Rodavi Staroslavenskog Instituta* IV (Zagreb, 1960).
Vita Constantini (Slavonic *Life of Constantine*), tr. M. Kantor, *Medieval Slavonic Lives of Saints and Princes* (Ann Arbor, 1983), 23–97.
William of Rubruck, *Itinerarium*, tr. W. Rockhill, *The Journey of William of Rubruck to the Eastern Parts of the World, 1253–55, as Narrated by Himself, with Two Accounts of the Earlier Journey of John of Pian de Carpine* (London, 1900).
Zosimus, *Vita*, eds Société des Bollandistes, *Vita S. Zosimo Episcopo Syracusano in Sicilia, Acta Sanctorum, Martii* III (Paris, 1865), 839–43.

Secondary and Archaeological Literature

Abdullin, Y., 'Islam in the History of the Volga Kama Bulgars and Tatars', *Central Asian Survey* 9/2 (1990), 1–11.

Afanas'ev, G., *Донские аланы (социальные структуры алано-ассо-буртасского населения бассейна среднего дона)* (Moscow, 1993).

Afanas'ev, G., 'Где же археологические свидетельства существования хазарского государства', РА 2 (2001), 43–55.

Afanas'ev, G., 'К проблеме локализации хазарии и фурт-асии (о противоречии данных археологии и письменных источников)', *Форум "идель–алтай"* (Kazan', 2009), 7–17.

Afanas'ev, G. and A. Atavin, *Что же такое хазарский погребальный обряд?* (Moscow, 2002).

Afanas'ev, G. and D. Korobov, 'Северокавказские аланы по данным палеогенетики', in Š. Gapurov and S. Magamadov (eds), *Этногенез и этническая история народов кавказа* (Groznyj, 2018), 180–91.

Afanas'ev, G., Š. Ven', S. Tun, L. Van, L. Vej, M. Dobrovol'skaja, D. Korobov, I. Rešetova and Kh. Li, 'Хазарские конфедераты в бассейне дона (археологические, антропологические и генетические аспекты)', in *Естественнонаучные методы исследования и парадигма современной археологии: материалы всероссийской научной конференции*, ed. M. Dobrovol'skaja (Moscow, 2015), 146–53.

Afinogenov, D., 'The History of Justinian and Leo', in C. Zuckerman (ed.), *La Crimée entre Byzance et le Khaganat Khazar* (Paris, 2006), 181–200.

Aga, Ju., 'Хронология хазар', *Хазары*, (2000–16), http://www.hagahan-lib.ru/index.html, accessed 7 December 2020.

Ajbabin, A., 'Early Khazar Archaeological Monuments in Crimea and to the North of the Black Sea', in C. Zuckerman (ed.), *La Crimée entre Byzance et le Khaganat Khazar* (Paris, 2006), 31–65.

Aksënov, V., 'Форпост верхний салтов', *ВК* 2 (2006), 72–6.

Album, S. and T. Goodwin, *Sylloge of Islamic Coins in the Ashmolean, I: Pre-Reform Coinage of the Early Islamic Period* (London, 2002).

Alcalay, A., *After Jews and Arabs: Remaking Levantine Culture* (Minneapolis, 1993).

Alekseenko, N., 'Херсонская родовая знат X–XI вв. в памятниках сфрагистики', *Материалы по археологии, истории и этнографии таврики* 7 (2000), 256–66.

Alekseenko, N., 'Les relations entre Cherson et l'empire, d'après le témoignage des sceaux des archives de Cherson', in J-C. Cheynet and C. Sode (eds), *SBS 8* (Munich, 2003), 75–83.

Alekseenko, N., 'Печать как иконографический источник: к вопросу о редких изображениях святых в византийской сфрагистике', *СЩ* 3 (2012), 23–31.

Alf'orov, O., 'Молівдовули київських князів другої половини XI–кінця XII століття (за матеріалами сфрагістичної колекції О. Шереметьєва)', *СЩ* 2 (2012), 5–74.

Alf'orov, O., 'Молівдовули митрополита Михаїла (1130–1145 рр)', *СЩ* 2 (2012), 151–8.

Alf'orov, O., 'Інсигнії влади на давньоруських печатках XI–XII ст.', *СЩ* 3 (2012), 32–46.

Alf'orov, O., 'Some New Lead Seals are from Archive of Kherson', *СЩ* 4 (2013), 360–7.

Alf'orov, O., 'A Seal of Michael, Archon and Doux of Matarcha and All Khazaria (in Oleksii Sheremetiev's Collection)', in H. Ivakin et al. (eds), *Byzantine and Rus' Seals* (Kiev, 2015), 97–106.

Alf'orov, O., 'Княжі знаки на печатках київської русі', *СЩ* 5 (2015), 102–34.

Ambroz, A., 'О вознесенском комплексе VIII в. на днепре: вопрос интерпретации', in *Древности эпохи великого переселения народов V–VIII вв.* (Moscow, 1982), 204–21.

Anderson, A., *Alexander's Gate, Gog and Magog, and the Inclosed Nations* (Cambridge, 1932).

Anderson, B., *Imagined Communities: Reflections on the Origins and Spread of Nationalism* (New York, 1991).

Anderson, P., *Passages from Antiquity to Feudalism* (London, 1974).

Androshchuk, A., 'Byzantium and the Scandinavian World in the 9th–10th Century: Material Evidence of Contacts', in L. Bjerg et al. (eds), *From Goths to Varangians: Communication and Cultural Exchange between the Baltic and the Black Sea* (Gylling, 2013), 147–92.

Androshchuk, A., 'Byzantine Imperial Seals in Southern Rus'', in H. Ivakin et al. (eds), *Byzantine and Rus' Seals* (Kiev, 2015), 43–54.

Angelov, D., 'The Introduction of Christianity into Rus': The Work of Cyril and Methodius', in Y. Hamant (ed.), *The Christianization of Ancient Russia: A Millennium: 988–1988* (Paris, 1992), 29–35.

Angelov, D., 'Asia and Europe Commonly Called East and West: Constantinople and Geographical Imagination in Byzantium', in S. Bazzaz et al. (eds), *Imperial Geographies in Byzantine and Ottoman Space* (Cambridge, 2013), 43–68.

Anievas, A. and K. Nişancioğlu, *How the West Came to Rule* (London, 2015).

Ankori, Z., *The Karaites in Byzantium* (New York, 1959).

Antalóczy, I., 'A nyíri izmaeliták központjának, Böszörmény falunak régészeti leletei II', *Hajdúsági Múzeum Çvkönyve* 4 (1980), 131–70.
Anthony, D., 'Migration in Archaeology: The Baby and the Bathwater', *American Anthropologist* 92 (1990), 895–914.
Anthony, D., *The Horse, the Wheel and Language: How Bronze-Age Riders from the Eurasian Steppes Shaped the Modern World* (Princeton, 2007).
Archibald, M., 'Islamic and Christian Gold Coins from Spanish Mints Found in England, Mid-Eleventh to Mid-Thirteenth Centuries', in R. Naismith et al. (eds), *Early Medieval Monetary History: Studies in Memory of Mark Blackburn* (Burlington, VT, 2016), 377–96.
Armarčuk, E., 'О журнале "Татарская археология"', *PA* 1 (2001), 133–7.
Armstrong, K., *The Great Transformation: The World in the Time of Buddha, Socrates, Confucius and Jeremiah* (London, 2006).
Arnason, J., *Civilizations in Dispute: Historical Questions and Theoretical Traditions* (Boston, 2003).
Arnason, J., 'Rehistoricizing the Axial Age', in R. Bellah and H. Joas (eds), *The Axial Age and Its Consequences* (Cambridge, MA, 2012), 337–65.
Arnason, J., 'Making Contact and Mapping the Terrain', in J. Arnason and C. Hann (eds), *Anthropology and Civilizational Analysis: Eurasian Explorations* (Albany, 2018), xiii–xlii.
Arnason, J., 'Mauss Revisited: The Birth of Civilizational Analysis from the Spirit of Anthropology', in J. Arnason and C. Hann (eds), *Anthropology and Civilizational Analysis: Eurasian Explorations* (Albany, 2018), 1–34.
Arnason, J., S. Eisenstadt and B. Wittrock, 'Introduction: Late Antiquity as a Sequel and Counterpoint to the Axial Age', in J. Arnason et al. (eds), *Axial Civilizations and World History* (Boston, 2005), 287–93.
Arnold, W., E. Naumova, V. Koloda and P. Gaengler, 'Tooth Wear in Two Ancient Populations of the Khazar Kaganat Region in Ukraine', *International Journal of Osteoarchaeology* 17 (2007), 52–62.
Arrignon, J-P., *La chaire métropolitaine de Kiev des origines à 1240* (Lille, 1987).
Artamonov, M., 'Саркел – белая вежа: труды волго-донской археологической экспедиции', *Материалы и исследования по археологии СССР* 62 (1958).
Artamonov, M., *История хазар* (Leningrad, 1962).
Aržanceva, I., 'Terenozhkin and Tolstov: Faustian Bargains in Soviet Archaeology', in V. Mordvintseva et al. (eds), *Archaeological and Linguistic Research: Materials of the Humboldt-Conference* (Kiev, 2014), 44–56.

Aržanceva, I., D. Deopik and V. Malashev, 'Zilgi: An Early Alan Proto-City of the First Millennium AD on the Boundary between Steppe and Hill Country', in M. Kazanski and V. Soupault (eds), *Les sites archéologiques en Crimée et au Caucase durant l'Antiquité tardive et le haut Moyen-Age* (Boston, 2000), 211–50.

Asadov, F., 'Khazar Studies Locked between the Scarcity of Research Sources and Contemporary Policy Concerns', *Eurasia Studies Society Journal* 2/3 (2013), 1–11.

Asadov, F., 'Khazaria, Byzantium, and the Arab Caliphate: Struggle for Control Over Eurasian Trade Routes in the 9th–10th Centuries', *Caucasus and Globalization* 6/4 (2012), 140–50.

Ascherson, N., *Black Sea* (New York, 1995).

Atanasov, G., 'Durostorum–Dorostol(os)–Drastar/Dristra–Silistra: The Danubian Fortress from the Beginning of the 4th to the Beginning of the 19th c', in R. Ivanov (ed.), *Corpus of Ancient and Medieval Settlements in Bulgaria: Thracian, Greek, Roman and Medieval Cities, Residences and Fortresses*, vol. 2 (Sofia, 2014), 493–587.

Avdev, S., Монетната система в средновековна българия през XIII–XIV в. (Sofia, 2005).

Bacharach, J., 'Signs of Sovereignty: The *Shahāda*, Qur'anic Verses, and the Coinage of 'Abd al-Malik', *Muqarnas* 27/1 (2010), 1–30.

Bachrach, B., 'Book Review: Medieval Identity: People and Place: *On Barbarian Identity: Critical Approaches to Ethnicity in the Early Middle Ages* by A. Gillett; and *Medieval Frontiers: Concepts and Practices* by D. Abulafia and N. Berend', *International History Review* 25/4 (2003), 866–70.

Bagge, S., 'Division and Unity in Medieval Norway', in I. Garipzanov et al. (eds), *Franks, Northmen, and Slavs: Identities and State Formation in Early Medieval Europe* (Turnhout, 2008), 145–66.

Bakos, M., 'Römische Münzfunde im Esztergom (Gran/Ungarn) im 18. Jahrhundert', *Gazette Numismatique Suisse* 43–7 (1995), 52–64.

Bálint, C., 'Some Archaeological Addenda to P. Golden's Khazar Studies', *ActaAntHung* 35/2–3 (1981), 397–412.

Bálint, C., *Die Archäologie der Steppe: Steppenvölker zwischen Volga und Donau vom 6. bis zum 10. Jahrhundert* (Vienna, 1989).

Bálint, C., 'A 9. Századi magyarság régészeti hagyatéka', in L. Kovács (ed.) *Honfoglalás és régészet: A honfoglalásról sok szemmel 1* (Budapest, 1994), 39–46.

Bálint, C., 'Węgierska archeologia i nacjonalizm', in A. Cetnarowicz et al. (eds), *Węgry-Polska w Europie Środkowej: historia, literatura: księga*

pamiątkowa ku czci Profesora Wacława Felczaka (Kraków, 1997), 254–9.
BAR (Biblical Archaeology Review) (eds), 'Strata: Is This What the Temple Menorah Looked Like?' *Biblical Archaeology Review* 37/6 (2011). Referenced via webpage: https://www.baslibrary.org/biblical-archaeology-review/37/6/22, accessed 7 December 2020.
Baranov, I., *Таврика в эпоху раннего средневековья (салтово-маяцкая культура)* (Kiev, 1990).
Barford, P., *The Early Slavs: Culture and Society in Early Medieval Eastern Europe* (Ithaca, 2001).
Bartha, A., *Hungarian Society in the 9th and 10th Centuries*, tr. K. Balázs (Budapest, 1975).
Bartlett, R., 'From Paganism to Christianity in Medieval Europe', in N. Berend (ed.), *Christianization and the Rise of Christian Monarchy: Scandinavia, Central Europe and Rus, c. 900–1200* (Cambridge, 2007), 47–72.
Bartusis, M., *Land and Privilege in Byzantium: The Institution of Pronoia* (Cambridge, 2012).
Baskakov, N., *Тюркские языки* (Moscow, 1960).
Bazin, L., 'Pour une nouvelle hypothèse sur l'origine des Khazar', *Materialia Turcica* 7–8 (1982), 51–71.
Beckwith, C., *Empires of the Silk Road: A History of Central Eurasia from the Bronze Age to the Present* (Princeton, 2009).
Behar, D., 'The Origins of Ashkenazi Levites', presented at *The 11th Genetic Genealogy Conference for Family Tree DNA Group Administrators* (Houston, 2015), https://www.slideshare.net/FamilyTreeDNA/the-origin-of-ashkenazi-levites, accessed 7 December 2020.
Behar, D., M. Thomas, K. Skorecki, M. Hammer, E. Bulygina, D. Rosengarten, A. Jones, K. Held, V. Moses, D. Goldstein, N. Bradman and M. Weale, 'Multiple Origins of Ashkenazi Levites: Y Chromosome Evidence for Both Near Eastern and European Ancestries', *American Journal of Human Genetics* 73 (2003), 768–79.
Behar, D., M. Metspalu, Y. Baran, N. Kopelman, B. Yunusbayev, A. Gladstein, S. Tzur, H. Sahakyan, A. Bahmanimehr, L. Yepiskoposyan, K. Tambets, E. Khusnutdinova, A. Kusniarevich, O. Balanovsky, E. Balanovsky, L. Kovacevic, D. Marjanovic, E. Mihailov, A. Kouvatsi, C. Traintaphyllidis, R. King, O. Semino, A. Torroni, M. Hammer, E. Metspalu, K. Skorecki, S. Rosset, E. Halperin, R. Villems, and N. Rosenberg, 'No Evidence from Genome-Wide Data of a Khazar Origin for the Ashkenazi Jews', *Human Biology* 85/6 (2013), 859–900.

Beletsky, S., 'Rus' Seals as Text', in H. Ivakin et al. (eds), *Byzantine and Rus' Seals* (Kiev, 2015), 235–44.

Beliaev, L. and A. Chernetsov, 'The Eastern Contribution to Medieval Russian Culture', *Muqarnas* 16 (1999), 97–124.

Bell-Fialkoff, A. (ed.), *The Role of Migration in the History of the Eurasian Steppe: Sedentary Civilization vs. 'Barbarian' and Nomad* (London, 2000).

Belÿkh, S., *История народов волго-уральского региона* (Iževsk, 2005).

Ben-Itto, H., *The Lie that Wouldn't Die: The Protocols of the Elders of Zion* (Portland, 2005).

Benovska-Sabkova, M., 'The "Orthodox", "Eurasian", or "Russian Orthodox" Civilization?', in J. Arnason and C. Hann (eds), *Anthropology and Civilizational Analysis: Eurasian Explorations* (Albany, 2018), 323–38.

Bensch, S., *Barcelona and Its Rulers, 1096–1291* (Cambridge, 2002).

Bereczki, Z. and A. Marcsik, 'Trephined Skulls from Ancient Populations in Hungary', *Acta Medica Lituanica* 12/1 (2005), 65–9.

Berend, N., 'Medievalists and the Notion of the Frontier', *Medieval History Journal* 2/1 (1999), 55–72.

Berend, N., *At the Gate of Christendom: Jews, Muslims and 'Pagans' in Medieval Hungary, c. 1000–1300* (Cambridge, 2001).

Berend, N., 'Introduction', in N. Berend (ed.), *Christianization and the Rise of Christian Monarchy* (Cambridge, 2003), 1–46.

Berend, N., 'Défense de la Chrétienté et naissance d'une identité: Hongrie, Pologne et péninsule Ibérique au Moyen Âge', *Annales. Histoire, Sciences Sociales* 58/5 (2003), 1009–27.

Berend, N. (ed.), *Christianization and the Rise of Christian Monarchy: Scandinavia, Central Europe and Rus', c. 900–1200* (Cambridge, 2003).

Berend, N., 'A Note on the End of Islam in Medieval Hungary: Old Mistakes and Some New Results', *Journal of Islamic Studies* 25/2 (2014), 201–6.

Berend, N., P. Urbańczyk and P. Wiszewski, *Central Europe in the High Middle Ages: Bohemia, Hungary and Poland c. 900– c.1300* (Cambridge, 2013).

Bernard, H., G. Shelley and P. Killworth, 'How Much of a Network Does the GSS and RSW Dredge Up?', *Social Networks* 9/1 (1987), 49–63.

Bibikov, M., 'Byzantinorossica: свод византийских свидетельств о руси', (2004), http://www.studfiles.ru/preview/4016922/, accessed 7 December 2020.

Bierbrauer, V., 'Zur ethnischen Interpretation in der frühgeschichtlichen Archäologie', in W. Pohl (ed.), *Die Suche nach den Ursprüngen: Von der Bedeutung des frühen Mittelalters* (Vienna, 2004), 45–84.

Biermann, F., 'Northwestern Slavic Strongholds of the 8th–10th Centuries', in N. Christie and H. Herold (eds), *Fortified Settlements in Early Medieval Europe: Defended Communities of the 8th–10th Centuries* (Philadelphia, 2016), 85–94.

Birkenmeier, J., *The Development of the Komnenian Army: 1081–1180* (Leiden, 2002).

Birnbaum, H., 'On Some Evidence of Jewish Life and Anti-Jewish Sentiments in Medieval Russia', *Viator* 4 (1973), 225–55.

Birnbaum, H., 'The Slavic Settlements in the Balkans and the Eastern Alps', in S. Vryonis, Jr (ed.), *Byzantine Studies: Essays on the Slavic World and the Eleventh Century* (New Rochelle, 1992), 1–14.

Bíró, A., 'Weapons in the 10–11th Century Carpathian Basin: Studies in Weapon Technology – Rigid Bow Applications and Southern Import Swords in the Archaeological Material', *Dissertationes Archaeologicae ex Instituto Archaeologico Universitatis de Rolando Eötvös Nominatae* 3/2 (Budapest, 2014), 519–39.

Blažejovs'kij, D., *Hierarchy of the Kyivan Church, 861–1990*, Виданния украітського католицького університету ІМ. СВ. Климента Папи // *Editiones Universitatis Catholicae Ucrainorum S. Clementis Papae* vol. 72 Sacrum Ucrainae Millenium, vol. 3 (Rome, 1990).

Boba, I., *Nomads, Northmen and Slavs: Eastern Europe in the Ninth Century* (Wiesbaden, 1967).

Bocharov, S. and A. Sitdikov (eds), *Genoese Gazaria and the Golden Horde* (Simferopol', 2015).

Boeck, E., 'Simulating the Hippodrome: The Performance of Power in Kiev's St. Sophia', *The Art Bulletin* 91/3 (2009), 283–301.

Boia, L., *History and Myth in Romanian Consciousness*, tr. J. Brown (Budapest, 2001).

Bökönyi, S., 'Recent Developments in Hungarian Archaeology', *Antiquity* 67/254 (1993), 142–5.

Bóna, I., 'Arpadenzeitliche Kirche und Kirchhof im südlichen Stadtgebiet von Dunaujváros', *Alba Regia* 16 (1978), 99–157.

Bóna, I., *A Magyarok és Európa a 9–10 században* (Budapest, 2000).

Bondarenko, D., A. Korotayev and N. Kradin, 'Introduction: Social Evolution, Alternatives, and Nomadism', in N. Kradin et al. (eds), *Nomadic Pathways in Social Evolution* (Moscow, 2003), 1–24.

Boschetti, A., 'The Beginnings of Medieval Fortifications in the Late Carolingian Period from a Swiss Perspective', in N. Christie and H. Herold (eds), *Fortified Settlements in Early Medieval Europe: Defended Communities of the 8th–10th Centuries* (Philadelphia, 2016), 121–35.

Bosworth, C., 'The Tahirids and Arabic Culture', *JSS* 14/1 (1969), 45–79.
Bosworth, C., 'The Ṭāhirids and Ṣaffārids', in R. Frye (ed.), *Cambridge History of Iran 4: From the Arab Invasion to the Saljuqs* (Cambridge, 1975), 90–135.
Bosworth, C., *The New Islamic Dynasties: A Chronological and Genealogical Manual* (Edinburgh, 1996).
Bosworth, C., 'The Coming of Islam to Afghanistan', in C. Bosworth (ed.), *The Arabs, Byzantium and Iran* (Aldershot, 1996), 1–22.
Bosworth, C. and G. Rispling, 'An 'Ayyār Coin from Sīstān', *Journal of the Royal Asiatic Society* 3/2 (1993), 215–17.
Bowlus, C., *The Battle of Lechfeld and its Aftermath, August 955: The End of the Age of Migrations in the Latin West* (London, 2006).
Brătianu, G., *La Mer Noire: Des origines à la conquête Ottomane* (Munich, 1969).
Breckinridge, J., *The Numismatic Iconography of Justinian II (685–695, 705–711 A.D.)* (New York, 1959).
Brink, S. 'People and *Land* in Early Scandinavia', in I. Garipzanov et al. (eds), *Franks, Northmen, and Slavs: Identities and State Formation in Early Medieval Europe* (Turnhout, 2008), 87–111.
Brook, K., 'The Origins of East European Jews', *RH* 30/1–2 (2003), 1–22.
Brook, K., *The Jews of Khazaria*, 3rd edn (New York, 2018).
Brook, K., 'The American Center for Khazar Studies: A Resource for Turkic and Jewish History in Russia and Ukraine', *Khazaria.com* (1995–2020), http://www.khazaria.com/, accessed 7 December 2020.
Broome, M., *A Handbook of Islamic Coins* (London, 1985).
Brown, E., 'The Trojan Origins of the French: The Commencement of a Myth's Demise, 1450–1520', in A. Smyth (ed.), *Medieval Europeans: Studies in Ethnic Identity and National Perspectives in Medieval Europe* (New York, 1998), 135–79.
Brown, P., 'Higden's Britain', in A. Smyth (ed.), *Medieval Europeans: Studies in Ethnic Identity and National Perspectives in Medieval Europe* (New York, 1998), 103–18.
Brownsworth, L., *Lost to the West: The Forgotten Byzantine Empire that Rescued Western Civilization* (New York, 2009).
Brubaker, L., *Inventing Byzantine Iconoclasm* (London, 2012).
Brubaker, L. and J. Haldon, *Byzantium in the Iconoclast Era, c. 680–850: A History* (Cambridge, 2011).
Brubaker, R., *Ethnicity without Groups* (Cambridge, 2004).
Brutzkus, J., 'The Khazar Origin of Ancient Kiev', *SEER* 22 (1944), 108–24.
Bubenok, O., *Ясы и бродники в степях восточной европы (VI–начало XIII вв.)* (Kiev, 1997).

Bubenok, O., 'Данные топонимии о миграциях адыгов на украинские земли в развитое и позднее средневековье', in B. Khačimovič and F. Aleksandrovič (eds), *Древняя и средневековая культура адыгов: материалы международной научно-практической конференции* (Nal'čik, 2014), 30–5.

Budak, N., 'Identities in Early Medieval Dalmatia (Seventh–Eleventh Centuries)', in I. Garipzanov et al. (eds), *Franks, Northmen, and Slavs: Identities and State Formation in Early Medieval Europe* (Turnhout, 2008), 223–42.

Bulan, R., *La présence byzantine en Crimée et les relations entre l'Empire byzantin, les Khazars et les peuples voisins (VIIe–Xe siècles)* (Toulouse, 2010).

Bulgakova, V., 'Софийский корпус печатей: древнерусские и византийские находки на территории софийского собора в киеве', *VizVrem* 62 (2003), 59–74.

Bulgakova, V., *Byzantinische Bleisiegel in Osteuropa: Die Funde auf dem Territorium Altrusslands* (Wiesbaden, 2004).

Bulliet, R., *Conversion to Islam in the Medieval Period: An Essay in Quantitative History* (New York, 1979).

Bulliet, R., *The Case for Islamo-Christian Civilization* (New York, 2004).

Bushkovitch, P., 'Towns and Castles in Kievan Rus': Boiar Residence and Landownership in the Eleventh and Twelfth Centuries', *RH* 7/3 (1980), 251–64.

Bushkovitch, P., 'Review of: *The Origins of the Slavic Nations: Premodern Identities in Russia, Ukraine, and Belarus* by S. Plokhy', *International History Review* 29/4 (2007), 846–8.

Butler, F., 'The Representation of Oral Culture in the *Vita Constantini*', *Slavic and East European Journal* 39/3 (1995), 367–84.

Bÿkov, A., 'Из истории денежного обращения хазарии', *Восточные источники по истории народов юго-восточной и центральной европы* 3 (1974), 26–71.

Cahill, T., *How the Irish Saved Civilization* (New York, 2011).

Callmer, J., 'From West to East: The Penetration of Scandinavians into Eastern Europe ca. 500–900', in M. Kazanski et al. (eds), *Les centres proto-urbains russes entre Scandinavie, Byzance et Orient* (Paris, 2000), 45–94.

Carile, A., 'Byzantine Political Ideology and the Rus' in the Tenth–Twelfth Centuries', *HUkSt* 12 (1988), 400–13.

Carmi, S., P. Palamara, V. Vacic, T. Lencz, A. Darvasi and I. Pe'er, 'The Variance of Identity-by-Descent Sharing in the Wright-Fisher Model', *Genetics* 193 (2013), 911–28.

Carter, J. and G. Mack (eds), *Crimean Chersonesos: City, Chora, Museum, and Environs* (Austin, 2003).

Černigovskij (Gumilevskij), F., *Избранные жития святых, изложенные по руководству четьих-миней* (Moscow, 2011).

Chadwick, N., *The Beginnings of Russian History: An Enquiry into Sources* (Cambridge, 1966).

Chapman, J., *Tensions at Funerals: Micro-Tradition Analysis in Later Hungarian Prehistory* (Budapest, 2000).

Chazan, R., *European Jewry and the First Crusade* (Berkeley, 1987).

Chazan, R., *The Jews of Medieval Western Christendom: 1000–1500* (New York, 2006).

Chekin, L., 'The Role of Jews in Early Russian Civilization in the Light of a New Discovery and New Controversies', *RH* 17/4 (1990), 379–94.

Chekin, L., 'Безбожные сыны измайловы. Половцы и другие народы степи в древнерусской книжной культуре', *Из истории русской культуры* 1 (Moscow, 2000), 691–716.

Cherniavsky, M., 'Khan or Basileus: An Aspect of Russian Medieval Political Theory', *Journal of the History of Ideas* 20 (1959), 459–76.

Cheynet, J-C., 'Les sceaux byzantins de Londres', in J-C. Cheynet and C. Sode (eds), *SBS 8* (Munich, 2003), 85–100.

Chitwood, Z., *Byzantine Legal Culture and the Roman Legal Tradition, 867–1056* (Cambridge, 2017).

Christian, D., *A History of Russia, Central Asia and Mongolia: Inner Eurasia from Prehistory to the Mongol Empire* I (London, 1998).

Christian, D., 'The Khaganate of the Rus': Non-Slavic Sources of Russian Statehood', in S. Wheatcroft (ed.), *Challenging Traditional Views of Russian History* (New York, 2002), 3–26.

Christian, D., *Maps of Time: An Introduction to Big History* (Berkeley, 2004).

Čkhaidze, V., 'Зихская епархия: письменные и археологические свидетельства', in A. Ajbabin et al., (eds), *ХΘИиП* (Sevastopol', 2013), 47–68.

Čkhaidze, V., 'Byzantine Lead Seals Addressed to Matarcha from the Sixth to the Twelfth Century', in H. Ivakin et al. (eds), *Byzantine and Rus' Seals* (Kiev, 2015), 61–70.

Čkhaidze, V., 'Феофано Музалон: новые находки – старые открыткия', *СЩ* 5 (2015), 268–93.

Čkhaidze, V., 'Таманские монеты XI в. – Original or Fake?', *IV международный нумизматический симпозиум 'ПриPONTийский меняла: деньги местного рынка' севастополь, государственный* музей-заповедник 'Херсонес Таврический' 4–8 сентября 2016 г., материалы научной конференции (2016), 113–19.

Čkhaidze, V., 'Византийская власть на боспоре (последняя четверть XI – начало XIII вв.)', *Материалы по археологии, истории и этнографии таврии* XXIII (Simferopol, 2018), 721–730.

Coakley, J., 'Mobilizing the Past: Nationalist Images of History', *Nationalism and Ethnic Politics* 10/4 (2004), 531–60.

Çoban, E., 'Eastern Muslim Groups among Hungarians in the Middle Ages', Bilig 63 (2012), 55–76.

Codeso, P., 'Las crónicas Griegas y la entrada de los Rusos en la historia', *Minerva* 20 (2007), 93–109.

Coene, F., *The Caucasus: An Introduction* (New York, 2010).

Colarusso, J., 'The Storehouse of History: Ancient Ethnonyms and other Names from the Caucasus', in B. Khačimovič and F. Aleksandrovič (eds), *Древняя и средневековая культура адыгов: материалы международной научно-практической конференции* (Nal'čik, 2014), 76–81.

Collins, R., 'Law and Ethnic Identity in the Western Kingdoms in the Fifth and Sixth Centuries', in A. Smyth (ed.), *Medieval Europeans: Studies in Ethnic Identity and National Perspectives in Medieval Europe* (New York, 1998), 1–23.

Connor, W., 'A Nation Is a Nation, Is a State, Is an Ethnic Group, Is a . . .', in J. Hutchinson and A. Smith (eds), *Oxford Readers: Nationalism* (New York, 1994), 36–46.

Coon, C., *The Races of Europe, the White Race and the New World* (New York, 1939).

Costa, M., J. Pereira, M. Pala, V. Fernandes, A. Olivieri, A. Achilli, U. Perego, S. Rychkov, O. Naumova, J. Hatina, S. Woodward, K. Eng, V. Macaulay, M. Carr, P. Soares, L. Pereira and M. Richards, 'A Substantial Prehistoric European Ancestry Amongst Ashkenazi Maternal Lineages', *Nature Communications* 4/2543 (2013), 1–10.

Cotsonis, J., 'Saints and Cult Centers: A Geographic and Administrative Perspective in Light of Byzantine Lead Seals', in J-C. Cheynet and C. Sode (eds), *SBS 8* (Munich, 2013), 9–26.

Coulson, C., '"National" Requisitioning for "Public" Use of "Private" Castles in Pre-Nation State France', in A. Smyth (ed.), *Medieval Europeans: Studies in Ethnic Identity and National Perspectives in Medieval Europe* (New York, 1998), 119–34.

Craig, W., 'Whitrow and Popper on the Impossibility of an Infinite Past', *British Journal for the Philosophy of Science* 30/2 (1979), 165–70.

Cresci, L., 'Michele Attaliata e gli "ethnè" scitici', *Nea Rhome* 1 (2004), 185–207.

Crossley, P., *Hammer and Anvil: Nomad Rulers at the Forge of the Modern World* (London, 2019).
CSEN (Center for the Study of Eurasian Nomads), 'Chastiye Kurgany 2001 Excavation Report', *CSEN Archives* (2001). Referenced via webpage: http://web.archive.org/web/20120515060227/http://www.csen.org/Archives/2001_Chastiye_Report/2001_Chastiye_Report.html, accessed 7 December 2020.
CSEN (Center for the Study of Eurasian Nomads), 'Lower Don Chastiye Kurgany 2004 Excavation Report', *CSEN Archives* (2004). Referenced via webpage: http://web.archive.org/web/20120515055919/http://www.csen.org/Chastiye_Kurgany_All_Files/Chastiye_2004_Report/2004_Chastiye_Report.html, accessed 7 December 2020.
Csepeli, G. and A. Örkény, 'The Changing Facets of Hungarian Nationalism', *Social Research* 63/1 (1996), 247–86.
Csiky, E., *A Magyar Pénzek verdehelyei történelmünkben* (Szeged, 1987).
Curta, F., 'Pots, Slavs and "Imagined Communities": Slavic Archaeologies and the History of the Early Slavs', *EJA* 4/3 (2001), 367–84.
Curta, F., *Southeastern Europe in the Middle Ages: 500–1250* (New York, 2006).
Curta, F., 'Qagan, Khan, or King? Power in Early Medieval Bulgaria (Seventh to Ninth Century)', *Viator* 37 (2006), 1–31.
Curta, F., 'The Archaeology of Identities in Old Russia (ca. 500 to ca. 650)', *RH* 34/1–4 (2007), 31–62.
Curta, F., 'Introduction', in F. Curta and R. Kovalev (eds), *The Other Europe in the Middle Ages: Avars, Bulgars, Khazars, and Cumans* (Boston, 2008), 1–12.
Curta, F., '"Slavic" Bow Fibulae: Twenty Years of Research', *Bericht der Römisch-Germanischen Kommission* 93 (2012), 1–108.
Curta, F., 'The Image and Archaeology of the Pechenegs', *Banatica* 23 (2013), 143–202.
Curta, F., 'Markets in Tenth-Century al-Andalus and Volga Bulghâria: Contrasting Views of Trade in Muslim Europe', *Al-Masaq* 25/3 (2013), 305–30.
Curta, F., '"An Hesitating Journey through Foreign Knowledge": Niculescu, the Ostrich, and Culture History', *Arheologia Moldovei* 37 (2014), 299–306.
Curta, F., 'Four Questions for Those Who Still Believe in Prehistoric Slavs and Other Fairy Tales', *Starohrvatska prosvjeta* 120 (2015), 286–303.
Curta, F., 'Burials in Prehistoric Mounds: Reconnecting with the Past in Early Medieval Greece', *Revue des Ètudes Byzantines* 74 (2016), 269–85.

Curta, F., *Eastern Europe in the Middle Ages (500–1300)* (Boston, 2019).
Danilova, L., Сельская община в средневековой руси (Moscow, 1994).
Das, R., P. Wexler, M. Pirooznia and E. Elhaik, 'Localizing Ashkenazic Jews to Primeval Villages in the Ancient Iranian Lands of Ashkenaz', *Genome Biology and Evolution* 8/4 (2016), 1132–49.
Davidescu, M., *The Lost Romans* (Lexington, 2014).
Davis, K., *Periodization and Sovereignty: How Ideas of Feudalism and Secularization Govern the Politics of Time* (Philadelphia, 2008).
Davis-Kimball, J., 'Ongoing Archaeological Excavations in the Lower Don Region, Russia', *Central Eurasian Studies Review* 1/2 (2002), 11–13.
Dawson, C., *The Making of Europe: An Introduction to the History of European Unity* (Washington, D C, 1932).
Deér, J., 'A honfoglaló Magyarság', in L. Ligeti (ed.), *A Magyarság őstörténete* (Budapest, 1943), 123–53.
Derks, T. and N. Roymans (eds), *Ethnic Constructs in Antiquity: The Role of Power and Tradition* (Amsterdam, 2009).
Devletşin, G., *Törki-Tatar Ruḫi Mädäniyate Tariḫı* (Kazan', 1999).
Devletşin, G., 'Russian–Volga Bulgarian Mutual Relations in the Sphere of Spiritual Culture', *Journal of Sustainable Development* 8/7 (2015), 76–82.
DeWeese, D., *Islamization and the Native Religion in the Golden Horde: Baba Tükles and Conversion to Islam in Historical and Epic Tradition* (University Park, 1994).
Diaconu, P., *Les Coumans au Bas-Danube aux XIe et XIIe siècles* (Bucharest, 1978).
Diamond, J., *Guns, Germs and Steel: The Fates of Human Societies* (New York, 1999).
Diamond, J., *Collapse: How Societies Choose to Fail or Succeed* (New York, 2005).
Dilke, O., 'Cartography in the Byzantine Empire', in J. Harley and D. Woodward (eds), *The History of Cartography. Vol. 1: Cartography in Prehistoric, Ancient, and Medieval Europe and the Mediterranean* (Chicago, 1987), 258–75.
Dimitrov, D., *The Proto-Bulgarians North and West of the Black Sea* (Varna, 1987).
Djuvara, N., *O scurtă istorie a românilor povestită celor tineri* (Istros, 2003).
Dobrovits, M., 'The Altaic World through Byzantine Eyes: Some Remarks on the Historical Circumstances of Zemarchus' Journey to the Turks (AD 569–570)', *ActaAntHung* 64/4 (2011), 373–409.
Dolukhanov, P., *The Early Slavs: Eastern Europe from the Initial Settlement to the Kievan Rus* (New York, 1996).

Doncheva-Petkova, L., 'Плиска и печенезите', Плиска-Преслав 9 (2003), 244–58.

Doncheva-Petkova, L., 'Zur ethnischen Zugehörigkeit einiger Nekropolendes 11. Jahrhunderts in Bulgarien', in J. Henning (ed.), *Post-Roman Towns, Trade and Settlement in Europe and Byzantium* (New York, 2007), 644–58.

Donner, F., 'Muhammad and the Caliphate: Political History of the Islamic Empire up to the Mongol Conquest', in J. Esposito (ed.), *The Oxford History of Islam* (Oxford, 1999), 1–61.

van Donzel, E., A. Schmidt and C. Ott, *Gog and Magog in Early Syriac and Islamic Sources: Sallam's Quest for Alexander's Wall* (Boston, 2009).

Dragadze, T., 'A Meeting of Minds: A Soviet and Western Dialogue', *Current Anthropology* 19/1 (1978), 119–28.

Dudek, J., *Chazarowie: Polityka, Kultura, Religia VII–XI Wiek* (Warsaw, 2016).

Dunbar, R., *How Many Friends Does One Person Need? Dunbar's Number and Other Evolutionary Quirks* (London, 2010).

Dunlop, D., *The History of the Jewish Khazars* (New York, 1954).

Dyer, G., *War* (New York, 1985).

Dzino, D., '"Becoming Slav", "Becoming Croat": New Approaches in Research of Identities in Post-Roman Illyricum', *Hortus Artium Medievalium* 14 (2008), 195–206.

Dzino, D., *Becoming Slav, Becoming Croat: Identity Transformations in Post-Roman and Early Medieval Dalmatia* (Boston, 2010).

Eaton, R., *The Rise of Islam and the Bengal Frontier, 1204–1760* (Berkeley, 1993).

Effros, B., 'Grave Goods and the Ritual Expression of Identity', in T. Noble (ed.), *From Roman Provinces to Medieval Kingdoms* (New York, 2006), 189–232.

Efron, J., 'Jewish Genetic Origins in the Context of Past Historical and Anthropological Inquiries', *Human Biology* 85/6 (2013), 901–18.

Eidel, E., 'Буллы князей Ярополка-Петра и Владимира-Василия: атрибуция и датировка', СЩ 3 (2012), 53–68.

Eidel, E., 'A Seal of Maximos, Metropolitan of Kyiv and All Rus'', in H. Ivakin et al. (eds), *Byzantine and Rus' Seals* (Kiev, 2015), 231–4.

Eisenstadt, S., 'Introduction: The Secondary Breakthrough in Ancient Israelite Civilization – The Second Commonwealth and Christianity', in S. Eisenstadt (ed.), *The Origins and Diversity of Axial Age Civilizations* (Albany, 1986), 227–40.

Eisenstadt, S., *Comparative Civilizations and Multiple Modernities* (Boston, 2003).

Eisenstadt, S., *Explorations in Jewish Historical Experience* (Boston, 2004).

Eisenstadt, S., 'Axial Civilizations and the Axial Age Reconsidered', in J. Arnason et al. (eds), *Axial Civilizations and World History* (Boston, 2005), 531–64.

Eisenstadt, S., 'The Axial Conundrum between Transcendental Visions and Vicissitudes of Their Institutionalizations: Constructive and Destructive Possibilities', in R. Bellah and H. Joas (eds), *The Axial Age and its Consequences* (Cambridge, MA, 2012), 277–93.

Elhaik, E., 'The Missing Link of Jewish Ancestry: Contrasting the Rhineland and the Khazarian Hypothesis', *Genome Biology and Evolution* 5/1 (2012), 61–74.

Elhaik, E., 'Diverse Genetic Origins of Medieval Steppe Nomad Conquerors: A Response to Mikheyev et al. (2019)', *bioRxiv* (2020) 2020.01.06.885103, https://www.biorxiv.org/content/10.1101/2020.01.06.885103v2, accessed 7 December 2020.

Eliade, M., *The Sacred and the Profane: The Nature of Religion*, tr. W. Trask (New York, 1961).

Eliade, M., *The Myth of the Eternal Return: Cosmos and History* (Princeton, 1971).

Engel, P., *The Realm of St. Stephen: A History of Medieval Hungary, 895–1526*, tr. T. Pálosfalvi and A. Ayton (New York, 2001).

Engel, P., Gy. Kristó and M. Ferenc (eds), *Korai magyar történeti lexikon (9–14. század)* (Budapest, 1994).

Epstein, L., *The Theory and Practice of Welcoming Converts to Judaism: Jewish Universalism*, (Lewiston, NY, 1992).

Erdal, M., *Die Sprache der Wolgabolgarischen Inschriften* (Wiesbaden, 1993).

Erdal, M., 'The Khazar Language', in D. Sinor and N. di Cosmo (eds), *The World of the Khazars, New Perspectives: Selected Papers from the Jerusalem 1999 International Khazar Colloquium* (Boston, 2007), 75–108.

Erdélyi, I., 'Кабары (кавары) в карпатском бассейне', СА 4 (1983), 174–81.

Erdélyi, I. and M. Benkő, 'Some Problems of the Khazar Archaeology', *Проблемы этногенеза и этнической истории народов евразии* (2012), 1–3. Referenced via webpage: http://www.repository.enu.kz:8080/bitstream/handle/123456789/3011/some-problems.pdf, accessed 7 December 2020.

Escalona, J., 'The Endings of Early Medieval Kingdoms: Murder or Natural Causes?', *Reti Medievali Rivista* 17/2 (2016), 1–11.

Faber, A. and R. King, 'Yiddish and the Settlement History of Ashkenazic Jews', *MQ* 24/4 (1984), 393–425.

Faruqui, M., 'The Forgotten Prince: Mirza Hakim and the Formation of the Mughal Empire in India', *JESHO* 48/4 (2005), 487–523.

Feissel, D., C. Morrisson, J-C. Cheynet and B. Pitarakis, *Trois donations byzantines au Cabinet des médailles: Froehner (1925), Schlumberger (1929), Zacos (1998)* (Paris, 2001).

Fejér, M. and L. Huszár, *Bibliographia Numismaticae Hungaricae* (Budapest, 1977).

Feldbrugge, F., *A History of Russian Law: From Ancient Times to the Council Code (Ulozhenie) of Tsar Aleksei Mikhailovich of 1649* (Boston, 2018).

Feldbrugge, F., *Law in Medieval Russia* (Boston, 2009).

Feldman, A. M., 'The Historiographical and Archaeological Evidence of Autonomy and Rebellion in Cherson: A Defense of the Revisionist Analysis of Vladimir's Baptism (987–989)', MRes thesis, University of Birmingham (2013), https://etheses.bham.ac.uk/id/eprint/4865/, accessed 7 December 2020.

Feldman, A. M., 'How and Why Vladimir Besieged Cherson: An Inquiry into the Latest Research on the Chronology of the Conversion of Vladimir, 987– 989 CE', *Byzantinoslavica* 73/1–2 (2015), 145–70.

Feldman, A. M., 'Bullion, Barter and Borders in the Rus' Coinless Period', *Midlands Historical Review* 2 (2018), 1–12.

Feldman, A. M., 'Local Families, Local Allegiances: Sigillography and Autonomy in the Eleventh–Twelfth Century Black Sea', *BMGS* 42/2 (2018), 202–18.

Feldman, A. M., 'The First Christian Rus' Generation: Contextualizing the Black Sea Events of 1016, 1024 and 1043', *Rossica Antiqua* 16 (2018), 3–25.

Feldman, A. M., 'Masonry, Medicine and Monotheism: The Conversion of the Volga Bulgars in the *Kyssa'i Yūsuf*, the *Risāla* of Ibn Fadlān and the *Tārīkh-i-Bulghār*', *Diogenes* 8 (2019), 3–15.

Feldman, A. M., 'Mercantilist Thought in Byzantium', *Journal of Archaeological Numismatics* (2022).

Ferguson, N., *Civilization: The West and the Rest* (New York, 2011).

Flërov, V., 'Крепости хазарии в долине нижнего дона (этюд к теме фортификации)', in V. Mikheev et al. (eds), *Хазарский альманах I* (Kharkov, 2002), 151–68.

Flërov, V., '"Хазарские города" Что это такое?', *Проблеми на прабългарската история и култура* 4–1 (Sofia, 2007), 53–75.

Flërov, V., 'Иудаизм, христианство, ислам в хазарском каганате по археологическим данным (краткий обзор)', *Приноси към българската археология* 8 (2018), 139–45, http://series.naim.bg/index.php/CBA/article/view/20/11, accessed 7 December 2020.

Flërov, V. and V. Flërova, 'Иудаизм в степной и лесостепной хазарии: проблема идентификации археологических источников', *Хазары: материалы первого и второго международных коллоквиумов* 16 (2005), 185–207.

Flërova, V., *Образы и сюжеты мифологии хазарии* (Moscow, 2001).

Fletcher, R., *The Barbarian Conversion from Paganism to Christianity* (New York, 1997).

Fodor, I., *Verecke híres útján a magyar nép őstörténete és a honfoglalás* (Budapest, 1975).

Fodor, I., *In Search of a New Homeland: The Prehistory of the Hungarian People and the Conquest*, tr. H. Tarnoy (Budapest, 1982).

Fodor, I., *A magyarság születése* (Budapest, 1992).

Fodor, I., 'Ein Ungarischer Fund aus dem 10. Jahrhundert in Kasan', *Acta-AntHung* 62/3 (2009), 303–13.

Fodor, I., 'Őstörténeti viták és álviták', *Csodaszarvas* IV (2012), 125–46.

Fodor, I., M. Wolf and I. Nepper (eds), *The Ancient Hungarians: Exhibition Catalogue* (Budapest, 1996).

Fomin, A., 'Рунические знаки и тамги на подражаниях куфическим монетам X в. заметки', *СА* 4 (1988), 187–98.

Forster, B. and J. Tabachnik, *Jews by Choice: A Study of Converts to Reform and Conservative Judaism* (Hoboken, NJ, 1991).

Fosbroke, T., *British Monachism, or, Manners and Customs of the Monks and Nuns of England* (London, 1843).

Foss, C., *Arab-Byzantine Coins* (Washington, DC, 2008).

Fowden, G., *Empire to Commonwealth: Consequences of Monotheism in Late Antiquity* (Princeton, 1993).

Frank, A., *Islamic Historiography and 'Bulgar Identity' among the Tatars and Bashkirs of Russia* (Leiden, 1998).

Frank, A., 'Historical Legends of the Volga-Ural Muslims concerning Alexander the Great, the City of Yelabuga, and Bāchmān Khān', *Revue des Mondes Musulmans et de la Méditerranée* 89–90 (2000), 89–107.

Franklin, S., 'The Empire of the "Romaioi" as Viewed from Kievan Russia: Aspects of Byzantino-Russian Cultural Relations', *Byzantion* 53 (1983), 518–28.

Franklin, S. 'The Invention of Rus(sia)(s): Some Remarks on Medieval and Modern Perceptions of Continuity and Discontinuity', in A. Smyth (ed.), *Medieval Europeans: Studies in Ethnic Identity and National Perspectives in Medieval Europe* (New York, 1998), 180–95.

Franklin, S., *Byzantium – Rus – Russia: Studies in the Translation of Christian Culture* (Burlington, VT, 2002).

Franklin, S., *Writing, Society and Culture in Early Rus, c. 950–1300* (Cambridge, 2002).
Franklin, S. and J. Shepard, *The Emergence of Rus: 750–1200* (New York, 1996).
Frankopan, P., *The Silk Roads* (London, 2015).
Freeman, C., *The Closing of the Western Mind: The Rise of Faith and the Fall of Reason* (New York, 2003).
Friedenberg, D., *Medieval Jewish Seals from Europe* (Detroit, 1987).
Gadlo, A., Этническая история северного кавказа IV–X вв. (Leningrad, 1979).
Gagin, I., 'Волжская булгария: от посольства багдадского халифа до походов князя Святослава (X в.)', *VoprIst* 3 (2008), 131–42.
Gajdukov, P. and V. Kalinin, 'Древнейшие русские монеты', *Русь в IX–X веках. Археологическая панорама* (Moscow, 2012), 402–35, http://www.poludenga.ru/srebrenik/mos.html, accessed 7 December 2020.
Gălăbov, G., 'Златна ли е златната монета на Йоан Асен II', *Минало* 4 (2004), 23–40.
Galkina, E., Территория хазарского каганата IX–первой половины X в. в письменных источниках', *VoprIst* 9 (2006), 132–45.
Garagozov, R., 'Collective Memory and the Russian "Schematic Narrative Template"', *Journal of Russian and East European Psychology* 40/5 (2003), 55–89.
Garipzanov, I., 'The Annals of St. Bertin (839) and *Chacanus* of the *Rhos*', *Ruthenica* 5/1 (2006), 7–11.
Garipzanov, I., 'Frontier Identities: Carolingian Frontier and the *gens Danorum*', in I. Garipzanov et al. (eds), *Franks, Northmen, and Slavs: Identities and State Formation in Early Medieval Europe* (Turnhout, 2008), 113–43.
Garkavy, A., *Сказания еврейских писателей о хазарах и хазарском царстве* (St Petersburg, 1874).
Garnier, S., 'La notice "ṣifat sadd Yāǧūǧ wa-Māǧūǧ" dans le Kitāb al-Masālik wa-l-mamālik d'Ibn Ḫurdāḏbih: une feintise réussie', *Arabica* 60 (2013), 602–37.
Gavrituhin, I., 'La date du "Trésor" de Pereščepina et la chronologie des antiquités de l'époque de formation du Khaganat Khazar', in C. Zuckerman (ed.), *La Crimée entre Byzance et le Khaganat Khazar* (Paris, 2006), 13–30.
Geary, P., *The Myth of Nations: The Medieval Origins of Europe* (Princeton, 2002).
Geary, P., 'The Crisis of European Identity', in T. Noble (ed.), *From Roman Provinces to Medieval Kingdoms* (New York, 2006), 33–42.

Geary, P., 'Slovenian Gentile Identity: From Samo to the Fürstenstein', in I. Garipzanov et al. (eds), *Franks, Northmen, and Slavs: Identities and State Formation in Early Medieval Europe* (Turnhout, 2008), 243–57.

Geary, P., 'Rethinking Barbarian Invasions through Genomic History', *HA* Autumn (2014), 1–8.

Gedai, I., *A magyar pénzverés kezdete* (Budapest, 1986).

Gedai, I., 'Pénzverés', in Gy. Kristó et al. (eds), *Korai magyar történeti lexikon (9–14. század)* (Budapest, 1994), 541–2.

Gellner, E., *Nations and Nationalism* (Ithaca, 1983).

Ghenghea, A., 'Review of: *A History of Central European Archaeology: Theory, Methods, and Politics*, ed. A. Gramsch', *Dacia* 57 (2013), 177–9.

Gibbon, E., *The Decline and Fall of the Roman Empire* I–VI (London, repr., 1776–1845).

Gil, M., 'The Râdhânite Merchants and the Land of Râdhân', *JESHO* 17/3 (1974), 299–328.

Gil, M., 'Did the Khazars Convert to Judaism?', *Revue des Études Juives* 170/3–4 (2011), 429–41.

Gillett, A., *On Barbarian Identity: Critical Approaches to Ethnicity in the Early Middle Ages* (Turnhout, 2002).

Gillett, A., 'Ethnogenesis: A Contested Model of Early Medieval Europe', *History Compass* 4/2 (2006), 241–60.

Glukhov, A., 'Погребения огузо-печенежского времени из могильника солодовка I', *Волго-донское археологическое общество* (2001–5), http://archeolog-vdao.narod.ru/bibliotec_2konferenc_gluchov.html, accessed 7 December 2020.

Goffart, W., *The Narrators of Barbarian History (A.D. 550–800): Jordanes, Gregory of Tours, Bede, and Paul the Deacon* (Princeton, 1988).

Goffart, W., 'Does the Distant Past Impinge on the Invasion Age Germans?', in T. Noble (ed.), *From Roman Provinces to Medieval Kingdoms* (New York, 2006), 91–109.

Goffart, W., 'The Barbarians in Late Antiquity and How They Were Accommodated in the West', in T. Noble (ed.), *From Roman Provinces to Medieval Kingdoms* (New York, 2006), 235–61.

Goitein, S., *A Mediterranean Society: The Jewish Communities of the Arab World as Portrayed in the Documents of the Cairo Geniza* (Berkeley, 1967–93).

Gold, D., 'Has the Textbook Explanation of the Origins of Yiddish and of Ashkenazic Jewry Been Challenged Successfully?', *MQ* 26/3 (1986), 339–63.

Golden, P., 'The Migrations of the Oğuz', *Archivum Ottomanicum* 4 (1972), 45–84.

Golden, P., *Khazar Studies: An Historico-Philological Inquiry into the Origins of the Khazars* (Budapest, 1980).

Golden, P., 'Review of: *Les Coumans au Bas-Danube aux XIe et XIIe siecles*', *American Historical Review* 85/2 (1980), 380.

Golden, P., 'Peoples and Cultures: Imperial Ideology and the Sources of Political Unity amongst the Pre-Činggisid Nomads of Western Eurasia', *AEMA* 2 (1982), 37–76.

Golden, P., 'The Question of the Rus' Qaghanate', *AEMA* 2 (1982), 77–92.

Golden, P., 'Judaism in Khazaria', *AEMA* 3 (1983), 127–56.

Golden, P., 'Aspects of the Nomadic Factor in the Economic Development of Kievan Rus", in I. Koropeckÿj (ed.), *Ukrainian Economic History: Interpretive Essays* (Cambridge, 1991), 58–101.

Golden, P., *An Introduction to the History of the Turkic Peoples: Ethnogenesis and State-Formation in Medieval and Early Modern Eurasia and the Middle East* (Wiesbaden, 1992).

Golden, P., 'The Codex Cumanicus', in H. Paksoy (ed.), *Central Asian Monuments* (Istanbul, 1992), 33–63.

Golden, P., 'Cumanica IV: The Tribes of the Cuman-Qïpčaqs', *AEMA* 9 (1997), 99–122.

Golden, P., 'Some Notes on the *Comitatus* in Medieval Eurasia with Special References to the Khazars', *Festschrift for Thomas S. Noonan, RH* 28 (2001), 153–70.

Golden, P., 'Nomads in the Sedentary World: The Case of Pre-Chinggisid Rus' and Georgia', in A. Khazanov and A. Wink (eds), *Nomads in the Sedentary World* (New York, 2001), 24–75.

Golden, P., 'The Qïpčaqs of Medieval Eurasia: An Example of Stateless Adaptation in the Steppes', in G. Seaman and D. Marks (eds), *Rulers from the Steppe: State Formation on the Eurasian Periphery* (Los Angeles, 2001), 132–57.

Golden, P., *Nomads and their Neighbours in the Russian Steppe: Turks, Khazars and Qipchaqs* (Burlington, VT, 2003).

Golden, P., 'Khazaria and Judaism', in P. Golden, *Nomads and their Neighbours in the Russian Steppe: Turks, Khazars and Qipchaqs* (Burlington, VT, 2003), 127–56.

Golden, P., 'The Polovci Dikii', in P. Golden, *Nomads and their Neighbours in the Russian Steppe: Turks, Khazars and Qipchaqs* (Burlington, VT, 2003), 296–309.

Golden, P., 'The Khazar Sacral Kingship', in K. Reyerson et al. (eds), *Pre-Modern Russia and Its World: Essays in Honor of Thomas S. Noonan* (Wiesbaden, 2006), 79–102.

Golden, P., 'Khazar Studies: Achievements and Perspectives', in D. Sinor and N. di Cosmo (eds), *The World of the Khazars, New Perspectives: Selected Papers from the Jerusalem 1999 International Khazar Colloquium* (Boston, 2007), 7–57.

Golden, P., 'The Conversion of the Khazars to Judaism', in D. Sinor and N. di Cosmo (eds), *The World of the Khazars, New Perspectives: Selected Papers from the Jerusalem 1999 International Khazar Colloquium* (Boston, 2007), 123–61.

Golden, P., 'Irano-Turcica: The Khazar Sacral Kingship Revisited', *ActaAntHung* 60 (2007), 161–94.

Golden, P., *Turks and Khazars: Origins, Institutions, and Interactions in Pre-Mongol Eurasia* (Burlington, VT, 2010).

Golden, P., 'The Turks: Origins and Expansion', in P. Golden, *Turks and Khazars: Origins, Institutions, and Interactions in Pre-Mongol Eurasia* (Burlington, VT, 2010), 1–33.

Golden, P., 'Some Notes on the Etymology of *Sabir*', in A. Sinicyn and M. Kholod (eds), *KOINON ΔΩPON: Исследования и эссе в честь 60-летнего юбилея Валерия Павловича Никонорова от друзей и коллег* (St Petersburg, 2013), 49–55.

Goldina, R. and E. Chernykh, 'Forest and Steppe: A Dialogue of Culture on Archaeological Materials from the Kama Region', *ActaAntHung* 58/1 (2005), 41–58.

Golev, K., 'On the Edge of Another World: A Comparison between the Balkan and the Crimean Peninsula as Contact Zones between Dašt-i Qipčaq and the Byzantine Empire', *EtBalk* 54/1 (2018), 89–126.

Golovina, E., 'Итиль найден? Учёные изучают крупное поселение хазар', *Russian Geographical Society* (2020), https://www.rgo.ru/ru/article/itil-nayden-uchyonye-izuchayut-krupnoe-poselenie-hazar, accessed 9 July 2021.

Golovnëv, A., *Антропология движения (древности северной евразии)* (Jekaterinburg, 2009).

Golovnëv, A., 'О традициях и новациях: признательность за дискуссию', *Этнографическое обозрение* 2 (2012), 84–6.

Golubovskij, P., *Печенеги, торки и половцы до нашествия татар. История южно-русских степей IX–XIII вв.* (Kiev, 1884).

Gombocz, Z., 'Die bulgarisch-türkischen Lehnwörter in der ungarischen Sprache', *Mémoires de la Société Finno-Ougrienne* 30 (Helsinki, 1912), 1–252.

Gončarov, E., 'Восточная нумизматика херсона: вторая половина XII–первая половина XV вв.', in S. Karpov (ed.), *Причерноморье в средние века* VII (St Petersburg, 2009), 118–32.

Gončarov, E. and V. Čkhaidze, 'Находки средневековых монет на территории таманского полуострова', *Материалы и исследования по археологии кубани* (Krasnodar, 2005), 343–7.

Goodacre, H., *A Handbook of the Coinage of the Byzantine Empire* (London, 1957).

Goodman, M., *Mission and Conversion: Proselytizing in the Religious History of the Roman Empire* (Oxford, 1991).

Goussous, N., *Umayyad Coinage of Bilad al-Sham* (Amman, 1996).

Grabar, O., 'Islamic Art and Byzantium', in M. Bonner (ed.), *Arab–Byzantine Relations in Early Islamic Times* (Burlington, VT, 2004), 263–94.

Grečkina, T. and E. Šnajdštejn, 'Археология астраханского края на рубеже тысячелетий', *Археология нижнего поволжья на рубеже тысячелетий. Материалы всероссийской научно-практической конференции* (Astrakhan', 2001).

Greenfeld, L., 'Types of European Nationalism', in J. Hutchinson and A. Smith (eds), *Oxford Readers: Nationalism* (New York, 1994), 165–71.

Grekov, B., *Киевская русь* (Leningrad, 1953).

Grekov, B. and N. Kalinin, 'Булгарское государство до монгольского завоевания', Материалы по истории татарии (Kazan', 1948), 97–185.

Grierson, P., 'The Monetary Reforms of 'Abd al-Malik: Their Metrological Basis and their Financial Repercussion', *JESHO* 3/3 (1960), 241–64.

Grierson, P., *Byzantine Coinage in the Dumbarton Oaks Collection. II: Phocas to Theodosius III, 602–717* (Washington, DC, 1968).

Grierson, P., *Byzantine Coins* (Berkeley, 1982).

Grierson, P., *Byzantine Coinage in its International Setting* (Cambridge, 1990).

Grierson, P., *Catalogue of the Byzantine Coins in the Dumbarton Oaks Collection. IV: Alexius I to Michael VIII, 1081–1261* (Washington, DC, 1999).

Grinberg, L., '"Is this City Yours or Mine?" Political Sovereignty and Eurasian Urban Centers in the Ninth through Twelfth Centuries', *CSSH* 55/4 (2013), 895–921.

Grousset, R., *The Empire of the Steppes: A History of Central Asia*, tr. N. Walford (New Brunswick, 1991).

von Grunebaum, G., *Medieval Islam: A Study in Cultural Orientation*, 2nd edn (Chicago, 1971).

Grynaeus, T., 'Skull Trephination in the Carpathian Basin (8th–13th Century A.D.)', *MQ* 40/2 (1999), 131–40.

Gubajdullin, A., *Фортификация городищ волжской булгарии* (Kazan', 2002).

Guldi, J. and D. Armitrage, *The History Manifesto* (Cambridge, 2014).

Gumilëv, L., 'Степная атлантида', *Опубликовано в журнале азия и африка сегодня* 2 (1962), 52–3.

Gumilëv, L., 'New Data on the History of the Khazars', *ActaAntHung* 19 (1967), 61–103.

Gumilëv, L., *Этногенез и биосфера земли* (Leningrad, 1989).

Gumilëv, L., *Древняя русь и великая степь* (Moscow, 2000).

Gunszt, P., *A magyar polgári történetírás* (Budapest, 1964).

Gurulëva, V. and T. Fëdorova, 'Шелонский клад конца XII–первой половины XIII в.: византийские монеты, болгарские и латинские имитации', *НиЭ* 19 (2015), 63–99.

Gurulëva, V., V. Kulešov and T. Jurčenko, 'Монеты из славянского (анастасиевского) клада', *НиЭ* 18 (2011), 136–86.

Gyóni, G., 'Hungarian Traces in Place-Names in Bashkiria', *Acta Ethnographica Hungarica* 53/2 (2008), 279–305.

Györffy, G., 'Monuments du lexique petchénègue', *ActaAntHung* 18 (1965), 73–82.

Györffy, G., *Anonymus: Rejtély vagy történeti forrás* (Budapest, 1988).

ter Haar Romeny, B. (ed.), *Religious Origins of Nations? The Christian Communities of the Middle East* (Boston, 2010).

Hahn, W., *Moneta Imperii Byzantini von Heraclius bis Leo III (610–720)* (Vienna, 1981).

Hajnóczi, Gy., T. Mezős, M. Nagy and Z. Visy (eds), *Pannonia Hungarica Antiqua*, tr. I. Bíró (Budapest, 1998).

Haldon, J., *The State and the Tributary Mode of Production* (New York, 1993).

Haldon, J., *Warfare, State and Society in the Byzantine World, 565–1204* (London, 1999).

Haldon, J., *The Empire that Would Not Die: The Paradox of Eastern Roman Survival, 640–740* (Cambridge, 2016).

Haldon, J., 'Bureaucracies, Elites and Clans: The Case of Byzantium, c.600–1100', in P. Crooks and T. Parsons (eds), *Empires and Bureaucracy in World History: From Late Antiquity to the Twentieth Century* (Cambridge, 2017), 147–69.

Haldon, J., H. Elton, S. Huebner, A. Izdebski, L. Mordechai and T. Newfield, 'Plagues, Climate Change, and the End of an Empire: A Response to Kyle Harper's *The Fate of Rome*' (1–3), *History Compass* 16/12 (2018), https://onlinelibrary.wiley.com/doi/abs/10.1111/hic3.12508, accessed 7 December 2020.

Halim, H., K. Yusoff and A. Ghazalli, 'Relations between Volga Bulgaria and Baghdad', *International Business Management* 7/1 (2013), 21–30.

Halperin, C., *Russia and the Golden Horde: The Mongol Impact on Medieval Russian History* (Bloomington, 1987).

Halperin, C., 'The Kipchak Connection: The Ilkhans, the Mamluks and Ayn Jalut', *BSO[A]S* 63/2 (2000), 229–45.

Halperin, C., 'National Identity in Premodern Rus'. Review of: *The Origins of the Slavic Nations: Premodern Identities in Russia, Ukraine and Belarus*, by S. Plokhy', *RH* 37 (2010), 275–94.

Halsall, G., 'Review of: *On Barbarian Identity. Critical Approaches to Ethnicity in the Early Middle Ages*, ed. A. Gillett', *EHR* 118/479 (2003), 1349–50.

Halsall, G., 'Movers and Shakers: The Barbarians and the Fall of Rome', in T. Noble (ed.), *From Roman Provinces to Medieval Kingdoms* (New York, 2006), 277–91.

Halsall, G., *Barbarian Migrations and the Roman West, 376–568* (Cambridge, 2007).

Hamant, Y. (ed.), *The Christianization of Ancient Russia: A Millennium: 988–1988* (Paris, 1992).

Hanak, W., *The Nature and the Image of Princely Power in Kievan Rus', 980–1054* (Leiden, 2014).

Hankey, T., 'Civic Pride versus Feelings for Italy in the Age of Dante', in A. Smyth (ed.), *Medieval Europeans: Studies in Ethnic Identity and National Perspectives in Medieval Europe* (New York, 1998), 196–216.

Hann, C., 'Anthropology, Eurasia, and Global History', in J. Arnason and C. Hann (eds), *Anthropology and Civilizational Analysis: Eurasian Explorations* (Albany, 2018), 339–54.

Hanson, V., *Carnage and Culture: Landmark Battles in the Rise to Western Power* (New York, 2007).

Härke, H., 'Archaeologists and Migrations: A Problem of Attitude?', in T. Noble (ed.), *From Roman Provinces to Medieval Kingdoms* (New York, 2006), 262–76.

Härke, H., 'Archaeology and Nazism: A Warning from Prehistory', in V. Mordvintseva et al. (eds), *Archaeological and Linguistic Research: Materials of the Humboldt-Conference* (Kiev, 2014), 32–43.

Harper, K., *The Fate of Rome* (Princeton, 2017).

Harris, J., *Byzantium and the Crusades* (New York, 2003).

Heather, P., '*Foedera* and *Foederati* of the Fourth Century', in T. Noble (ed.), *From Roman Provinces to Medieval Kingdoms* (New York, 2006), 292–308.

Heather, P., 'Ethnicity, Group Identity, and Social Status in the Migration Period', in I. Garipzanov et al. (eds), *Franks, Northmen, and Slavs:*

Identities and State Formation in Early Medieval Europe (Turnhout, 2008), 17–49.

Heather, P., *Empires and Barbarians: Migrations, Development and the Birth of Europe* (London, 2009).

Heather, P., *The Restoration of Rome: Barbarian Popes and Imperial Pretenders* (London, 2013).

Hellebrandt, M., *Celtic Finds from Northern Hungary*, tr. M. Seleanu (Budapest, 1999).

Hellie, R., 'Rewriting Pre-Mongol Russian History Once Again', *RH* 16/1 (1989), 67–76.

Hendy, M., *Coinage and Money in the Byzantine Empire (1081–1261)* (Washington, DC, 1969).

Hendy, M., *Catalogue of the Byzantine Coins in the Dumbarton Oaks Collection and in the Whittemore Collection: 1081–1261*, vol. 4/1 (Washington, DC, 1999).

Herold, H., 'The Natural Environment, Anthropogenic Influences and Supra-Regional Contacts at 9th- to 10th-Century Fortified Elite Settlements in Central Europe', in N. Christie and H. Herold (eds), *Fortified Settlements in Early Medieval Europe: Defended Communities of the 8th–10th Centuries* (Philadelphia, 2016), 107- 20.

Hildinger, E., *Warriors of the Steppe: A Military History of Central Asia, 500 B.C. to 1700 A.D.* (New York, 1997).

Hlebionek, M., 'Herb Ziemi Kijowskiej na pieczęciach władlów rzeczpospolitej', СЩ 2 (2012), 82–98.

Hobsbawm, E., *Nations and Nationalism since 1780: Programme, Myth, Reality* (Cambridge, 1990).

Hofer, T., 'Ethnography and Hungarian Prehistory', *Budapesti Könyvszemle* (1996), 301–3, http://www.c3.hu/scripta/books/96/03/02hofer.htm, accessed 7 December 2020.

Holland, T., *Millennium: The End of the World and the Forging of Christendom* (London, 2008).

Holló, G., L. Szathmáry, A. Marcsik and Z. Barta, 'History of the Peoples of the Great Hungarian Plain in the First Millennium: A Craniometric Point of View', *Human Biology* 80/6 (2008), 655–67.

Holmes, C. and N. Standen, 'Defining the Global Middle Ages', *Medieval Worlds* 1 (2015), 106–17.

Holo, J., 'A Genizah Letter from Rhodes Evidently Concerning the Byzantine Reconquest of Crete', *Journal of Near Eastern Studies* 59 (2000), 1–13.

Holo, J., *Byzantine Jewry in the Mediterranean Economy* (New York, 2009).

Holtorf, C., 'Academic Critique and the Need for an Open Mind (A Response to Kristiansen), *Antiquity* 82 (2008), 490–2.
Hóman, B., *Magyar Pénztörténet, 1000–1325* (Budapest, 1916).
Honeychurch, W., 'Alternative Complexities: The Archaeology of Pastoral Nomadic States', *Journal of Archaeological Research* 22/4 (2014), 277–326.
Horváth, C., 'The Cemeteries and Grave Finds of Győr and Moson Counties from the Time of the Hungarian Conquest and the Early Árpádian Age', *Dissertationes Archaeologicae ex Instituto Archaeologico Universitatis de Rolando Eötvös Nominatae* 3/1 (Budapest, 2013), 331–8.
Howard-Johnston, J., 'The *De Administrando Imperio*: A Re-Examination of the Text and a Re-Evaluation of its Evidence about the Rus', in M. Kazanski et al., (eds), *Les centres proto-urbains russes entre Scandinavie, Byzance et Orient* (Paris, 2000), 301–36.
Howard-Johnston, J., 'Byzantine Sources for Khazar History', in D. Sinor and N. di Cosmo (eds), *The World of the Khazars, New Perspectives: Selected Papers from the Jerusalem 1999 International Khazar Colloquium* (Boston, 2007), 163–93.
Humphreys, M., 'The "War of Images" Revisited: Justinian II's Coinage Reform and the Caliphate', *NC* 173 (2013), 229–44.
Huntington, S., *The Clash of Civilizations and the Remaking of World Order* (New York, 1996).
Hurwitz, E., 'Kievan Rus' and Medieval Myopia', *RH* 5/2 (1978), 176–87.
Hurwitz, E., 'Metropolitan Hilarion's *Sermon on Law and Grace*: Historical Consciousness in Kievan Rus'', *RH* 7/3 (1980), 322–33.
Hurwitz, E., 'Review of: *Kievskaia Rus' i kochevniki. Pechenegi, torki i polovtsy*, by R. Mavrodina', *Russian Review* 44/1 (1985), 102–3.
Huszár, L., *Münzkatalog Ungarn von 1000 bis Heute* (Munich, 1979).
Hutchinson, J. and A. Smith (eds), *Oxford Readers: Nationalism* (New York, 1994).
Huxley, G., 'The Scholarship of Constantine Porphyrogenitus', *Proceedings of the Royal Irish Academy: Archaeology, Celtic Studies, History, Linguistics, Literature* 80C (1980), 29–40.
Huxley, G., 'Byzantinochazarika', *Hermathena* 148 (1990), 69–87.
Ignác, R., 'Egy miniszter a tévesztett úton; eredeti közlés: Élet és tudomány', *Vörösvári Újság* (2006), http://pilisvorosvar.hu/vorosvariujsag-regi/2006/augusztus/7.htm, accessed 7 December 2020.
Ilisch, L., "Abd al-Malik's Monetary Reform in Copper and the Failure of Centralization', in J. Haldon (ed.), *Money, Power and Politics in Early Islamic Syria: A Review of Current Debates* (New York, 2010), 125–46.
Inge, W., *The End of an Age and Other Essays* (London, 1949).

Inkov, A., *Древняя русь и половцы во второй половине XI–первой трети XIII века* (Saransk, 2001).
Insoll, T., *The Archaeology of Islam* (Oxford, 1999).
Ioannisyan, O., 'Archaeological Evidence for the Development and Urbanization of Kiev from the 8th to the 14th Century', tr. K. Judelson, in D. Austin and L. Alcock (eds), *From the Baltic to the Black Sea: Studies in Medieval Archaeology* (Boston, 1990), 285–312.
Ioffe, D., 'Jews, Khazars and the Issues of Slavic Cultural History', in M. de Dobbeleer and S. Vervaet (eds), *(Mis)Understanding the Balkans: Essays in Honour of Raymond Detrez* (Ghent, 2013), 385–405.
Iotov, V., 'A Note on the "Hungarian Sabers" of Medieval Bulgaria', in F. Curta and R. Kovalev (eds), *The Other Europe in the Middle Ages: Avars, Bulgars, Khazars, and Cumans* (Boston, 2008), 327–38.
Ivakhiv, A., 'Nature and Ethnicity in East European Paganism: An Environmental Ethnic of the Religious Right?', *Pomegranate* 7/2 (2005), 194–225.
Ivakin, H., N. Khrapunov and W. Seibt (eds) *Byzantine and Rus' Seals* (Kiev, 2015).
Ivanova, M., I. Zhurbin and A. Kirillov, 'Fortifications at Idnakar Settlement: The Findings of Interdisciplinary Research', *Archaeology, Ethnology and Anthropology of Eurasia* 41/2 (2013), 108–19.
Ivik, O. and V. Ključnikov, Хазары (Moscow, 2013).
Iwanus, J., *Democracy, Federalism, and Nationality: Ukraine's Medieval Heritage in the Thought of N. I. Kostomarov* (Edmonton, 1986).
Izdebski, A., J. Pickett, N. Roberts and T. Waliszewski, 'The Environmental, Archaeological and Historical Evidence for Regional Climatic Changes and Their Societal Impacts in the Eastern Mediterranean in Late Antiquity', *Quaternary Science Reviews* 30 (2015), 1–20.
Izmajlov, I., 'Ислам в волжской булгарии', *Восток. Афро-азиатские общества: история и современность* 2 (2009), 5–12.
Jaffrelot, C., 'For a Theory of Nationalism', *Questions de Recherche* 10 (2003), 1–51.
Jakhšijan, O., 'Общинное самоуправление и государственное управление: соотношение в эпоху этнополитогенеза', *Теоретический и научно-методический журнал* 20 (2013), 285–91.
Jakubovskij, A., 'Феодальное общество азии и его торговля с восточной европой в 10–15 вв', in A. Samojlovič (ed.), *Материалы по истории узбекской, таджикской и туркменской ССР 1: торговля с московским государством и международное положение средней азии в XVI–XVII вв.* (Leningrad, 1932), 18–28.

James, P., *Globalism, Nationalism, Tribalism: Bringing Theory Back In* (London, 2006).

Janin, V., *Денежно-весовые системы домонгольской руси и очерки истории денежной системы средневекового новгорода* (Moscow, 1956).

Janin, V., *Актове печати древней руси I* (Moscow, 1970).

Janin, V. and P. Gajdukov, *Актове печати древней руси x–XV вв. III: печати, зарегистрированные в 1970–1996 гг.* (Moscow, 1998).

Jankowiak, M., 'Two Systems of Trade in the Western Slavic Lands in the 10th Century', in M. Bogucki and M. Rębkowski (eds), *Economies, Monetisation and Society in West Slavic Lands 800–1200 ad* (Szczecin, 2013), 137–48.

János, I., L. Szathmáry and L. Hüse, 'Pagan–Christian Change in Northeastern Hungary in the 10th–13th Centuries AD: A Palaeodemographic Aspect', *Collegium Antropologicum* 38/1 (2014), 305–18.

Jaspers, K., *The Origin and Goal of History* (New York, 1953).

Jerusalimskaja, A., *Кавказ на шелковом пути* (St Petersburg, 1992).

Jeszensky, G., 'Az első Magyar rézpénzek', *Numizmatikai Közlöny* 34/35 (1938), 3–46.

Joas, H., 'The Axial Age Debate as Religious Discourse', in R. Bellah and H. Joas (eds), *The Axial Age and Its Consequences* (Cambridge, MA, 2012), 9–29.

Jones, T. and A. Ereira, *Barbarians: An Alternative Roman History* (London, 2006).

Jordanov, I., *Монетни и монетно обръщение в средновековна българия: 1081–1261* (Sofia, 1984).

Jordanov, I., 'Sceau d'archonte de PATZINAKIA du XIe siècle', *EtBalk* 2 (1992), 79–82.

Jordanov, I., 'Byzantine Lead Seals from the Village of Melnitsa (District of Elkhovo, Bulgaria), Part II', in J-C. Cheynet and C. Sode (eds), *SBS 10* (Berlin, 2010), 33–59.

Jordanov, I., 'Взаимоотношения киевской руси, византии и болгарии X–XII значение сфрагистики', *СЩ* 4 (2013), 368–75.

Kaiser, D., *The Growth of Law in Medieval Russia* (Princeton, 1980).

Kakhovskij, B. and V. Kakhovskij, 'Изучение булгарских памятников на территории чувашии', in F. Khuzin (ed.), *Археология волжской булгарии: проблемы, поиски, решения* (Kazan', 1993), 32–46.

Kakhovskij, V., *Происхождение чувашского народа* (Šupaškar, 2003).

Kaldellis, A., *Hellenism in Byzantium: The Transformations of Greek Identity and the Reception of the Classical Tradition* (Cambridge, 2007).

Kaldellis, A., *Ethnography after Antiquity: Foreign Lands and Peoples in Byzantine Literature* (Philadelphia, 2013).

Kaldellis, A., *Romanland: Ethnicity and Empire in Byzantium* (London, 2019).

Kálnoky, N., 'Des princes scythes aux capitaines des Iasses', *Droit et Cultures* 52 (2006), 65–84.

Kamenceva, E. and N. Ustjugov, Русская сфрагистика и геральдика (Moscow, 1974).

Kaplan, F., 'The Decline of the Khazars and the Rise of the Varangians', *SEER* 13/1 (1954), 1–10.

Karpat, K., *Studies on Turkish Politics and Society: Selected Articles and Essays* (Leiden, 2004).

Kazakov, E., *О взаимодействии волжских булгар с тюркоязычным населением юго- восточной европы в IX–XI вв.* (Kazan', 1991).

Kazakov, E., *Культура ранней волжской болгарии. Этапы этнокультурной истории* (Moscow, 1992).

Kazakov, E., 'Волжская булгария и финно-угорский мир', *Finno-Ugrica* 1 (1997), 33–53.

Kazakov, E., 'The Nature and Chronology of Ninth- and Tenth-Century Volga Bulgar Trade', paper presented at the conference *Lost in Translation? Ibn Fadlan and the Great Unwashed*, Corpus Christi College, University of Oxford, 14–15 March (2016).

Kazanski, M., A. Nercessian and C. Zuckerman (eds), *Les centres protourbains russes entre Scandinavie, Byzance et Orient* (Paris, 2000).

Keating, S., 'Revisiting the Charge of Taḥrīf: The Question of Supersessionism in Early Islam and the Qurʾān', in I. Levy et al. (eds), *Nicholas of Cusa and Islam: Polemic and Dialogue in the Late Middle Ages* (Boston, 2014), 202–17.

Kent, J., *A Selection of Byzantine Coins in the Barber Institute of Fine Arts* (Birmingham, 1985).

Khakimzjanov, F., *Эпиграфические памятники волжской булгарии и их язык* (Moscow, 1987).

Khalikov, A., *Ранние болгары на волге* (Moscow, 1964).

Khalikov, A., 'История изучения билярского городища и его исторического топография', in V. Sedov (ed.), *Исследования великого города. Сборник статей* (Moscow, 1976), 33–46.

Khalikov, A., *Татарский народ и его предки* (Kazan', 1989).

Khalikov, A., '*Ислам и урбанизм в волжской булгарии*', in P. Starostin et al. (eds), Биляр - столица домонгольской болгарии (Kazan', 1991).

Khalikova, E., *Мусульманские некрополи волжской булгарии X–начала XIII в.* (Kazan', 1986).

Khaljavrin, N., 'Проблема становления новгородской архиепископии в трудах отечественных историков', *Вестник удмуртского университета* 26/4 (2016), 23–30.

Khazanov, A., *Nomads and the Outside World*, tr. J. Crookenden (New York, 1983).

Khazanov, A., 'Nomads in the History of the Sedentary World', in A. Khazanov and A. Wink (eds), *Nomads in the Sedentary World* (New York, 2001), 1–23.

Khotko, S., 'Опыт критического осмысления новой концепции этнической истории северо-западного кавказа в хазарское время (VIII–X вв.)', in B. Khačimovič and F. Aleksandrovič (eds), *Древняя и средневековая культура адыгов: материалы международной научно-практической конференции* (Nal'čik, 2014), 181–9.

Khromov, K., 'Находки исламских медных монет второй половины XII–первой половины XIII в. на территории киевского княжества', *Эпиграфика востока* 30 (2013), 1–11.

Khuzin, F., 'On the Process of Sedentarization of Volga Bulgars', *Journal of Sustainable Development* 8/7 (2015), 68–74.

Kiernowski, R., 'Teksty pisane na polskich monetach wczesnośredniowiecznych', *Wiadomości Numizmatyczne* 3 (1959), 4–22.

Killworth, P. and H. Bernard, 'A Pseudomodel of the Small World Problem', *Social Forces* 58/2 (1979), 477–505.

Killworth, P., C. McCarty and H. Bernard, 'Measuring Patterns of Acquaintanceship', *Current Anthropology* 25/4 (1984), 381–97.

King, C., *The Black Sea: A History* (New York, 2004).

King, G., 'Islam, Iconoclasm, and the Declaration of Doctrine', *BSO[A]S* 48/2 (1985), 267–77.

Kirk, G., *Myth: Its Meaning and Functions in Ancient and Other Cultures* (Berkeley, 1973).

Kirk, G., *The Nature of Greek Myths* (New York, 1974).

Kirpičnikov, A. and N. Kazanskij, 'Византийская митрополичья печать, найденная в старой ладоге', in D. Mačinskij (ed.), *Ладога и эпоха викингов: четвертые чтения памяти Анны Мачинской, материалы к чтениям* (St Petersburg, 1998), 78–85.

Kizilov, M. and D. Mikhaylova, 'The Khazar Kaganate and the Khazars in European Nationalist Ideologies and Scholarship', *AEMA* 14 (2005), 31–53.

Klaniczay, G., 'The Birth of a New Europe about 1000 CE: Conversion, Transfer of Institutional Models, New Dynamics', *Medieval Encounters* 10/1–3 (2004), 99–129.

Klausner, C., *The Seljuk Vezirate: A Study of Civil Administration, 1055–1194* (Cambridge, 1973).

Klejn, L., 'The Russian Controversy over the Varangians', in L. Bjerg et al. (eds), *From Goths to Varangians: Communication and Cultural Exchange between the Baltic and the Black Sea* (Gylling, 2013), 27–38.

Klejn, L., G. Lebedev and V. Nazarenko, 'Норманские древности киевской руси на современном этапе археологического изучения', in N. Nosov and I. Šaskol'ckij (eds), *Исторические связи скандинавии и россии IX–XX вв.* (Leningrad, 1970), 226–52.

Kleščevskij, A., 'Россия – тысячелетнее имя руси. Часть 2', *Кузнецкая сечь* 3/3 (2015), 12.

Klier, J., 'Review of: *The Myth of the Khazars and Intellectual Antisemitism in Russia, 1970s–1990s*, by V. Shnirelman', *SEER* 83/4 (2005), 779–81.

Klima, L., *The Linguistic Affinity of the Volgaic Finno-Ugrians and their Ethnogenesis* (Budapest, 1996).

Klima, L., 'The History of Research on the Ancestral Uralic Homeland', in G. Nanovfszky (ed.), *The Finno-Ugric World* (Budapest, 2004), 15–24.

Klyashtorny, S., 'The Terkhin Inscription', *ActaAntHung* 36/1–3 (1982), 335–66.

Klyosov, A. and T. Faleeva, 'Excavated DNA from Two Khazar Burials', *Advances in Anthropology* 7 (2017), 17–21.

Kobiščankov, Ju., *Полюдье: явление отечественной и всемирной истории цивилизации* (Moscow, 1999).

Koç, D., 'Bulgar boylarının orta idil bölgesine göçü ve novinkovsk kurganları', *Karadeniz Araştırmaları* 27 (2010), 37–58.

Koder, J., 'Die räumlichen Vorstellungen der Byzantiner von der Ökumene (4. bis 12. Jahrhundert)', *Anzeiger der phil.-hist. Klasse der Österreichischen Akademie der Wissenschaften* 137/2 (2002), 15–34.

Koestler, A., *The Thirteenth Tribe* (New York, 1976).

Kohen, E., *History of the Byzantine Jews: A Microcosmos in the Thousand Year Empire* (New York, 2007).

Kolčin, B., *Древняя русь: город, замок, село* (Moscow, 1985).

Komar, A., *Степи европы в эпоху средневековья: хазарское время 5* (Donetsk, 2006).

Komatina, P., 'Date of the Composition of the Notitiae Episcopatuum Ecclesiae Constantinopolitanae nos. 4, 5 and 6', *ЗРВИ* 50 (2013), 195–214.

Konjavskaja, E., 'Половцы в ранних летописях: оценки и интерпретации летописцев', *Slověne* 1 (2015), 180–90, http://slovene.ru/2015_1_Konyavskaya.pdf, accessed 7 December 2020.

Köpeczi, B., L. Makkai, A. Mócsy, Z. Szász and G. Barta (eds), *History of Transylvania*, tr. B. Kovrig and P. Szaffkó (Budapest, 1994).

Koptev, A., 'The Story of "Chazar Tribute": A Scandinavian Ritual Trick in the Russian Primary Chronicle', *Scando-Slavica* 56/2 (2010), 189–212.

Koptev, A., 'A "Khazar Prince" at the Walls of Medieval Kiev: The Collision of Princely Succession in the Russian *Primary Chronicle*', *Mirator* 15/2 (2014), 84–120.

Korobeinikov, D., 'A Broken Mirror: The Kıpçak World in the Thirteenth Century', in F. Curta and R. Kovalev (eds), *The Other Europe in the Middle Ages: Avars, Bulgars, Khazars, and Cumans* (Boston, 2008), 379–412.

Kostomarov, N., *Исторические монографии и исследования* (St Petersburg, 1903).

Kosztolyik, Z., 'Magyar Beginnings in the Reports of Hungarian and Byzantine Chroniclers', *Cithara* 19/1 (1979), 40–9.

Kouřil, P., 'Staří Maďaři a Morava z pohledu archeologie', in J. Klápště et al. (eds), *Dějiny ve věku nejistot. Sborník k příležitosti 70. Narozenin Dušana Třeštíka* (Prague, 2003), 110–46.

Kovács, L., 'Coinage and Other Forms of Currency in Hungary', in A. Wieczorek and H-M. Hinz (eds), *Europe's Centre around 1000 AD* (Stuttgart, 2000), 125–6.

Kovalenko, V., 'Scandinavians in the East of Europe: In Search of Glory or a New Motherland?', in L. Bjerg et al. (eds), *From Goths to Varangians: Communication and Cultural Exchange between the Baltic and the Black Sea* (Gylling, 2013), 257–94.

Kovalev, R., 'Critica: S. A. Pletneva, Sarkel I "shelkovyi' put"', *AEMA* 10 (1999), 245–54.

Kovalev, R., 'Zvenyhorod in Galicia: An Archaeological Survey (Eleventh–Mid-Thirteenth Century)', *Journal of Ukrainian Studies* 24/2 (1999), 7–36.

Kovalev, R., 'Mint Output in Tenth-Century Bukhārā: A Case Study of Dirham Production and Monetary Circulation in Northern Europe', *RH* 28/1–4 (2001), 245–71.

Kovalev, R., 'Dirham Mint Output of Sāmānid Samarqand and its Connection to the Beginnings of Trade with Northern Europe (10th Century)', *Histoire et Mesure* 17/3–4 (2002), 197–216.

Kovalev, R., 'What Does Historical Numismatics Suggest about the Monetary History of Khazaria in the Ninth Century? Question Revisited', *AEMA* 13 (2004), 97–129.

Kovalev, R., 'Creating Khazar Identity through Coins: The Special Issue Dirhams of 837/8', in F. Curta (ed.), *East Central and Eastern Europe in the Early Middle Ages* (Ann Arbor, 2005), 220–52.

Kovalev, R., 'Commerce and Caravan Routes along the Northern Silk Road (Sixth–Ninth Centuries), Part 1: The Western Sector', *AEMA* 14 (2005), 55–105.

Kovalev, R., 'Review Article of: *Reimagining Kievan Rus'* [in Unimagined Europe]', by C. Raffensperger', *RH* 42 (2015), 158–87.

Kovalev, R., 'What Do "Official" Volga Bulġār Coins Suggest about the Political History of the Middle Volga Region during the Second Half of the 10th Century?', *Turcologica* 108 (2016), 193–207.

Kovalevskaja, V., 'Возникновение местного производства стеклянных бус на Кавказе (к вопросу об алано-хазарских взаимоотношениях)', *Хазары* (Moscow, 2005).

Kradin, N., *Кочевые общества* (Vladivostok, 1992).

Kradin, N., 'Nomads and the Theory of Civilizations', in J. Arnason and C. Hann (eds), *Anthropology and Civilizational Analysis: Eurasian Explorations* (Albany, 2018), 303–22.

Kralides, A., 'Οἱ Χάζαροι καί τό Βυζάντιο: Ιστορική και Θρησκειολογική Προσέγγιση', PhD thesis, Aristoteleio University of Thessaloniki (2001).

Kravčenko, È., 'Городища среднего течения Северского Донца', in V. Mikheev et al. (eds), *Хазарский альманах* 3 (Kharkov, 2004), 242–75.

Kravčenko, E., and V. Kul'baka, 'Погребение хазарского времени из мариуполя', in V. Petrukhin et al. (eds), *Хазары: миф и история* (Moscow, 2010), 275–82.

Krekovič, E., 'Who Was First? Nationalism in Slovak and Hungarian Archaeology and History', *Archaeologies: Journal of the World Archaeological Congress* 3/1 (2007), 59–67.

Kristiansen, K., 'Should Archaeology be in the Service of "Popular Culture"? A Theoretical and Political Critique of Cornelius Holtorf's Vision of Archaeology', *Antiquity* 82 (2008), 488–90.

Kristó, Gy., *Hungarian History in the Ninth Century*, tr. Gy. Novák and E. Kelly (Szeged, 1996).

Kristó-Nagy, I., 'Conflict and Cooperation between Arab Rulers and Persian Administrators in the Formative Period of Islamdom, c.600–c.950 CE', in P. Crooks and T. Parsons (eds), *Empires and Bureaucracy in World History: From Late Antiquity to the Twentieth Century* (Cambridge, 2017), 54–80.

Kriwaczek, P., *Yiddish Civilization: The Rise and Fall of a Forgotten Nation* (London, 2005).

Kropotkin, V., 'Клады византийских монет на территории СССР', *Археология СССР: свод археологических источников* 4/4 (1962), 1–89.

Kropotkin, V., 'Новые находки византийских монет на территории СССР', *VizVrem* 26 (1965), 166–89.

Krsmanović, B., *The Byzantine Province in Change: On the Threshold between the 10th and 11th Centuries* (Athens, 2008).

Kruglov, E., 'О культурно-хронологической атрибуции кургана 27 Царевского могильника', *Степи европы в эпоху средневековья* 4 (2005), Donetsk.

Krumova, T., 'Pecheneg Chieftains in the Byzantine Administration in the Theme of Paristrion in the Eleventh Century', *Annual of Medieval Studies at the Central European University* 11 (2005), 207–21.

Kulakov, V., 'Запад и восток: король без войска и дружина без князя', *Экономика и социум* 1 (2011), 164–70.

Kulešov, V., 'Манкус барселонского графства XI в. из киевского клада 1899 г', in D. Ëlšin (ed.), *Первые каменные храмы древней руси: материалы архитектурно-археологического семинара* (St Petersburg, 2012), 211–17.

Kulešov, V., 'Средиземноморье, балканы и восточная европа: памятники монетного обращения Еврейских общин (VIII–XIII века)', in V. Zalesskaja et al. (eds), *Белградский сборник: к XXIII международному конгрессу византинистов, белград, сербия* (St Petersburg, 2016), 85–104.

Kulik, A., 'The Earliest Evidence of the Jewish Presence in Western Rus", *HUkSt* 27/1 (2005), 13–24.

Kulik, A., 'Judeo-Greek Legacy in Medieval Rus", *Viator* 39/1 (2008), 51–64.

Kulik, A., 'The Jews of *Slavia Graeca*: The Northern Frontier of Byzantine Jewry?" in R. Bonfil, O. Irshai, G. Stroumsa and R. Talgam (eds), *Jews in Byzantium: Dialectics of Minority and Majority Cultures* (Boston, 2012), 297–314.

Kungurov, A., *Киевской руси не было, или что скрывают историки* (Moscow, 2014).

Kunkova, V., 'Торговые отношения арабов до династии Аббасидов', *Общество. Среда. Развитие (Terra Humana)* 1 (2001), 57–60.

Kupoveckij, M., 'Социокультурный анализ формирования коллективной памяти и мифология о происхождении евреев восточного кавказа до 80-х годов XIX в', *Этнографическое обозрение* 6 (2009), 58–73.

Kwanten, L., *Imperial Nomads* (Leicester, 1979).

Langer, L., "The Historiography of the Preindustrial Russian City', *Journal of Urban History* 5/2 (1979), 209–40.

Langó, P., *Amit elrejt a föld: A 10. századi magyarság anyagi kultúrájának régészeti kutatása a Kárpát-medencében* (Budapest, 2007).

Langó, P., 'Relations between the Carpathian Basin and South East Europe during the 10th Century: The Evidence of Minor Objects', *Dissertationes Archaeologicae ex Instituto Archaeologico Universitatis de Rolando Eötvös Nominatae* 3/1 (Budapest, 2013), 321–30.

Langó, P., 'Review of: *Peoples of Eastern Origin in Medieval Hungary: The Cultural Heritage of Pechenegs, Uzes, Cumans and the Jász*, by A. Horváth', *HA* Spring (2015), 1–5.

de Lapouge, G., *L'Aryen: Son rôle social* (Paris, 1899).

Laszlovszky, J., 'Social Stratification and Material Culture in 10th–14th Century Hungary', in A. Kubinyi and J. Laszlovszky (eds), *Alltag und Materielle Kultur im Mittelalterlichen Ungarn* (Krems, 1991), 32–67.

Laurent, V., *La collection C. Orghidan* (Paris, 1952).

Laurent, V., *Le corpus des sceaux de l'empire byzantin: L'église, I–II* (Paris, 1963–5).

Le Calloc'h, B., *Des Asiatiques en Hongrie: Khazars, Kabars et Alains* (Paris, 2013).

Leidholm, N., 'Political Families in Byzantium: The Social and Cultural Significance of the Genos as Kin Group, c. 900–1150', PhD thesis, University of Chicago (2016).

Leiser, G. (tr.), *A History of the Seljuks: İbrahim Kafesoğlu's Interpretation and the Resulting Controversy* (Carbondale, IL, 1988).

Leskov, A., *The Maikop Treasure* (Philadelphia, 2008).

Levy-Coffman, E., 'We Are Not Our Ancestors: Evidence for Discontinuity between Prehistoric and Modern Europeans', *Journal of Genetic Genealogy* 1 (2005), 40–50.

Limonov, Ju., *Владимиро-суздальская русь* (Leningrad, 1987).

Lind, J., 'The Russo-Byzantine Treaties and the Early Urban Structure of Rus', *SEER* 62/3 (1984), 362–70.

Lougges, T., *Η Ιδεολογία της Βυζαντινής Ιστοριογραφίας* (Thessalonike, 1990).

Lowick, N., *Coinage and History of the Islamic World* (Aldershot, 1990).

Lozovsky, N., 'Geography and Ethnography in Medieval Europe: Classical Traditions and Contemporary Concerns', in K. Raaflaub and R. Talbert (eds), *Geography and Ethnography: Perceptions of the World in Pre-Modern Societies* (Oxford, 2010), 627–62.

Lübke, C., 'Christianity and Paganism as Elements of Gentile Identities to the East of the Elbe and Saale Rivers', in I. Garipzanov et al. (eds), *Franks, Northmen, and Slavs: Identities and State Formation in Early Medieval Europe* (Turnhout, 2008), 189–203.

Ludwig, D., *Struktur und Gesellschaft des Chazaren-Reiches im Licht des Schriftlichen Quellen* (Münster, 1982).

Lund, N., 'The Presence of Chiasmus in the Old Testament', *American Journal of Semitic Languages and Literatures* 46/2 (1930), 104–26.
Macartney, C., *The Magyars in the Ninth Century* (Cambridge, 1930).
Macartney, C., *The Medieval Hungarian Historians: A Critical and Analytical Guide* (Cambridge, 1953).
McCarthy, C., P. Killworth, H. Bernard, E. Johnsen and G. Shelley, 'Comparing Two Methods for Estimating Network Size', *Human Organization* 60/1 (2000), 28–39.
Mačinskij, D., 'Некоторые предпосылки, движущие силы и исторический контекст сложения русского государства в середине VIII–середине XI в.', in B. Korotkevič et al. (eds), *Сложение русской государственности в контексте раннесредневековой истории старого света: материалы международной конференции* (St Petersburg, 2009), 460–538.
MacMaster, T., 'The Origin of Origins, Trojans, Turks and the Birth of the Myth of Trojan Origins in the Medieval World', *Atlantide* 2 (2014), 1–12.
MacMaster, T., 'The Pogrom that Time Forgot: The Ecumenical Anti-Jewish Campaign of 632', in Y. Fox and E. Buchberger (eds), *Inclusion and Exclusion in Mediterranean Christianities, 400–800* (Turnhout, 2019), 217–35.
Maczel, M., G. S. Kocsis, A. Marcsik and E, Molnár, 'Dental Disease in the Hungarian Conquest Period', *Bulletins et Mémoires de la Société d'Anthropologie de Paris* 10/3 (1998), 457–70.
Madgearu, A., 'The Periphery against the Centre: The Case of Paradunavon', ЗРВИ 40 (2003), 49–56.
Madgearu, A., *The Romanians in the Anonymous Gesta Hungarorum: Truth and Fiction* (Cluj-Napoca, 2005).
Madgearu, A., 'The Pechenegs in the Byzantine Army', in V. Spinei et al. (eds), *The Steppe Lands and the World Beyond Them: Studies in Honor of Victor Spinei on his 70th Birthday* (Iași, 2013), 207–18.
Madgearu, A., *Byzantine Military Organization on the Danube, 10th–12th Centuries* (Boston, 2013).
Magdalino, P., 'Constantine VII and the Historical Geography of Empire', in S. Bazzaz et al. (eds), *Imperial Geographies in Byzantine and Ottoman Space* (Cambridge, 2013), 23–41.
Magdalino, P. and R. Nelson, 'Introduction: μωσέα τὸν μέγαν οὐ λάβεν εἰς τύπον ἄρκιον οὐδείς', in P. Magdalino and R. Nelson (eds), *The Old Testament in Byzantium* (Washington, DC, 2010), 1–38.
Magomedov, M., *Образование хазарского каганата* (Moscow, 1983).
Magomedov, M., S. Kasparov and N. Tupik, 'Каспийская атлантида', Научная мысль кавказа 4 (1997), 51–60.

Magosci, P., *The Shaping of a National Identity: Subcarpathian Rus', 1848–1948* (London, 1978).
Magoulias, H., *Byzantine Christianity: Emperor, Church, and the West* (Chicago, 1970).
Makarov, N., 'Rural Settlement and Trade Networks in Northern Russia, AD 900–1250', in M. Mango (ed.), *Byzantine Trade, 4th–12th Centuries: The Archaeology of Local, Regional and International Exchange. Papers of the Thirty-Eighth Spring Symposium of Byzantine Studies* (Burlington, VT, 2009), 443–61.
Makarov, N., E. Nosov and V. Yanin, 'The Beginning of Rus' through the Eyes of Modern Archaeology', tr. B. Alekseev, *Вестник российской академии наук* 83/6 (2013), 496–507.
Makk, F., *Vom mythischen Vogel Turul bis zum Doppelkreuz* (Herne, 2012).
Mako, G., 'The Islamization of the Volga Bulghars: A Question Reconsidered', *AEMA* 18 (2011), 199–223.
Mako, G., *Two Examples of Nomadic Conversion in Eastern Europe: The Christianization of the Pechenegs, and the Islamization of the Volga Bulghars (Tenth to Thirteenth Century A.D.)* (Cambridge, 2011).
Malamut, E., 'L'image byzantine des Petchénègues', *BZ* 88 (1995), 105–47.
Malinova, O., 'Obsession with Status and Ressentiment: Historical Backgrounds of the Russian Discursive Identity Construction', *Communist and Post-Communist Studies* 47/3–4 (2014), 291–303.
Malmer, B., 'Some Observations on the Importation of Byzantine Coins to Scandinavia in the Tenth and Eleventh Centuries and the Scandinavian Response', *RH* 28/1–4 (2001), 295–302.
Mănucu-Adameșteanu, G., 'Les invasions des Petchénègues au Bas Danube, 1027–1048', *EtByz* 4 (2001), 87–112.
March, A., 'Genealogies of Sovereignty in Islamic Political Theology', *Social Research* 80/1 (2013), 293–322.
Marey, A., 'Socio-Political Structure of the Pecheneg', in N. Kradin et al. (eds), *Alternatives of Social Evolution* (Vladivostok, 2000), 450–6.
Margoliouth, D., 'The Russian Seizure of Bardha-ah in 943 A.D.', *BSO[A]S* 1/2 (1918), 82–95.
Marinich, V., 'Revitalization Movements in Kievan Russia', *Journal for the Scientific Study of Religion* 15/1 (1976), 61–8.
Marjanović-Vujović, G., 'Archaeological Proving the Presence of the Pechenegs in Beograd Town', *Balcanoslavica* 3 (1974), 183–8.
Martin, J., *Medieval Russia: 980–1584* (New York, 1995).
Martín, M. and S. Martín, 'El hallazgo de monedas almohades de Priego de Córdoba: Aspectos ideológicos', *Antiqvitas* 15 (2003), 73–8.

Martínez, C. M., 'Un mancús de Ramon Berenguer I', *Annals de l'Institut d'Estudis Gironins* 30 (1995), 47–53.

Marvakov, T., 'Селищни структури на първото българско царство и кримска хазария. Проблемът за аулите', in R. Rašev (ed.), *Проблеми на прабългарската история и култура* 4–2, (Sofia, 2007), 205–11.

Marx, A., *Faith in Nation: Exclusionary Origins of Nationalism* (New York, 2003).

Maslovskij, A., 'Археологические исследования в азове и азовском районе в 2005 году', in V. Kiaško (ed.), *Историко-археологические исследования в г. азове и на нижнем дону в 2005 г.* 22 (Azov, 2006), 102–26.

Mason, R., 'The Religious Beliefs of the Khazars', *Ukrainian Quarterly* 60/4 (1995), 383–415.

Matolcsy, J., 'A Kazár állattartás és a Magyar honfoglalók háziállatai', *Élet és Tudomány* 30/34 (1975), 1589–92.

Matyushko, I., 'Nomads of the Steppe near the Ural Mountains in the Middle Ages', in Á. Pető and A. Barczi (eds), *Kurgan Studies: An Environmental and Archaeological Multiproxy Study of Burial Mounds in the Eurasian Steppe Zone, BAR International 2238* (Oxford, 2011), 155–67.

Mauss, M., *The Gift: The Form and Reason for Exchange in Archaic Societies*, tr. W. Halls (New York, repr. 2002).

Mavrodina, R., *Киевская русь и кочевники: печенегы, торки, половцы. Историографически очерк* (Leningrad, 1983).

Maxwell, A., 'Contemporary Hungarian Rune-Writing: Ideological Linguistic Nationalism within a Homogenous Nation', *Anthropos* 99 (2004), 161–75.

Maxwell, A., 'Multiple Nationalism: National Concepts in Nineteenth-Century Hungary and Benedict Anderson's "Imagined Communities"', *Nationalism and Ethnic Politics* 11/3 (2005), 385–414.

Mell, J., 'Cultural Meanings of Money in Medieval Ashkenaz: On Gift, Profit, and Value in Medieval Judaism and Christianity', *Jewish History* 28 (2014), 125–58.

Melnikova, E., 'Mental Maps of the Old Russian Chronicle-Writer of the Early Twelfth Century', in L. Bjerg et al. (eds), *From Goths to Varangians: Communication and Cultural Exchange between the Baltic and the Black Sea* (Gylling, 2013), 317–40.

Metcalf, D., *Coinage in South-Eastern Europe: 820–1396* (London, 1979).

Meyendorff, J., *Byzantium and the Rise of Russia: A Study of Byzantino-Russian Relations in the Fourteenth Century* (New York, 1981).

Mezentsev, V., 'The Emergence of the Podil and the Genesis of the City of Kiev: Problems of Dating', *HUkSt* 10/1 (1986), 48–70.

Miftakhov, Z., 'The First Islamic State in the Itil Basin', *History of Tatar People: Lecture Course* State Pedagogical University (Kazan', 1998–2002). Referenced via webpage: http://s155239215.onlinehome.us/turkic/11Miftakhov/Lecture_9En.htm, accessed 7 December 2020.

Mikhajlova, T., 'Късно номадски гробове в дворцовия център на плиска', *Плиска-Преслав* 9 (2003), 259–66.

Mikheyev, A., L. Qiu, A. Zarubin, N. Moshkov, Y. Orlov, D. Chartier, I. Kornienko, T. Faleeva, V. Klyuchnikov, E. Batieva and T. Tatarinova, 'Diverse Genetic Origins of Medieval Steppe Nomad Conquerors', *bioRxiv* (2019) 2019.12.15.876912, https://www.biorxiv.org/content/10.1101/2019.12.15.876912v1, accessed 7 December 2020.

Mil'khov, V., G. Aksenova, G. Barankova, S. Mil'khova, A. Makarov, M. Neborsckij, A. Petrov, A. Frolov and S. Jakunin, *Древняя русь: пересечение традиций* (Moscow, 1997).

Miller, D., 'The Kievan Principality on the Eve of the Mongol Invasion: An Inquiry into Recent Research and Interpretation', *HUkSt* 10/1 (1986), 215–40.

Miller, D., 'Monumental Building and Its Patrons as Indicators of Economic and Political Trends in Rus, 900–1262', *JbGOst* 38/3 (1990), 321–55.

Milner-Gulland, R., 'Ultimate Russia, Ultimate Byzantium', presented at the *50th Spring Symposium of Byzantine Studies* (Birmingham, 2017).

Mjusse, L., *Варварские нашествия на западную европу* (St Petersburg, 2006).

Mocja, O., 'Le rôle des élites guerrières dans la formation des centres urbains de la Rus' kiévienne', in M. Kazanski et al., (eds), *Les centres proto-urbains russes entre Scandinavie, Byzance et Orient* (Paris, 2000), 267–82.

Mogaričev, Ju. and V. Majko, 'Фулы и крымская хазария: еще раз о локализации фульской епархии', in S. Posokhov et al. (eds), *Laurea I. Античный мир и средние века: чтения памяти профессора Владимира Ивановича Кадеева. материалы* (Kharkov, 2015), 130–4.

Montgomery, J., 'Ibn Faḍlān and the Rūsiyyah', *Journal of Arabic and Islamic Studies* 3 (2000), 1–25.

Montinaro, F., 'Les premiers commerciaires byzantins', *Travaux et Mémoires* 17 (2013), 351–538.

Moór, E., 'Die Vorfahren der Ungarn überschreiten die Wolga', in Gy. Ortutay (ed.), *Papers of the Congressus Internationalis Fenno-Ugristarum, Budapestini Habitus* (Budapest, 1963), 420–7.

Moravcsik, Gy., 'Byzantine Christianity and the Magyars in the Period of their Migration', *SEER* 5/3–4 (1946), 29–45.

Moravcsik, Gy., 'Byzantinische Mission im Kreise der Türkervölker an der Nordküste des Schwarzen Meeres', in J. Hussey et al. (eds), *Proceedings of the XIII International Congress of Byzantine Studies, Oxford*, (Oxford, 1967), 22–4.

Morgenthau, H., *Politics among Nations* (New York, 1948).

Morris, A., 'The Medieval Emergence of the Volga-Oka Region', *Annals of the Association of American Geographers* 61/4 (1971), 697–710.

Morris, I., *Why the West Rules – for Now: The Patterns of History, and What They Reveal about the Future* (New York, 2010).

Morrisson, C., *Catalogue des Monnaies Byzantines de la Bibliothèque Nationale* (Paris, 1970).

Mošin, V., 'Варяго-русский вопрос', *Slavia* 10/3 (1931), 109–36.

Mukhamadiev, A., Булгаро-татарская монетная система XII–XV вв. (Moscow, 1983).

Nagy, P., *Islamic Art and Artefacts in Twelfth- and Thirteenth-Century Hungary* (Budapest, 2015).

Naumenko, V., 'Византийско-хазарские отношения в середине IX века', in V. Petrukhin et al. (eds), *Хазары. Евреи и славяне* 16 (Moscow, 2005), 231–44.

Nazarenko, A., 'Западноевропейские источники', in E. Mel'nikova (ed.), *Древняя русь в свете зарубежных источников* (Moscow, 1999), 259–406.

Nazarenko, A., 'Архиепископы в русской церкви домонгольского времени', *Древняя русь. Вопросы медиевистики* 4/62 (2015), 67–76.

Nebel, A., D. Filon, M. Faerman, H. Soodyall and A. Oppenheim, 'Y Chromosome Evidence for a Founder Effect in Ashkenazi Jews', *European Journal of Human Genetics* 13 (2005), 388–91.

Nelson, J., 'Frankish Identity in Charlemagne's Empire', in I. Garipzanov et al. (eds), *Franks, Northmen, and Slavs: Identities and State Formation in Early Medieval Europe* (Turnhout, 2008), 70–83.

Németh, Gy., 'Die petschenegischen Stammesnamen', *Ungarische Jahrbücher* 10 (1930), 27–34.

Németh, Gy., *A honfoglaló magyarság kialakulása* (Budapest, 1991).

Neumann, I. and E. Wigen, *The Steppe Tradition in International Relations: Russians, Turks and European State-Building 4000 bce–2018 ce* (Cambridge, 2018).

Nicol, N., *Sylloge of Islamic Coins in the Ashmolean II: Early Post-Reform Coinage* (London, 2009).

Niculescu, G., 'Culture-Historical Archaeology and the Production of Knowledge on Ethnic Phenomena', *Dacia* 55 (2011), 5–24.

Niebuhr, R., *Faith and History: A Comparison of Christian and Modern Views of History* (New York, 1949).

Nikolov, A., 'Making a New Basileus: The Case of Symeon of Bulgaria (893–927) Reconsidered', in M. Salamon et al. (eds), *Rome, Constantinople and Newly Converted Europe: Archeological and Historical Evidence* (Kraków, 2012), 101–8.

Nikulina, Ju. and L. Kravčenko, 'Візантійські хроніки як джерело з історії давньої русі', in M. Šepelěv and S. Ševcov (eds), *Матеріали: другої всеукраїнської науково-практичної конференції з міжнародною участю 'Науковий діалог "Схід-Захід"'* (Dnipropetrovs'k, 2013), 164–8.

Noonan, T., 'The Circulation of Byzantine Coins in Kievan Rus', *Études Byzantines* 7/2 (1980), 143–81.

Noonan, T., 'Did the Khazars Possess a Monetary Economy? An Analysis of the Numismatic Evidence', *AEMA* 2 (1982), 219–67.

Noonan, T., 'Why Dirhams Reached Russia: The Role of Arab–Khazar Relations in the Development of the Earliest Islamic Trade with Eastern Europe', *AEMA* 4 (1984), 151–282.

Noonan, T., 'The Monetary History of Kiev in the Pre-Mongol Period', *HUkSt* 11 (1987), 384–461.

Noonan, T., 'Rus', Pechenegs, and Polovtsy: Economic Interaction along the Steppe Frontier in the Pre-Mongol Era', *RH* 19/1–4 (1992), 301–26.

Noonan, T., 'Byzantium and the Khazars: A Special Relationship?', in J. Shepard and S. Franklin (eds), *Byzantine Diplomacy* (Aldershot, 1992), 109–32.

Noonan, T., 'The Khazar-Byzantine World of the Crimea in the Early Middle Ages: The Religious Dimension', *AEMA* 10 (1999), 207–30.

Noonan, T., 'The Impact of Islamic Trade upon Urbanization in the Rus' Lands: The Tenth and Early Eleventh Centuries', in M. Kazanski et al. (eds), *Les centres proto-urbains russes entre Scandinavie, Byzance et Orient* (Paris, 2000), 379–94.

Noonan, T., 'The Tenth-Century Trade of Volga Bulghāria with Sāmānid Central Asia', *AEMA* 11 (2000–1), 140–219.

Noonan, T., 'The Khazar Qaghanate and its Impact on the Early Rus' State: The *Translatio Imperii* from Ītil to Kiev', in A. Khazanov and A. Wink (eds), *Nomads in the Sedentary World* (New York, 2001), 76–102.

Noonan, T., 'The Dirham Output and Monetary Circulation of a Secondary Sāmānid Mint: A Case Study of Balkh', in R. Kiersnowski et al. (eds), *Moneta Mediavalis: Studia numizmatyczne i historyczne ofiarowane Profesorowi Stanisławowi Suchodolskiemu w 65. rocznicę urodzin* (Warsaw, 2002), 163–74.

Noonan, T., 'Some Observations on the Economy of the Khazar Khaganate', in D. Sinor and N. di Cosmo (eds), *The World of the Khazars, New*

Perspectives: Selected Papers from the Jerusalem 1999 International Khazar Colloquium (Boston, 2007), 207–44.

Noonan, T. and R. Kovalev, 'The Dirham Output of the Spanish Umayyad Emirate, ca. 756–ca. 929', in M. Hipólito et al. (eds), *Homenagem a Mário Gomes Marques* (Sintra, 2000), 253–60.

Noonan, T. and R. Kovalev, 'Prayer, Illumination, and Good Times: The Export of Byzantine Wine and Oil to the North of Russia in Pre-Mongol Times', in J. Shepard (ed.), *The Expansion of Orthodox Europe* (Burlington, VT, 2007), 73–96.

Nosov, E., 'Rjurikovo Gorodišče et Novgorod', in M. Kazanski et al. (eds), *Les centres proto-urbains russes entre Scandinavie, Byzance et Orient* (Paris, 2000), 143–72.

Novosel'cev, A., 'Хазария в системе международных отношений VII–IX веков', *VoprIst* 2 (1987), 20–32.

Novosel'cev, A., *Хазарское государство и его роль в истории восточной европы и Кавказа* (Moscow, 1990).

Obolensky, D., *The Byzantine Commonwealth: Eastern Europe, 500–1453* (New York, 1971).

Obolensky, D., 'Cherson and the Conversion of Rus': An Anti-Revisionist View', *BMGS* 13 (1989), 244–56.

Obolensky, D., *Byzantium and the Slavs* (New York, 1994).

Odnoroženko, O., 'Зображення щитів на руських печатках XI–XIII ст', *СЩ* 5 (2015), 150–267.

Ödön, G., 'Magyarország barbárpénzeinek áttekintése', *Az Érem* (1925), 59–63.

Oikonomides, N. et al. (eds), *Studies in Byzantine Sigillography* (Berlin, Munich, Paris, Washington, DC, 2003–19).

Olsson, J., 'Coup d'état, Coronation and Conversion: Some Reflections on the Adoption of Judaism by the Khazar Khaganate', *Journal of the Royal Asiatic Society* 23 (2013), 495–526.

Olster, D., 'Ideological Transformation and the Evolution of Imperial Presentation in the Wake of Islam's Victory', in E. Grypeou et al. (eds), *The Encounter of Eastern Christianity with Early Islam* (Leiden, 2006), 45–72.

Ostrowski, D., 'The Account of Volodimer's Conversion in the "Povest' Vremennykh Let": A Chiasmus of Stories', *HUkSt* 28/1 (2006), 567–80.

Oța, S., *The Mortuary Archaeology of the Medieval Banat (10th–14th Centuries)* (Boston, 2015).

Pačkalov, A., *Средневековые города нижнего поволжья и северного кавказа* (Moscow, 2018).

Page, G., *Being Byzantine: Greek Identity before the Ottomans* (Cambridge, 2008).

Pálóczi Horváth, A., *Pechenegs, Cumans, Iasians: Steppe Peoples of Medieval Hungary*, tr. T. Wilkinson (Budapest, 1989).

Papageorgiou, S., *Άπο το γένος στο έθνος: Η θεμελίωση του ελληνικού κράτους* (Athens, 2005).

Pappas, N., *English Refugees in the Byzantine Armed Forces: The Varangian Guard and Anglo-Saxon Ethnic Consciousness* (Huntsville, TX, 2004), http://deremilitari.org/2014/06/english-refugees-in-the-byzantine-armed-forces-the-varangian-guard-and-anglo-saxon-ethnic-consciousness/, accessed 7 December 2020.

Paroń, A., 'The Nomadic State of Early Medieval Europe on the Background of the Eurasian Steppes' Political Structures: An Essay', in A. Paroń et al. (eds), *Potestas et Communitas* (Warsaw, 2010), 163–82.

Paroń, A., 'Power and Social Structures: Final Remarks', in A. Paroń et al. (eds), *Potestas et Communitas* (Warsaw, 2010), 357–62.

Paroń, A., S. Rossignol, B. Szmoniewski and G. Vercamer (eds), *Potestas et Communitas: Interdisciplinary Studies of the Constitution and Demonstration of Power Relations in the Middle Ages East of the Elbe* (Warsaw, 2010).

Paszkiewicz, H., *The Origin of Russia* (London, 1954).

Pauliny, J., *Arabské správy o Slovanoch (9–12. storočie)* (Bratislava, 1999).

Pavlova, E., 'The Coinless Period in the History of Northeastern Rus': Historiography Study', *RH* 21/4 (1994), 375–92.

Petkov, K., 'Review of: *The Romanians and the Turkic Nomads North of the Danube Delta from the Tenth to the Mid-Thirteenth Century*, by V. Spinei', *Speculum* 86/2 (2011), 554–6.

Petrukhin, V., 'The Normans and the Khazars in the South of Rus': The Formation of the "Russian Land" in the Middle Dnepr Area', *RH* 19/1–4 (1992), 393–400.

Petrukhin, V., 'Русь и хазария: к оценке исторических взаимосвязей', in V. Petrukhin et al. (eds), *Хазары. Евреи и славяне* 16 (Moscow, 2005), 69–100.

Petrukhin, V., 'Феодализм перед судом русской историографии', *Одиссей: Человек в истории* 1 (2006), 161–70.

Petrukhin, V., 'Khazaria and Rus': An Examination of their Historical Relations', in D. Sinor and N. di Cosmo (eds), *The World of the Khazars, New Perspectives: Selected Papers from the Jerusalem 1999 International Khazar Colloquium* (Boston, 2007), 245–68.

Petrukhin, V., 'Sacral Kingship and the Judaism of the Khazars', in L. Słupecki and R. Simek (eds), *Conversions: Looking for Ideological Change in the Early Middle Ages* (Vienna, 2013), 291–301.

Petrukhin, V. and V. Flërov, 'Иудаизм в хазарии по данным археологии', in A. Kulik (ed.), *История еврейского народа* (Moscow, 2010), 151–62.

Pettersson, A-M. (ed.), *The Spillings Hoard: Gotland's Role in Viking Age World Trade* (Visby, 2009).

Pilipenko, A., G. Kubarev, V. Molodin, S. Čerdancev and R. Trapezov, 'Генофонд митохондриальной днк древнетюркского населения алтая (первые резултаты)', *Проблемы археологии, этнографии, антропологии сибири и сопредельных территорий* (Novosibirsk, 2014), 267–9.

Pleszczynski, A., *The Birth of a Stereotype: Polish Rulers and Their Country in German Writings c. 1000 A.D.* (Boston, 2011).

Pletnëva, S., *От кочевий к городам: салтово-маяцкая культура* (Moscow, 1967).

Pletnëva, S., *Хазары* (Moscow, 1976).

Pletnëva, S., *Маяцкое городище* (Moscow, 1984).

Pletnëva, S., *На славяно-хазарском пограничье: дмитриевский археологический комплекс* (Moscow, 1989).

Pletnëva, S., *Половцы* (Moscow, 1990).

Pletnëva, S., *Саркел и "шелковый" путь* (Voronež, 1996).

Pletnëva, S., *Очерки хазарской археологий* (Moscow, 1999).

Pletnëva, S., 'О заселении славянами саркела-белой вежи', in A. Prjakhin and M. Cÿbin (eds), *Евразийская степь и лесостепь в эпоху раннего средневековья* (Voronež, 2000), 82–98.

Pletnëva, S., 'Города в хазарском каганате (доклад к постановке проблемы)', in V. Mikheev et al. (eds), *Хазарский альманах* 1 (Kharkov, 2002), 110–24.

Pletnëva, S., *Кочевники южнорусских степей в эпоху средневековья IV–XIII века* (Voronež, 2003).

Pletnëva, S. and T. Makarova, 'Пояс знатного воина из саркела', *CA* 2 (1983), 62–77.

Plokhy, S., *The Origins of the Slavic Nations: Premodern Identities in Russia, Ukraine and Belarus* (Cambridge, 2006).

Poddubnÿj, V., 'Историография. И. А. Гагин. Волжская булгария: очерки истории средневековой дипломатии (X–первая треть XIII в.)', *VoprIst* 5 (2006), 168–70.

Pohl, W., 'Deliberate Ambiguity: The Lombards and Christianity', in G. Armstrong and I. Wood (eds), *Christianizing Peoples and Converting Individuals* (Turnhout, 2000), 47–58.

Pohl, W. (ed.), *Die Suche nach den Ursprüngen: Von der Bedeutung des frühen Mittelalters* (Vienna, 2004).

Pohl, W., 'Telling the Difference: Signs of Ethnic Identity', in T. Noble (ed.), *From Roman Provinces to Medieval Kingdoms* (New York, 2006), 120–67.

Pohl, W., 'Gender and Ethnicity in the Early Middle Ages', in T. Noble (ed.), *From Roman Provinces to Medieval Kingdoms* (New York, 2006), 168–88.

Pohl, W. and G. Heydemann (eds), *Strategies of Identification: Ethnicity and Religion in Early Medieval Europe* (Turnhout, 2013).

Popov, V. (ed.), *Потестарность: генезис и эволюция* (St Petersburg, 1997).

Popov, V., 'Концепт "племя", или этничность и потестарность "в одном флаконе"', *Studia Slavica et Balcanica Petropolitana* 2 (2015), 13–20.

Popova, L., 'Blurring the Boundaries: Foragers and Pastoralists in the Volga-Urals Region', in B. Hanks and K. Linduff (eds), *Social Complexity in Prehistoric Eurasia: Monuments, Metals and Mobility* (Cambridge, 2009), 296–320.

Poppe, A., *Państwo i Kościoł na Rusi w XI wieku* (Warsaw, 1968).

Poppe, A., 'The Political Background to the Baptism of Rus': Byzantine–Russian Relations between 986–89', *DOP* 30 (1976), 195–244.

Poppe, A., 'Once Again Concerning the Baptism of Olga, Archontissa of Rus'', in A. Poppe (ed.), *Christian Russia in the Making* (Burlington, VT, 2007), 271–7.

Poppe, N., 'Die mongolischen Lehnwörter im Komanischen', in M. Mansuroğlu et al. (eds), *Németh Armağani* (Ankara, 1962), 331–40.

Popper, K., *The Open Society and Its Enemies*, new edn (Princeton, 2013).

Postică, G. and I. Tentiuc, 'Amulete-calareti de bronz din perioada medievală timpurie în spațiul carpato-nistrean', *Tyragetia* 8/1 (2014), 45–72.

Preiser-Kapeller, J., 'A Jewish Empire? Religion and Mission in the Khanate of the Khazars', (2020), https://www.dasanderemittelalter.net/news/a-jewish-empire/, accessed 24 November 2020.

Prinzing, G., 'Die autokephale byzantinische Kirchenprovinz Bulgarien/Ohrid: Wie unabhängig waren ihre Erzbischöfe?', in *Proceedings of the 22nd International Congress of Byzantine Studies, Plenary Papers* (Sofia, 2011), 389–413.

Pritsak, O., *The Pečenegs: A Case of Social and Economic Transformation* (Lisse, 1976).

Pritsak, O., 'The Khazar Kingdom's Conversion to Judaism', *HUkSt* 2/3 (1978), 261–81.

Pritsak, O., 'What Really Happened in 988?', in D. J. Goa (ed.), *The Ukrainian Religious Experience: Tradition and the Canadian Cultural Context* (Edmonton, 1989), 5–19.

Pritsak, O., *The Origins of the Old Rus' Weights and Monetary Systems: Two Studies in Western Eurasian Metrology and Numismatics in the Seventh to Eleventh Centuries* (Cambridge, 1998).

Prozorova, Y., 'Civilizational Analysis and Archaeology: Prospects for Collaboration', in J. Arnason and C. Hann (eds), *Anthropology and Civilizational Analysis: Eurasian Explorations* (Albany, 2018), 53–74.

Pylypčuk, Ja., *Дешт-и-кыпчак на стыке цивилизаций* (Ufa, 2015).

Pylypčuk, Ja. and Ž. Sabitov, *Очерки этнополитической истории кыпчаков* (Astana, 2015).

Quinn, D., *Ishmael* (New York, 1992).

Raffensperger, C., *Reimagining Europe: Kievan Rus' in the Medieval World* (Cambridge, 2012).

Rasovskij, D., *Половцы. Черные клобуки: печенеги, торки и берендеи на руси и в венгрии* (Moscow, 2012).

Rąszkowski, W., '"The German School of Archaeology" in its Central European Context: Sinful Thoughts', in A. Gramsch and U. Sommer (eds), *A History of Central European Archaeology: Theories, Methods, and Politics* (Budapest, 2011), 197–214.

Reher, G. and M. Fernández-Götz, 'Archaeological Narratives in Ethnicity Studies', *Archeologické Rozhledy* 67 (2015), 400–16.

Reimitz, H., '*Omnes Franci*: Identifications and Identities of the Early Medieval Franks', in I. Garipzanov et al. (eds), *Franks, Northmen, and Slavs: Identities and State Formation in Early Medieval Europe* (Turnhout, 2008), 51–69.

Renan, E., *Qu'est-ce qu'une nation?* (Paris, 1882).

Rešetova, I., 'Описание индивидов с трепанированными черепами среди носителей салтово-маяцкой культуры: медицинская практика или культ?', *Этнографическое обозрение* 5 (2012), 151–7.

Rešetova, I., 'Trephination Cases from the Early Bulgarian Population (Saltovo-Mayaki Culture)', *European Archaeologist* 38 (2013), 9–14.

Réthy, L. and G. Probszt, *Corpus Nummorum Hungariae* (Graz, 1958).

Reuter, T., 'The Making of England and Germany, 850–1050: Points of Comparison and Difference', in A. Smyth (ed.), *Medieval Europeans: Studies in Ethnic Identity and National Perspectives in Medieval Europe* (New York, 1998), 53–70.

Révész, L., '"The Cemeteries of the Conquest Period", tr. N. Horton et al., in Z. Visy and M. Nagy (eds), *Hungarian Archaeology at the Turn of the Millennium* (Budapest, 2003), 338–43.

Rice, T., *The Seljuks in Asia Minor* (London, 1961).
Richter, M., 'National Identity in Medieval Wales', in A. Smyth (ed.), *Medieval Europeans: Studies in Ethnic Identity and National Perspectives in Medieval Europe* (New York, 1998), 71–84.
Ripley, W., *The Races of Europe: A Sociological Study* (New York, 1899).
Rispling, G., 'Khazar Coins in the Name of Moses and Muhammad', *Acta-AntHung* (2002).
Rispling, G., 'Osteuropäische Nachahmungen islamischer Münzen', in T. Mayer (ed.), *Sylloge der Münzen des Kaukasus und Osteuropas im Orientalischen Münzkabinett Jena* (Wiesbaden, 2005), 172–220.
Robinson, C., *'Abd al-Malik* (Oxford, 2005).
Rogers, J., 'Inner Asian States and Empires: Theories and Synthesis', *Springer Science & Business Media* (2012). Referenced via webpage: https://repository.si.edu/bitstream/handle/10088/18890/anth_rogers_J_archaeol_res_2012.pdf?sequence=1&isAllowed=y, accessed 7 December 2020.
Romašov, S., 'Историческая география хазарского каганата (V–XIII вв.)', *AEMA* 11–14 (2000–5), 219–338, 81–221, 185–264, 107–93.
Róna-Tas, A., 'A kazár népnévről', *Nyelvtudományi Közlemények* 84 (1982), 349–80.
Róna-Tas, A., *Hungarians and Europe in the Early Middle Ages: An Introduction to Early Hungarian History*, tr. N. Bodoczky (New York, 1999).
Róna-Tas, A., 'The Khazars and the Magyars', in D. Sinor and N. di Cosmo (eds), *The World of the Khazars, New Perspectives: Selected Papers from the Jerusalem 1999 International Khazar Colloquium* (Boston, 2007), 269–78.
Rootsi, S., D. Behar, M. Järve, A. Lin, N. Myres, B. Passarelli, G. Poznik, S. Tzur, H. Sahakyan, A. Pathak, S. Rosset, M. Metspalu, V. Grugni, O. Semino, E. Metspalu, C. Bustamante, K. Skorecki, R. Villems, T. Kivisild and P. Underhill, 'Phylogenetic Applications of Whole Y-Chromosome Sequences and the Near Eastern Origin of Ashkenazi Levites', *Nature Communications* 4 (2013), 1–9.
Rossman, V., 'Lev Gumilev, Eurasianism and Khazaria', *East European Jewish Affairs* 32/1 (2002), 30–51.
Roth, A., *Chasaren: Das vergessene Grossreich der Juden* (Frankfurt, 2006).
Rózsa, Z., J. Balázs, V. Csányi and B. Tugya, 'Árpád Period Muslim Settlement and Cemetery in Orosháza', *HA* Autumn (2014), 1–7.
Rudenko, K., 'Волжская булгария, северо-восточная русь и прикамье: проблемы исследования этнокультурных контактов и взаимовлиянии в XI–XIV вв. (по археологическим материалам)', *Археология и этнография марийского края* 27 (2004), 105–15.

Rÿbakov, B., 'К вопросу о роли хазарского каганата в истории Руси', CA 18 (1953), 128–50.
Rÿbakov, B., 'Древние Руси', CA 17 (1953), 23–104.
Šabaev, Ju., N. Šilov and A. Sadokhin, '"Финно-угорский мир": миф, макроидентичность, политический проект?', *Общественные науки и современность* 1 (2010), 147–55.
Sabatier, J., *Description générale des monnaies byzantines* (Graz, 1955).
Sakharov, A., *Дипломацията на древна русия IX–първата половина на X век* (Sofia, 1984).
Šakhmatov, A., *Разыскания о древнейших русских летописных сводах* (St Petersburg, 1908).
Salmin, A., 'The Iranian Chapter in the History of the Chuvash', *Archaeology, Ethnology and Anthropology of Eurasia* 41/3 (2013), 112–19.
Salmin, A., *Savirs – Bulgars – Chuvash* (Saarbrücken, 2014).
Sand, S., *The Invention of the Jewish People*, tr. Y. Lotan (New York, 2009).
Šandrovskaja, V., 'Печати с изображениями анаргиров', in V. Zalesskaja (ed.), *Пилигримы: историко-культурная роль паломничества: к XX международный конгрессу византинистов* (St Petersburg, 2001), 69–78.
Sardelić, M., 'Kumani-Kipčaci između Azije i Europe u razvijenome i kasnome srednjem vijeku', *Migracijske i etničke teme* 31/2 (2015), 247–74.
Šarifullin, R., 'О ранних жилищах волжских булгар (X–начало XIII вв.)', in F. Khuzin (ed.), *Археология волжской булгарии: проблемы, поиски, решения* (Kazan', 1993), 63–76.
Sarris, P., *Empires of Faith: The Fall of Rome to the Rise of Islam, 500–700* (New York, 2001).
ŠČapov, Ja., 'Церковь и становление древнерусской государственности', *VoprIst* 11 (1969), 55–64.
ŠČapov, Ja., *Древнерусские княжеские уставы XI–XV вв.* (Moscow, 1976).
ŠČapov, Ja., *Государство и церковь древней руси X–XIII вв.* (Moscow, 1989).
ŠČerbak, A., *Печенежский язык. Языки мира: тюркские языки* (Moscow, 1997).
Schama, S., *The Story of the Jews: Finding the Words (1000 BCE–1492 CE)* (London, 2013).
Scherb, V., 'Assimilating Giants: The Appropriation of Gog and Magog in Medieval and Early Modern England', *Journal of Medieval and Early Modern Studies* 32/1 (2002), 59–84.
Schiffman, D., 'The Valuation of Coins in Medieval Jewish Jurisprudence', *Journal of the History of Economic Thought* 27/2 (2005), 141–60.

Schirrmacher, T., 'Die osteuropäischen Juden: Nachfahren der mittelalterlichen Khasaren?', *Martin Buber Seminar Texte* 23 (2004), 3–7. https://www.contra-mundum.org/schirrmacher/mbstexte023.pdf, accessed 7 December 2020.

Schmitt, O., 'Die Petschenegen auf dem Balkan von 1046 bis 1072', in S. Conrad et al. (eds), *Pontos Euxeinos: Beiträge zur Archäologie und Geschichte des antiken Schwarzmeer- und Balkanraumes (Manfred Opermann zum 65. Geburtstag von Kollegen, Freuden und Schülern)* (Langenweißbach, 2006), 473–90.

Schorkowitz, D., 'Cultural Contact and Cultural Transfer in Medieval Western Eurasia', *Archaeology, Ethnology and Anthropology of Eurasia* 40/3 (2012), 84–94.

Sear, D., *Byzantine Coins and their Values* (London, 1987).

Sears, S., *A Monetary History of Iraq and Iran, ca. CE 500 to 750* (Chicago, 1997).

Sedov, V., *Восточные славяне в VI–XIII вв.* (Moscow, 1982).

Sedov, V., 'Распространение христианства в древней руси', *Краткие сообщения института археологии* 208 (1993), 3–11.

Sedov, V., 'К этногенезу волжских болгар', *РА* 2 (2001), 5–15.

Sedov, V., *Sloveni u ranom srednjem veku* (Novi Sad, 2013).

Sedykh, V., 'On the Function of Coins in Graves in Early Medieval Rus'', *RH* 32/3–4 (2005), 471–8.

Seibt, W., 'Some Interesting Byzantine Seals with Surnames in the Collection of Oleksii Sheremetiev', in H. Ivakin et al. (eds), *Byzantine and Rus' Seals* (Kiev, 2015), 83–95.

Seidel, E., 'Cases and Converts in Jewish History', in W. Homolka et al. (eds), *Not by Birth Alone: Conversion to Judaism* (Washington, DC, 1997), 103–28.

Šelekhan', O., 'Свастика в матеріальній культурі ранніх слов'ян та київської русі', *СЩ* 3 (2012), 69–88.

Semenov, A., 'New Evidence on the Slavyansk (Anastasiyevka) Hoard of the 8th Century AD Byzantine and Arab Coins', in A. Kozincev (ed.), *New Archaeological Discoveries in Asiatic Russia and Central Asia* (St Petersburg, 1994), 82–5.

Semënov, I., 'Образование хазарского каганата', *VoprIst* 8 (2008), 118–27.

Semënov, I., 'Происхождение и значение титула "хазар-эльтебер"', *VoprIst* 9 (2009), 160–3.

Senga, T., 'The Toquz Oghuz Problem and the Origin of the Khazars', *Journal of Asian History* 24/2 (1990), 57–69.

Ševčenko, I., *Byzantium and the Slavs: In Letters and Culture* (Cambridge, 1991).

Shake, G., *Coins of the Khazar Empire* (Allen, TX, 2000).
Shams-Eshragh, A., *Silver Coinage of the Caliphs* (London, 2010).
Shapira, D., 'Judaization of Central Asian Traditions as Reflected in the So-Called Jewish-Khazar Correspondence, with Two Excurses: A. Judah Halevy's Quotations; B. Eldad ha-Dani (Ju daeo-Turkica VI) with an Addendum', in V. Petrukhin et al. (eds), *Хазары. Евреи и славяне* 16 (Moscow, 2005), 503–21.
Shapira, D., 'Iranian Sources on the Khazars', in D. Sinor and N. di Cosmo (eds), *The World of the Khazars, New Perspectives: Selected Papers from the Jerusalem 1999 International Khazar Colloquium* (Boston, 2007), 291–306.
Shapira, D., 'Armenian and Georgian Sources on the Khazars: A Re-Evaluation', in D. Sinor and N. di Cosmo (eds), *The World of the Khazars, New Perspectives: Selected Papers from the Jerusalem 1999 International Khazar Colloquium* (Boston, 2007), 307–52.
Sharf, A., *Byzantine Jewry: From Justinian to the Fourth Crusade* (London, 1971).
Shaw, D., 'The Nature of the Russian City', *Journal of Historical Geography* 3/3 (1977), 267–70.
Shboul, A., *Al-Mas'ūdī and his World: A Muslim Humanist and his Interest in Non-Muslims* (London, 1979).
Shepard, J., 'Another New England? Anglo-Saxon Settlement on the Black Sea', *Byzantine Studies* 1/1 (1974), 18–39.
Shepard, J., 'The Khazar s' Formal Adoption of Judaism and Byzantium's Northern Policy', *Oxford Slavonic Papers* 31 (1998), 9–34.
Shepard, J., 'Rus'', in N. Berend (ed.), *Christianization and the Rise of Christian Monarchy: Scandinavia, Central Europe and Rus', c. 900–1200* (Cambridge, 2003), 369–414.
Shepard, J., 'Close Encounters with the Byzantine World: The Rus at the Straits of Kerch', in K. Reyerson et al. (eds), *Pre-Modern Russia and Its World: Essays in Honor of Thomas S. Noonan* (Wiesbaden, 2006), 15–78.
Shepard, J., 'The Byzantine Commonwealth 1000–1550', in M. Angold (ed.), *The Cambridge History of Christianity V: Eastern Christianity* (Cambridge, 2006), 1–52.
Shepard, J. (ed.), *The Expansion of Orthodox Europe: Byzantium, the Balkans and Russia* (Burlington, VT, 2007).
Shepard, J., 'The Viking Rus and Byzantium', in S. Brink and N. Price (eds), *The Viking World* (New York, 2008), 496–516.
Shepard, J., 'The Coming of Christianity to Rus: Authorized and Unauthorized Versions', in C. Kendall et al. (eds), *Conversion to Christianity from*

Late Antiquity to the Modern Age: Considering the Process in Europe, Asia, and the Americas (Minneapolis, 2009), 185–222.

Shepard, J., '"Mists and Portals": The Black Sea's North Coast', in M. Mango (ed.), *Byzantine Trade, 4th–12th Centuries: The Archaeology of Local, Regional and International Exchange. Papers of the Thirty-Eighth Spring Symposium of Byzantine Studies* (Burlington, VT, 2009), 421–41.

Shepard, J., *Emergent Elites and Byzantium in the Balkans and East-Central Europe* (Burlington, VT, 2011).

Shepard, J., 'Review Article. Back in Old Rus and the USSR: Archaeology, History and Politics', *EHR* 131/549 (2016), 384–405.

Shnirelman, V., *The Myth of the Khazars and Intellectual Antisemitism in Russia, 1970s–1990s* (Jerusalem, 2002).

Shnirelman, V., 'The Story of a Euphemism: The Khazars in Russian Nationalist Literature', in D. Sinor and N. di Cosmo (eds), *The World of the Khazars, New Perspectives: Selected Papers from the Jerusalem 1999 International Khazar Colloquium* (Boston, 2007), 353–72.

Shnirelman, V., 'Ancestral Wisdom and Ethnic Nationalism: A View from Eastern Europe', *Pomegranate* 9/1 (2007), 41–60.

Siapkas, J., 'Ancient Ethnicity and Modern Identity', in J. McInerney (ed.), *A Companion to Ethnicity in the Ancient Mediterranean* (Oxford, 2014), 66–81.

Siebers, T. (ed.), *Religion and the Authority of the Past* (Ann Arbor, 1993).

Siklódi, C., *Between East and West: Everyday Life in the Hungarian Conquest Period*, tr. M-B. Davis (Budapest, 1996).

Silagi, G., 'Die Ungarnstürme in der ungarischen Geschichtsschreibung', *Settimane di Studio del Centro Italiano di Studi sull' Alto Medioevo* 35 (1988), 245–72.

Silagi, G., 'Zum Text der Gesta Hungarorum des anonymen Notars', *Deutsches Archiv fur Erforschung des Mittelalters* 45/2 (1989), 173–80.

Silman, Y., *Philosopher and Prophet: Judah Halevi, the Kuzari, and the Evolution of His Thought*, tr. L. Schramm (Albany, 1995).

Simmons, S., 'Rus' Dynastic Ideology in the Frescoes of the South Chapels in St. Sophia, Kiev', in N. Matheou et al. (eds), *From Constantinople to the Frontier: The City and the Cities* (Boston, 2016), 207–25.

Sinor, D. 'The Outlines of Hungarian Prehistory', *Cahiers d'Histoire Mondial* 4/3 (1958), 513–40.

Sinor, D. (ed.), *The Cambridge History of Early Inner Asia* (Cambridge, 1990).

Sitdikov, A. and F. Khuzin, 'Some Results of Archeological Study of the Kazan Khanate's Kremlin', *AAoE* 48/2 (2009), 51–72.

Sitdikov, A., I. Izmailov and R. Khayrutdinov, 'Weapons, Fortification and Military Art of the Volga Bulgaria in the 10th–the First Third of the 13th Centuries', *Journal of Sustainable Development* 8/7 (2015), 167–77.

Sivertsev, A., *Judaism and Imperial Ideology in Late Antiquity* (Cambridge, 2011).

Skinner, J., *The Invention of Greek Ethnography: From Homer to Herodotus* (New York, 2012).

Skržinskaja, E., 'Половцы. Опыт исторического исследования этникона', *VizVrem* 46 (1986), 255–69.

Sljadz', A., 'Предыстория византийской аннексии приазовья: князь-изгой Ростислав тмутараканский', *Проблемы истории, филологии, культуры* 2 (2015), 161–74.

Smirnov, A., 'Труды государственного исторического музея', *Работы археологических экспедиции* 16 (1941), 135–70.

Smirnov, A., 'Некоторые спорные вопроси истории волжских болгар', in D. Avdusin and V. Janin (eds), *Историо-археологическии сборник* (Moscow, 1962), 160–74.

Smirnov, A., 'Об этническом составе волжской булгары', in V. Janin (ed.), *Новое в археологии* (Moscow, 1972), 302–7.

Smith, A. D., *The Ethnic Origins of Nations* (Oxford, 1986).

Smolij, V., H. Borjak, O. Šeremet'jev et al. (eds), *1000 Years of Ukrainian Seal* (Kiev, 2013).

Šmurȳgina, O., 'О содержательном потенциале концепта потестарности', *Социум и власть* 2 (2012), 34–7.

Smyčkov, K., 'Несколько моливдовулов с территории древней руси и херсонеса (по материалам частного собрания)', in A. Ajbabin et al. (eds), *ХΘИиП* (Sevastopol', 2013), 331–48.

Smyčkov, K., 'Несколько византийских печатей с фамильными именами', *СЩ* 4 (2013), 476–83.

Smyth, A., 'The Emergence of English Identity, 700–1000', in A. Smyth (ed.), *Medieval Europeans: Studies in Ethnic Identity and National Perspectives in Medieval Europe* (New York, 1998), 24–52.

Sneath, D., *The Headless State: Aristocratic Orders, Kinship Society, and Misrepresentations of Nomadic Inner Asia* (New York, 2007).

Solov'ev, K., *Властители и судьи: легитимация государственной власти в древней и средневековой руси. IX–I половина XV в.* (Moscow, 1999).

Solev'ëv, S., *История россии с древнейших времён* (St Petersburg, 1879).

Soloviev, A., 'L'influence du droit byzantin dans les pays orthodoxes', in G. Sansoni (ed.), *Relazione del X Congresso Internationale di Scienze Storiche VI* (Florence, 1955), 599–650.

Soloviev, A., 'Metropolitensiegel des kiewer Russland', *BZ* 55 (1962), 292–301.

Somogyi, P., 'New Remarks on the Flow of Byzantine Coins in Avaria and Walachia during the Second Half of the Seventh Century', in F. Curta and R. Kovalev (eds), *The Other Europe in the Middle Ages: Avars, Bulgars, Khazars, and Cumans* (Boston, 2008), 83–149.

Sorlin, I., 'Voies commerciales, villes et peuplement de la *Rôsia* au Xe siècle d'après le *De administrando imperio* de Constantin Porphyrogénète', in M. Kazanski et al. (eds), *Les centres proto-urbains russes entre Scandinavie, Byzance et Orient* (Paris, 2000), 337–56.

Soročan, S., 'Случайность или система? Раннесредневековый византийский меркантилизм', *Древности-1995. Харьковский историко-археологический ежегодник* (1995), 122–32.

Soročan, S., '"Дело" епископа Иоанна Готского в связи с историей византино-хазарских отношений в таврике', in V. Mikheev et al. (eds), *Хазарский альманах 2* (Kharkov, 2004), 77–98.

Soročan, S., 'Еще раз о византийско-хазарском кондоминиуме в крыму в конце VII–первой половине VIII в.', *VizVrem* 73/98 (2014), 278–97.

Soteri, N., 'Khazaria: A Forgotten Jewish Empire', *History Today* 45/4 (1995), 10–12.

Sotnikova, M., 'A Seal of Jaroslav the Wise (Kyiv, 1019–1054)', in H. Ivakin et al. (eds), *Byzantine and Rus' Seals* (Kiev, 2015), 221–30.

Spassky, I., *The Russian Monetary System*, tr. Z. Gorishin (Amsterdam, 1967).

Spinei, V., *The Great Migrations in the East and South East of Europe from the Ninth to the Thirteenth Century*, tr. D. Badulescu (Amsterdam, 2003).

Spinei, V., 'The Cuman Bishopric: Genesis and Evolution', in F. Curta and R. Kovalev (eds), *The Other Europe in the Middle Ages: Avars, Bulgars, Khazars, and Cumans* (Boston, 2008) 379–412.

Spinei, V., *The Romanians and the Turkic Nomads North of the Danube Delta from the Tenth to the Mid-Thirteenth Century* (Leiden, 2009).

Stadnik, O. and A. Stadnik, 'Красногоровский грунтовый могильник салтово-маяцкой культуры на р. айдар', *Матеріали та дослідження з археології східної україни* 12 (2013), 254–63.

Stampfer, S., 'Did the Khazars Convert to Judaism?', *Jewish Social Studies* 9/3 (2013), 1–72.

Starostin, P., 'О раннем болгаре', in I. Belocerkovskaja (ed.), *Научное наследие А. П. Смирнова и современные проблемы археологии волго-камья. Сборник тезисов докладов конференции, посвященной*

100 летию так дня вождения Алексея Петровича Смирнова (Moscow, 1999), 99–101.

Starr, J., *The Jews in the Byzantine Empire: 641–1204* (Athens, 1939).

Stein-Wilkeshuis, M., 'Scandinavians Swearing Oaths in Tenth-Century Russia: Pagans and Christians', *JMedHist* 28 (2002), 155–68.

Stender-Peterson, A., *Varangica* (Aarhus, 1953).

Stepanenko, V., 'The Image of the Horseman Triumphant in the Sphragistics and Numismatics of Byzantium and the Countries of the Byzantine Cultural Milieu', in W. Seibt (ed.), *SBS* 7 (Washington, DC, 2002) 65–77.

Stepanenko, V., '"Portraits" of Princes in the Sigillography of Rus' from the Eleventh and the Twelfth Century', in H. Ivakin et al. (eds), *Byzantine and Rus' Seals* (Kiev, 2015), 245–60.

Stepanov, S., 'Цивилизационно равнище на българите до X век: другите за нас и ние за себе си', in *История на българите. Изкривявания и фалшификации* I (Sofia, 2002), 23–38.

Stepanov, S., *Българите и степната империя през ранното средновековие* (Sofia, 2005).

Stepanova, E., 'The Image of St. Nicholas on Byzantine Seals', in J-C. Cheynet and C. Sode (eds), *SBS* 9 (Berlin, 2006), 185–96.

Stephenson, P., *Byzantium's Balkan Frontier: A Political Study of the Northern Balkans, 900–1204* (New York, 2000).

Stephenson, P., 'Byzantine Conceptions of Otherness after the Annexation of Bulgaria (1018)', in D. Smythe (ed.), *Strangers to Themselves: The Byzantine Outsider. Papers from the 32nd Spring Symposium of Byzantine Studies, University of Sussex, Brighton* (Burlington, VT, 2000), 245–58.

Stern, S., 'The Coins of Āmul', in S. Stern (ed.), *Coins and Documents from the Medieval Middle East* (London, 1986), 205–78.

Stojanov, Ju., *Другият Бог: дуалистичните религии от античността до катарската ерес* (Sofia, 2006).

Stoljarik, E., *Essays on Monetary Circulation in the North-Western Black Sea Region in the Late Roman and Byzantine Periods: Late 3rd Century–Early 13th Century AD*, tr. V. Petljučenko (Odessa, 1992).

Stouraitis, I., '"Just War" and "Holy War" in the Middle Ages: Rethinking Theory through Case Study', *Jahrbuch des Österreichisches Byzantinistik* 62 (2012), 227–64.

van Straten, J., 'The Origin of East European Ashkenazim via a Southern Route', Aschkenas 27/1 (2017), 239–70.

Štulrajterova, K., 'Convivenza, Convenienza and Conversion: Islam in Medieval Hungary (1000–1400 CE)', *Journal of Islamic Studies* 24/2 (2013), 175–98.

Suchodolski, S., *Moneta polska w X/XI wieku* (Warsaw, 1967).
Suchodolski, S., 'Początki rodzimego mennictwa', in H. Samsonowicz (ed.), *Ziemie polskie w X wieku i ich znaczenie w kształtowaniu się nowej mapy Europy* (Krakow, 2000), 351–60.
Suchodolski, S., 'Czy orzeł polski ma już tysiąc lat? Uwagi o zwierzyńcu numizmatycznym Tomasza Panfila ', *Biuletyn Numizmatyczny* 1/321 (2001), 1–12.
Sudár, B. and Z. Petkes (eds), *A honfoglalók viselete* (Budapest, 2015).
Sullivan, R., 'Khan Boris and the Conversion of Bulgaria: A Case Study of the Impact of Christianity on a Barbarian Society', *Studies in Medieval and Renaissance History* 3 (1966), 55–139.
Šušarin, V., 'О сущности и формах современного норманизма', *VoprIst* 8 (1960), 65–93.
Szabó, M., *Les Celtes en Pannonie: Contribution à l'histoire de la civilization celtique dans la cuvette des Karpates* (Paris, 1988).
Szathmáry, L., 'Observations on Anthropological Research Concerning the Period of Hungarian Conquest and the Arpadian Age', *Acta Biologica Szegediensis* 44/1–4 (2000), 95–102.
Szczesniak, B., 'The Dependency of Kievan Rus on King Bolesław the Great: Numismatic Evidence', *Polish Review* 18/3 (1973), 31–43.
Szentgáli, K., 'Az "Árpádok" specializálása', *Az Érem* (1922), 20–3.
Szentgáli, K., 'Bizanc pénzei', *Az Érem* (1936), 187–209.
Szöke, B., *A honfoglaló és kora Árpad-kori Magyarország emlékei* (Budapest, 1962).
Szücs, J., 'Sur le concept de nation', *Recherche en Sciences Sociales* 64 (1986), 51–62.
Szyszyman, S., 'La question des Khazars: Essai de mise au point', *Jewish Quarterly Review* 73/2 (1982), 189–202.
Tachiaos, A-E. (ed.), *The Legacy of Saints Cyril and Methodius to Kiev and Moscow, Proceedings of the International Congress on the Millennium of the Conversion of Rus' to Christianity* (Thessalonike, 1992).
Takács, M., 'Review: *The Attire of the Conquering Hungarians – Ancient Hungarian History 1*, eds B. Sudár and Z. Petkes', *HA* Spring (2014), 1–3.
Taube, M., 'Transmission of Scientific Texts in 15th-Century Eastern Knaan', *Aleph: Historical Studies in Science and Judaism* 10/2 (2020), 315–53.
Tekin, T., *Volga Bulgar Kitabeleri ve Volga Bulgarcası* (Ankara, 1988).
Terras, V., 'Leo Diaconus and the Ethnology of Kievan Rus", *Slavic Review* 24 (1965), 395–406.

Thomas, N., 'Râdhânites, Chinese Jews, and the Silk Road of the Steppes', *Sino-Judaica: Occas ional Papers of the Sino-Judaic Institute* 1 (1991), 1–25.

Thomov, T., 'Four Scandinavian Ship Graffiti from Hagia Sofia', *BMGS* 38/2 (2014), 168–84.

Thompson, M., 'Byzantine Coins in Russia', *Medieval Archaeology* 10 (1966), 145–6.

Thomsen, V., *The Relations between Ancient Russia and Scandinavia and the Origin of the Russian State* (Oxford, 1877).

Thomson, F., 'The Bulgarian Contribution to the Reception of Byzantine Culture in Kievan Rus': The Myths and the Enigma', in F. Thomson (ed.), *The Reception of Byzantine Culture in Medieval Russia* (Brookfield, 1999), 214–61.

Thomson, F., 'The Distorted Mediaeval Russian Perception of Classical Antiquity: The Causes and the Consequences', in F. Thomson (ed.), *The Reception of Byzantine Culture in Medieval Russia* (Brookfield, 1999), 303–64.

Tiguncev, Ju., 'Власть и церковь в киевской руси XI–XII вв.: один взгляд на проблему взаимоотношений по сфрагистиким материалам', *СЩ* 4 (2013), 185–90.

Tihanyi, B., Z. Bereczki, E. Molnár, W. Berthon, L. Révész, O. Dutour and G. Pálfi, 'Investigation of Hungarian Conquest Period (10th c. AD) Archery on the Basis of Activity-Induced Stress Markers on the Skeleton: Preliminary Results', *Acta Biologica Szegediensis* 59/1 (2015), 65–77.

Tikhomirov, M., *The Towns of Ancient Rus*, tr. Y. Sdobnikov, ed. D. Skvirsky (Moscow, 1959).

Tilly, C., *Identities, Boundaries and Social Ties* (Boulder, 2005).

de Tocqueville, A., *Democracy in America* (Philadelphia, 1840).

Todorov, B., 'The Value of Empire: Tenth-Century Bulgaria between Magyars, Pechenegs and Byzantium', *JMedHist* 36 (2010), 312–26.

Toločko, A., *Очерки начальной руси* (St Petersburg, 2015).

Toločko, O., 'The *Primary Chronicle*'s "Ethnography" Revisited: Slavs and the Varangians in the Middle Dnieper Region and the Origin of the Rus' State', in I. Garipzanov et al. (eds), *Franks, Northmen, and Slavs: Identities and State Formation in Early Medieval Europe* (Turnhout, 2008), 169–88.

Toločko, P., 'Киевская земля', in L. Beskrovnÿj (ed.), *Древнерусские княжества X–XIII вв.* (Moscow, 1975), 5–56.

Toločko, P. (ed.), *Новое в археологии киева* (Kiev, 1981).

Toločko, P., *Древний киев* (Kiev, 1983).

Toločko, P., *Древняя русь: очерки социально-политической истории* (Kiev, 1987).
Toločko, P., *Древнерусский феодальный город* (Kiev, 1989).
Toločko, P. (ed.), *Южная русь и византия: сборник научных трудов (к XVIII конгрессу византинистов)* (Kiev, 1991).
Toločko, P., *Кочевые народы степей и киевская русь* (St Petersburg, 2003).
Tolstoï, I., *Византійскія монеты* (St Petersburg, 1912).
van der Toorn, K., B. Becking and P. van der Horst (eds), *Dictionary of Deities and Demons in the Bible*, 2nd edn (Leiden, 1999).
Tor, D., 'The Islamization of Central Asia in the Sāmānid Era and the Reshaping of the Muslim World', *BSO[A]S* 72/2 (2009), 279–99.
Tortika, A., *Северо-западная хазария в контексте истории восточной европы (вторая половина VII–третья четверть X вв.)* (Kharkov, 2006).
Tóth, V., *Strata of Ethnics, Languages and Settlement Names in the Carpathian Basin* (Debrecen, 2014).
Toynbee, A., *Constantine Porphyrogenitus and His World* (New York, 1973).
Treadwell, L., "Abd al-Malik's Coinage Reforms: The Role of the Damascus Mint', *Revue Numismatique* 6/165 (2009), 357–81.
Treadwell, L., 'Byzantium and Islam in the Late 7th Century AD: A "Numismatic War of Images"?', in T. Goodwin (ed.), *Arab-Byzantine Coins and History: Papers Presented at the 13th Seventh Century Syrian Numismatic Roundtable held at Corpus Christi College, Oxford* (Oxford, 2012), 145–55.
Trencsényi, B., '"Imposed Authenticity": Approaching Eastern European National Characterologies in the Inter-War Period', *Central Europe* 8/1 (2010), 20–47.
Trjarski, E., 'Les religions des Petchénègues', in A. Françoise (ed.), *Traditions religieuses et para-religieuses des peuples altaïques: Communications présentées au XIIIe Congrès de la Permanent International Altaistic Conference* (Paris, 1972), 139–48.
Tuganaev, A. and V. Tuganaev, *Состав, структура и эволюция агроэкосистем европейской России (лесная и лесостепная зоны) в средневековье (VI–XVI вв. н. э.)* (Iževsk, 2007).
Turčaninov, G., *Древние и средневековые памятники осетинского письма и языка* (Vladikavkaz, 1990).
Turchin, P., 'A Theory for the Formation of Large Agrarian Empires', *Journal of Global History* 4 (2009), 191–217.
Türk, A., 'The New Archaeological Research Design for Early Hungarian History', *HA* Summer (2012), 1–6.

Türk, A., 'Some Remarks on the Khwarazmian–Hungarian Connections in the Middle Ages', in S. Prozorov (ed.), *Medieval Cities of Turkmenistan in the System of the Eurasian Civilization* (Ashgabat, 2012), 242–3.

Ul'janovskij, V., 'Новая булла Феофано Музалон и загадка "археонтессы Росии": почти крамольные заметки историка на сфрагистическую тему', *СЩ* 4 (2013), 54–87.

Unger, E. (ed.), *Magyar éremhatározó* I–IV (Budapest, 1974).

Urazmanova, R., 'Симбиоз этнического и конфессионального в современной праздничной культуре татар', *Этнографическое обозрение* 2 (2010), 69–83.

Urbańczyk, P., 'Slavic and Christian Identities during the Transition to Polish Statehood', in I. Garipzanov et al. (eds), *Franks, Northmen, and Slavs: Identities and State Formation in Early Medieval Europe* (Turnhout, 2008), 205–22.

Urbańczyk, P., 'Early Medieval Strongholds in Polish Lands', in N. Christie and H. Herold (eds), *Fortified Settlements in Early Medieval Europe: Defended Communities of the 8th–10th Centuries* (Philadelphia, 2016), 95–106.

Urbańczyk, P. and S. Rosik, 'The Kingdom of Poland, with an Appendix on Polabia and Pomerania between Paganism and Christianity', in N. Berend (ed.), *Christianization and the Rise of Christian Monarchy: Scandinavia, Central Europe and Rus', c. 900–1200* (Cambridge, 2003), 263–318.

Usmanov, M., *Татарские исторические источники XVII–XVIII вв.* (Kazan', 1972).

Uspenskij, P., 'Могильники с трупосожжениями VIII–XIII вв. на северо-западном кавказе (динамика ареала погребального обряда)', *РА* 4 (2013), 86–98.

Vachkova, V., 'Danube Bulgaria and Khazaria as Parts of the Byzantine *Oikoumene*', in F. Curta and R. Kovalev (eds), *The Other Europe in the Middle Ages: Avars, Bulgars, Khazars, and Cumans* (Boston, 2008), 339–62.

Vágner, Z., 'Medieval Pottery Kilns in the Carpathian Basin', *EJA* 5/3 (2002), 309–42.

Valiev, R., 'Leatherworking in the Kazan Khanate', *AAoE* 48/2 (2009), 73–95.

Vásáry, I., *Cumans and Tatars: Oriental Military in the Pre-Ottoman Balkans, 1185–1365* (Cambridge, 2005).

Vasiliev, A., *The Goths in the Crimea* (Cambridge, 1936).

Vasil'iev, D., 'Итиль-мечта: на раскопках древнего центра хазарского каганата', *Лехаим* 10 (2006), 174.

Vasil'iev, D. (ed.), *Самосдельское городище: вопросы изучения и интерпретации* (Astrakhan, 2011).
Vasil'iev, D. and E. Zilivinskaja, 'Городище в дельте Волги', *BK* 2/25 (2006), 42–54.
Vasjutin, S., 'Typology of Pre-States and Statehood Systems of Nomads', in N. Kradin et al. (eds), *Nomadic Pathways in Social Evolution* (Moscow, 2003), 50–62.
Veres, P., 'The Uralic and Hungarian Ancestral Homeland: The State of Current Research', in G. Nanovfszky (ed.), *The Finno-Ugric World* (Budapest, 2004), 31–6.
Vernadsky, G., *A History of Russia* (New Haven, 1948).
Vernadsky, G., *Kievan Russia* (New Haven, 1959).
Vértes, E., 'Randbemerkungen zu den neuesten Forschungen auf dem gebiete der ungarischen Vorgeschichte', *Acta Linguistica* 4 (1954), 427–62.
Veszprémy, L., 'Conversion in Chronicles: The Hungarian Case', in G. Armstrong and I. Wood (eds), *Christianizing Peoples and Converting Individuals* (Turnhout, 2000), 133–46.
Vinnikov, A, 'Контакты донских славян с алано-болгарским миром', *CA* 3 (1990), 124–37.
Visi, T., *On the Peripheries of Ashkenaz: Medieval Jewish Philosophers in Normandy and in the Czech Lands from the Twelfth to the Fifteenth Century* (Olomouc, 2011).
Voegelin, E., *Collected Works. Vol. 18: Order and History: In Search of Order* (London, 1999).
Vojnikov, Ž., *Титли и имена в първата българска държава: сравнителен анализ* (Sofia, 2018).
Voorheis, P., *The Perception of Asiatic Nomads in Medieval Russia: Folklore, History and Historiography* (Bloomington, 1982).
Vörös, G., 'Relics of the Pecheneg Language in the Works of Constantine', in H. Güzel et al. (eds), *The Turks: Early History* (Ankara, 2002), 617–31.
Vrij, M., 'The Numismatic Iconography of the Period of Iconomachy (610–867)', PhD thesis, University of Birmingham (2017).
Vryonis, S., Jr, 'The Slavic Pottery (Jars) from Olympia, Greece', in S. Vryonis, Jr (ed.), *Byzantine Studies: Essays on the Slavic World and the Eleventh Century* (New Rochelle, NY, 1992), 15–42.
Walker, J., *A Catalogue of the Arab-Byzantine and Post-Reform Umaiyad Coins* (London, 1956).
Walker, J., *A Catalogue of the Arab-Sassanian Coins* (London, 1967).
Wasserstein, D., 'The Khazars and the World of Islam', in D. Sinor and N. di Cosmo (eds), *The World of the Khazars, New Perspectives: Selected*

Papers from the Jerusalem 1999 International Khazar Colloquium (Boston, 2007), 373–86.

Wasserstrom, S., 'Review: *Philosopher and Prophet: Judah Halevi, the Kuzari, and the Evolution of His Thought*, by Y. Silman', *Medieval Encounters* 3/3 (1997), 284–317.

Wassiliou-Seibt, A-K., 'A Kommerkiarios Seal from the Last Year of Constans II's Reign (667/68) Found in the Upper Dniester Region', in H. Ivakin et al. (eds), *Byzantine and Rus' Seals* (Kiev, 2015), 37–41.

Websdale, N., '"Multi-Ethnic Empire", "Nation-State" or "Agents of Imperialism"? Some Remarks on *Romanland* by Anthony Kaldellis', *Medioevo Greco* 20 (2020), 319–34.

Webster, B., 'John of Fordun and the Independent Identity of the Scots', in A. Smyth (ed.), *Medieval Europeans: Studies in Ethnic Identity and National Perspectives in Medieval Europe* (New York, 1998), 85–102.

Weickhardt, G., 'Early Russian Law and Byzantine Law', *RH* 32/1 (2005), 1–22.

Weinryb, B., 'Solving the "Khazar Problem": A Study in Soviet Historiography', *Judaism* 13/4 (1964), 431–43.

Weiss, J., 'Fortress Forever at the Ready: The Jewish Ethos in the Byzantine Mind and its Ruthenian Translation', *GOTR* 46/3–4 (2001), 287–344.

Wells, P., *Barbarians to Angels: The Dark Ages Reconsidered* (New York, 2008).

Werbart, B., 'Khazars or "Saltovo-Majaki Culture"? Prejudices about Archaeology and Ethnicity', *Current Swedish Archaeology* 4 (1996), 199–221.

Werbart, B., 'The Invisible Identities: Cultural Identity and Archaeology', in V. Herva (ed.), *People, Material Culture and Environment in the North: Proceedings of the 22nd Nordic Archaeological Conference* (Oulu, 2006), 83–99.

Wexler, P., *The Ashkenazic Jews: A Slavo-Turkic People in Search of a Jewish Identity* (Columbus, 1993).

Wexler, P., *Two-Tiered Relexification of Yiddish: Jews, Sorbs, Khazars, and the Kiev-Polessian Dialect* (Berlin, 2002).

Wexler, P., 'Yiddish Evidence for the Khazar Component in the Ashkenazic Ethnogenesis', in D. Sinor and N. di Cosmo (eds), *The World of the Khazars, New Perspectives: Selected Papers from the Jerusalem 1999 International Khazar Colloquium* (Boston, 2007), 387–98.

Whitting, P., *Byzantine Coins* (London, 1973).

Whittle, A., 'Fish, Faces and Fingers: Presences and Symbolic Identities in the Mesolithic–Neolithic Transition in the Carpathian Basin',

Documenta Praehistorica: Poročilo o Raziskovanju Paleolitika, Neolitika in Eneolitika v Sloveniji 25 (1998), 133–50.

Whittow, M., 'Early Medieval Byzantium and the End of the Ancient World', *Journal of Agrarian Change* 9/1 (2009), 134–53.

Wickham, C., 'The Donkey and the Boat: Mediterranean Economic Expansion in the 11th Century', presented at *The Birmingham Research Institute for History and Cultures (BRIHC) Annual Lecture*, University of Birmingham, 27 February 2017.

Wilk, M., *The Journals of a White Sea Wolf*, tr. D. Stok (London, 2005).

Wilkinson, D., 'Cities, Civilizations and Oikumenes: I–II', *Comparative Civilizations Review* (1992–3), 27–8, 51–87; 41–72.

Wimmer, A., *Ethnic Boundary Making: Institutions, Power, Networks* (New York, 2013).

Le Winter, O., 'Among the Khazars', *Hudson Review* 16/3 (1963), 380–1.

Wittrock, B., 'The Meaning of the Axial Age', in J. Arnason et al. (eds), *Axial Civilizations and World History* (Boston, 2005), 51–85.

Wittrock, B., 'The Axial Age in Global History: Cultural Crystallizations and Societal Transformations', in R. Bellah and H. Joas (eds), *The Axial Age and its Consequences* (Cambridge, MA, 2012), 102–25.

Wolf, J., *Abeceda národů* (Prague, 1984).

Wolf, M., '10th–11th Century Settlements, Earthen Forts and Crafts', tr. N. Horton et al., in Z. Visy and M. Nagy (eds), *Hungarian Archaeology at the Turn of the Millennium* (Budapest, 2003), 326–32.

Wolfram, H., 'Gothic History as Historical Ethnography', in T. Noble (ed.), *From Roman Provinces to Medieval Kingdoms* (New York, 2006), 43–69.

Wolfram, H., '*Origo et Religio*: Ethnic Traditions and Literature in Early Medieval Texts', in T. Noble (ed.), *From Roman Provinces to Medieval Kingdoms* (New York, 2006), 70–90.

Wołoszyn, M., 'Byzantine Archaeology: Selected Problems', tr. M. Kozub, *Analecta Archaeologica Ressoviensia* 1 (2006), 259–92.

Wood, I., 'Introduction', in G. Armstrong and I. Wood (eds), *Christianizing Peoples and Converting Individuals* (Turnhout, 2000), ix–x.

Wood, I., 'Defining the Franks: Frankish Origins in Early Medieval Historiography', in T. Noble (ed.), *From Roman Provinces to Medieval Kingdoms* (New York, 2006), 110–19.

Wood, I., 'Barbarians, Historians, and the Construction of National Identities', *Journal of Late Antiquity* 1/1 (2008), 61–81.

Woodfin, W., Y. Rassamakin and R. Holod, 'Foreign Vesture and Nomadic Identity on the Black Sea Littoral in the Early Thirteenth Century: Costume from the Chungrul Kurgan', *Ars Orientalis* 38 (2010), 155–86.

Woods, J., J. Pfeiffer and E. Tucker (eds), 'The Chinese Chroniclers of the Khazars: Notes on Khazaria in Tang Period Texts', *AEMA* 14 (2005), 231–61.

Wooster, S., 'From the Enlightenment to Genocide: The Evolution and Devolution of Romanian Nationalism', *McNair Scholars Journal* 16/1 (2012), 80–99, http://scholarworks.gvsu.edu/cgi/viewcontent.cgi?article=1402&context=mcnair, accessed 7 December 2020.

Wyszomirska, B., 'Religion som enande politisk-social länk – exemplet: Det Kazariska riket', in L. Larsson and B. Wyszomirska (eds), *Arkeologi och Religion: Rapport från Arkeologi Dagarna 16–18 januari 1989* (Lund, 1989), 135–48.

Ya'ari, E., 'Skeletons in the Closet: Who's Afraid of the Khazar Jewish Empire?', *Jerusalem Report*, Jerusalem, 9 July 1995, 29–30.

Yashaeva, T., E. Denisova, N. Ginkut, V. Zalesskaya and D. Zhuravlev, *The Legacy of Byzantine Cherson* (Austin, 2011).

Yasmann, V., 'The Rise of the Eurasians', *Radio Free Europe/Radio Liberty Security Watch* (2001), reproduced in *The Eurasian Politician* 4, http://users.jyu.fi/~aphamala/pe/issue4/yasmann.htm, accessed March 2022.

Zalesskaja, V., 'Byzantine White-Clay Painted Bowls and Cylix-Type Cups', in R. Morris (ed.), *Church and People in Byzantium* (Birmingham, 1986), 215–24.

Zalesskaja, V., I. Zaseckaja, K. Kasparova, Z. Lvova, B. Maršak, I. Sokolova and M. ŠČukin, *Съкровище на хан Кубрат: Култура на българи, хазари, славяни* (Sofia, 1989).

Zancani, D., 'The Notion of "Lombard" and "Lombardy" in the Middle Ages', in A. Smyth (ed.), *Medieval Europeans: Studies in Ethnic Identity and National Perspectives in Medieval Europe* (New York, 1998), 217–32.

Zernatto, G. and A. Mistretta, 'Nation: The History of a Word', *Review of Politics* 6/3 (1944), 351–66.

Zguta, R., 'Kievan Coinage', *SEER* 53/133 (1975), 483–92.

Zhivkov, B., *Khazaria in the Ninth and Tenth Centuries*, tr. D. Manova (Boston, 2015).

Zimonyi, I., *The Origins of the Volga Bulghars* (Szeged, 1990).

Zimonyi, I., *Muszlim Források a honfoglalás előtti magyarokról: A Ğayhānī-hagyomány magyar fejezete* (Budapest, 2003).

Zongzheng, X., *A History of Turks* (Beijing, 1992).

Zuckerman, K., 'On the Date of the Khazars' Conversion to Judaism and the Chronology of the Kings of the Rus Oleg and Igor: A Study of the Anonymous Khazar *Letter* from the Genizah of Cairo', *Revue des Études Byzantines* 53 (1995), 237–70.

Zuckerman, K., 'Русь, византия и хазария в середине X века: проблемы хронологии', *Славяне и их соседи* 6 (1996), 68–80.

Zuckerman, K., 'Two Notes on the Early History of the *thema* of Cherson', *BMGS* 21 (1997), 210–22.

Zuckerman, K., 'Deux étapes de la formation de l'ancien état russe', in M. Kazanski et al. (eds), *Les centres proto-urbains russes entre Scandinavie, Byzance et Orient* (Paris, 2000), 95–120.

Zuckerman, K., 'Byzantium's Pontic Policy in the *Notitiae Episcopatuum*', in C. Zuckerman (ed.), *La Crimée entre Byzance et le Khaganat Khazar* (Paris, 2006), 201–30.

Zuckerman, K., 'The Khazars and Byzantium: The First Encounter', in D. Sinor and N. di Cosmo (eds), *The World of the Khazars, New Perspectives: Selected Papers from the Jerusalem 1999 International Khazar Colloquium* (Boston, 2007), 399–432.

Zuckerman, K., 'The End of Byzantine Rule in North-Eastern Pontus', *Материалы по археологии, истории и этнографии таврии* XXII (Simferopol', 2017), 311–36.

Index

'Abbasid dynasty, 25, 65, 154, 158–60, 179
'Abd al-Malik (Islamic caliph), 152–4
Abrahamic faiths, 2, 6, 36, 60, 80, 82, 152, 171, 182, 189, 193
Adyges, 51, 76
Aeolians, 93
Afanas'ev, Gennadij, 48, 51, 198
Afghanistan, 158–9
Africa, 3, 94, 170, 193
Agura, Moshe, 35
Akerovič, Petro (metropolitan of Rus'), 144
Akropolites, Georgios, 21
al-Andalus, 57, 92, 102, 159
Alans, 30, 34, 51, 53, 61, 65, 73, 75–6, 87, 173
al-Baladhuri, 153
Albanians, 173, 205
al-Dīmašqi, 35
Alexander of Macedon (the Great), 26, 105, 188
Alexios III Angelos, 163
al-Gardīzī, 141
al-Garnatī, 55, 57–8, 105–6, 113, 119
al-Hamdānī, 52
al-Istakhrī, 23–4, 53, 61, 70, 88–9, 100
al-Kāšgarī, 124

al-Mas'ūdī, 24, 34, 36–7, 40, 44, 52, 73, 76, 78, 88–9, 100–1, 169
al-Muqaddasī, 24, 52, 75, 89, 200
Almuš, 2, 14, 25, 38, 74–6, 89, 99, 103–7, 135, 159, 199
Almušid dynasty, 2, 38, 83–4, 98, 101–3, 106, 150, 157, 159, 166, 170–1
al-Nuwayri, 189
Amartolos, Georgios, 130
American exceptionalism, 93
Americas, the, 3, 93, 170–1, 179
Ananias of Širak, 100
Anastasius Bibliothecarius (the Librarian), 202
Anatolia, 1, 14, 85, 93, 126, 145, 197
Anderson, Benedict, 109, 116, 167, 174
Andreas (king of Hungary), 162
Anglia, 62, 68
Anglican Christianity, 171
Anglo-Saxons, 173
Annales Bertiniani, 141
Antes, 174
antiquity, 3–8, 11–12, 15, 59, 66, 80, 91, 94–5, 162, 168, 170–1, 175–83, 191, 204
anti-Semitism, 172, 187, 191–2, 194, 196, 201

INDEX

Arabia, 193
Arabic sources, 14, 19, 21, 23–4, 32, 41, 62, 76, 90, 102, 104–5, 152, 158, 196
Aral Sea, 24–5
Ardabīl (Erbil), 39
Armenia, 22, 32, 35
Armenians, 1, 10, 39–40, 130, 197
Árpád dynasty, 15, 38, 43, 109, 118, 120, 122, 150, 157, 160–2, 166
Artamonov, Mikhail, 20, 29, 37, 43, 48–9, 61, 66, 69–71, 76, 88, 100, 125, 141, 155
Asenid dynasty, 162–3
Ashkenazim, 17–18, 29, 31, 81, 165, 193–200, 203–5
Asia, 2–3, 6–7, 80, 94, 126–7, 157, 159, 170, 182–3, 189
Āšĭnà dynasty, 2, 20, 24, 32, 35, 37, 46, 142, 150, 155
Attaleiates, Michael, 124, 126, 128, 130
Avars, 15, 42, 75, 80
axial age, 177–8, 182

Bağatur (khağan), 39
Baghdad, 25, 34, 103, 159, 171
Balanjar, 46
Balkans, 14, 59, 61, 67, 72, 80, 87, 94–5, 98–9, 108, 124, 129, 132, 145, 169, 205
Balts, 3, 41, 100, 138, 142, 156
Banská Štiavnica, 162
Bar Kokhba Revolt, 17, 194
Barber Institute of Fine Art (UoB), 152–3, 162
Basileios II Porphyrogennetos, 1–2, 143, 146
Baškīrs, 23, 25, 100, 113, 138
Bašqortostan, 21
Basques, 92
Battle of Agincourt, 180
Battle of Guadalete, 180

Battle of Lebounion, 130–3
Battle of Lechfeld, 108, 114, 120
Battle of Lepanto, 180
Battle of Salamis, 180
Battle of the Kalka River, 168
Battle of the Somme, 180
Battle of Waterloo, 180
beg, 22–3, 37, 45
Belgorod, 48, 145–6
Belgrade, 129
Benevento, 27
Berend, Nora, 85, 95, 108, 111, 112, 113, 116, 117, 118, 119, 121–3, 135, 160–3
Berengar, 92
Beta Israel, 193
Big History, 182
Biliar, 102, 106, 122
Bjelo-Brdo archaeological culture, 111, 113, 116
Black Bulgars, 86–7, 95
blood-and-soil nationality, 91, 193
boat-burning burial, 25
Bolesław (the Brave), 160–1
Bolgar, 2, 25, 72, 75, 102, 106, 122, 159
Book of Ezekiel, 187
Boris, *khağan* of Danube Bulgaria, 27, 43, 45, 96, 162
Bosnians, 205
Botaneiates, Nikephoros III, 146
Britannia, 194
Brook, Kevin, 19, 36, 52, 54, 71, 85, 90, 155, 196, 204
Buddhism, 171
Bukhārā, 25, 159
Bulan-Sabriel, 31, 33, 36, 39–41, 45, 52, 62, 78
Bulgarian imitative coinage, 163, 165
Burtās, 23, 51, 76, 87
Byzantine commonwealth, 11, 20, 77, 83–7, 94–6, 99, 124, 151, 157
Byzantinists, 7

Byzantium (Eastern Roman/Byzantine empire), 2, 7–9, 11, 15–17, 19–20, 27, 30, 32, 34–7, 41–2, 44–5, 47–8, 55–7, 59, 67–9, 72–3, 75, 77, 80, 82, 83–8, 90–6, 98–100, 106–8, 112, 124–6, 128–33, 135–8, 140–1, 143–9, 151–4, 161–6, 169, 171, 173, 176, 179–81, 183–4, 195–7, 204

Cairo Geniza, 28, 35
Caliphate (Islamic), 14, 19, 21, 23, 32, 34–7, 52, 55–6, 59, 73, 82, 89, 126, 141, 154, 157–8, 166, 179, 188
Caliphate of Córdoba, 28, 30
Cambodia, 188
Carpathian Mountains, 3, 73, 98, 107–8, 114, 116–17, 123
Carthage, 153
Caspian Sea, 22, 24, 47, 52, 56–8, 85, 89–90, 184
catacombs, 46, 53, 55, 61, 71
Catalans, 92
Caucasus, 3, 6, 30, 32, 35–7, 39, 47, 50, 52, 61, 68, 71, 73–4, 76, 86–7, 89, 98, 194–5, 197–8
Čečens, 197
Čelarevo, burial site in Serbia, 42, 49
Celtiberians, 173
Celts, 11, 120, 138, 173
Čerkess (Circasians), 77
Černigov, 139, 144–6
Červona (Nova) Gusarivka (Ukraine), 70
Charlemagne, 80, 173, 179
Cherson, 2, 13, 38, 44, 47, 71, 85–6, 91, 94, 106, 111, 128, 135, 142–3, 146, 148, 161, 202
Chiasmus (rhetorical technique), 13, 188–9
China, 24, 175, 180, 193

Chinese sources, 19–20, 28, 37
Christendom, 9, 26, 32, 83, 95, 108, 111–12, 116, 120–1, 123, 149, 151, 165, 171, 178–9, 194
Christian of Stavelot, 26–7, 44–5, 53, 79, 200–1
Chronicle of Ahima'az, 33
Čiček (Khazar princess), 20
Cimljansk *gorodišče* and reservoir region in southern Russia, 48, 50, 70–1, 86
circumstantial ethnicity, 5, 8, 115, 139, 171, 202, 205
CIS (Commonwealth of Independent States), 191
Čistoj Banki, 56–7
civilisational analysis, 168, 178–82
Čkhaidze, Viktor, 84, 86, 88, 90, 145, 148, 165
Classicists, 7
Classics, 180–1
Constantine-Cyril (Konstantinos-Kyrillos), 13, 21, 45, 86, 96
Constantinople, 1, 10, 13, 20, 30, 37, 88, 90, 96, 127, 144, 148, 153, 165, 169, 171
constitutive descent, 96
Cossacks, 170
Council in Trullo, 153
craniometry, 115, 117
Crimea, 1, 34, 36–8, 46–7, 49–51, 55–6, 61, 71, 73–4, 81, 84–6, 88, 90, 95–6, 98, 124, 128, 146, 149, 164–5, 174, 196, 204–5
Croatians, 92–3, 95, 171, 174, 205
culture-history, 15, 111–13, 116–17, 119, 129, 136–7, 174, 176, 178
Cumania, 130, 134–5
Cuman-Qıpčaqs (also Polovcÿ), 10, 12, 15, 17, 42, 47, 51, 64, 71, 73, 76, 79–80, 95, 107–8, 114, 119–20, 122–3, 125, 127–35, 169, 178, 184, 189, 191–2

Curta, Florin, 15, 43, 45, 47, 57–8, 60–1, 94–5, 99, 102, 114, 124, 127–30, 134, 139–40, 145, 159, 174–6
Čuvaš, 100, 138

Dacians, 111
Dalmatians, 174
Danube Bulgaria, 10, 36, 41, 47, 62, 65–6, 80, 99, 154
Danube Bulgars, 72, 157
Danube River, 3, 98–9, 128, 134, 162, 172
Dār al-Bābūnaj, 36
Davidic dynasty, 53, 61, 154
De Administrando Imperio, 14, 30, 42, 62, 76–7, 84, 86–7, 90–5, 107, 109–10, 116, 123–7, 138, 192, 199
De Ceremoniis, 14, 87, 151
De Thematibus, 14, 93–4
de Tocqueville, Alexis, 93
Derevlians, 174
DeWeese, Devin, 31–3, 35, 38–9, 43–5, 56, 60–1, 63, 65, 72, 103, 105–6, 189
Diamond, Jared, 179–80
Dimitrievskij Complex, 48–9, 51, 61
dispensationalism, 176
DNA (as genetic evidence), 194–5, 197–9, 201, 203, 205
Dniepr River, 2, 27, 51, 71, 77, 165
Dniestr River, 114, 165
Don River, 15, 22, 44, 49, 61–2, 70–1, 73, 76, 86
Donec River, 73
Dorians, 93
Doros (Mangup), 85
družina, 139
duck test, 203
Dunlop, Douglas, 19–20, 34–6, 39, 42, 52, 57, 70, 73, 75, 88, 196, 204
Dunn, Archie, 58
Durkheim, Émile, 182

Ecumenism, 9, 35, 95, 143, 145, 149, 152, 161–2, 166, 168, 171, 175, 180, 183
Egypt, 165
el'teber, 25, 47–8, 75
Elhaik, Eran, 195, 197, 199
Eliade, Mircea, 68
Ellas (Byzantine Greece), 93
epigraphy, 8, 49–50, 58, 69, 79, 136
Epiros, 169
Erakleios (Heraclius), Roman/Byzantine emperor, 20
eschatology, 67, 187–8
Esztergom, 13, 72, 122
ethnos, 14, 91–5
etrog (Jewish ceremonial citrus), 42, 166
Etruscans, 173
eugenics, 112, 115
Eurasianism, 134, 172, 181, 190–1
Europe, 2–3, 6–7, 13, 37, 41, 43, 45, 47, 54, 57–8, 65, 67, 71, 80, 94–5, 99–100, 113–17, 121–4, 127, 130, 133–4, 139, 143, 148–9, 157, 160–3, 169–71, 175, 177, 179–80, 183–4, 194–5, 198, 204–5
European Union, 116
Extremadurans, 92

Ferguson, Niall, 179–80
fibulae, 139
Finno-Ugrians, 100, 113, 201
foederati, 128, 175
Fourth Crusade, 169
Francia, 62, 68
Franklin, Simon, 15–16, 27, 50–1, 64, 67, 71–3, 77, 89, 100, 133, 135–7, 140–2, 144–5, 149, 174
Franks, 13, 92–3, 117, 120, 173
Fukuyama, Francis, 179
funerary archaeology, 25, 51, 76, 101, 118, 136, 139, 198

Galicians, 92
Gaul (region), 173, 194
Geary, Patrick, 96, 174, 177, 199
Gellner, Ernest, 8, 174
genealogy, 91, 94–5, 132, 157–8
Genoese Crimea, 90
genos, 91–3, 138
Georgia, 39–40, 85, 165, 197
Germania, 62
Germanic peoples, 173, 184
Germany, 68, 173, 194, 197
Gesta Hungarorum, 13, 108–12, 116, 124
Getica, 13, 191
Gibbon, Edward, 84, 176
Gil, Moshe, 37, 81, 189, 199–200
Gilgamesh, 182
Gniezno, 13, 160
Gog and Magog, 22, 26–7, 187–9
Gökturk *khağanate*, 20, 32
Golden Horde, 43, 57, 62, 79, 191
Golden, Peter, 19–20, 23, 27, 29, 36–44, 46–7, 50–4, 60–2, 66–7, 71–3, 76–7, 88, 90, 99–101, 106, 108, 124–7, 132–5, 141, 155, 169, 190, 196
Gončarov, Evgenij, 54, 58, 165
Gordian knot, 168, 178
Gotland, 41, 137, 143, 154
Gotthia, 36, 84–6, 145, 150
Great Walls (of China), 73, 189
Greece, 12, 34, 40, 87, 93, 178, 183
Greek sources, 1, 19–20, 26–7, 32, 34, 62, 68, 76, 94, 109, 147–9, 152, 161, 165, 196, 202, 204
Gregory of Tours, 13
Gumilëv, Lev, 56–8, 89, 172, 190–2

Halakhic Law, 54, 203
Haldon, John, 16, 35, 74, 90, 92, 142, 146, 152–3, 166, 175–6, 183
HaLevi, Yehuda, 26, 28, 30–1, 67

Hanson, Victor, 180
Hartvic (Christian bishop), 117, 122
Hebrew sources, 19, 26, 28–34, 41–2, 44–5, 49–51, 54–5, 60–3, 67–8, 72, 76, 79, 86–7, 91, 141, 165, 187, 195–6, 200, 202
Herodotus, 94, 96
Hezekiah (king in the *Tanakh*/Old Testament), 33
Hinduism, 171
Hispania, 194
Hobsbawm, Eric, 174
Honfoglalás, 19, 107–9, 115–16
Howard-Johnston, James, 20, 75, 85–7, 91, 94–5, 100, 125
Ḥudūd al-ʿĀlam, 15, 23–4, 36, 73, 101, 124–5, 138, 141, 188
Hugh of Arles, 93
Humbert, cardinal, 182
Hungarian prehistory, 109, 113, 115, 117, 120
Hungary, 4, 6, 15, 54, 62, 67, 85, 98, 107, 113, 115–16, 118–19, 122–3, 133–5, 138, 140, 142, 150, 157, 160, 162, 166
Huns, 76, 86, 112, 138, 191
Huntington, Samuel, 179

Iberians, 92
ibn Aʿtham, 39
ibn al-Athīr, 36, 39
ibn al-Faqīh, 22, 52–3, 200–1
ibn al-Nadim, 28
ibn Fadlān, 13, 22–6, 36, 40, 43, 47, 52–3, 75–6, 88–9, 100–1, 105, 138, 141, 188–9, 196, 199
ibn Hauqal, 24, 88–9
ibn Hussein, Ṭāhir, 157–8
ibn Jaʿfar, 203
ibn Khurradādhbih, 22–4, 47, 188–9, 203
ibn Qutayba, 189

ibn Rusta, 23, 36, 47, 52–3, 61, 105, 141, 201
ibn Šaprut, Hasdai, 28–31, 67
ibn Saruq, Menahem, 28
ibn Ziyād, Tariq, 180
iconoclasm, 85, 152–4
Idnakar, 102–3
Ilarion, metropolitan of Rus', 140–1, 144–5
Illyrians, 173
Imen'kov (archaeological culture), 100, 102
India, 24, 175, 193
Ioannes of Gotthia, 46, 85
Ionia, 32
Iran, 21, 37, 42–3, 54, 100, 152, 158, 197–8
Ireland, 179
īšā, 37, 47–8, 52
Isaakios II Angelos, 163
Israel, 18, 33–4, 41, 50, 60, 67, 177, 182, 187, 193–4, 205
Italy, 19, 27, 33, 68, 90, 117, 137, 165, 173, 179, 194
Itīl', 2, 19, 23, 25, 36–8, 46, 55–9, 72–4, 77–9, 85, 87–8, 122, 141, 155
Ivan II Asen, 163
Ivan III of Moscow, 169

Jakov the monk, 88, 132
Jankowiak, Marek, 16, 89, 102, 156, 159
Jaroslav the Wise (Kievan Rus' prince), 132, 141, 144, 148–9, 161
Jaspers, Karl, 177–8, 180
John F. Kennedy, 188–9
Jordanes (chronicler), 13, 110–11, 191
Josephus (Jewish chronicler), 188
Josiah (king in the *Tanakh*/Old Testament), 33
Ĵuanšer (Georgian ruler), 39

Judaism, 2, 5–6, 10–12, 15, 17, 18–19, 21–3, 26–42, 44–7, 49–56, 59–64, 66–8, 71–2, 76–82, 84–8, 90, 98, 104–5, 107, 116, 122, 135, 141, 150–1, 155–6, 158, 170–2, 189, 193–205
Justinian II, 20, 153–4

Kaifeng Jews, 193
Kaldellis, Anthony, 9–10, 59, 91, 93–5, 124, 128, 138, 183
Kalmyk *khağanate*, 175
Kalojan Asen, 163
Kama River, 25, 98–9, 102–3
Karaite Jews, 41, 196, 204
Kartlis Cxovreba, 39–40, 78
Kasogs, 76–7, 88
Kazakhs, 170
Kazakhstan, 4, 6, 191
Kazan', 72, 101–2
Khazar Correspondence, 29, 67, 154–5
Khazar-Ashkenazi descent theory, 17, 29, 81, 193–205
Khazaria, 2–3, 6, 10, 15, 17, 18–82, 83–90, 94, 97–100, 103–4, 107–8, 110–13, 115–16, 118, 121–9, 132, 134–5, 140–2, 145, 150, 151–2, 154–9, 161, 164–5, 169–73, 181, 187–9, 191, 194–205
Khazarian Pečenegs, 24, 125
Khazars, 10, 12–13, 15, 17, 19–81, 85–9, 99–100, 106, 109, 116, 120, 129, 135, 140–1, 155–6, 171–3, 176, 184, 188–9, 191, 196–205
Khwărazmia/Khorosan, 23–5, 28, 42, 85, 89, 99, 102, 119, 157–9
Kiev, 2, 13–14, 29–30, 43, 46, 51, 55, 57, 72, 76–7, 88, 128, 132, 135–6, 140–1, 143–9, 160–1, 191, 195–6
Kievan Letter, 28–9, 33, 50, 67, 195–6, 202

King Joseph's Reply, 28–31, 33, 36,
    39–41, 44–5, 52, 55, 60, 63, 67,
    70, 72–6, 125, 196, 202
Kitâb al-Buldân, 23, 52, 200
Klaniczay, Gabor, 37, 43, 65, 123, 177
Knaanic, 195–6
Kochinim, 183
Koestler, Arthur, 194–5
Komnene, Anna, 128, 130–1
Komnenian dynasty, 130, 132, 163
Komnenos, Alexios I, 146
Komnenos, Manouel I, 146, 163
Konstantinos IX Monomachos, 143
Konstantinos VII Porphyrogennetos,
    14, 21, 30, 42, 62, 76, 84,
    86–7, 90–6, 107, 110, 126–7,
    138, 151, 203
Köten, *khağan* of the Cuman-Qıpčaqs,
    169
Kotrag, *khağan* of the Bulgars, 99
Kovalev, Roman, 15–16, 20, 41, 43, 50,
    74, 76–9, 96, 99–100, 102, 136,
    142, 144, 149, 154–5, 158–9
Kubrat, *khağan* of the Bulgars, 98–9
Kulešov, Vjačeslav, 155, 164–5
Kulik, Alexander, 27, 32, 76,
    195–6, 204
kurgans, 14–15, 46, 51, 53–4, 59, 61,
    69, 101, 129
Kyssa'i Yusuf, 103–5

Ladino, 195
Lakapenos, Romanos, 34
Langobard, Lombards, Lombardy, 67,
    117, 173
laos, 91–3
Latin Christianity, 2, 6–7, 11–13, 38,
    82, 95, 113, 120, 122–3, 134–5,
    162, 168, 170–2, 179, 195
Latin sources, 13, 19, 107, 109, 113,
    122, 152, 160, 162, 201–2
Leon Diakonos, 2, 21, 88, 91, 106,
    130, 137

Levant, 49, 198, 205
Life of St. Abo, 39, 44, 78, 85
Lithuania, 67
Liudprand of Cremona, 107, 109
loros (imperial vestment), 154, 163
Lydians, 93–4, 187

Macedonia, 32, 87, 105, 188, 205
Magyars, 10–13, 15, 17, 19, 42–3, 51,
    71–3, 75–6, 80, 86, 93–4, 97–8,
    100, 107–29, 134–5, 138–40,
    161–2, 192
Majackij *gorodišče*, 49, 51, 61, 69, 71
Manzikert, 180
Mariupol', 49, 169
Marxist archaeology, 9, 12, 111
Matthew of Edessa, 130
Mauss, Marcel, 171, 182–3
Maximos of Arta, 7
McLuhan, Marshall, 202
Medievalists, 7
Meiji Reformation, 178
menorah (Jewish candelabra), 42, 49,
    55, 166
mercantilism, 164
Merv, 158
Michael III, 153
Michael the Syrian, 33
middle ages, 3–7, 11, 127, 164,
    168, 170, 174–7, 180, 182,
    184, 200
Middle East, 3, 6, 171
Mieszko I, 160
Mieszko II, 160
migration era *(völkerwanderung)*,
    11–12, 30, 32–5, 58–9, 80, 98,
    100, 107, 109, 119, 124–6, 130,
    175–7, 184, 194, 197, 204
miliaresia (Byzantine silver coins),
    143, 156
Mishnah, 41, 54, 196
mixobarbaroi, 94
Mizrahim, 193, 204–5

modernity, 4–5, 8–9, 18, 46, 73, 75, 80–1, 93, 98, 105–6, 109, 112, 157, 160, 168, 176–7, 181–3
Mohammed (Islamic Prophet), 3, 93, 152, 155–6
Moldova, 133
Mongolia, 19, 115, 182
Mongols, 76, 100, 102, 105, 135, 145, 169, 175, 191
Moravians, 92, 109, 116
Mordvians, 100, 138–9, 142
Moščevaja Balka, 50–1
Moscow, 57, 144, 147
Moses coins, 40–4, 49, 55, 78, 81, 141, 151, 154–6, 165, 200–1
Mouzalonissa, Theophano, 88, 148
Mt. Athos (the Holy Mountain), 133
Mycenae, 178

Narentines, 91
Nazi archaeology, 15, 112, 174, 176, 178
Nicholas Mystikos, patriarch of Constantinople, 21, 44, 86, 202
Nikaea, 169
Nikephoros, patriarch of Constantinople, 20, 98
Nishapur, 158
Noah (Old Testament Prophet), 31, 187
Noonan, Thomas, 16, 47, 59, 64, 72, 74–5, 77, 85, 89–90, 96, 101, 133, 136, 141, 143–4, 158–9, 161, 164
Normanist debate, 136–7, 199
Notitiae Episcopatuum, 10, 14, 21, 36, 47, 85–6, 96, 145
Novgorod, 139, 145, 147–8
Novgorod First Chronicle, 168–9
Novosel'cev, Anatolij, 20, 37–8, 43, 47, 66, 76, 87
numismatics, 15, 41, 58, 89, 101, 135, 141, 143, 146, 152–5, 157–8, 162–3, 165–6

Obadiah, 31, 40–3, 62, 78
Obolensky, Dimitri, 11, 20, 83–6, 94–5, 99, 124, 135–6, 149
ochlos, 92
Odysseus, 182
Oğuz, 15, 25, 51, 57–8, 73, 80, 87, 100, 122, 125–7, 129, 132–3, 190–2
oikoumene, 9–10, 13–14, 17, 35, 59, 83, 113, 144–6, 149–50, 151, 154, 157, 160–6, 167–8, 178–9, 183–4, 193
Old Great Bulgaria, 20, 76, 80, 98–9
Old Testament *(Tanakh)*, 13, 33, 41, 67–8, 96, 187–9
Oleg (Rus' prince), 34, 87
Olsson, Joshua, 35, 37–8, 40, 42–4, 46–7, 85–6, 156
Onoğurs, 42, 85
Orthodox Christianity, 2, 6, 9–13, 30, 35, 38, 83–4, 122, 134–5, 144, 149, 162, 168–72, 178, 182, 191, 205
otherisation, 174, 189
ouroboros, 178
Ovid, 180

Palaiologan dynasty, 145
Pálóczi-Horváth, András, 15, 42, 47, 64, 71, 73, 76, 95, 108, 114, 119, 122–3, 129–30, 133–4
palynology, 121
Pannonia, 73, 85, 107, 110–11, 113–15, 117, 119–22, 139, 162, 192
Parallelism (rhetorical technique), 188
Patzinakia, 123, 126, 128, 130, 134–5
Paul the Deacon (chronicler), 13
Pečenegs, 10, 12, 15, 17, 23–5, 42, 47, 51, 64, 71, 73, 76, 80, 87, 91–2, 94–5, 97, 107–9, 114–15, 119–20, 122–35, 138–9, 169, 184, 190–2
Persia, 12, 21–2, 25, 36, 48, 65, 158, 160, 171
Persian sources, 19–23, 90

Peter, Doge of Venice, 34
Petrukhin, Vladimir, 15, 27, 33, 36–7, 41–2, 45, 55, 71, 74, 77, 88–9, 128, 141–2, 156
phossatos, 92
Photios, patriarch of Constantinople, 47
Phoullai, 85, 145
Phrygians, 93–4
phylon, 92
Piast dynasty, 15, 84, 157, 160–2, 166, 170–1, 194
pit-graves, 46, 53, 55, 61, 69
Plato, 31, 180, 193
Pletnëva, Svetlana, 43, 46–51, 55, 61–2, 66, 71, 73–4, 76, 88, 125, 130, 133–4
Plutarch, 94
Poland, 15, 122, 157, 160–1, 197
Poland-Lithuania, 195
Poles, 173
politeia, 9–10
Poljanians, 174
poljud'e, 74, 128
Portuguese, 92
potestarian state formation, 66, 80, 95, 170
Poznań, 160
Preslav, 72
primordial ethnicity, 5–6, 8, 10–11, 91, 94–6, 101, 110–15, 117, 120, 122–3, 130, 134–40, 142, 145, 168, 170–2, 174–5, 178–80, 182, 184, 191–2, 195, 197–9, 205
Prinzing, Günter, 10
Priscus, 110
Pritsak, Omeljan, 16, 23, 29–34, 37–40, 44–5, 60–3, 67–8, 72, 76, 84, 87, 125, 135–6, 141, 161, 196, 202
Protestant Christianity, 171, 179
Protocols of the Elders of Zion, 192, 194
Psellos, Michael, 124, 130, 137

pseudo-Kallisthenes, 188
Ptolemy, 94
putative descent, 91, 93, 96
PVL (Russian Primary Chronicle), 2, 25, 27, 29, 39, 43, 76–9, 87–9, 106, 110, 124, 130, 132, 137, 141, 190, 200, 204

Qabars, 42–3, 62, 95, 116
Qur'an, 97, 188

Rabbinical Judaism, 41, 54, 60, 196
Radanites, 22, 28, 36–7, 164, 198
Radimichians, 77
Raffensperger, Christian, 67, 133, 148–9
Ravenna, 153
Regino of Prüm, 107, 109–10
Renaissance, 119, 179
Rhineland, 194–5, 197
Risāla, 13, 25–6, 36, 43, 47, 52, 75–6, 89, 101, 105–6, 124, 138, 199–200, 202–3
Rjurikid dynasty, 15, 38, 84, 135, 142–3, 149–50, 157, 160–1, 170–1
Rjurikovo gorodišče, 139
Roman *Limes*, 73
Romania, 32, 133, 147
Romans, 2, 7–9, 22, 30–5, 42, 92–6, 101, 110, 120–6, 130–1, 134, 137, 151–4, 166, 170, 173–9, 184, 194
Rome (city), 13, 153, 171, 175–6
Romulus Augustulus, 179
Róna-Tas, András, 20, 41, 43, 54, 75, 100, 113, 121–2
Rosia (Byzantine metropolitanate), 145
Rus', 10, 12–17, 22–7, 34, 36, 43, 56, 59, 62, 64, 67, 71–7, 83–4, 87–91, 94, 96, 97–8, 100, 103, 108, 116, 120, 122, 127–9, 132–50, 154–5, 161–5, 169, 174, 184, 190–1, 195–6, 201, 204

Rus'sia (or Russia), 4, 6–7, 15, 39,
    48, 67, 75, 86, 89, 101, 135–6,
    138–9, 143–50, 157, 160, 164,
    180, 182, 191
Russians, 109, 129, 136, 170, 173–4
Russologists, 7

Safavid dynasty, 171
Ṣaffārid dynasty, 16, 157–9, 166
St. Augustine of Hippo, 7
St. Gall, 107–9
St. Maximos (metropolitan of Rus'),
    144, 147
St. Sophia cathedral (Kiev), 132, 144
St. Stephen (first Christian Magyar
    king), 38, 43, 72, 107, 117–23,
    135, 161–2, 192
St. Vladimir of Kiev (first Christian
    Rus' prince), 2, 13, 27, 38, 57, 91,
    96, 106, 135, 140, 143, 146, 148–9,
    161, 189, 204
Saksin (see Itīl'), 55–9, 79
Sallām the Interpreter, 22, 47, 188–9
Saltovo-Majackij Culture *(SMC)*,
    47–9, 53, 58–61, 65, 69–72, 81,
    116–17
Samandar, 46
Sāmānid dynasty, 2, 16, 102,
    157–60, 166
Samarqand, 16, 158–9
Samosdel'ka, 38, 56–9, 69, 79, 81
Ṣaqāliba, 22–6, 99–101, 138
Saracens, 30, 92, 132
Sardinia, 153, 165
Sarkel, 44–51, 55, 61–2, 69–71, 73,
    86–8, 122, 155
Sasanian dynasty, 21, 152
Sava River, 114
Scandinavia, 16, 136, 143, 158,
    164, 173
Scandinavians, 11, 101, 136–40, 143,
    145, 164
Schama, Simon, 32, 36, 52, 56, 63

Schechter Text, 13, 28–39, 44–5,
    60–3, 67–8, 72, 76, 87, 106, 141,
    155, 202
Scythians, 27, 59, 101, 109–10, 126,
    130–3, 188
Sea of Azov, 98, 169
Sefer Yosippon, 68
Sefer Yuhasin, 34
Selčuq Turks, 24, 80, 126–7, 165, 169
Semibugrÿ, 56–9, 79, 81
Semikarakorsk *gorodišče*, 62
Sephardim, 26, 31, 193, 195, 204–5
Septuagint, 187
Serbs, 14, 42, 49, 92–3, 205
Šestovica (burial site), 139
settlement-archaeology, 15, 36, 49,
    57–9, 69–72, 79, 101, 113, 116,
    118, 120–4, 135, 138, 144, 195–6
shahada, 2, 41, 102, 152, 160
Shapira, Dan, 21–2, 39–41, 152
Shepard, Jonathan, 10, 15–16, 27, 44,
    47, 50–4, 64, 71–3, 77, 85–6, 89,
    96, 100, 133, 135–7, 139, 141–2,
    144–5, 173, 204
Shi'a Islam, 12, 171
shofar (Jewish ceremonial ram's horn),
    42, 166
Siberia, 177
Sicily, 33, 68, 165
sigillography, 16, 58, 146, 148
Silk Roads, 53, 16, 74, 99–102, 175,
    180, 198
Sīstān, 158–9
skull trephination, 48, 53–4, 71,
    117, 134
Skylitzes, Ioannes, 21, 88, 124, 137–8
slavery, 24–6, 74, 89, 101–2, 128,
    155–9
Slavonic sources, 13, 19, 21, 27, 44–5,
    86, 202
Slavs, 11, 13, 73, 77, 80, 95, 98–101,
    111–12, 116–17, 121, 136–42,
    145, 149–50, 171–6, 195–7, 204

Slovakia, 162
Smolensk, 145
Smoljatič, Kliment (metropolitan of Rus'), 144
Sochi, 50
Solov'ov, Damir, 58, 79
Soloveckij monastery, 149
Sougdaia, 85, 145
Soviet archaeology, 9, 49, 74, 97, 101, 112, 133, 136, 143, 190–1
Spain, 205
Spanish, 66, 92, 158, 165
Spillings Hoard, 41, 154
Sredna Gora, 162–3
Stampfer, Shaul, 29, 81, 199–204
Staraja Ladoga, 146
Stephenson, Paul, 59, 67, 72, 87, 94–5, 98–9, 108, 124, 132, 169
Stouraitis, Yannis, 175, 183
Strabo, 94
stratos, 92
Sumer, 178
Sunni Islam, 12, 14, 36, 38, 98, 158, 170–2
Suwār, 75, 102, 159
Suwārs, 51, 76
Suzdal', 145
Svjatopolk Vladimirovich (Kievan Rus' prince), 161
Svjatoslav (Rus' prince), 39, 43, 57, 77, 79, 87–9, 141, 204
swastika, 15, 174, 178
Sweden, 41, 137, 143
Switzerland, 114, 139
synagogues, 36, 50, 54–5, 63
syncretism, 54, 60, 63–4
Syr Darya River, 124
Syracuse, 33, 153

Table of Nations (*Genesis* 10), 33, 67, 95, 137, 187
Ṭāhirid dynasty, 16, 24, 157–60, 166
Taḥrīf, 104–5

Tajikistan, 166
Talmud, 18, 41, 54, 196
Taman', 36–8, 46–51, 55–6, 71, 81, 84, 90, 164–5, 196, 204–5
Tamatarcha (Tmutarakan'), 86, 90, 141, 145
tamga symbols, 48–51, 61, 141–2, 155
Tanzimat, 178
Tārīkh Nāma-yi Bulghār, 149
Tārīkh-i-Bulghār, 13–14, 105–6
tarkhān, 22, 47–8
Tashkent, 158
Tatars, 98–9, 103, 107, 130, 169, 178
Tatarstan, 6, 21, 98, 103–7
Tauroscythians, 91, 137
taxation, 16, 74, 81, 97, 102, 128, 140, 144, 161–3, 170
Teimanim, 193
teleology, 3, 7–8, 18, 65, 171, 176, 179, 181, 201
Terek River, 85–6
Terkhin Inscription, 19
themata, 9–10, 14, 44, 86, 90, 93, 123, 126–7, 145, 183
Theophanes Omologetes (the Confessor), 20, 33, 47, 75–6, 153
Theophilos of Edessa, 20–1
Theophilos, Byzantine emperor, 86
Timurid dynasty, 130, 175
Togarmah, 31, 67–8, 187
Torah, 54, 67
Trebizond, 149, 165
tribalism, 10, 68, 72–3, 97, 99–101, 107, 109–10, 125, 127, 132, 145, 168, 172–5, 183
tribute, 16, 19–20, 24–5, 27, 30, 72–7, 80–1, 89, 97–8, 124, 127–8, 138, 140–4, 153, 170, 191, 199
trident (symbol of power), 141–2, 148, 155

tripartite division of history, 8, 94, 168, 176–9
Tudor dynasty, 171
tudun, 47–8
Turkey, 93, 147
Turkic languages, 19–20, 29, 33, 41–2, 47, 62–3, 67, 73, 76, 99, 101, 110, 115, 124–5, 134, 136–7, 156, 195–8
Turkic Pečenegs, 125
Turkic runiform, 19, 29, 115, 195
Turkmenistan, 158

Udmurt Republic, 103
Uiğur *khağanate*, 19, 21
Ukraine, 4, 9, 14, 133, 142, 146–8, 150, 174
Ukrainians, 9, 11, 14, 136, 142, 146–8, 173–4, 197
Umayyad dynasty, 158
ummah, 10, 17, 59, 106, 151, 154, 157, 160, 163–6, 167, 178, 183, 188, 193
University of Birmingham, 7, 84, 152, 162
Urban II, pope of Rome, 182
Uzbekistan, 159, 166

Valencians, 92
Vandals, 173
Varangians (also Viking/Norman), 2, 27, 41, 64–6, 77, 109, 136–8, 142, 150, 175
Vasil'ev, Dmitrij, 54–8, 69, 79
Venetians, 34, 92, 137, 169
Vernadsky, George, 39, 144
Vienna, 114
Visigoths, 173
Vita Basilii, 14
Vita Constantini, 13, 21, 44–5, 79, 86, 202
Vladimir Monomakh (Kievan Rus' prince), 148

Volčansk, 70
Volga River, 2–3, 25–6, 36, 38, 56–9, 64, 71, 79, 85–6, 98–106, 113, 144, 159, 172, 188
Volga Bulgaria, 15–16, 25, 56, 62, 67, 72, 74–5, 80, 89, 97–108, 111, 118, 120–3, 134–5, 137–8, 140, 142, 150, 154, 156, 158–9
Volga Bulgars, 10, 12–14, 17, 23, 25, 43, 72–3, 75, 98–107, 113, 116, 120, 129, 135, 140, 157–9, 199
Volgograd, 49, 129
Volhynia, 146
Vrij, Maria, 153–4, 163

Washington, George, 171
Werbart, Bozena, 34, 48, 65, 70, 72, 129, 172, 176, 195, 198
Western Civilisation, 3, 5–9, 65, 67, 71, 74, 80, 82, 94, 115–16, 137–8, 143, 162, 165, 168–9, 175–84, 191, 194–5, 198, 204–5
Westphalian sovereignty, 171
Wexler, Paul, 195, 197
William of Rubruck, 133
Wood, Ian, 94, 110, 112, 173, 177
World War II, 8, 14, 112, 136, 174, 196

Yehuda ben Barzillai, 31, 35
Yiddish, 52, 195–7

Zachlumians, 92
Zaranj, 158
Zhivkov, Boris, 15, 19–20, 33, 36–47, 50–1, 54, 57–8, 60–77, 80–1, 86–90, 94, 98–102, 108, 110, 112–13, 115–16, 124–9, 135, 142, 155–6, 159, 169–73, 188, 191

Zichia, 90, 141, 145
Zichians, 76
Zilivinskaja, Emma, 57–8
Zoroastrianism, 21–2

Zosimo, *Vita*, 48, 33
Zuckerman, Constantin, 10, 16, 20, 29, 32, 34, 40, 44, 46–7, 52, 75, 77, 84–8, 96, 100, 141–2, 145

EU representative:
Easy Access System Europe
Mustamäe tee 50, 10621 Tallinn, Estonia
Gpsr.requests@easproject.com